Surveys in Economic Growth

T0299439

Surveys in Economic Growth

Theory and Empirics

Edited by

Donald A. R. George, Les Oxley and Kenneth I. Carlaw

Blackwell
Publishing

First published as a special issue of *Journal of Economic Surveys*, 2003

350 Main Street, Malden, MA 02148-5018, USA
108 Cowley Road, Oxford OX4 1JF, UK
550 Swanston Street, Carlton, Victoria 3053, Australia

First published 2004 by Blackwell Publishing Ltd

Reprinted 2004

Library of Congress Cataloging-in-Publication Data has been applied for

ISBN 1-4051-0881-9

A catalogue record for this title is available from the British Library.

Set by Integra Software Services Pvt. Ltd, India

For further information on
Blackwell Publishing, visit our website:
http://www.blackwellpublishing.com

CONTENTS

PREFACE

This is the sixth book in the series *Surveys of Recent Research in Economics*. Its theme is economic growth, a subject which has developed rapidly in the last fifteen years. The central ideas of endogenous growth are now essential tools for all economists, and the analysis of economic growth has important policy applications.

The contributors to this book discuss recent work on economic growth from both the theoretical and empirical points of view. They cover topics such as human capital, convergence, international trade, fiscal policy, unemployment and technical progress. A theme of the book is the distinction between steady state analysis and transitional dynamics. It could well be argued that the latter now deserves more attention from economists and, in particular, the linearised saddlepoint dynamics, ubiquitous in the economic growth literature, may have outlived their usefulness.

All the contributions to this volume have been selected to be accessible to the technically competent non-specialist economist. Our thanks to all those at Blackwell who helped pilot the book through the production process.

Donald A R George, Les Oxley and Kenneth I Carlaw

1

ECONOMIC GROWTH IN TRANSITION

Donald A. R. George

University of Edinburgh

Les Oxley

University of Canterbury, New Zealand

Kenneth I. Carlaw

University of Canterbury, New Zealand

1. Introduction

The analysis of economic growth has come a long way since Solow's and Swan's famous contributions (Solow, 1956 and Swan, 1956) and developments have been particularly rapid since the mid 1980's. The contributors to this *Special Issue* tackle selected aspects of this large and rapidly growing literature. This introductory article sets their contributions in context.

Solow's (1956) constant savings ratio is easily replaced with an infinite horizon Ramsey utility function and augmented with Harrod-neutral technical progress (see Barro and Sala-I-Martin, 1995 for example). We list below some of this model's central features, many of which reappear in the more recent models discussed by the contributors to this issue.

1. It is a dynamic general equilibrium model, involving aggregate variables. The assumption of *competitive* general equilibrium often has to be dropped in more modern models, to admit monopoly power, externalities or public goods, but the dynamic, aggregate, general equilibrium approach remains.
2. Momentary equilibrium is unique and is achieved instantaneously in all markets, by a smoothly functioning price mechanism, perhaps involving a Walrasian auctioneer.
3. The classical theorems of welfare economics can be invoked but, because of the 'representative dynasty' summarised by the Ramsey utility function, efficiency can be analysed while equity cannot.
4. The model has a unique long-run steady state. This long-run equilibrium is stable and the method of comparative dynamics is used to make predictions (i.e.

one steady-state is compared with another). By contrast with momentary equilibrium, this dynamic stability does not require the invocation of an auctioneer.

5. The model displays *saddlepoint* dynamics. Transition to the steady state
   involves a jump in one or more variables (consumption per head in the
   Solow/Swan/Ramsey model), allowing the economy to move to a stable
   manifold (stable *branch* in the Solow/Swan/Ramsey model): thereafter, it
   moves in the stable manifold towards the long-run equilibrium (steady
   state). These particular transitional dynamics arise because of the Ramsey
   utility function and are not present in the simpler version of the model, with
   a constant savings ratio. They are usually ignored in the formulation of
   predictions, in favour of the comparative dynamics approach, and rarely
   have much of a role in empirical work.

2. Endogenous Growth

It is usually argued that the Solow/Swan/Ramsey model can explain Kaldor's
stylised facts (Kaldor, 1961), but in a very unsatisfactory way. The long-run
equilibrium growth rate of per capita GDP is determined exogenously (it is the
rate of Harrod-neutral technical progress). It is therefore independent of the
savings ratio, depreciation rate, level of productivity or any other economic
variable, and is immune to policy variations. Of course, the short-run growth
rate responds to these variables, but with the focus on the steady-state, short-run
effects are deemed to be of no consequence. Actual technical progress involves the
use of economic resources and is the outcome of (possibly profit-maximising)
decision-taking (for example in research and development departments). Thus a
good model of economic growth should include an analysis of technical progress,
preferably including innovation and diffusion of new knowledge.

A related, but distinct objection is that technical progress in the Solow/Swan/
Ramsey model *must* be Harrod-neutral for a steady-state to exist. (Alternatively, the
production function could be Cobb-Douglas, in which case each variety of neutrality
implies all the others.) There is no reason to believe that actual technical progress is
Harrod-neutral or that the aggregate production function is Cobb-Douglas. The
Kennedy/von Weizsacker invention possibility frontier (Kennedy, 1964 and von
Weiszacker, 1966) is an interesting attempt to resolve this difficulty, and could be
seen as an early model of endogenous technical progress. However it is based on
restrictive assumptions and cannot be seen as a fully satisfactory approach.

Moreover, empirical studies have raised doubts as to whether long-run growth in
per capita GDP can always be attributed to technical progress. The question therefore arises as to whether a plausible model *without* technical progress can be constructed in which there is long-run growth in per capita GDP, at a rate which depends
on economic variables, possibly including policy variables (i.e. *endogenous growth*).
This turns out, in theory at least, to be remarkably easy: all that is required is a factor
of production whose marginal product does not diminish as it is accumulated relative
to labour. The obvious candidate is human capital. Taking the marginal product of
human capital as *exactly* constant allows endogenous growth, for example in the

famous model due to Uzawa (1965) and Lucas (1988). However if this marginal product diminishes even slightly, endogenous growth disappears, and if it increases even slightly, growth is explosive and no steady state exists. Thus, this route to endogenous growth appears to depend on a *knife-edge* assumption and thus to be less than satisfactory. In *The Long-Run Implications of Growth Theories* Jonathan Temple discusses the methodological importance of knife-edge assumptions and points out that the Harrod-neutrality of technical progress is itself such an assumption, commonly made in models of *exogenous* growth.

A model of endogenous growth without technical progress is clearly *possible* but is it *plausible*? It could be argued that constant returns to human capital is implausible in the absence of technical progress, because specific types of human capital are closely linked to specific technologies. Imagine an economy with the technology of 1900 held constant, but with the human capital associated with it being accumulated. Is such an economy really likely to experience long-run growth?

Of course it is always possible that technical progress is the outcome of economic decision-taking, but that the long-run equilibrium growth rate is still independent of economic variables (including policy variables). This is the case of *semi-endogenous growth* (see, for example Li, 2000). Temple argues that some of the recent literature attributes too much significance to this distinction between endogenous and semi-endogenous growth.

3. Branches of the Literature

Technical progress and human capital provide two potential sources of endogenous growth, but there are many other branches of the literature. A major feature shared by virtually all branches of this literature is that one-shot changes in *levels* of economic variables can bring about changes in the long-run growth *rate*. Thus small changes in economic variables (including policy variables), combined with the passage of time, can bring about dramatic effects. The endogenous growth framework can be applied to an enormous variety of issues (including policy issues) within economics, sometimes with counter-intuitive results. For example, in the Uzawa/Lucas model of human capital, discussed above, a one-shot increase in the productivity of human capital *in the 'education sector'* causes an increase in the long-run growth rate of the economy, but a similar productivity increase in the 'final goods sector' has only a short-run effect.

We list below the main branches of the endogenous growth literature:

1. Endogenous technical progress, including both innovation and diffusion of new knowledge.
2. Human capital. The Dearing Report (Dearing, 1997) on higher education in the UK contains an appendix on endogenous growth, and argues for the introduction of tuition fees for university courses.
3. Policy and its effect on growth, including the relationship between growth and unemployment, and the effect of competition on growth rates.
4. Endogenous labour supply, including migration and choice of fertility.

5. Endogenous growth and globalisation. This literature raises the possibility, sensed by the protestors of Seattle and Prague that international trade may not always benefit all the countries involved.
6. Endogenous growth and cycles. This literature suggests that recessions may be *good* for us, because they sharpen technological competition and raise the long-run growth rate.

The contributors to this *Special Issue* tackle various aspects of this wide and heterogeneous subject. An issue which emerges clearly from their contributions is the methodological one of 'long-run equilibrium versus transitional dynamics'. As long ago as the 1970's Atkinson (1969) and Sato (1966) asked 'How Long is the Long-Run?' They carried out some numerical experiments with the Solow/Swan model and discovered that, on plausible assumptions, adjustment times between steady states were extremely long, so that (a) new shocks would be bound to hit the economy before it had completed more than a tiny fraction of its adjustment and (b) any conceivable time series of data would be too short to make meaningful tests of the theory. In the light of this, perhaps transitional dynamics deserve more attention from theorists and econometricians. Ken Carlaw and Richard Lipsey in 'Productivity, Technology and Economic Growth: What is the Relationship?', describe why technological change is not captured by the usual measure of total factor productivity. They offer some alternatives to TFP as measures of technological change and then develop a model of general purpose technology (GPT) driven growth and relate technological growth to TFP under a variety of measurement methodologies. Growth is sustained in their framework only through the arrival of GPTs and the long run equilibrium is non-stationary in both levels and rates. This means that the system never converges to a constant growth rate or constant levels of output and inputs. This property of the model is by design since the observed growth rate of economies may or may not display stationarity and in the authors view the arrival of new pervasive technologies has disrupted stability of economies through the millennia. Thus, their model is one in which the economy is always in a transitional dynamic, moving in a recursive fashion through epochs associated with each GPT. They use this model to simulate artificial data and ask under what (if any conditions) conventional measures of TFP are related to the actual rate of technological change in the system. We return to the question of long-run versus transitional dynamics in section 6.

The focus on long-run equilibrium is not confined to theorists. The appeal to cointegration methods, so popular in the empirical study of economic growth, is based on the idea that a long-run equilibrium relationship exists in the data, and the econometrician's task is to establish its empirical form and ideally one that has a structural interpretation see Wickens (1996).

4. Empirical Studies

Economic growth is typically presented as a long-run equilibrium concept, however, in real-time the main observable features are transitional ones – an economy in motion.

An important empirical analogue to transitional dynamics is the issue of convergence. This area of empirical economic growth has attracted an enormous literature and the paper by Nazrul Islam entitled, *What Have We Learnt from the Convergence Debate?* provides an excellent survey of this strand of that literature. Convergence testing can be traced back to Baumol (1986), DeLong (1988), Dowrick and Nguyen (1989) and Barro (1991), however, the major contributors to this empirical production line were Barro and several co-authors see Barro (1991), Barro and Lee (1993, 1996, 2001) and Barro and Sala-i-Martin (1992, 1995, 1997). This empirical research agenda is based upon a simple economic model and a simple easily testable hypothesis that could be tested via a single OLS regression. The 'convergence hypothesis' (and Islam identifies its many forms) is one of the more robust implications of the original Solow (1956) model.

Combining simplicity of theory and econometrics with the ready availability of Summers and Heston (1988, 1991) data, created a research industry. In particular, using cross-section or small-t panels, the following model was estimated

$$g_{i,T} = \alpha + \beta y_{i,0} + \varepsilon_{i,T}$$

where $g_{i,T} = T^{-1}(y_{i,T} - y_{i,0})$ denotes the average growth rate for each of I economies and T is a fixed horizon. Support for *convergence* implies a $\beta < 0$, whereas the null hypothesis of *non*-convergence sets $\beta \geq 0$.

In a series of papers, however, including Bernard and Durlauf (1995, 1996), Durlauf and Johnson (1995), and Quah (1993a,b, 1996a,b,c) the economic and empirical underpinnings of the cross-section/panel tests of convergence were challenged and undermined.

Bernard and Durlauf (1995, 1996) use time series tests to consider convergence based upon differences between countries GDP per capita over time. Let y_i be the log real GDP per capita in country i and likewise y_j for country j. Define the differences in real GDP per capita in countries i and j, $y_i - y_j$. Define I_t as the information set available at period t. Then Bernard and Durlauf (1995), define five types of convergence, catching-up or common trends; *convergence in output; convergence in multivariate output; convergence as catching-up; common trends in output* and *common trends in multivariate output* where each is defined, using their notation and numbering, in turn as:

Definition 2.1. Convergence in Output. *Countries i and j converge if long-term forecasts of output for both countries are equal at some fixed time t:*

$$\lim_{k \Rightarrow \infty} E(y_{i,t+k} - y_{j,t+k} | I_t) = 0$$

Definition 2.1'. Convergence in Multivariate Output. *Countries $p = 1, \ldots n$ converge if long-term forecasts of output for all countries are equal at some fixed time t:*

$$\lim_{k \Rightarrow \infty} E(y_{i,t+k} - y_{j,t+k} | I_t) = 0 \quad \forall p \neq 1$$

Definition 2.1″. Convergence as Catching-up. Countries i and j converge between dates t and t + T if the deviation in output between country I and country j is expected to decrease. If $y_{i,t} > y_{j,t}$:

$$\lim_{k \Rightarrow \infty} E(y_{i,t+T} - y_{j,t+T}|I_t) < y_{i,t} - y_{j,t}$$

Definition 2.2. Common Trends in Output. Countries i and j contain a common trend if long-term forecasts of output are proportional at a fixed time t:

$$\lim_{k \Rightarrow \infty} E(y_{i,t+k} - ay_{j,t+k}|I_t) = 0$$

Definition 2.2′. Common Trends in Multivariate Output. Countries $p = 1, \ldots n$ contain a single common trend if long-term forecasts of output are proportional at a fixed time t, let $\bar{y}_t = [y_{2,t}, y_{3,t}, \ldots y_{p,t}]$:

$$\lim_{k \Rightarrow \infty} E(y_{i,t+k} - a_p^t \bar{y}_{j,t+k}|I_t) = 0$$

Their arguments are compelling and question the usefulness and relevance of the 'Barro-type' tests of 'convergence'. The topic is pursued further in Islam's article.

One of the other big empirical issues stemming from the endogenous growth literature is the role of human capital in the economic growth process. Although this has been championed recently by Rebelo (1991) and Romer (1986, 1989), it has a long history stretching back as far as, at least, Smith (1776).

In two papers in this issue the important area of *measuring human capital* is surveyed. Ludger Wößmann in *Specifying Human Capital* and Trinh Le, John Gibson and Les Oxley, in *Cost- and Income-based Measures of Human Capital* cover the current literature on this topic. Woessmann concentrates on the larger literature which proxies human capital with some measure of educational experience, whereas Le, Gibson and Oxley cover the cost- and income-based measures whose heritage stretches back to 1690 and the work of Petty.

Both papers have a strong empirical focus and argue forcefully about the need to measure the important variable with minimum error and identify some of the consequences of ignoring this advice. Taken together, the two papers present an extensive and up-to-date review of the 'measuring human capital' literature.

Continuing the empirical theme and the issue of long-run, dynamic effects, Joshua Lewer and Hendrik Van den Berg ask the question, *How Large is International Trade's Effect on Economic Growth?* As they state, the estimated static welfare gains from international trade are very small such that the case for free trade is increasingly linked to trade's positive effects on economic growth. However, how large are these effects? Lewer and Van den Berg's paper surveys the vast empirical literature on the trade and growth issue focussing not simply on statistical significance, but more specifically on the size of the relationship. They identify through careful review that many empirical studies show considerable consistency in measuring the trade and growth relationship, in particular, a one percentage point increase in the growth of exports is associated with a one-fifth percentage point increase in economic growth, which over time can be a very potent engine for growth.

5. Economic Policy and Unemployment

Endogenous growth theory suggests an obvious approach to fiscal policy, namely to analyse the effects of one-shot changes in fiscal policy instruments on the long-run equilibrium growth rate. In *Fiscal Policy and Economic Growth* Martin Zagler and Georg Durnecker draw attention to the externalities and credit market imperfections which justify the public provision of education. Other channels of influence for public expenditure include public infrastructure, research and development and the provision of health care, all of which are discussed in their article. They also discuss the effects of taxation, pointing out that it can, in principle, internalise the externalities which are often to be found in endogenous growth models. Finally, they consider the effects of public debt on economic growth in a non-Ricardian economy. They conclude by calling for further research on the effects of fiscal policy on innovation driven economic growth, arguing that a reproducible factor with a non-diminishing marginal product is *not* in fact required to explain long-run growth.

In the Solow/Swan/Ramsey model momentary equilibrium is achieved instantaneously and costlessly by a smoothly functioning price mechanism (perhaps implemented by a hyper-efficient auctioneer). This feature is also found in more complicated neo-classical models such as Uzawa's (1962) two-sector model, in which the price mechanism also allocates the factors of production between sectors, instantaneously and costlessly. In models such as these, labour can never be unemployed even for a split second.

Persistent unemployment of labour is clearly a central policy concern, particularly for European governments, so it is a topic which should concern growth theorists. Fabio Arico turns to these matters in *Growth and Unemployment: Towards a Theoretical Integration*. He considers Pissarides' (1990) claim that a relationship exists between growth and unemployment based on a 'capitalisation effect'. Schumpeter's idea of 'creative destruction', as developed by Aghion and Howitt (1992), provides another possible approach to unemployment in the growth context, as does Acemoglu's (1997) model of strategic complementarity and co-ordination failure. Arico gives considerable attention to the role of human capital and argues for more work on microfoundations of growth theory. He draws attention to the likelihood of multiple equilibria, which may be Pareto-ranked. In which case, Arico argues, the policy-maker's job is to select the Pareto-dominant equilibrium, possibly using policies not aimed directly at the labour-market.

6. Saddlepoint stability

Even a cursory glance at the endogenous growth literature reveals that the interesting dynamic effects arise on the production side of the economy, for example via unusual factors of production such as human capital, or the stock of knowledge and ideas. The consumption side of the economy does relatively little analytical work. An infinitely long-lived, utilitarian dynasty, which discounts the future[1] at a rate greater than the population growth rate, chooses a consumption/savings path which allows the model to be closed. In some models the dynasty may have more work to do, for example allocating its human capital between the various sectors of the economy. The standard mathematical approach to this kind of problem is to invoke Pontryagin's maximum principle[2] and formulate a Hamiltonian. For good mathematical reasons, the resulting dynamics almost always take saddlepoint form, as described in section 1 above. Provided the number of jump variables is equal to the dimension of the unstable manifold, there exists a unique jump, placing the economy in its stable manifold and forcing convergence to the long-run equilibrium. It is a wonder of economic theory that this happy equality always prevails, so that the long-run equilibrium is stable and the method of comparative dynamics can be applied.

This argument is supported by appeal to the transversality condition, which arises from the Hamiltonian problem. This condition requires that the discounted shadow value of the state variables (usually stocks such as physical or human capital) tends to zero as time tends to infinity. Since some of the endogenous variables are jump variables, they cannot have initial conditions, apparently leaving the solution of the dynamical system undetermined. But the transversality condition provides an extra boundary condition (in fact a terminal condition), allowing the solution path to picked from the phase portrait. By a happy coincidence, divergent paths violate the transversality condition but convergent ones do not. Thus the long-run equilibrium methodology is preserved: all that is required is that the economy be controlled by an infinitely long-lived Ramsey dynasty, with perfect foresight, preferably discounting the future at a rate greater than the population growth rate.

This dynamic story is of course pure fantasy: and has at least four major difficulties as a basis for growth theory:

1. The Ramsey dynasty is supposed to be a *representative* agent, not a controlling one. Short of a centrally-planned economy, it is not clear how or by whom the appropriate jumps are supposed to be brought about.
2. The transversality condition is *not* in general a necessary condition for the solution of the Pontryagin problem (e.g. see Halkin, 1974). This has led some theorists to impose a 'no Ponzi games' condition in the credit market. This, they suggest, allows the invocation of the transversality condition (e.g. see Barro and Sala-i-Martin, 1995). This approach requires a substantial set of extra assumptions, in addition to those relating directly to economic growth.

3. If the Ramsey dynasty has a *finite* horizon the transversality condition will be satisfied on divergent paths but not convergent ones.

4. In models with multiple equilibria, the transversality condition may be satisfied on paths which converge to stable equilibria (see e.g. George, Oxley and Williamson, forthcoming), thus removing the need for jump variables.

It seems then that the conventional approach to transitional growth dynamics has arisen largely as a methodological by-product of theorists' wish to preserve the long-run equilibrium approach and the method of comparative dynamics. But we have seen that there is a compelling case, on both theoretical and empirical grounds, to shift the focus of attention towards transitional dynamics. The mathematical and computing tools are now available to do this, and we suspect that future models of economic growth will dispense with the saddlepoint/jump variables fairy story.

7. Conclusions

The analysis of economic growth has developed rapidly in the last twenty years, on both the theoretical and empirical fronts. Unusually in economics, theoretical and empirical work have interacted in a way which has actually generated intellectual progress. Models of economic growth are now essential tools for the analysis of an enormous variety of important economic questions, including human capital, technical progress, international trade, fiscal policy, unemployment, migration, choice of fertility and economic fluctuations. Thus far economists have tended to concentrate on long-run equilibrium growth, but that is gradually changing. There are compelling reasons, theoretical and empirical, to believe that transitional dynamics are far more important than hitherto believed. Future research is likely to reflect this fact and, in particular, it can reasonably be expected that the superstitious belief in saddlepoints and jump variables will soon be consigned to the dustbin of history.

Acknowledgements

Financial support from the Royal Society of New Zealand Marsden Fund, grants UOC101 and UOC108 aided completion of this work.

Notes

1. Against Ramsey's moral instincts: he saw discounting as 'ethically indefensible and arising only from a deficiency of the imagination.' Abandoning discounting would mean appeal to the 'overtaking criterion' and a consequent increase in analytical difficulty.

2. One of the authors was once forbidden by his Head of Department from teaching
   Pontryagin's Principle to undergraduates. In fact they take to it with great ease: it is
   *post*graduates who find it baffling.

References

Acemoglu, D. (1997) Technology, Unemployment and Efficiency. *European Economic
Review*, 41, 525–533.

Aghion, P. and Howitt, P. (1992) A Model of Growth Through Creative Destruction.
Econometrica, 60, 323–51.

Atkinson, A. B. (1969) The Timescale of Economic Models: How Long is the Long-Run?
Review of Economic Studies, 137–52.

Barro, R. J., (1991) Economic Growth in a Cross Section of Countries. *Quarterly Journal
of Economics*, 106, 2 (May), 407–443.

Barro, R. J. (1999) Human capital and growth in cross-country regressions. *Swedish
Economic Policy Review*, 6 (2), 237–277.

Barro, R. J. and Lee, J-W. (1993) International comparisons of educational attainment.
Journal of Monetary Economics, 32 (3), 363–394.

Barro, R. J. and Lee, J-W. (1996) International measures of schooling years and schooling
quality. *American Economic Review*, 86 (2), 218–223.

Barro, R. J. and Lee, J-W. (2001) International data on educational attainment: updates
and implications. *Oxford Economic Papers*, 53 (3), 541–563.

Barro, R. J., and Sala-i-Martin, X. (1992) Convergence. *Journal of Political Economy*,
L, 223–51.

Barro, R. J. and Sala-i-Martin, X. (1995) *Economic Growth*, McGraw-Hill, New York.

Barro, R. J., and Sala-i-Martin, X. (1997) Technological Diffusion, Convergence, and
Growth. *Journal of Economic Growth*, 2, 1, 1–27.

Baumol, W. J. (1986) Productivity Growth, Convergence, and Welfare: What the Long
Long-Run Data Show. *American Economic Review*, 76, 1072–85.

Bernard, A., and Durlauf, S. N. (1995) Convergence in International Output. *Journal of
Applied Econometrics*, 10, 97–108.

Bernard, A., and Durlauf, S. N. (1996) Interpreting Tests of the Convergence Hypothesis.
Journal of Econometrics, 71, 161–173.

Dearing, R. (1997) *Higher Education in the Learning Society*, HMSO.

DeLong, B. J. (1988) Productivity Growth, Convergence, and Welfare. *American Economic
Review*, 78, 1138–54.

Dowrick, S. and Nguyen, D. T. (1989) 'OECD Comparative Economic Growth 1950–1985:
Catch-Up and Convergence'. *American Economic Review*, 79, 1010–30.

Durlauf, S., and Johnson, P. A. (1995) Multiple Regimes and Cross-Country Growth
Behavior. *Journal of Applied Econometrics*, 1995, 10, 365–384.

George, D. A. R., Oxley, L. T. and Williamson, P. (in preparation) Nonlinearity and
Hyperinflation, *University of Edinburgh Discussion Paper*.

Halkin, H. (1974) Necessary Conditions for Optimal Control Problems with Infinite
Horizons. *Econometrica*, 42, 267–272.

Kaldor, N. (1961) Capital Accumulation and Economic Growth. In *The Theory of Capital*,
F. A. Lutz and D. C. Hague (eds.), St. Martins, New York.

Kennedy, C. (1964) Induced Bias in Innovation and the Theory of Distribution. *Economic
Journal*, 541–547.

Li, C. W. (2000) Endogenous v. Semi-Endogenous growth in a Two-R & D-sector Model.
Economic Journal, 110, C109–C122.

Lucas, R. E. (1988) On the Mechanics of Development Planning. *Journal of Monetary Economics*, 22, 3–42.

Pissarides, C. A. (1990) *Equilibrium Unemployment Theory*, Blackwell, Oxford.

Quah, D. (1993a) Galton's Fallacy and Tests of the Convergence Hypothesis. *Scandinavian Journal of Economics*, 95, 4, 427–443.

Quah, D. (1993b) Empirical Cross-Section Dynamics in Economic Growth. *European Economic Review*, 37, 426–434.

Quah, D. (1996a) Empirics for Economic Growth and Convergence. *European Economic Review*, 40, 6, 1353–75.

Quah, D. (1996b) Twin Peaks: Growth and Convergence in Models of Distribution Dynamics. *Economic Journal*, 106, 1045–1055.

Quah, D. (1996c) Convergence Empirics Across Economies with (Some) Capital Mobility. *Journal of Economic Growth*, 1, 95–124.

Rebelo, S. (1991) Long Run Policy Analysis and Long Run Growth. *Journal of Political Economy*, XCIX, 500–21.

Romer, P. (1986) Increasing returns and long run growth. *Journal of Political Economy*, 94 (5), 1002–1037.

Romer, P. (1989) Human capital and growth: theory and evidence. *National Bureau of Economic Research Working Paper* No. 3173.

Sato, K. (1966) On the Adjustment Time in Neoclassical Growth Models. *Review of Economic Studies*, 263–8.

Solow, R. M. (1956) A Contribution to the Theory of Economic Growth. *Quarterly Journal of Economics*, 70, 65–94.

Summers, R. and Heston, A. (1988) A New Set of International Comparisons of Real Product and Price Levels Estimates for 130 Countries, 1950–1985. *Review of Income and Wealth*, 34(1), March, 1–25.

Summers, R. and Heston, A. (1991) The Penn World Table (Mark 5): an Expanded Set of International Comparisons, 1950–1988. *Quarterly Journal of Economics*, 106(2), May, 327–68.

Swan, T. W. (1956) Economic Growth and Capital Accumulation. *Economic Record*, 32, 334–361.

Uzawa, H. (1962) On a Two-Sector model of Economic Growth. *Review of Economic Studies*, 40–7.

Uzawa, H. (1965) Optimal Technical Change in an Aggregative Model of Economic Growth. *International Economic Review*, 6, 18–31.

Von Weiszacker, C. C. (1966) Tentative Notes on a Two-Sector Model with Induced Technical Progress. *Review of Economic Studies*, 245–51.

2

SPECIFYING HUMAN CAPITAL

Ludger Wößmann

Ifo Institute for Economic Research, Munich

1. Introduction

The acquisition of knowledge and skills is an investment in the sense that people forego consumption in order to increase future income. Because workers have invested in themselves to different extents through education, one hour of labour input does not yield the same output across all workers. Education increases future labour productivity and future income and can thus be seen as an investment in human capital, which then is embodied in the human being. This idea can already be found in Adam Smith's (1776/1976, p. 118) classical Inquiry into the Nature and Causes of the Wealth of Nations:

'A man educated at the expence of much labour and time to any of those employments which require extraordinary dexterity and skill, may be compared to [an] expensive machin[e]. The work which he learns to perform, it must be expected, over and above the usual wages of common labour, will replace to him the whole expence of his education, with at least the ordinary profits of an equally valuable capital.'

And in his Principles of Economics, Alfred Marshall (1890/1922, p. 564) stated that

'The most valuable of all capital is that invested in human beings'.

While these citations demonstrate an early awareness of the importance of human capital in the economics profession, it was not before the second half of the twentieth century that economists such as Theodore W. Schultz, Gary S. Becker, and Jacob Mincer developed a thorough theory of human capital.[1]

This paper reviews attempts to derive a measure of the stock of human capital in *empirical* work and provides some extensions, focusing on education as the central means to accumulate human capital. It should be clear from the outset that the paper does *not* give a survey of 'human capital and growth,' but that it pursues a much more limited task: to survey empirical specifications of measures of the stock of human capital. In his review article of the new empirical evidence in the economics of growth, Temple (1999a, p. 139) points out that '[t]he literature uses somewhat dubious proxies for aggregate human capital.' Likewise, Borghans *et al.* (2001, p. 375) state that 'in relation to th[e] far-reaching theoretical and practical importance [of skills], economic science is hampered by the fact that procedures for the empirical measurement of skills are comparatively under-developed.' A survey of human capital measurement, combined with a critique of commonly used proxies and suggestions for improvement, may thus be a helpful device at the current state of the literature.

There may be two types of measurement error in the measurement of any variable. Data recording errors constitute a first reason for mismeasurement. But even when the data are perfectly recorded, the measured variable may still be a poor measure of the true variable. These second measurement errors due to using an imperfect proxy for the true stock of human capital are the focus of this paper.

The main reason for the use of poor proxies of the stock of human capital is that in most empirical growth studies, the choice of the human capital proxy is hardly reflected upon and depends very much on data availability. Instead of being based on an ad-hoc choice, however, the search for a proxy for the stock of human capital should be led by economic theory. Human capital theory offers a specification of the human capital function which represents the stock of human capital, expressed in money units, as a function of the measured variable of education, expressed in units of time. Therefore, the task of deriving a viable measure of the stock of human capital embodied in the labour force is mainly a task of correctly *specifying* the form of the relationship between education and human capital. The objective of this paper is to survey and relate the different specifications of the human capital measure used in the literature, to show that there are potentially huge specification errors in the human capital proxies currently used in applied work, and to present theoretically founded improvements of the specification of human capital measures.

Section 2 reviews the measures of the stock of human capital used in the literature from early growth accounting to the cross-country growth regressions of the mid-1990s, evaluates their merits and shortcomings, and shows how the different measures are interrelated. These measures include education-augmented labour input, adult literacy rates, school enrollment ratios, and average years of schooling of the working-age population, which is currently the proxy most commonly employed.

Human capital theory can be used to show that the stock of human capital is misspecified by the simple use of the proxy 'average years of schooling' because this includes an incorrect specification of the functional form of the education-human capital relationship (Section 3). Therefore, I present some extensions of the specification of human capital which yield measures which accord to human capital theory. A first extension, proposed by Bils and Klenow (2000), is to account for decreasing returns to investment in education by combining years of education with rates of return to education in a Mincer specification of the function linking education to human capital. Further extensions, based in part on Gundlach *et al.* (2002), try to account for cross-country differences in the quality of education, especially through the inclusion of a cognitive-skill index into the human capital function.

A comparison of measures of the stock of human capital based on the different specifications reveals that for virtually all countries in the world, specification issues strongly matter for the estimated stock of human capital, both in absolute and relative terms (Section 4). A low cross-country correlation between the preferred quality-adjusted measure of human capital and previously used measures shows that there is much scope for misspecifcation of the human capital variable, and development-accounting results suggest that this misspecification may cause severe underestimation of the development impact of human capital in empirical growth research. Section 5 concludes.

2. Human Capital Specification from Early Growth Accounting to Current Cross-Country Growth Regressions

2.1. *Education-Augmented Labour Input in Early Growth Accounting*

The only factor inputs which were accounted for in the earliest growth accounting studies were physical capital and labour. Thus, the total labour force, which is the linear sum of all workers, was the only measure of input embodied in human beings, implying the assumption that workers are homogeneous. However, Solow (1957, p. 317, footnote 8) was already aware of the importance of skill accumulation as a form of capital formation, conceding in passing that 'a lot of what appears as shifts in the production function must represent improvement in the quality of the labour input, and therefore a result of real capital formation of an important kind.'

Subsequent growth accounting studies tried to account for the heterogeneity of labour by considering differences in the quality of labour input. Labour input was augmented by considering differences across workers with respect to categories of characteristics, where education was one of several categories including gender, age, and occupational characteristics. In that sense, human capital specification has its predecessors in early growth accounting. Denison (1967) augments labour input to reflect differences in the quality of labour by adjusting total employment for hours worked, age-sex composition, and education. The effect of differences in the gender, age, and educational composition of hours worked upon the average quality of labour is estimated by the use of earnings weights. Assuming that wage differences reflect differences in the marginal product of labour, differences in the wages earned by different labour force groups make it possible to measure differences in their human capital. By using data on the distribution of the labour force across worker categories and weighting each category by its relative average wages, an aggregate labour quality index is constructed which reflects differences in the labour force with respect to the categories, weighted by market returns.

Denison (1967) argues that not the whole wage differential by level of education represents differences which are due to differences in education, because some of the wage differential may represent rewards for intelligence, family background, or credentialism. Therefore, he does not use average wages directly as educational weights, but instead makes the ad-hoc assumption that only three-fifth of the reported wage differentials between the group with eight years of education and each other group represents wage differences due to differences in education as distinguished from other associated characteristics. As education weights, he and many subsequent studies use the ensuing compressed income differentials. Denison (1967) also makes some allowance for differences in days of schooling per year.

Jorgenson and co-authors elaborate on this specification of education-augmented labour input in numerous contributions, many of which are collected in Jorgenson (1995). Especially, they disaggregate the analysis to the level of individual industries and break down the labour input not only by gender, age, and education, but also by such characteristics as employment status and occupational group. This leads to a myriad of labour input categories which are then aggregated on the basis of wage weights to yield a constant quality measure of overall labour input. Dagum and Slottje (2000) combine this earnings-based method to calculate macroeconomic average stocks of human capital with a microeconomic estimation of human capital as a latent variable on the basis of survey data on a set of human-capital indicators. This allows them to calculate not only the average level of human capital, but also the distribution of human capital among households.

The detailed data required for these calculations is only available in a few advanced countries. Since most of the early growth-accounting literature was interested mainly in within-country intertemporal comparisons of indices of the quality of labour, difficulties in cross-country comparisons, stemming mainly from informational deficiencies and measurement differences, were not addressed. Therefore, measures of total labour input adjusted for quality differences, and especially education-augmented labour input, are available only for very few countries.

2.2. *Adult Literacy Rates*

The availability of national accounts data for a large number of countries and years in the Penn World Table compiled by Summers and Heston (1988; 1991) has initiated a huge literature of cross-country growth regressions, which from the outset considered the inclusion of a measure of human capital. The early contributions to the literature specified the stock of human capital in the labour force by proxies such as adult literacy rates and school enrollment ratios. In most studies, this choice of specification reflects ease of data availability and a broad coverage of countries by the available data (usually coming from UNESCO Statistical Yearbooks) rather than suitability for the theoretical concept at hand. It soon became apparent that specification by these proxies does not yield very satisfactory measures of the stock of human capital available in production.

Studies such as Azariadis and Drazen (1990) and Romer (1990) use the adult literacy rate as a human capital proxy. Literacy is commonly defined as the ability to read and write, with understanding, a simple statement related to one's daily life. The adult literacy rate then measures the number of adult literates (e.g., in the population aged 15 years and over) as a percentage of the population in the corresponding age group:

$$l = \frac{M_A}{P_A} \tag{1}$$

where l is the adult literacy rate, M_A is the number of literates in the adult population, and P_A is the total adult population.

There has been some discussion about the international comparability of the thus defined variable because it is not easily applied systematically, but adult literacy rates certainly reflect a component of the relevant stock of human capital. However, they miss out most of the investments made in human capital because they only reflect the very first part of these investments. Any educational investment which occurs on top of the acquisition of basic literacy – e.g., the acquisition of numeracy, of logical and analytical reasoning, and of scientific and technical knowledge – is neglected in this measure. Hence using adult literacy rates as a proxy for the stock of human capital implies the assumption that none of these additional investments directly adds to the productivity of the labour force. Therefore, adult literacy rates can only stand for a minor part of the total stock of human capital. Accordingly, adult illiteracy rates $(1 - l)$ have later been used in the construction of school attainment measures to proxy for the percentage of the population without any schooling (see Section 2.4).

2.3. *School Enrollment Ratios*

School enrollment ratios, a further human capital proxy used in the literature, measure the number of students enrolled at a grade level relative to the total population of the corresponding age group:

$$e_g = \frac{E_g}{P_g} \tag{2}$$

where e_g is the enrollment ratio in grade level g, E_g is enrollment (the number of students enrolled) at grade level g, and P_g is the total population of the age group that national regulation or custom dictates would be enrolled at grade level g. Gross enrollment ratios take the total number of students enrolled at the grade level as the numerator, while net enrollment ratios take only those students enrolled at the grade level who belong to the corresponding age group P_g. Enrollment ratios have been used to proxy for human capital in the seminal studies of Barro (1991) and Mankiw *et al.* (1992)[2] and in the sensitivity study by Levine and Renelt (1992), among many others.

Although some researchers interpret enrollment ratios as proxies for human capital stocks, they may be a poor measure of the stock of human capital available for current production. Enrollment ratios are flow variables, and the children currently enrolled in schools are by definition not yet a part of the labour force, so that the education they are currently acquiring cannot yet be used in production. Current school enrollment ratios do not necessarily have an immediate and stable relationship to the stock of human capital embodied in the current productive labour force of a country. The accumulated stock of human capital depends indirectly on lagged values of school enrollment ratios, where the time lag between schooling and future additions to the human capital stock can be very long and also depends on the ultimate length of the education phase.

Enrollment ratios may thus be seen as – imperfect – proxies of the flow of human capital investment. However, the stock of human capital is changed by the net additions to the labour force, which are determined by the difference between the human capital embodied in the labour force entrants and the human capital embodied in those who retire from the labour force. Therefore, enrollment ratios may only poorly proxy for the relevant flows. First, they do not measure the human capital embodied in the entrants of the labour force this year, but the human capital acquired by current students who might enter the labour force at some time in the future. Second, the education of current students may not at all translate into additions to the human capital stock embodied in the labour force because graduates may not participate in the labour force and because part of current enrollment may be wasted due to grade repetition and dropping out. Third, net investment flows would have to take account of the human capital content of the workers who are retiring from the labour force that year. In sum, enrollment ratios may not even accurately represent changes in the human capital stock, especially during periods of rapid educational and demographic transition (Hanushek and Kimko, 2000).[3]

2.4. *Levels of Educational Attainment and Average Years of Schooling*

Both adult literacy rates and school enrollment ratios seem to have major deficiencies as proxies for the concept of human capital highlighted in theoretical models. Since the inadequacies of these proxies have motivated improvements in the specification of the human capital stock, it cannot be recommended to use either of them as a human capital measure. When looking for a measure of the stock of human capital that is currently used in production, it seems sensible to quantify the accumulated educational investment embodied in the current labour force. Therefore, several studies have tried to construct data on the highest level of educational attainment of workers to quantify the average years of schooling in the labour force. Educational attainment is clearly a stock variable, and it takes into account the total amount of formal education received by the labour force. So average years of schooling have by now become the most popular and most commonly used specification of the stock of human capital in the literature, including studies such as Barro and Sala-i-Martin (1995), Barro (1997; 2001), Benhabib and Spiegel (1994), Gundlach (1995), Islam (1995), Krueger and Lindahl (2001), O'Neill (1995), and Temple (1999b).[4]

2.4.1 *Perpetual Inventory Method*

Three main methods have been used in the construction of data sets on years of educational attainment in the labour force, each building in one way or another on the data on enrollment ratios discussed previously. The first method to get from school enrollment to average years of schooling, used by Lau *et al.* (1991) and refined by Nehru *et al.* (1995), is the perpetual inventory method. If sufficiently long data series on school enrollment ratios are available, the perpetual inventory method (superscript *PIM*) can be used to accumulate the total number of years of schooling S embodied in the labour force at time T by

$$S^{PIM} = \sum_{t=T-A_h+D_0}^{T-A_l+D_0} \sum_g E_{g,t+g-1}\left(1 - r_g - d\right)p_{g,t+g-1} \qquad (3)$$

where $E_{g,t}$ is total (gross) enrollment at grade level g at time t as in equation (2), A_h is the highest possible age of a person in the labour force, A_l is the lowest possible age of a person in the labour force, D_0 is the age at which children enter school (typically six), r_g is the ratio of repeaters to enrollments in grade g (assumed to be constant across time), d is the drop-out rate (assumed to be constant across time and grades), and $p_{g,t}$ is the probability of an enrollee at grade g at time t to survive until the year T.[5] By assuming $A_l = 15$ and $A_h = 64$, the studies count all persons between age 15 and 64 inclusive as constituting the labour force. The probability of survival $p_{g,t}$ is calculated on the basis of age-specific mortality rates in each year, which implicitly assumes that the mortality rate is independent of the level of schooling attained. The total number of years of schooling S can then be normalized by the population of working age P_w to obtain the average years of schooling of the working-age population s:

$$s^{PIM} = \frac{S^{PIM}}{P_w}. \qquad (4)$$

Much of the data on enrollment rates, repeater rates, age-specific mortality rates, and drop-out rates necessary to implement the calculation on the basis of the perpetual inventory method are not available and have therefore been 'statistically manufactured.' E.g., enrollment ratios and repeater rates have to be extrapolated backwards, and data gaps have to be closed by interpolations. Both problems are especially severe in the case of tertiary education. Age-specific survival rates have been constructed for a 'representative' country in each world region only.

2.4.2 *Projection Method*

In a second method to get from school enrollment ratios to years of schooling, Kyriacou (1991) builds on information on average years of schooling in the labour force available for the mid-1970s from Psacharopoulos and Arriagada (1986) based on direct census evidence of worker's attainment levels (see below).

Data on lagged enrollment ratios are then used to project (superscript *PRO*) average years of schooling in the labour force s for further countries and years T:

$$s_T^{PRO} = \alpha_0 + \alpha_1 e_{pri,T-15} + \alpha_2 e_{sec,T-5} + \alpha_3 e_{hig,T-5} \qquad (5)$$

where $e_{a,t}$ is the enrollment ratio at attainment level a (primary, secondary, and higher) at time t, and the αs are estimated in a regression of the value of the attainment-data based years of schooling in the mid-1970s (i.e., between 1974 and 1977) on prior enrollment rates:

$$s_{1975}^{ATT} = \alpha_0 + \alpha_1 e_{pri,1960} + \alpha_2 e_{sec,1970} + \alpha_3 e_{hig,1970} + \varepsilon \qquad (6)$$

where ε is an error term.[6]

Kyriacou (1991) finds that this relationship is rather strong across the 42 countries in the mid-1970s for which the respective data is available, with an R^2 of 0.82. For the projection, it has to be assumed that the relationship between average years of schooling in the labour force and lagged enrollment ratios is stable over time and across countries.

2.4.3 *Attainment Census Method*

The third method applied in the construction of attainment data sets is to use direct measures of levels of educational attainment from surveys and censuses. Psacharopoulos and Arriagada (1986) collected information on the educational composition of the labour force from national census publications for six levels of educational attainment a: no schooling, incomplete primary, complete primary, incomplete secondary, complete secondary, and higher. Based on these direct data on attainment levels (superscript *ATT*), average years of schooling s in the labour force can be calculated as

$$s^{ATT} = \sum_a \left[n_a \left(\sum_{i=1}^{a} D_i \right) \right] \qquad (7)$$

where n_a is the fraction of the labour force for whom attainment level a is the highest level attained ($n_a = N_a/L$ with N_a as the number of workers for whom a is the highest level attained and L as the labour force) and D_a is the duration in years of the ath level of schooling.[7] For fractions of the labour force who have achieved an attainment level only incompletely, half the duration of the corresponding level is attributed. The main shortcoming of the data set of Psacharopoulos and Arriagada (1986) is that the year of observation varies greatly across the countries covered, with most of the countries providing only one observation, so that a cross-country analysis is hard to obtain.

Barro and Lee (1993) apply basically the same methodology based on census and survey data on educational attainment levels, but they are able to greatly extent the coverage of countries and years. The greater coverage is partly achieved through a focus on the adult population as a substitute for the labour force (they use $n_a = N_a/P_A$ with P_A as the total adult population), so that their s^{ATT} represents average years of schooling in the working-age population, i.e. the population aged 25 (or 15) years and over, instead of the actual labour force. Barro and Lee's (1993) attainment levels are based on UNESCO's International Standard Classification of Education (ISCED) and are: no schooling, incomplete first level, complete first level, entered first cycle of second level, entered second cycle of second level, and entered higher level.

Barro and Lee (1993) also use data on adult illiteracy rates – $(1 - l)$ from equation (1) – to estimate the fraction of the working-age population with no schooling in those instances where direct data from censuses or surveys is not available. Since they observe a high correlation between the no-schooling fraction n_0 and adult illiteracy rates $(1 - l) - 0.95$ for the 158 observations where both data are available – they estimate missing values of the fraction of the working-age population with no schooling n_0 at time T for countries which report both a value for the no-schooling fraction n_0 and a value for adult illiteracy $(1 - l)$ in another year $T \pm t$ based on

$$n_{0,T} = (1 - l_T) \frac{n_{0,T \pm t}}{(1 - l_{T \pm t})}. \qquad (8)$$

When measured at four broad attainment levels (no schooling, first, second, and higher level), 40 percent of all possible data cells (for a total of 129 countries at six points in time) are filled out by available census or survey data, and an additional 16 percent of the cells are filled out by using adult illiteracy rates.

Barro and Lee (1993) go on to estimate the missing observations based on data on school enrollment ratios. They use the perpetual inventory method (see above), starting with the directly observed data points as benchmark stocks and estimating changes from these benchmarks on the basis of school enrollment ratios and data on population by age to estimate survival rates. In Barro and Lee (1993), repeater ratios r and drop-out rates d were neglected in the estimation (see equation (3)), while the revised version of the data set in Barro and Lee (1996) takes account of them. Barro and Lee (2001) additionally account for variations in the duration D_a of schooling levels over time within a country.

De la Fuente and Doménech (2000; 2001) point out that there is still a lot of data recording and classification error in the available data sets, giving rise to severe differences in country rankings across data sets and to implausible jumps and breaks in the time-series patterns. They construct a revised version of the Barro and Lee (1996) data set for OECD countries, relying on direct attainment data and using interpolation and backward projection instead of the perpetual inventory method with enrollment data to fill in missing observations. They collect additional attainment data from national sources, reinterpret some of the data when data points seem unreasonable, and choose the figure which they deem most plausible when different estimates are available. Their treatment of data inconsistencies includes a fair amount of subjective guesswork, so that their heuristic method comes short of a sound scientific methodology. Nevertheless, their revised data set may give a hint to what extent previous data sets are plagued with data recording errors.

2.4.4 *Evaluation of the Construction Methods*

Before coming to a fundamental critique of the *specification* of human capital by years of schooling in Section 3.1, some further criticism of the methods used to *construct* years-of-schooling data sets and of their implementation is warranted, especially as years-of-schooling data will turn out to be an important ingredient of a well-specified measure of human capital. In addition to the limited availability of the data necessary to implement the first method (plain perpetual inventory method), another severe shortcoming is its lack of benchmarking against the available census data on educational attainment. By disregarding the only direct information available on the variable of interest, it is inferior to the third method which combines the perpetual inventory method with census information. The second method (projection method) is the only method that involves making parametric assumptions. It is based on the assumption that the relationship between average years of schooling in the labour force and lagged enrollment ratios is a stable one. The available data on school attainment in the labour force from censuses and on school enrollment ratios gives ample evidence that this relationship varies over time and across countries, leaving the assumption erroneous and the projections unreliable. Furthermore, if the enrollment rates on which the projection method is based are measured with error, the coefficient estimates will be biased downward, yielding inconsistent predictions even if the stability assumption was correct.

Given these shortcomings of the first two methods, the attainment census method seems to be the most elaborate to date. However, even the Barro and Lee data set has some measurement weaknesses. It represents average years of schooling in the adult population, but not in the labour force. It therefore includes adults who are not labour force participants and it may exclude some of the members of the labour force (Gemmell 1996). The step from reported attainment levels to average years of schooling includes mismeasurement because it is only known whether a person has started and/or completed any given level. For people not completing a level, it is simply assumed that they stayed on for half the years required for the full cycle. For higher education, Barro and Lee (1993) simply assume a duration D_{hig} of four years for all countries. Furthermore, the original censuses and surveys often use varying definitions for the variables collected (Behrman and Rosenzweig, 1994).

A direct data recording problem of the Barro and Lee (1993) data set is the poor coverage of the basic data. While 77 of the 129 countries in their data set have three or more census or survey observations since 1945, only nine countries have more than four observations of the 9 potential data points from 1945 to 1985, and only three countries more than five. For any given five-year period since 1960, the number of countries for which census or survey data is available ranges from a minimum of 14 countries (in the period surrounding 1985) to a maximum of 78 (1980) out of the 129 countries in the data set. To give an example from the de la Fuente and Doménech (2000) data set, only 40 of the 147 observations (21 countries times 7 points in time) on secondary attainment in the data set – or 27 percent – are original observations taken directly from censuses or surveys, while the rest is interpolated in one way or the other. It would be reasonable to conclude that such a coverage does not provide a sensible basis for panel estimation. Accordingly, Krueger and Lindahl (2001) substantiate severe data measurement errors in panel data on average years of schooling. Hence, de la Fuente and Doménech's (2000, p. 12) conclusion is correct that 'a fair amount of detailed work remains to be done before we can say with some confidence that we have a reliable and detailed picture of worldwide educational achievement levels or their evolution over time.' By contrast, basically all observations in the OECD sample for 1990 are direct census or survey observations, allowing for a reasonable data quality at least for this sample at this specific point in time.

3. A Critique and Two Extensions

3.1. *Critique of Schooling Years as a Specification of Human Capital*

Apart from the problems of *recording* average years of schooling in the labour force, there are more fundamental problems with the *specification* of the stock of human capital by average years of schooling (cf. Mulligan and Sala-i-Martin, 2000). Although it is the most commonly employed measure, using the unweighted sum of schooling years linearly as a measure of the stock of human capital lacks a sound theoretical foundation. There are two major criticisms which render years of schooling a poor proxy for the human capital stock. First, one year of schooling does not raise the human capital stock by an equal amount regardless of whether it is a person's first or seventeenth year of schooling. Second, one year of schooling does not raise the human capital stock by an equal amount regardless of the quality of the education system in which it takes place.[8]

As for the first point, specifying human capital by average years of schooling implicitly gives the same weight to any year of schooling acquired by a person i.e., productivity differentials among workers are assumed to be proportional to their years of schooling. This disregards the findings of a whole microeconometric literature on wage rate differentials which shows that there are decreasing returns to schooling (Psacharopoulos 1994). Therefore, a year of schooling should be weighted differently depending on how many years of schooling the person has already accumulated.

As for the second point, using years of schooling as a human capital measure gives the same weight to a year of schooling in any schooling system at any time i.e., it is assumed to deliver the same increase in skills regardless of the efficiency of the education system, of the quality of teaching, of the educational infrastructure, or of the curriculum. In cross-country work, a year of schooling in, say,

Papua New Guinea is assumed to create the same increase in productive human capital as a year of schooling in, say, Japan. Instead, a year of schooling should be weighted differently depending on the quality of the education system in which it has taken place. In the following two sub-sections, I propose specifications of the human capital stock which deal with these two criticisms.

3.2. The Mincer Specification and Decreasing Returns to Education

The stock of human capital embodied in the labour force is a variable expressed in money units. To transform a measure of education measured in units of time into the stock of human capital expressed in units of money, each year of schooling should be weighted by the earnings return it generates in the labour market. Human capital theory offers a straightforward specification of the functional form of this relationship between education and the stock of human capital, the human capital earnings function (Mincer, 1974; cf. Chiswick, 1998). Assuming that the total cost C to an individual of investing into a year of schooling lies in the earnings which he or she foregoes during that year, annual earnings W after t years of schooling are equal to annual earnings with $t-1$ years of schooling plus the cost of the investment ($C_t = W_{t-1}$) times the rate of return r on that investment:

$$W_t = W_{t-1} + r_t W_{t-1}. \tag{9$'$}$$

By mathematical induction, it follows that earnings after s years of schooling are given by:

$$W_s = W_0 \prod_{t=1}^{s} (1 + r_t). \tag{9$''$}$$

Taking natural logarithms and applying the approximation that, for small values of r, $\ln(1+r) \approx r$, yields

$$\ln W_s = \ln W_0 + \sum_{t=1}^{s} r_t. \tag{9$'''$}$$

For $r = r_t$ being constant across levels of schooling, this is equal to

$$\ln W_s = \ln W_0 + rs. \tag{9}$$

Thereby, the relationship in equation (9)$'$ between earnings and investments in education measured in money units is converted to the relationship in equation (9) between the natural logarithm of earnings and investments in education measured in time units. That is, the logarithm of individuals' earnings is a linear function of their years of schooling. This log-linear formulation suggests that each additional year of schooling raises earnings by r percent.

Mincer (1974) estimated the rate of return to education r for a cross-section of workers as the regression coefficient on years of schooling in an earnings function like (9), controlling for work experience of the individuals. A whole literature of micro labour studies has confirmed that this log-linear specification gives the best fit to the data (cf. Card, 1999; Krueger and Lindahl, 2001). To be able to interpret the schooling coefficient in an earnings function as the rate of return to education, however, the assumption must hold that total costs of investment in the tth year of schooling C_t are equal to foregone earnings W_{t-1}. If the opportunity cost of schooling is a full year's earnings, this would imply that there are no direct costs such as tuition, school fees, books, and other school supplies. Furthermore, the regression coefficient in the earnings function method is a biased measure of the rate of return if age-earnings profiles are not constant for different levels of education.

Therefore, rates of return estimated by the elaborate discounting method, which can account both for the total cost of schooling and for variable age-earnings profiles, are superior to estimates based on the earnings function method. The elaborate discounting method consists in calculating the discount rate r which equates the stream of costs of education to the stream of benefits from education:

$$\sum_{t=1}^{s} (C_{h,t} + W_{l,t})(1+r)^t = \sum_{t=s+1}^{A_h} (W_{h,t} - W_{l,t})(1+r)^{-t} \qquad (10)$$

where C_h is the resource cost of schooling incurred to achieve a higher level h from a lower level l, W_l are the foregone earnings of the student while studying, $(W_h - W_l)$ is the earnings differential between a person with a higher level of education and a person with a lower level of education, s is years of schooling, and A_h is the highest possible working age.

By counting both private and public educational expenditures as the cost of schooling C, the elaborate discounting method is able to estimate social rates of return to education. Social – as opposed to private – rates of return are the relevant choice when dealing with questions from a society's point of view. The estimated rates of return are 'narrow-social,' taking account of the full cost of education to the society (including public expenditure) while disregarding any potential external benefits. Recent studies by Heckman and Klenow (1997), Acemoglu and Angrist (2001), and Ciccone and Peri (2000) show that there is little evidence in favor of such external returns to education.[9]

As first suggested by Bils and Klenow (2000), the micro evidence derived from the log-linear Mincer formulation can be used to specify the aggregate human capital stock in macro studies as

$$H^M = e^{\phi(s)} L \quad \Leftrightarrow \quad h^M = e^{\phi(s)} \qquad (11)$$

where H^M is the stock of human capital based on the Mincer specification, L is labour as measured by the number of workers,[10] and $h \equiv H/L$ is the stock of human capital per worker. The function $\phi(s)$ reflects the efficiency of a unit of labour with s years of schooling relative to one with no schooling. With $\phi(s) = 0$, the specification melts down to one with undifferentiated labour as in the earliest growth-accounting studies (Section 2.1). Furthermore, the derivative of this function should equal the rate of return to education as estimated in the labour literature, so that $\phi'(s) = r$. In the simplest specification, this would imply

$$\phi(s) = rs. \tag{12}$$

Thereby, a human capital measure can be constructed for every country by combining data on years of schooling with rates of return estimated in micro labour studies which weight each year of schooling by its market return.[11] This approach of specifying human capital stocks based on the Mincer regression has already been used in several studies, including Bils and Klenow (2000), Klenow and Rodríguez-Clare (1997), Hall and Jones (1999), and Jovanovic and Rob (1999).[12] Note that this approach is similar to weighting worker categories by relative wage rates as applied by the growth-accounting literature in the construction of education-augmented labour input (see Section 2.1).

In addition to taking account of the log-linear relationship between earnings and schooling, this specification can also be used to include decreasing returns to education. While the original work by Mincer entered schooling linearly over the whole range of schooling years, international evidence as collected by Psacharopoulos (1994) suggests that rates of returns to education are decreasing with the acquisition of additional schooling. Therefore, one year of schooling should be weighted differently depending on whether it is undertaken by a student in primary school, in high school, or in college. The available evidence allows a piecewise linear specification for the primary, secondary, and higher level of schooling:

$$\phi(s) = \sum_a r_a s_a \quad \Rightarrow \quad H_i^M = e^{\sum_a r_a s_{ai}} L_i \quad \Leftrightarrow \quad h_i^M = e^{\sum_a r_a s_{ai}} \tag{13}$$

where r_a is the rate of return to education at level a and s_{ai} is years of schooling at level a in country i.[13]

Barro and Lee (2001) argue that there are potential problems with the available estimates of returns to education because of biases through unmeasured characteristics like ability and because of disregard of social benefits. However, ample research in the modern labour literature has shown at least for the United States that the upward ability bias is offset by a downward bias of about the same order of magnitude due to measurement error in years of education (cf. Card, 1999). Estimates based on siblings or twin data and instrumental variable estimates based on family background or institutional features of the school system are of about the same magnitude as rates of return to education estimated by cross-sectional regressions of earnings on schooling, suggesting that rates of return to education reflect real productivity enhancements. Furthermore, recent studies have found no evidence in favour of externalities to education (see above).[14]

3.3. *The Quality of Education*

While several studies have by now taken on the Mincer specification to deal with the first criticism, the second criticism of qualitative differences in a year of schooling has as yet not led to a generally accepted refinement in human capital measurement. However, it is not just the *quantity* of education, i.e. the average years of schooling *s* embodied in the labour force, which differs across countries, but also the *quality* of each year of schooling, i.e. the cognitive skills learned during each of these years. One year of schooling is not the same everywhere because one unit of *s* may reflect different amounts of acquired knowledge in different countries. Estimated development effects of human capital based on merely quantitative measures may be strongly misleading if qualitative differences do not vary with years of education. Therefore, differences in the quality of education should be introduced into the human capital measure in addition to differences in the mere quantity of education to account for how much students have learned in each year. In what follows, three suggestions are made as to how to adjust the specification of the human capital function for quality differences.

3.3.1 *Educational Inputs*

The first attempt to account for differences in educational quality is to use proxies for the quality of educational inputs. These measures of the amount of inputs used per student in the education system are then entered as separate explanatory variables in growth regression analyses, presumably reflecting an additional effect of human capital. Barro (1991) already added student-teacher ratios to his analysis as a crude proxy for the quality of schooling, Barro and Sala-i-Martin (1995) use the ratio of government spending on education to GDP, and Barro and Lee (1996) collect data on educational expenditure per student, student-teacher ratios, teacher salaries, and length of the school year to proxy for the quality of educational inputs.

However, it has repeatedly been shown that such measures of educational inputs are not strongly and consistently linked to acquired cognitive skills, rendering them a poor proxy for educational quality (Hanushek, 1996). The input measures disregard the huge differences in the effectiveness with which inputs are put to use in different schooling systems, caused mainly by differences in institutional features of the education systems such as centralization of examinations or extent of school autonomy (Wößmann, 2003).

3.3.2 *Country-Specific Rates of Return to Education*

Because of the lack of a systematic relationship between resource inputs and educational quality, a second specification to account for qualitative differences in a year of schooling can be thought of building on country-specific rates of return to education. Under the assumptions that global labour markets are perfectly competitive, that labour is perfectly mobile internationally, and that employers are perfectly informed about the human capital quality of workers, differences in the quality of education of the work force would be captured by differences in the rates of return to education. Therefore, country-specific rates of return may already reflect differences in the quality of education across countries. A quality-adjusted measure of the human capital stock could then be specified as

$$h_i^r = e^{\sum_a r_{ai}s_{ai}} \tag{14}$$

where h_i^r is the stock of human capital per worker (based on country-specific measures of r) in country i, r_{ai} is the rate of return to education at level a in country i, and s_{ai} is average years of schooling at level a in country i.

Unfortunately, the data which are available on country-specific rates of return to education seem to be plagued with a high degree of measurement error and may presumably contain more noise than information. The figures collected by Psacharopoulos (1994) show a degree of variation which is difficult to interpret in terms of differences in schooling quality (see Section 4.1). Furthermore, the three assumptions mentioned which underlie the hypothesis that country-specific rates of return to education capture cross-country differences in the quality of human capital are undoubtedly wrong. Labour markets are not very competitive in many countries, given collective bargaining mechanisms and uniform wage setting. Labour is highly immobile across countries, and employers are not perfectly informed about the acquired skills of potential employees. Consequently, qualitative differences in education are probably not well captured by the available data on country-specific rates of return to education.

3.3.3 Direct Tests of Cognitive Skills

Neither educational input measures nor country-specific rates of return appear to give good proxies for accumulated cognitive skills. Therefore, the most promising way to introduce an adjustment for differences in the quality of education builds on direct measures of the cognitive skills of individuals obtained from tests of cognitive achievement (Gundlach et al., 2002). There are two international organizations which have conducted a series of standardized international tests in varying sets of countries to assess student achievement in the fields of mathematics and natural sciences. The International Assessment of Educational Progress (IAEP), which builds on the procedures developed for the main national testing instrument in the United States, administered two international studies in 1988 and 1991, both encompassing mathematics and science tests. The International Association for the Evaluation of Educational Achievement (IEA), an agency specializing in comparative education research since its establishment in 1959, conducted cross-country mathematics studies in 1964 and 1981, cross-country science studies in 1971 and 1984, and the Third International Mathematics and Science Study (TIMSS) in 1995. Most studies include separate tests for students in different age groups (primary, middle, and final school years) and in several subfields of the subjects.

Hanushek and Kimko (2000) combine all of the available information on mathematics and science scores up to 1991 to construct a single measure of educational quality for each country. All together, they use 26 separate test score series (from different age groups, subfields, and years), administered at six points in time between 1965 and 1991, and encompassing a total of 39 countries which have participated in an international achievement test at least once. To splice these test results together for each country, they first transform all test scores into a 'percent correct' format. To account for the different mean percent correct of the test score series, their quality index $QL2^*$ makes use of intertemporally comparable time series information on student performance in the United States provided by the National Assessment of Educational Progress (NAEP). These national tests establish an absolute benchmark of performance to which the US scores on international tests can be keyed. Thus, the results of the different test series are combined by allowing the mean of each international test series to drift in accordance with the US NAEP score drift and the US performance on each international comparison. The constructed quality measure is a weighted average of all available transformed test scores for each country, where the weights are the normalized inverse of the country-specific standard error of each test, presuming that a high standard error conveys less accurate information. By combining tests from the relevant time range when current workers were students, the measure tries to approximate the cognitive skills embodied in the current labour force.[15]

To incorporate the thus measured cross-country differences in educational quality into measures of the stock of human capital, I normalize Hanushek and Kimko's (2000) educational quality index for each country relative to the measure for the United States. This measure of relative quality can then be viewed as a quality weight by which each year of schooling in a country can be weighted, where the weight for the United States is unity. Using the United States as the reference country seems warranted by the fact that the returns to schooling should be relatively undistorted on the competitive US labour market. To obtain a quality-adjusted human capital specification, the quality and quantity measures of education are combined with world-average rates of return to education at the different education levels in a Mincer-type specification of the human capital function:

$$h_i^Q = e^{\sum_a r_a Q_i s_{ai}} \tag{15}$$

where r_a is the world-average rate of return to education at level a and Q_i is Hanushek and Kimko's (2000) educational quality index for country i relative to the US value. That is, the measure of quality-adjusted years of schooling Qs enters a Mincer-type equation with rates of return r.

One virtue of this quality adjustment of the human capital specification is that one may think of the quality of human capital to rise continually and without an upper bound. By contrast, the growth in pure quantity specifications of human capital is bounded because educational attainment is asymptotically a constant. Such a specification is hard to reconcile with most models of economic growth, where the stock of physical capital also has no natural upper bound. A further virtue of the final specifications of h_i^r and h_i^Q is that they yield one single human capital variable. Since human capital is embodied in the labour force, it is more natural to think of it as one combined factor of production, rather than as several independent factors. By combining information on the labour force, quantity of education, rates of return to these educational investments, and quality of this education, the final quality-adjusted human capital specification is more readily interpreted in growth and development applications.

4. Comparison of Human Capital Measures

4.1. *Human Capital Data*

To be able to compare the different measures of human capital proposed in the literature, several data sources are exploited, using data for 1990 or the most recent year available. Adult literacy rates l and school enrollment ratios e are taken from the UNESCO (2000) World Education Indicators. Adult literacy rates l refer to the population aged 15 years and over and are for both sexes in 1990. School enrollment ratios e are gross enrollment ratios in primary, secondary, and tertiary education for both sexes in 1990. e^{MRW} refers to the indicator used by Mankiw *et al.* (1992), which is the average percentage of the working-age population enrolled in secondary school for 1960–1985.

Average years of schooling calculated by the perpetual inventory method s^{PIM} are for total (primary, secondary, and tertiary) education in 1987 as calculated by Nehru *et al.* (1995). s^{PRO} are Kyriacou's (1991) projected average years of schooling for 1985, as reported in Benhabib and Spiegel (1994). Average years of schooling based on the attainment census method s^{ATT} are taken from Barro and Lee (2001) and refer to years of total (primary, secondary, and higher) education in the total population aged 15 and over in 1990. s^{DD} is the revision of Barro and Lee's average years of schooling in 1990 for OECD countries by de la Fuente and Doménech (2000).

In calculating the human capital specifications of Sections 3.2 and 3.3, I use average years of schooling s_a^{ATT} separately at the primary, secondary, and higher level for 1990 from Barro and Lee (2001). Years of schooling in the population aged 15 and over are taken because this age group corresponds better to the labour force for most developing countries than the population aged 25 and over. The rates of return to education r_a used in h^M and h^Q are world-average social rates of return at the primary, secondary, and higher level of education estimated by the elaborate discounting method. As reported by Psacharopoulos (1994, Table 2), the world-average social rate of return to education is 20.0 percent at the primary level, 13.5 percent at the secondary level, and 10.7 percent at the higher level.

Instead of using equation (13) as the function $\phi(s)$ which links the stock of human capital to average years of schooling in equation (11), Hall and Jones (1999) and Gundlach *et al.* (2002) use

$$\phi^{HJ}(s) = \begin{cases} r^{Pri}s & \text{if } s \leq D_{pri} \\ r^{Pri}D_{pri} + r^{Sec}(s - D_{pri}) & \text{if } D_{pri} < s \leq D_{pri} + D_{sec} \\ r^{Pri}D_{pri} + r^{Sec}D_{sec} + r^{High}(s - D_{pri} - D_{sec}) & \text{if } s > D_{pri} + D_{sec} \end{cases} \Rightarrow h^{HJ} = e^{\phi^{HJ}(s)}. \quad (16)$$

Hall and Jones (1999) additionally assume that $D_{pri} = D_{sec} = 4$ for each country. This equation yields a biased allocation of level-specific rates of return to respective schooling years. For example, all the schooling years in a country whose average years of schooling are less than 4 will be weighted by the rate of return to primary education, although presumably some of the years which make up the total stock will have been in secondary or higher education. By just looking at the average and not splitting down the acquired years of education into those acquired at the primary, secondary, and higher levels, this method allocates the wrong rates of return to a substantial part of the acquired schooling years. Furthermore, Hall and Jones (1999) employ private rates of return to education calculated on the basis of the earnings function method, also reported in Psacharopoulos (1994), using the ad-hoc assumption that the rate of return to primary education equals the average rate of return in Sub-Saharan Africa (13.4 percent), the rate of return to secondary education equals the world-average rate of return (10.1 percent), and the rate of return to higher education equals the average rate of return in OECD countries (6.8 percent).[16] To be able to compare my estimates of h^M, h^r, and h^Q to the method used by Hall and Jones (1999), I also report their measure as h^{HJ}, updated to 1990 with years of schooling from Barro and Lee (2001).

In calculating h^r, country-specific social rates of return to education at the three levels estimated by the elaborate discounting method – on which the world-average rates used in h^M and h^Q are based – are taken. However, the country-specific rates of return reported by Psacharopoulos (1994) include an implausible range of values, with rates of return to primary education ranging from 2 percent in Yemen to 66 percent in Uganda. Yemen's low figure makes it the country with the lowest h^r in the sample, while Uganda's and Botswana's high figures make them the countries with the highest h^r. Morocco's high figure stems from a reported rate of return to primary education of 50.5 percent, which compares to a regional average of 15.5 percent and an income-group average of 18.2 percent. These implausible results make a sensible use of country-specific rates of return virtually impossible.

As the quality measure Q for the quality-adjusted human capital specification h^Q, I use Hanushek and Kimko's (2000) index of educational quality $QL2^*$, relative to the US value. To obtain a full set of human capital estimates, some values for s and Q (and for r in h^r) have been imputed. The imputation takes the mean of the respective regional average and the respective income-group average for any country with a missing value on one of these variables, using the World Bank's (1992) classification of countries by major regions and income groups.[17]

4.2. *Comparison of the Different Human Capital Specifications*

Table 1 presents the measures of human capital stocks based on the different specifications. To facilitate comparisons of the different specifications, values are reported relative to the United States, while the first row in each column shows the absolute US value. Countries are ranked according to output per worker based on the Summers and Heston (1991) data.[18]

The results in Table 1 show that the different specifications can yield very different measures of the human capital stock of a country. Even among the different estimation methods of average years of schooling s, large differences exist. E.g., while Mauritania's s^{ATT} is 2.42 years and Switzerland's s^{ATT} is 10.14 years, their s^{PIM} is about the same (6.66 and 6.96 years). Likewise, Spain's s^{PRO} of 9.70 years is 3.26 years higher than its s^{ATT} of 6.44 years, while Taiwan's s^{PRO} of 4.67 years is 3.31 years lower than its s^{ATT} of 7.98 years. Even between the two measures based on the attainment census method (s^{ATT} and s^{DD}), France shows a difference of 3.92 years.

To allow for an overall cross-country comparison of the different specifications, Table 2 reports correlation coefficients among the 11 human capital measures. Because the data sets cover different samples of countries, the number of countries covered jointly by each pair of measures is reported in brackets below the correlation coefficients. For example, there is no country jointly covered by the l and s^{DD} data sets, because the UNESCO does not report adult literacy rates l for advanced countries and de la Fuente and Doménech's (2000) data set s^{DD} is available only for OECD countries.

The correlation between the enrollment ratio e and the three broad-sample schooling years variables s^{PIM}, s^{PRO}, and s^{ATT} range between 0.83 and 0.90, suggesting that enrollment ratios may not be an altogether bad proxy for the quantity of schooling after all. The correlations among the three broad-sample schooling-years variables s range from 0.88 to 0.90, showing a comparable broad-sample distributions. When compared to the revised OECD sample data set s^{DD}, however, the correlation is very low (0.35, 0.47, and 0.79, respectively). Both s^{DD} and h^r in general show a low correlation to all other human capital specifications. Barro and Lee's (2001) s^{ATT} and the Mincer specification h^M are highly correlated (0.97), as are the two measures based on the Mincer specification, h^M and h^{HJ} (0.98). The correlation between the quality-adjusted human capital specification h^Q and most other specifications is relatively low.

In sum, there seem to be substantial differences between the different measures of the stock of human capital, and even between those measures which do not take into account differences in the quality of education. Given that the human capital specification which takes account of international differences in the educational quality is relatively weakly related to the other specifications, the recognition of international differences in the quality of education seems to introduce a substantial amount of additional information into the measure of human capital. The differences in the human capital measures may lead to largely different results in an empirical application of the different measures, and thus to diverging conclusions on the importance of human capital for economic growth.

Table 1. Data on Human Capital Specifications
Relative to the United States. Absolute U.S. values reported in the first row. (Countries ranked by output per worker.)

	[1] l^1	[2] e	[3] e^{MRW}	[4] s^{PIM}	[5] s^{PRO}	[6] s^{ATT}	[7] s^{DD}	[8] h^{HJ}	[9] h^M	[10] h^r	[11] h^Q	[12] Note: Q
United States (Abs.)	–	91.1	11.9	11.6	12.1	11.7	12.9	3.3	6.9	4.3	6.9	46.77
Luxembourg	–	–	0.420	–	0.571	–	–	0.820	0.662	0.708	0.615	0.951
United States	–	1.000	1.000	1.000	1.000	1.000	1.000	1.000	1.000	1.000	1.000	1.000
Qatar	0.770	0.840	–	–	–	–	–	0.698	0.484	0.598	0.444	0.929*
United Arab E.	0.770	0.776	–	–	–	–	–	0.698	0.484	0.598	0.444	0.929*
Canada	–	1.093	0.891	0.862	0.826	0.936	0.991	0.950	0.898	0.864	1.216	1.167
Switzerland	–	0.783	0.403	0.599	–	0.864	0.971	0.897	0.804	0.819	1.370	1.312
Belgium	–	0.901	0.782	0.721	0.774	0.756	0.756	0.823	0.704	0.862	0.997	1.220
Netherlands	–	0.947	0.899	0.725	0.784	0.745	0.848	0.816	0.665	0.604	0.856	1.166
Italy	–	0.773	0.597	0.684	0.756	0.552	0.620	0.665	0.446	0.529	0.475	1.056
France	–	0.910	0.748	0.732	0.789	0.592	0.842	0.697	0.486	0.564	0.616	1.197
Australia	–	0.834	0.824	0.654	0.722	0.884	0.951	0.911	0.888	0.923	1.427	1.262
Germany, West	–	0.833	0.706	0.731	0.855	0.827	1.006	0.871	0.684	0.733	0.728	1.041
Bahamas	0.980	–	–	–	–	–	–	0.717	0.514	0.881	0.530	1.025*
Norway	–	0.899	0.840	0.817	0.764	0.985	0.794	0.988	1.052	0.862	2.231	1.380
Sweden	–	0.813	0.664	0.848	0.797	0.810	0.807	0.859	0.735	0.776	1.062	1.228
Finland	–	0.980	0.966	0.844	0.896	0.799	0.765	0.852	0.734	0.763	1.141	1.273
Oman	–	0.600	0.227	–	–	–	–	0.617	0.402	0.506	0.341	0.837*
United Kingdom	–	0.818	0.748	0.879	0.703	0.747	0.847	0.817	0.695	0.704	1.175	1.337
Austria	–	0.870	0.672	0.754	0.709	0.661	0.848	0.757	0.523	0.599	0.685	1.210
Spain	–	0.920	0.672	0.616	0.802	0.549	0.550	0.662	0.454	0.588	0.515	1.110
Puerto Rico	–	–	–	–	–	–	–	0.633	0.427	1.136	0.397	0.934*
Kuwait	0.760	–	0.807	–	0.572	0.510	–	0.633	0.372	0.490	0.229	0.481
New Zealand	–	0.877	1.000	0.762	0.767	0.958	0.938	0.967	1.049	1.345	2.468	1.434
Iceland	–	0.886	0.857	0.791	0.708	0.691	–	0.781	0.609	0.664	0.697	1.095
Denmark	–	0.894	0.899	0.787	0.571	0.816	0.847	0.863	0.751	0.775	1.270	1.321
Singapore	0.890	0.673	0.756	0.631	0.570	0.507	–	0.631	0.420	0.428	0.746	1.542
Ireland	–	0.886	0.958	1.083	0.731	0.748	0.729	0.818	0.669	0.712	0.748	1.073
Israel	–	0.839	0.798	0.620	0.830	0.798	–	0.851	0.781	0.840	1.029	1.164
Saudi Arabia	0.590	0.542	0.261	–	0.244	–	–	0.617	0.402	0.506	0.341	0.837*
Hong Kong	0.910	–	0.605	–	0.645	0.780	–	0.839	0.682	1.159	1.560	1.536
Japan	–	0.844	0.916	0.946	0.783	0.763	0.871	0.828	0.687	0.528	1.279	1.400
Bahrain	0.820	0.903	1.017	–	–	0.423	–	0.571	0.354	0.459	0.226	0.496
Trinidad & Tobago	0.970	0.761	0.739	–	0.489	0.610	–	0.713	0.517	0.661	0.512	0.993
Taiwan	–	–	–	–	0.386	0.679	–	0.774	0.581	1.301	0.771	1.204
Malta	–	0.827	0.597	–	0.565	–	–	0.737	0.567	0.655	0.766	1.222
Cyprus	–	0.796	0.689	0.660	–	0.742	–	0.814	0.662	0.445	0.651	0.989
Greece	–	0.845	0.664	0.753	0.695	0.681	0.613	0.775	0.605	0.654	0.686	1.088
Venezuela	0.900	0.772	0.588	0.569	0.571	0.422	–	0.570	0.357	0.615	0.308	0.836
Mexico	0.880	0.718	0.555	0.511	0.584	0.572	–	0.681	0.480	0.683	0.377	0.796
Portugal	–	0.785	0.487	0.493	0.539	0.418	0.497	0.567	0.342	0.436	0.327	0.945
Korea, Rep.	0.970	0.866	0.857	0.665	0.657	0.847	–	0.885	0.789	0.908	1.207	1.252
Syria	0.660	0.752	0.739	–	0.548	0.435	–	0.579	0.361	0.510	0.262	0.646
U.S.S.R. (Rus. Fed.)	–	0.923	–	–	–	–	–	0.737	0.567	0.749	0.713	1.168
Barbados	0.970	–	1.017	–	0.663	0.674	–	0.769	0.576	0.726	0.844	1.279
Argentina	0.960	–	0.420	0.652	0.664	0.693	–	0.782	0.638	0.450	0.674	1.037

(continued)

Table 1. *Continued.*

	[1]	[2]	[3]	[4]	[5]	[6]	[7]	[8]	[9]	[10]	[11]	[12]
	l^1	e	e^{MRW}	s^{PIM}	s^{PRO}	s^{ATT}	s^{DD}	h^{HJ}	h^M	h'	h^Q	Note: Q
Bulgaria	–	0.801	–	–	–	–	–	0.691	0.509	0.682	0.526	1.026*
Jordan	0.820	0.598	0.908	0.424	0.618	0.506	–	0.630	0.407	0.568	0.369	0.904
Malaysia	0.800	0.645	0.613	0.534	0.474	0.514	–	0.636	0.430	0.661	0.512	1.161
Algeria	0.550	0.711	0.378	0.354	0.385	0.362	–	0.531	0.310	0.447	0.229	0.600
Iraq	0.520	–	0.622	0.360	0.377	0.278	–	0.469	0.262	0.365	0.206	0.588
Chile	0.940	–	0.647	0.618	0.576	0.593	–	0.698	0.515	0.438	0.284	0.529
Uruguay	0.970	0.847	0.588	0.679	0.634	0.604	–	0.707	0.507	0.775	0.587	1.118
Fiji	0.890	0.806	0.681	–	0.549	0.669	–	0.764	0.636	0.958	0.910	1.242
Iran	–	0.720	0.546	0.328	0.476	0.338	–	0.515	0.294	0.439	0.192	0.390
Belize	0.300	–	–	–	–	–	–	0.594	0.383	0.567	0.333	0.855*
Brazil	0.810	0.739	0.395	0.380	0.458	0.342	–	0.519	0.305	0.761	0.260	0.783
Hungary	–	0.743	–	–	–	0.761	–	0.826	0.764	0.818	1.276	1.309
Mauritius	0.800	0.645	0.613	–	0.522	0.474	–	0.607	0.396	0.692	0.472	1.175
Colombia	0.900	0.622	0.513	0.436	0.540	0.400	–	0.556	0.333	0.520	0.284	0.810
Costa Rica	0.940	0.684	0.588	–	0.681	0.473	–	0.606	0.394	0.448	0.389	0.987
Yugoslavia	–	–	–	–	–	0.601	–	0.705	0.541	0.291	0.662	1.154
South Africa	0.800	0.874	0.252	–	–	0.460	–	0.596	0.399	0.730	0.440	1.097
Namibia	–	–	–	–	–	–	–	0.520	0.305	0.519	0.270	0.834*
Seychelles	–	–	–	–	–	–	–	0.555	0.340	0.538	0.316	0.913*
Ecuador	0.870	0.772	0.605	0.493	0.725	0.503	–	0.627	0.413	0.529	0.347	0.834
Tunisia	0.600	0.677	0.361	0.415	0.468	0.335	–	0.513	0.296	0.429	0.269	0.866
Turkey	0.790	0.606	0.462	0.387	0.523	0.353	–	0.525	0.309	0.434	0.276	0.849
Gabon	0.560	–	0.218	–	0.663	–	–	0.555	0.340	0.538	0.316	0.913*
Yemen	–	–	0.050	–	–	0.126	–	0.370	0.191	0.266	0.179	0.758*
Panama	0.890	0.739	0.975	0.644	0.661	0.688	–	0.779	0.619	0.885	0.619	1.000
Czechoslovakia	–	0.787	–	–	–	–	–	0.737	0.567	0.655	0.654	1.105*
Suriname	0.920	–	0.681	–	0.503	–	–	0.633	0.427	0.564	0.397	0.934*
Poland	–	0.829	–	–	–	0.806	–	0.857	0.858	1.059	1.673	1.376
Guatemala	0.530	–	0.202	0.303	0.304	0.259	–	0.455	0.256	0.390	0.236	0.855*
Reunion	–	–	–	–	–	–	–	0.555	0.340	0.538	0.316	0.913*
Dominican Rep.	0.800	–	0.487	–	–	0.378	–	0.541	0.320	0.483	0.283	0.841
Egypt	0.480	0.737	0.588	0.412	0.471	0.363	–	0.532	0.307	0.483	0.222	0.565
Peru	0.860	0.854	0.672	0.565	0.657	0.529	–	0.647	0.434	0.641	0.381	0.880
Morocco	–	–	0.303	0.208	0.288	–	–	0.553	0.336	1.387	0.276	0.763*
Thailand	0.930	–	0.370	0.493	0.456	0.476	–	0.607	0.414	1.065	0.409	0.989
Solomon Is.	–	–	–	–	–	–	–	0.526	0.308	0.522	0.289	0.917*
Botswana	0.650	0.739	0.244	–	0.292	0.455	–	0.593	0.396	2.135	0.287	0.678
Western Samoa	–	–	–	–	–	–	–	0.591	0.377	0.583	0.361	0.954*
Grenada	–	–	–	–	–	–	–	0.594	0.383	0.567	0.333	0.855*
Paraguay	0.910	0.615	0.370	0.500	0.510	0.523	–	0.642	0.442	0.709	0.376	0.854
Swaziland	0.720	0.720	0.311	–	0.447	0.450	–	0.590	0.398	0.685	0.346	0.861
Dominica	–	–	–	–	0.550	–	–	0.594	0.383	0.567	0.333	0.855*
Tonga	–	–	–	–	–	–	–	0.591	0.377	0.583	0.361	0.954*
St. Vincent & Gre.	–	–	–	–	–	–	–	0.594	0.383	0.567	0.333	0.855*
Sri Lanka	0.890	0.728	0.697	0.540	0.499	0.517	–	0.638	0.421	0.728	0.382	0.910
El Salvador	0.690	0.620	0.328	0.428	0.349	0.362	–	0.531	0.324	0.454	0.228	0.560
St. Lucia	–	–	–	–	–	–	–	0.594	0.383	0.567	0.333	0.855*
Bolivia	0.790	0.693	0.412	0.544	0.444	0.428	–	0.574	0.364	0.368	0.249	0.587
Vanuatu	–	–	–	–	–	–	–	0.591	0.377	0.583	0.361	0.954*
Jamaica	0.830	0.697	0.941	0.693	0.488	0.404	–	0.558	0.336	0.457	0.347	1.040
Indonesia	0.820	0.673	0.345	0.381	0.370	0.341	–	0.518	0.302	0.494	0.285	0.919
Djibouti	0.410	0.215	–	–	–	–	–	0.520	0.305	0.519	0.270	0.834*

	[1]										
Bangladesh	0.350	0.381	0.269	0.269	0.288	0.187	–	0.407	0.217	0.358	0.210	0.917*
Philippines	0.940	0.847	0.891	0.667	0.734	0.620	–	0.721	0.532	0.562	0.369	0.717
Pakistan	0.340	0.339	0.252	0.182	0.210	0.353	–	0.525	0.293	0.369	0.276	0.917*
Congo	0.680	0.822	0.319	–	–	0.437	–	0.580	0.357	0.621	0.386	1.088
Honduras	0.690	–	0.311	0.383	0.467	0.358	–	0.528	0.317	0.508	0.235	0.611
Nicaragua	0.640	0.617	0.487	–	0.498	0.311	–	0.494	0.284	0.430	0.215	0.584
Romania	–	0.729	–	–	–	–	–	0.691	0.509	0.682	0.526	1.026*
Mongolia	0.800	0.719	–	–	–	–	–	0.591	0.377	0.583	0.361	0.954*
India	0.480	0.568	0.429	0.305	0.393	0.349	–	0.523	0.308	0.654	0.203	0.445
Cote d'Ivoire	0.340	–	0.193	0.181	0.340	–	–	0.520	0.305	0.519	0.270	0.834*
Papua New Guinea	0.680	–	0.126	–	0.232	0.196	–	0.412	0.226	0.319	0.180	0.483
Guyana	0.970	–	0.983	–	0.514	0.484	–	0.614	0.416	0.689	0.462	1.101
Laos	0.520	–	–	–	–	–	–	0.526	0.308	0.522	0.289	0.917*
Cape Verde Is.	0.630	0.605	–	–	–	–	–	0.520	0.305	0.519	0.270	0.834*
Cameroon	0.570	0.577	0.286	0.269	0.449	0.262	–	0.457	0.258	0.432	0.244	0.906
Sierra Leone	0.270	0.314	0.143	0.190	0.164	0.182	–	0.403	0.215	0.360	0.199	0.796*
Zimbabwe	0.820	0.754	0.370	0.389	0.402	0.429	–	0.575	0.356	0.726	0.311	0.848
Senegal	0.290	0.338	0.143	0.173	0.205	0.193	–	0.410	0.222	0.369	0.207	0.834*
Sudan	0.400	0.341	0.168	0.160	0.173	0.140	–	0.378	0.197	0.322	0.185	0.796*
Nepal	0.240	0.603	0.193	–	0.168	0.132	–	0.373	0.190	0.311	0.186	0.917*
China	0.780	0.587	–	0.448	–	0.498	–	0.624	0.416	0.722	0.618	1.377
Liberia	0.340	–	0.210	–	0.267	0.183	–	0.404	0.215	0.487	0.199	0.796*
Nigeria	0.490	–	0.210	0.210	0.166	–	–	0.447	0.249	0.426	0.228	0.832
Lesotho	0.670	0.665	0.168	–	0.404	0.334	–	0.512	0.312	0.366	0.339	1.111
Zambia	0.730	0.618	0.202	0.388	0.317	0.356	–	0.527	0.325	0.608	0.273	0.783
Haiti	0.410	–	0.160	0.226	0.220	0.248	–	0.447	0.249	0.406	0.226	0.817*
Benin	–	0.333	0.151	–	0.193	0.166	–	0.393	0.209	0.358	0.194	0.796*
Ghana	0.580	0.493	0.395	0.391	0.319	0.308	–	0.492	0.278	0.422	0.208	0.547
Kenya	0.720	0.637	0.202	0.356	0.285	0.311	–	0.494	0.292	0.518	0.227	0.636
Gambia	0.340	–	0.126	–	0.128	0.138	–	0.377	0.196	0.332	0.184	0.796*
Mauritania	0.350	0.285	0.084	0.573	0.085	0.206	–	0.419	0.230	0.402	0.209	0.796*
Somalia	–	–	0.092	–	0.068	–	–	0.447	0.249	0.398	0.224	0.796*
Guinea	0.310	0.211	–	–	–	–	–	0.447	0.249	0.444	0.224	0.796*
Togo	0.450	0.598	0.244	–	–	0.250	–	0.449	0.249	0.442	0.212	0.699
Madagascar	–	0.462	0.218	0.300	0.356	–	–	0.447	0.249	0.444	0.224	0.796*
Mozambique	0.350	–	0.059	0.226	0.174	0.077	–	0.342	0.174	0.288	0.162	0.597
Rwanda	0.540	–	0.034	0.239	0.268	0.179	–	0.401	0.220	0.381	0.202	0.796*
Bhutan	0.370	–	–	–	–	–	–	0.526	0.308	0.522	0.289	0.917*
Guinea-Biss.	0.500	–	–	–	0.190	0.055	–	0.330	0.165	0.270	0.161	0.796*
Angola	–	0.378	0.151	0.157	0.305	–	–	0.520	0.305	0.519	0.270	0.834*
Myanmar (Burma)	0.810	0.494	0.294	0.222	0.409	0.211	–	0.422	0.228	0.377	0.220	0.917*
Comoros	0.540	–	–	0.679	–	–	–	0.447	0.249	0.444	0.224	0.796*
Central Afr. R.	0.500	0.345	0.118	–	0.295	0.200	–	0.415	0.223	0.388	0.183	0.530
Malawi	0.520	0.436	0.050	0.293	0.163	0.231	–	0.436	0.248	0.348	0.222	0.796*
Chad	0.430	–	0.034	–	0.151	–	–	0.447	0.249	0.444	0.224	0.796*
Uganda	0.570	0.437	0.092	0.216	0.243	0.278	–	0.469	0.271	1.672	0.239	0.796*
Tanzania	0.620	0.371	0.042	0.216	0.152	0.237	–	0.440	0.251	0.439	0.225	0.796*
Zaire (Congo, D. R.)	0.720	–	0.303	0.344	0.358	0.239	–	0.441	0.246	0.436	0.212	0.717
Mali	0.250	0.151	0.084	0.097	0.119	0.057	–	0.331	0.165	0.271	0.161	0.796*
Burundi	0.310	0.348	0.034	–	0.143	0.118	–	0.364	0.190	0.321	0.180	0.796*
Burkina Faso	0.160	0.181	0.034	–	0.061	–	–	0.447	0.249	0.444	0.224	0.796*
Niger	0.120	0.159	0.042	–	0.069	0.070	–	0.338	0.170	0.280	0.165	0.796*
Ethiopia	0.310	0.206	0.092	0.049	0.094	–	–	0.447	0.249	0.415	0.224	0.796*

Notes: [1]l (column [1]): Absolute value of the adult literacy rate.
* Imputed Q data.

Table 2. Correlation between Human Capital Specifications
Correlation coefficents; number of joint observations in brackets below.

	[1] l	[2] e	[3] e^{MRW}	[4] s^{PIM}	[5] s^{PRO}	[6] s^{ATT}	[7] s^{DD}	[8] h^{HJ}	[9] h^{M}	[10] h^{r}	[11] h^{Q}
[1] l	1										
	[96]										
[2] e	0.828	1									
	[67]	[103]									
[3] e^{MRW}	0.738	0.817	1								
	[83]	[90]	[117]								
[4] s^{PIM}	0.770	0.858	0.863	1							
	[55]	[69]	[81]	[83]							
[5] s^{PRO}	0.846	0.902	0.872	0.878	1						
	[79]	[83]	[108]	[79]	[111]						
[6] s^{ATT}	0.841	0.830	0.819	0.890	0.896	1					
	[77]	[86]	[102]	[76]	[96]	[108]					
[7] s^{DD}	–	0.300	0.383	0.345	0.471	0.791	1				
	[0]	[21]	[21]	[21]	[20]	[21]	[21]				
[8] h^{HJ}	0.789	0.809	0.806	0.863	0.872	0.999	0.789	1			
	[96]	[103]	[117]	[83]	[111]	[108]	[21]	[152]			
[9] h^{M}	0.759	0.736	0.753	0.822	0.819	0.973	0.697	0.976	1		
	[96]	[103]	[117]	[83]	[111]	[108]	[21]	[152]	[152]		
[10] h^{r}	0.395	0.447	0.344	0.373	0.361	0.574	0.579	0.558	0.554	1	
	[96]	[103]	[117]	[83]	[111]	[108]	[21]	[151]	[151]	[151]	
[11] h^{Q}	0.562	0.576	0.623	0.695	0.661	0.846	0.503	0.845	0.916	0.510	1
	[96]	[103]	[117]	[83]	[111]	[108]	[21]	[151]	[151]	[151]	[151]

4.3. *Impact on the Results of Growth Research*

To show the importance of an improved specification of the stock of human capital in growth research, Table 3 reports results of development-accounting exercises for the human-capital specifications which are based on Mincerian human-capital theory. The development-accounting exercises, which look at sources of differences in levels of economic development across countries in 1990, use the covariance measure proposed by Klenow and Rodríguez-Clare (1997) to decompose the international variance in output per worker y into the relative contributions of differences in human capital stocks, in physical capital stocks, and in levels of total factor productivity in a simple neoclassical growth framework. The covariance measure calculates the respective average fraction of output dispersion across countries which can be statistically attributed to international differences in human capital stocks h and in physical capital-output ratios k/y, leaving the rest to be explained by residual total factor productivity A. Details on the development-accounting methodology and on the data on output and physical capital can be found in Wößmann (2002).

In the broadest sample of countries for which the output and physical-capital data is available ($n = 132$), differences in human capital per worker h^{HJ} account

Table 3. Development-Accounting Results

Covariance measure: $\frac{\text{cov}(\ln(y),\ln(Z))}{\text{var}(\ln(y))}$ with Z given in each column.

	h^X	$(k/y)^{\frac{\alpha}{1-\alpha}}$	A	Sample Size
Human capital specification:				
$X = HJ$	0.21	0.19	0.60	132
$X = M$	0.33	0.19	0.48	132
$X = r$	0.18	0.19	0.63	132
$X = Q$	0.45	0.19	0.36	132
Different samples of countries:	h^Q			
Non-imputed s^{ATT} data	0.51	0.19	0.30	104
PWT benchmark study and non-imputed s^{ATT} and Q data	0.60	0.13	0.27	64
PWT benchmark, non-imputed s^{ATT} data, and non-projected Q data	0.61	0.13	0.26	29

Note: For h^{HJ}, h^M, h^r, and h^Q, see equations (13) to (16).

for 21 percent of the international variation in output per worker when the stock of human capital is measured as in Hall and Jones (1999). Since another 19 percent can be attributed to differences in the physical capital-output ratio, 60 percent remain as differences in residual total factor productivity. With the human capital specification h^M, which attributes rates of return to years of schooling through equation (13) instead of equation (16) and uses social rates of return estimated by the elaborate discounting method, 33 percent of development differences are accounted for by human capital differences. Using country-specific social rates of return in the specification h^r, the share attributed to human capital is only 18 percent. This should reflect the substantial measurement errors in many of the country-specific estimates of rates of return, as well as the fact that there is certainly no world-wide competitive labour market.

Since cognitive skills are not well proxied by measures of mere school quantities or country-specific rates of return to education, results based on the quality-adjusted human capital specification h^Q are reported in the fourth row of Table 3. The adjustment of the human capital specification for differences in the quality of schooling boosts the share of variation in development levels attributed to human capital differences to 45 percent. This evidence shows that the assumption implicit in all previous specifications, that differences in educational quality can be neglected in the specification of human capital stocks, can give rise to misleading results on the development effect of human capital in empirical growth research. Furthermore, the empirical merits of different theories of economic growth and development may be severely misjudged when using misspecified measures of human capital.

Further results on the quality-adjusted human capital specification for different sub-samples of countries reveal that the share attributed to human capital seems to be additionally understated through the use of non-original human capital data. When countries with imputed values on years of schooling s^{ATT} are excluded ($n = 104$), the share of development variation accounted for by human capital exceeds 50 percent. In the sample which excludes countries which never participated in one of the benchmark studies underlying the Penn World Tables (PWT) and countries which have imputed s^{ATT} or Q data ($n = 64$), the share attributed to quality-adjusted human capital rises to 60 percent. Furthermore, of the 88 available values of the quality index Q, more than half had been projected in Hanushek and Kimko (2000) on the basis of observed country and education-system characteristics. When confining the sample to the 29 countries which do not have any imputed or projected human capital data (s^{ATT} and Q) and which participated in a PWT benchmark study, similarly 61 percent of the international variation in the level of economic development are accounted for by differences in quality-adjusted human capital. All this shows that the development impact of human capital seems to be severely understated by previous human capital specifications and by misreported human capital data.

Likewise, in the sample of OECD countries, whose economies work under a relatively similar open institutional framework, the share of development variation accounted for by differences in human capital stocks increases from 39 percent with the h^{HJ} measure to 100 percent with the h^{Q} measure (for details, see Wößmann, 2002). That is, the covariance between the quality-adjusted human capital specification and output per worker in the OECD sample is just as large as the variance of output per worker, so that the whole variation in OECD development levels can be accounted for by differences in human capital once the human capital measure is adjusted for differences in the quality of schooling. Furthermore, Wößmann (2002) shows that the effect on development-accounting results of the specification error introduced by the use of inferior rate of return estimates and by the disregard of differences in educational quality is far greater than that of the recording errors in the data on educational quantity which have recently been stressed by Krueger and Lindahl (2001) and de la Fuente and Doménech (2000).

5. Conclusion

The review of human capital specification has shown how the implementation of the concept of human capital has evolved in the empirical growth literature. In light of the differences among the different specifications, one should not wonder that different studies have found very different results on growth and development effects of human capital. Two crucial aspects of human capital specification which can strongly influence the estimated growth effect of human capital are the correct inclusion of rates of return to education and the consideration of the quality of education. The development-accounting results show that the development impact of human capital seems to be severely understated by human capital specifications which neglect these specification issues. Using the quality-adjusted measure of human capital h^{Q}, cross-country differences in the stock of human capital can account for about half the world-wide dispersion of levels of economic development and for virtually all the development differences across OECD countries – compared to less than a quarter and less than half, respectively, with human capital measured as h^{HJ}.

The preferred human capital specification h^Q presented in this paper is certainly not the last word in the academic quest for improvements in human capital measurement. The quality of the estimates of rates of return to education and of the measures of educational quality are without doubt limited, and the construction and method of inclusion of the quality weights employed in calculating h^Q is rather ad-hoc. Nevertheless, the quality-adjusted human capital specification based on a Mincer specification with decreasing returns to education constitutes a substantial advancement over the most commonly used proxy, average years of schooling, and the relevance of the adoption of the improvements is highlighted by the development-accounting results. In light of the gradual advancements in the specification of human capital surveyed in this review, it may be hoped that future improvements in the quality of the underlying data and in the specification of the human capital measure may further increase our knowledge of human capital issues.

While this paper has focussed on education as a means to accumulate human capital, an encompassing specification of human capital should also consider the whole range of other investments which people make to improve their productivity. In addition to formal education, these investments include informal education acquired parallel to schooling, skills acquired after schooling through training on the job, and the experience gained through learning by doing. Furthermore, medical care, nutrition, and improvements in working conditions which avoid activities with high accident rates can be viewed as investments to improve health. While the variable 'age minus pre-schooling years minus years of schooling' has been used as a proxy for experience and the variables 'life expectancy' and 'infant mortality rate' have been used as proxies for health status, these are probably not very good measures of the productively available human capital accumulated through after-school skill acquisition and through health investments. A further complication lies in the fact that knowledge can not only be gained, but also lost after it has been acquired in school. Nevertheless, the focus on the mere formal education component of human capital seems warranted, also because education increases people's ability to learn later in live and to live healthier lives.

Even more, education is an especially crucial aspect in development because it is not only important for human capital in the narrow sense that it augments future production possibilities, but also for human capabilities in the broader sense of ability and freedom of people to lead the kind of lives they value. When understanding development as a broader concept of freedom expansion as in Sen (1999), where economic growth is not an end in itself but a means to expanding the freedoms that people enjoy, the benefits of education exceed its role as human capital in economic production. The abilities to read, communicate, and argue, to choose in a more informed way, or to be taken more seriously by others are among such additional benefits of education as valued by the broader human-capability perspective.

Acknowledgements

I would like to thank Erich Gundlach and Jon Temple for their detailed comments and helpful discussion on an earlier version of this paper, and an associate editor and an anonymous referee for several helpful suggestions.

Notes

1. For a history of the concept of human capital, see Kiker (1968). For a brief exposition of the history of human capital estimation, see Dagum and Slottje (2000), who include the highly problematic retrospective cost-of-production approach in addition to the prospective income-based approach and the proxy educational-stock approach which are dealt with in this paper.
2. Mankiw *et al.* (1992) use the proportion of the working-age population enrolled in secondary school as their proxy, obtained by multiplying secondary school enrollment ratios by the fraction of the working-age population which is of school age.
3. See Pritchett (2001) for an illustration why enrollment ratios can – and in reality seem to – be *negatively* correlated with true accumulation rates of human capital; see also Gemmell (1996) for a critique of the use of enrollment ratios as human capital measures.
4. For an application which uses data on levels of educational attainment directly, see Temple (2001a).
5. Note that the perpetual inventory formula given in Nehru *et al.* (1995) is erroneous.
6. Kyriacou (1991) does not give an explicit rationale for the lag structure chosen between years of schooling and enrollment rates, or specifically for choosing the same lag for the enrollment ratios at the secondary and higher level, but only reports that he heuristically found a strong relationship of the form of equation (6).
7. Several studies use years of schooling at the different levels separately (e.g., Barro and Sala-i-Martin, 1995; Barro, 1997). This seems problematic since, e.g., years of primary schooling can only increase up to universal coverage. The variation across countries with basically universal coverage is mainly caused by cross-country differences in the duration of the primary level D_{pri}, which will depend primarily on an education system's classification of different levels. Therefore, it is not quite clear what, e.g., estimated coefficients in a growth regression really show.
8. Additionally, using average years of schooling assumes perfect substitutability of workers across attainment levels and a constant elasticity of substitution across sub-groups of workers at any time and place (Mulligan and Sala-i-Martin, 2000).
9. Note that if there were signalling effects in the private rate of return, the social rate of return might be overstated (cf. Weiss, 1995). See Temple (2001b) for a discussion of the issues involved.
10. Note that in this work, no adjustment is made for differences in hours worked, as the early growth accounting studies did (Section 2.1).
11. In addition to rates of return to each year of education, Bils and Klenow (2000) introduce an influence of teachers' education, measured by the stock of human capital 25 years earlier, into their measure of human capital. However, it is not clear why teachers' education should have an influence on the level of human capital apart from the one reflected in the returns to education. They also include a wage effect of experience, measured by age less years of schooling less 6, whereas the current paper focuses on the human capital accumulated through education.

12. Jones (1996), Topel (1999) and Krueger and Lindahl (2001) also specify the relation-
    ship between income and years of schooling in a log-linear way.
13. Bils and Klenow (2000) suggest decreasing returns to schooling of the form $\phi(s) =$
    $\frac{\alpha}{1-\beta}s^{1-\beta}$, $\beta > 0$, which in applied terms becomes broadly equivalent to equation (13).
14. Mulligan and Sala-i-Martin (1997) also suggest a measure of human capital based on
    labour income, namely the ratio of the average wage of the labour force to the wage of
    a person without any schooling. This wage of a person with zero years of schooling is
    measured as the exponential of the constant term α_0 from a Mincer regression like
    equation (9). This method weights different segments of the labour force by the income
    at different levels of education. While Mulligan and Sala-i-Martin (1997) calculate
    stocks of human capital for the states of the United States, the lack of the detailed
    labour-income data necessary to pursue this method in most countries of the world will
    make it impossible to apply such measures in cross-country research in the near future.
    In any event, for the calculation of the aggregate stock of human capital, this approach
    should yield estimates equivalent to using estimated rates of return to education in
    equation (13). Mulligan and Sala-i-Martin (2000) further expand on the idea of
    aggregating heterogeneous workers into a stock of human capital based on their
    educational attainment, yielding optimal index numbers for human capital stocks
    which minimize an expected-error function.
15. Hanushek and Kimko (2000) show that such quality measures of education matter more
    in growth regressions than quantity measures, a finding also confirmed by Barro (2001).
16. Note that while in general, narrow-social rates of return must be lower than private
    rates, the reported private estimates based on the earnings function method are even
    lower than the narrow-social estimates based on the elaborate discounting method.
17. The regions used are Asia, Latin America, Sub-Saharan Africa, North Africa, Middle
    East, Eastern Europe, and OECD. The income groups are low, lower-middle, upper-
    middle, and high income.
18. To allow for an evaluation of the quality component of the quality-adjusted human
    capital specification h^Q, column [12] of Table 1 reports Hanushek and Kimko's (2000)
    index of educational quality.

References

Acemoglu, D. and Angrist, J. (2001) How Large are Human Capital Externalities? Evi-
    dence from Compulsory Schooling Laws. In B. S. Bernanke and K. Rogoff (eds.),
    NBER Macroeconomics Annual 2000. Cambridge, MA: MIT Press, 9–59.
Azariadis, C. and Drazen, A. (1990) Threshold Externalities in Economic Development.
    Quarterly Journal of Economics, 105, 2, 501–526.
Barro, R. J. (1991) Economic Growth in a Cross Section of Countries. *Quarterly Journal of
    Economics*, 106, 2, 407–443.
Barro, R. J. (1997) *Determinants of Economic Growth: A Cross-Country Empirical Study*.
    Cambridge, MA: MIT Press.
Barro, R. J. (2001) Human Capital and Growth. *American Economic Review, Papers and
    Proceedings*, 91, 2, 12–17.
Barro, R. J. and Lee, J.-W. (1993) International Comparisons of Educational Attainment.
    Journal of Monetary Economics, 32, 3, 363–394.
Barro, R. J. and Lee, J.-W. (1996) International Measures of Schooling Years and School-
    ing Quality. *American Economic Review, Papers and Proceedings*, 86, 2, 218–223.
Barro, R. J. and Lee, J.-W. (2001) International Data on Educational Attainment: Updates
    and Implications. *Oxford Economic Papers*, 53, 3, 541–563.

Barro, R. J. and Sala-i-Martin, X. (1995) *Economic Growth*. New York: McGraw-Hill.

Behrman, J. R. and Rosenzweig, M. R. (1994) Caveat Emptor: Cross-Country Data on Education and the Labour Force. *Journal of Development Economics*, 44, 1, 147–171.

Benhabib, J. and Spiegel, M. M. (1994) The Role of Human Capital in Economic Development: Evidence from Aggregate Cross-Country and Regional U.S. Data. *Journal of Monetary Economics*, 34, 2, 143–173.

Bils, M. and Klenow, P. J. (2000) Does Schooling Cause Growth? *American Economic Review*, 90, 5, 1160–1183.

Borghans, L., Green, F. and Mayhew, K. (2001) Skills Measurement and Economic Analysis: An Introduction. *Oxford Economic Papers*, 53, 3, 375–384.

Card, D. (1999) The Causal Effect of Education on Earnings. In O. Ashenfelter and D. Card (eds.), *Handbook of Labour Economics, Volume 3A*. Amsterdam: North-Holland, 1801–1863.

Chiswick, B. R. (1998) Interpreting the Coefficient of Schooling in the Human Capital Earnings Function. *Journal of Educational Planning and Administration*, 12, 2, 123–130.

Ciccone, A. and Peri, G. (2000) Human Capital and Externalities in Cities. Barcelona: Universitat Pompeu Fabra, Mimeo.

Dagum, C. and Slottje, D. J. (2000) A New Method to Estimate the Level and Distribution of Household Human Capital with Application. *Structural Change and Economic Dynamics*, 11, 1, 67–94.

de la Fuente, A. and Doménech, R. (2000) Human Capital in Growth Regressions: How Much Difference Does Data Quality Make? CEPR Discussion Paper 2466. London: Centre for Economic Policy Research.

de la Fuente, A. and Doménech, R. (2001) Schooling Data, Technological Diffusion, and the Neoclassical Model. *American Economic Review, Papers and Proceedings*, 91, 2, 323–327.

Denison, E. F. (1967) *Why Growth Rates Differ: Postwar Experience in Nine Western Countries*. Washington, D.C.: The Brookings Institution.

Gemmell, N. (1996) Evaluating the Impacts of Human Capital Stocks and Accumulation on Economic Growth: Some New Evidence. *Oxford Bulletin of Economics and Statistics*, 58, 1, 9–28.

Gundlach, E. (1995) The Role of Human Capital in Economic Growth: New Results and Alternative Interpretations. *Weltwirtschaftliches Archiv*, 131, 2, 383–402.

Gundlach, E., Rudman, D. and Wößmann, L. (2002) Second Thoughts on Development Accounting. *Applied Economics*, 34, 11, 1359–1369.

Hall, R. E. and Jones, C. I. (1999) Why do Some Countries Produce So Much More Output per Worker than Others? *Quarterly Journal of Economics*, 114, 1, 83–116.

Hanushek, E. A. (1996) Measuring Investment in Education. *Journal of Economic Perspectives*, 10, 4, 9–30.

Hanushek, E. A. and Kimko, D. D. (2000) Schooling, Labour-Force Quality, and the Growth of Nations. *American Economic Review*, 90, 5, 1184–1208.

Heckman, J. J. and Klenow, P. J. (1997) Human Capital Policy. University of Chicago, Mimeo.

Islam, N. (1995) Growth Empirics: A Panel Data Approach. *Quarterly Journal of Economics*, 110, 4, 1127–1170.

Jones, C. I. (1996) Human Capital, Ideas, and Economic Growth. Stanford University, Mimeo.

Jorgenson, D. W. (1995) *Productivity. Volume 1: Postwar U.S. Economic Growth. Volume 2: International Comparisons of Economic Growth*. Cambridge, MA: MIT Press.

Jovanovic, B. and Rob, R. (1999) Solow vs. Solow. New York University, Mimeo.

Kiker, B. F. (1968) *Human Capital: In Retrospect*. Essays in Economics No. 16. Columbia, South Carolina: University of South Carolina.

Klenow, P. J. and Rodríguez-Clare, A. (1997) The Neoclassical Revival in Growth Economics: Has it Gone Too Far? In B. S. Bernanke and J. J. Rotemberg (eds.), *NBER Macroeconomics Annual 1997*. Cambridge, MA: MIT Press, 73–103.

Krueger, A. B. and Lindahl, M. (2001) Education for Growth: Why and For Whom? *Journal of Economic Literature*, 39, 4, 1101–1136.

Kyriacou, G. A. (1991) Level and Growth Effects of Human Capital: A Cross-Country Study of the Convergence Hypothesis. Economic Research Reports 19–26, C.V. Starr Center for Applied Economics, New York University.

Lau, L. J., Jamison, D. T. and Louat, F. F. (1991) Education and Productivity in Developing Countries: An Aggregate Production Function Approach. World Bank PRE Working Paper Series 612. Washington, D.C.

Levine, R. E. and Renelt, D. (1992) A Sensitivity Analysis of Cross-Country Growth Regressions. *American Economic Review*, 82, 4, 942–963.

Mankiw, N. G., Romer, D. and Weil, D. N. (1992) A Contribution to the Empirics of Growth. *Quarterly Journal of Economics*, 107, 2, 408–437.

Marshall, A. (1890/1922) *Principles of Economics: An Introductory Volume*. Eighth Edition. London: Macmillan.

Mincer, J. (1974) *Schooling, Experience, and Earnings*. New York: National Bureau of Economic Research.

Mulligan, C. B. and Sala-i-Martin, X. (1997) A Labour Income-Based Measure of the Value of Human Capital: An Application to the States of the United States. *Japan and the World Economy*, 9, 2, 159–191.

Mulligan, C. B. and Sala-i-Martin, X. (2000) Measuring Aggregate Human Capital. *Journal of Economic Growth*, 5, 3, 215–252.

Nehru, V., Swanson, E. and Dubey, A. (1995) A New Database on Human Capital Stock in Developing and Industrial Countries: Sources, Methodology, and Results. *Journal of Development Economics*, 46, 2, 379–401.

O'Neill, D. (1995) Education and Income Growth: Implications for Cross-Country Inequality. *Journal of Political Economy*, 103, 6, 1289–1301.

Pritchett, L. (2001) Where Has All the Education Gone? *World Bank Economic Review*, 15, 3, 367–391.

Psacharopoulos, G. (1994) Returns to Investment in Education: A Global Update. *World Development*, 22, 9, 1325–1343.

Psacharopoulos, G. and Arriagada, A. M. (1986) The Educational Composition of the Labour Force: An International Comparison. *International Labour Review*, 125, 5, 561–574.

Romer, P. (1990) Human Capital and Growth: Theory and Evidence. *Carnegie-Rochester Conference Series on Public Policy*, 32, 251–286.

Sen, A. (1999) *Development as Freedom*. Oxford: Oxford University Press.

Smith, A. (1776/1976) *An Inquiry into the Nature and Causes of the Wealth of Nations*. Glasgow Edition (R.H. Campbell, A.S. Skinner, eds.). Oxford: Clarendon Press.

Solow, R. M. (1957) Technical Change and the Aggregate Production Function. *Review of Economics and Statistics*, 39 3, 312–320.

Summers, R. and Heston, A. W. (1988) A New Set of International Comparisons of Real Product and Price Levels: Estimates for 130 Countries, 1950–1985. *The Review of Income and Wealth*, 34, 1, 1–25.

Summers, R. and Heston, A. W. (1991) The Penn World Table (Mark 5): An Expanded Set of International Comparisons, 1950–1988. *Quarterly Journal of Economics*, 106, 2, 327–368.

Temple, J. (1999a) The New Growth Evidence. *Journal of Economic Literature*, 37, 1, 112–156.

Temple, J. (1999b) A Positive Effect of Human Capital on Growth. *Economics Letters*, 65, 1, 131–134.

Temple, J. R. W. (2001a) Generalizations That Aren't? Evidence on Education and Growth. *European Economic Review*, 45, 4–6, 905–918.

Temple, J. (2001b) Growth Effects of Education and Social Capital in the OECD Countries. *OECD Economic Studies*, 33, 2, 57–101.

Topel, R. (1999) Labour Markets and Economic Growth. In O. C. Ashenfelter and D. Card (eds.), *Handbook of Labour Economics, Volume 3C*. Amsterdam: North-Holland, 2943–2984.

UNESCO (2000) *World Education Indicators*. Available at: http://unescostat.unesco.org/en/stats/stats0.htm.

Weiss, A. (1995) Human Capital vs. Signalling Explanations of Wages. *Journal of Economic Perspectives*, 9, 4, 133–154.

World Bank (1992) *World Development Report*. Oxford: Oxford University Press.

Wößmann, L. (2003) Schooling Resources, Educational Institutions, and Student Performance: The International Evidence. Oxford Bulletin of Economics and Statistics, 64, 2, forthcoming.

Wößmann, L. (2002) *Schooling and the Quality of Human Capital*. Berlin: Springer.

3

COST- AND INCOME-BASED MEASURES OF HUMAN CAPITAL

Trinh Le, John Gibson

Department of Economics, University of Waikato, New Zealand

Les Oxley

Department of Economics, University of Canterbury, New Zealand

1. Introduction

Economic growth has, once again, taken centre-stage in macroeconomics. Part of the resurgence in interest undoubtedly stems from a number of theoretical developments proposed by for example, Baumol (1990), Romer (1986, 1989), Lucas (1988), Jones and Manuelli (1990), Aghion and Howitt (1998), and Rebelo (1991). Common features of these new developments are the crucial and separate roles for Research and Development (R&D), and human, as distinct from physical capital, in the growth process. Such issues though not new see Ricardo (1951–1973) and Smith (1776), they are in sharp contrast to the traditional features of neoclassical, exogenous technological progress, growth models.

Central to any empirical debate on the role of human capital in the growth process is the issue of how the input is measured. For example, much of the recurring controversy on the magnitude of Total Factor Productivity (TFP) revolves around how factor inputs, particularly human capital, are measured.

Following the insights of Adam Smith, the creation of specialised labour is seen to require the use of scarce inputs, typically education/learning. This emphasis on 'education' has led to a research agenda where human capital is proxied by some (possibly weighted) measure of school experience. This approach, popularized by Barro and Lee (1993, 1996, 2001) and Lee and Barro (2001), in its simplest form is measured by 'years of schooling'. However, this is only one of several approaches to the measurement of human capital see Temple (2000), Pritchett (2001), Krueger and Lindahl (2001), Wolff (2000) and the excellent critical survey by Wößmann (2003), for a thorough discussion of this strand of the human capital literature. Recently, some improvements have been made to this form of human capital measurement, including Oxley *et al.* (1999, 1999–2000), de la Fuente and Doménech (2000), Cohen and Soto (2001), Barro and Lee (2001), and Wößmann (2003), yet they still suffer from drawbacks. In particular, by focusing on education *so far experienced*, these new measures fail to capture the richness of knowledge embodied in humans.

In this paper we concentrate on an alternative approach to measuring the stock of human capital which builds upon Smith, Ricardo and modern labour economics more generally. *In particular we consider measures of human capital which are based on cost- or income-based measures of heterogeneous labour.* This differs from much of the current research agenda on human capital stock measurement which is based upon educational experiences, but has a rich and long intellectual pedigree and the advantage of easily permitting monetary values to be assigned to the stock both at the individual and aggregate level and thus, if one wishes, then comparing its (monetary) value with physical capital.

Shultz (1961a), identifies Smith's (1776) work in this area as a major precursor, however, the origins can be found in Petty (1690), where he estimated the total human capital of this country to be £520 million, or £80 per capita. In a similar exercise, Farr (1853) estimated that the average net human capital of an English agricultural labourer was £150.

This 'old' research agenda has been resurrected under the banner of the 'knowledge economy' where human capital has increasingly attracted both academic and public interest. Understanding human capital must therefore be of great interest to politicians, economists, and development strategists.

> Enhancing individuals' capacity to succeed in the labour market is a major objective of both families and policy makers, one which in recent years has assumed special urgency with respect to those with low earnings. According to the canonical model, earnings are determined by human capital, which consists of capacities to contribute to production, generically called skills. (Bowles *et al.*, 2001)

The need for a reliable measure of human capital is reinforced by the fact that even in countries where attempts are made to estimate the value of human capital, it is not yet standard practice for official statistical agencies to include human capital in their capital stock measures see Wei, (2001). This is a surprising omission because estimates of the value of human capital, as mentioned above, predate the formal development of National Accounts statistics.

In part because of the deficiencies in the educational stock-based approach, Jorgenson and Fraumeni (1989, 1992) returned to the earlier approaches to valuing human capital, introduced by Farr (1853) and Dublin and Lotka (1930). The basic idea, as will be shown in detail below, is to value the human capital embodied in individuals as the total income that could be generated in the labour market over their lifetime. These expected labour earnings contribute to an extended notion of capital, which Jorgenson and Fraumeni include in a proposed new system of national accounts for the US economy. Outside the United States, this method has been applied to the estimate the human capital stock for Sweden (Ahlroth *et al*, 1997), Australia (Wei, 2001), and New Zealand (Le, Gibson and Oxley, 2002) where, in all cases, the stock of human capital greatly exceeds that of physical capital.

The remainder of this paper is organised as follows. Section 2 outlines the models underpinning the cost- and income-based measures of human capital and critically reviews the empirical results they underpin. Section 3 will present some results for forward-looking measures of human capital in New Zealand and Section 4 concludes.

2. Measuring Human Capital – A Review of the Literature

2.1 *Definition of human capital*

Shultz (1961a) classified *skills and knowledge* that people acquire as a form of human capital, and in so doing revived interest in the notion of human capital. Recently, however, the concept of human capital has been extended to incorporate non-market activities, and a broader definition of human capital is 'the knowledge, skills, competencies and attributes embodied in individuals that facilitate the creation of personal, social and economic well-being' (OECD, 2001, p18). Laroche *et al.* (1999)[1] further extend the notion to also include 'innate abilities'. As defined, human capital is a complex concept; it has many dimensions and can be acquired in various ways, including at home, at school, at work, and so on.

It is also clear from the definitions that human capital is *intangible*, the stock of which is not directly observable, hence all estimates of the stock must be constructed indirectly. The common approaches to measuring human capital that have been documented in the literature include the 'cost-based approach', the 'income-based approach', and the commonly applied 'educational stock-based approach'. In this paper we will consider the first two approaches referring interested readers to Wößmann (2003) for an excellent review of the third, educational stock-based approach.

Table 1 in the Appendix, presents a summary of human capital measurement using the cost-, income-based, and integrated approaches and could usefully be referenced while reading Section 2, below.

2.2 *The cost-based approach to human capital measurement*

This approach has its origins in the cost-of-production method of Engel (1883), who estimated human capital based on child rearing costs to their parents. According to Engel, the cost of rearing a person was equal to the summation of costs required to raise them from conception to the age of 25, since he considered a person to be fully produced by the age of 26. Assuming that the cost of rearing a person aged $x < 26$, belonging the ith class ($i = 1, 2, 3$ for the lower, middle and upper class respectively) consisted of a cost at birth of c_{oi} and annual costs of $c_{oi} + x c_{oi} k_i$ a year, Engel derived the formula:

$$c_i(x) = c_{oi} + c_{oi}[x + \frac{1}{2}k_i x(x+1)] = c_{oi}[1 + x + \frac{1}{2}k_i x(x+1)] \qquad (1)$$

where it was empirically observed that $c_{03} = 100$, $c_{02} = 200$, $c_{03} = 300$ marks; $k_i = k = 0.1$.

However, as Dagum and Stottje (2000) stress, this approach should not be construed as an estimation of individual human capital as it is merely a summation of historical costs which ignores the time value of money and the social costs that are invested in people. More recently, Machlup (1962), and Schultz (1961a), augmented Engel's approach to create what is now commonly taken to be the 'cost-based method' to measuring human capital. This approach estimates human capital based on the assumption that the depreciated value of the dollar amount spent on those items defined as investments in human capital is equal to the stock of human capital.

Kendrick (1976) and Eisner (1985) are among the seminal examples of systematically measuring the stock of human capital by a cost-based approach. Kendrick divided human capital investments into tangible and intangible where the tangible components consist of those costs required to produce the physical human including child rearing costs to the age of fourteen. Intangible investments are the costs to enhance the quality or productivity of labour. These involve expenditures on health and safety, mobility, education and training, plus the opportunity costs of students attending school.

This approach provides a measure of the current flow of resources invested in the education and other human capital related sectors, which can be very useful for cost-benefit analyses. It is also very easy to apply because of the ready availability of data on public and private spending.

However, there are several limitations with the method. Firstly, as is well known when evaluating physical capital by costs, there is no necessary relationship between investment and the quality of output: the value of capital is determined by the demand for it, not by the cost of production. This problem is more serious when measuring human capital and thus renders cross-sectional and temporal comparisons less robust. For example, an innately less able and less healthy child is more costly to raise, so the cost-based approach will over-estimate his human capital while underestimating well-endowed children who, all else equal, should incur fewer rearing and educational expenses. This bias is probably the main reason why Wickens (1924) found the value of the Australian stock of capital to triple when the income-based procedure was used in place of the cost-based procedure.

Secondly, the components entering into the production of human capital and their prices are not well-identified for a cost-based estimate of human capital to be useful. For example, Kendrick assumed that all costs of raising children to the age of fourteen are human capital investments. His reason was that these expenses, typically on necessities such as food and clothing, compete with other types of investment. This contradicts Bowman (1962) who argued that those costs should not be treated as investment unless the men were slaves. Machlup (1984) concurred with this view, maintaining that basic expenditures should be considered consumption rather than investment. There is a similar problem with determining the marginal contributions to human capital of different types of investments.

The lack of empirical evidence means that the researcher may have to allocate household spending quite arbitrarily between investment and consumption. Kendrick, for instance, attributed 50 percent of outlays for health and safety as human capital investment. Since most expenditures on people have both *consumption* effects (satisfying consumer preferences) and *investment* effects (enhancing productivity), cost-based measures are sensitive to the researcher's explicit assumptions about the type of spending and the share of various household and public expenditures that should be construed as human capital investment. The inseparability of the consumption and investment effects of 'expenditures on man' means that what should be considered human capital investment is controversial.[2]

Thirdly, the depreciation rate matters a great deal to cost-based estimates of the human capital stock. Typically, simple tax accounting rules have been chosen. In particular, Kendrick estimated depreciation on human capital by the (modified) double declining balance method. This is because physical capital depreciates faster in early years of life, so the double declining balance schedule is appropriate. To be consistent across different types of capital, Kendrick applied this method to depreciate human capital. By contrast, Eisner simply used the straight-line practice. Appreciation is often ignored, despite empirical evidence that showed human capital appreciating at younger ages then depreciating later in life (Mincer, 1958 and 1970). Graham and Webb (1979), who found evidence of human capital appreciation when using the income-based approach to measuring the stock of human capital in the United States, criticised Kendrick for under-estimating the US's human capital by not accounting for appreciation while over-depreciating it. Moreover, cost-based estimates of investment in education fail to account for the crucial time dimension of educational investment (Jorgenson and Fraumeni, 1989). Indeed, there is a long lag between the current outlays of educational institutions and the emergence of human capital embodied in their graduates. That is, a large share of educational investment goes to individuals who are still enrolled in school and whose human capital is yet to be realised.

Another limitation, as stressed by Jorgenson and Fraumeni (1989), is that by evaluating human capital based on costs of education and rearing rather than lifetime labour incomes, the cost-based approach disregards the value of non-market activities. It has been widely recognised that the external benefits of education, such as opportunity for self-fulfilment, enjoyment and its development of individual capabilities, are substantial (Haveman and Wolf, 1984).

Turning to empirical issues, there are several measures of the stock of human capital based upon the cost approach, though typically for the United States. Shultz (1961a), for example, tentatively estimated that the stock of education in the US labour force increased by about eight and a half times over the period 1900–1956 while the stock of reproducible capital grew only half as fast. Kendrick (1976) and Eisner (1985) provided more comprehensive measures, opening the way to the construction of human capital time series using the perpetual inventory method.

Kendrick estimated the United States' national wealth for every year from 1929 to 1969 and found that except in 1929 and 1956, the stock of human capital well exceeded that of physical, making the US's wealth more than double as a result of including human capital in the national accounts. In 1969, for example, the US's non-human capital stock totalled $3,220 billion, whereas human capital was valued at $3,700 billion. In constant prices, the stock of human capital more than tripled over the period 1929–1969, at a growth rate of 6.3 percent a year, and outperformed non-human capital which expanded by only 4.9 percent per year. Education and training accounted for about 40–60 percent of the stock of human capital and this share increased consistently over time.[3]

Eisner (1985) followed Kendrick's approach but with some modifications. In particular, Eisner made some allowance for the value of non-market household contributions to investment in child rearing. Investment in research and development counted as human capital investment in Eisner's estimates. Unlike Kendrick, who divided human capital into tangibles and intangibles, Eisner classified all human capital as intangibles. Furthermore, as mentioned earlier, Eisner applied the straight line rule to depreciate all human capital over a fifty year life. His results showed that of the $23,746 billion worth of total capital in 1981, $10,676 billion was human capital. In real terms, human capital grew at 4.4 percent a year from 1945 to 1981 while capital in general increased at a slower rate, 3.9 percent a year. When put in the same price base, Kendrick's and Eisner's estimates are very similar, except that Kendrick's estimates of human capital often exceeded those of physical capital stocks, whereas the opposite was true of Eisner's estimates.[4]

2.3 The income-based approach to human capital measurement

2.3.1 Early studies

Petty (1690) was the first researcher to apply this procedure to estimate a country's stock of human capital. He calculated the human capital stock in England and Wales by capitalising the wage bill, defined as the difference between the estimated national income (£42 million) and property income (£16 million, for both land and profit), to perpetuity at a five percent interest rate. This gave a result of £520 million, or £80 per capita. Petty's method was crude as it did not account for the heterogeneity of the population. Simple as it was, it raised the issue of estimating the monetary value of a country's labourers and provided an answer with a meaningful economic and social interpretation.

The first truly scientific procedure to estimating the money value of a human being, according to Kiker (1966), was that developed by Farr (1853). Farr estimated the capitalised value of earning capacity by calculating the present value of an individual's future earnings net of personal living expenses, adjusted for deaths in accordance with a life table. Using a discount rate of five percent, he estimated the average net human capital of an agricultural labourer to be £150, which is the difference between the average salary of £349 and the average maintenance cost of £199. Farr's approach provided a rigorous standard which has been adhered to by many succeeding researchers. The underlying assumption of this model is to value the human capital embodied in individuals as the total income that could be generated in the labour market over their lifetime.

Dublin and Lotka (1930) followed Farr and devised a formula for estimating the value of an individual at birth, V_0, as:

$$V_0 = \sum_{x=0}^{\infty} \frac{P_{0,x}(y_x E_x - c_x)}{(1+i)^x} \tag{2}$$

where i is the interest rate, $P_{0,x}$ is the probability at birth of an individual surviving to age x, y_x is the annual earnings per individual from age x to $x+1$, E_x is the annual employment rate at age x, and c_x is the cost of living for an individual from age x to age $x+1$. As can be seen, equation (2) is a formal statement of Farr's method, except that Dublin and Lotka allow for unemployment, rather than assuming full employment.

The above formula can be modified to obtain the money value of an individual at a particular age a:

$$V_a = \sum_{x=a}^{\infty} \frac{P_{a,x}(y_x E_x - c_x)}{(1+i)^{x-a}} \tag{3}$$

Similarly, the net cost of rearing a person up to age a is:

$$C_a = \sum_{x=0}^{a-1} \frac{P_{a,x}(c_x - y_x E_x)}{(1+i)^{x-a}} \tag{4}$$

Equation (3) can be expanded to:

$$V_a = \sum_{x=a}^{\infty} \frac{P_{a,x}(y_x E_x - c_x)}{(1+i)^{x-a}} = \sum_{x=0}^{\infty} \frac{P_{a,x}(y_x E_x - c_x)}{(1+i)^{x-a}} - \sum_{x=0}^{a-1} \frac{P_{a,x}(y_x E_x - c_x)}{(1+i)^{x-a}}$$

$$= \sum_{x=0}^{\infty} \frac{P_{0,x}(y_x E_x - c_x)(1+i)^a}{P_{0,a}(1+i)^x} + \sum_{x=0}^{a-1} \frac{P_{a,x}(c_x - y_x E_x)}{(1+i)^{x-a}}$$

$$= \frac{(1+i)^a}{P_{0,a}} \sum_{x=0}^{\infty} \frac{P_{0,x}(y_x E_x - c_x)}{(1+i)^x} + \sum_{x=0}^{a-1} \frac{P_{a,x}(c_x - y_x E_x)}{(1+i)^{x-a}} \tag{5}$$

Combining (5) with (2) and (3), we have:

$$V_a = \frac{(1+i)^a}{P_{0,a}} V_0 + C_a \tag{6}$$

Equivalently,

$$C_a = V_a - \frac{(1+i)^a}{P_{0,a}} V_0 \tag{7}$$

Indeed, this formula has a very intuitive interpretation: the cost of producing an individual up to age a is equal to the difference between his value at age a and the present value, at age a, of his value at birth, adjusted for his survival probability to age a. The gross human capital value at age a can be obtained by setting maintenance cost c_x to be zero:

$$Gross\ V_a = \sum_{x=a}^{\infty} \frac{P_{a,x} y_x E_x}{(1 + i)^{x-a}} \tag{8}$$

Prior to this study, Dublin (1928) estimated the human wealth of the United States in 1922 to be five times that of material wealth, but it is not clear how this figure was obtained (Kiker, 1966).

Wittstein (1867) combined Engel's cost-of-production approach with Farr's prospective method and developed an interesting procedure to estimate the human capital of an individual for different ages. However, he was criticised for the unjustified postulate that lifetime earnings and lifetime maintenance costs are equal.

Nicholson (1891) computed the value of the stock of human capital for Great Britain by capitalizing the wage bill, the earnings of management, the earnings of capitalists, the earnings of salaried government officials, and adding these up with what he termed 'domesticated humanity' (the costs of producing wage earners). He claimed that the value of the United Kingdom's stock of living capital was about five times that of the stock of conventional capital. But by combining the prospective and retrospective methods, Nicholson was criticised for duplicating values. This is because the costs of producing wage earners, which were already counted in the 'domesticated humanity', were also included in the capitalised value of their earnings.

De Foville (1905) believed that the prospective method overestimates human capital by not deducting consumption expenditures from earnings. By applying Petty's approach to labour earnings net of maintenance, he obtained the net stock of human capital, which was more comparable to conventional capital (i.e. physical capital) than other income-based measures of human capital.

Barriol (1910) used Farr's approach to evaluate the 'social value' of male French labourers. Assuming that lifetime income equals lifetime expenditures, Barriol computed this value by discounting their future expenditures, adjusted for deaths, at a three percent interest rate. This estimate differed from Farr's in that maintenance costs were not subtracted from earnings, but what made Barriol's method innovative was that he estimated the social value by age groups by assuming certain scales. In addition, Barriol used an interesting procedure to obtain the per capita social value of other countries. First, the weighted per capita average social value of the country in calculated by applying the age distribution of its population to the social values of male French labourers. This figure was then adjusted to account for the discrepancy in economic development (particularly the differences in wage levels), and gender differences in wage and labour force participation rates between France and that country. Although these figures were questionable, Barriol's adjusting procedure was interesting and indeed was followed by many subsequent analysts.

In the United States, early estimates date back to Fisher (1908) who followed Farr's approach and estimated the value of human capital in order to assess the costs of preventable illness. Also based on a Farr-type method, Huebner (1914) calculated the US stock of human capital in 1914 to be six to eight times the value of the stock of conventional capital. Woods and Metzger (1927) used five methods, including those due to Petty and Farr, to address this issue, but as Kiker (1966) stresses, these analyses contained several erroneous assumptions.

Treadgold (2000) identified Wickens (1924) as a pioneer in the field of human capital measurement. Applying the capitalization of earnings method, Wickens sought to evaluate the stock of wealth in Australia by estimating the total discounted value of all future streams of services expected to be generated by the country's citizens. Wickens divided the population into three broad groups: adults of working age (males aged 18–64 and females aged 18–59), juveniles (younger than 18), and the aged. The value of the services a person brings to the society in annual terms was assumed to be equal to the weighted average annual gross earnings, with no allowance being made for maintenance costs. These figures, corresponding to £133 and £65 for males and females respectively, were estimated from official weekly rates, with four weeks deducted from the working year to account for such factors as unemployment and unpaid holidays. Wickens further postulated that all surviving males would continue to earn £133 a year and females £65 until the retirement age. Combining these figures with the Australian life table and an interest rate of five percent, the author computed the present values of earnings that working-age men and women would generate throughout their working life. A similar procedure was applied to the aged, except that old-age pensions were used instead of earnings. The 'juveniles' were assigned a 'pure endowment' of £2,245 for males and £1,082 for females, which was equal to the 'wealth' value just computed for those aged 18. Therefore, human wealth values were obtainable for males and females at every age from 0 to 104.

Having human wealth values for males and females at every age from 0 to 104, Wickens identified a median age for each of the three new broad age groups (under 15, 15–64, and older than 64) then multiplied the wealth value of the median age in each group by the population size of that group. It was found that in 1915 Australia had a total human capital of £6,211 million, or £1,246 per capita (£1,923 for males and £928 for females). In addition, the Australian human capital stock was observed to be three times as large as the physical capital stock. However, the estimate of the human capital stock was questionable, since Wickens used such an unjustified short-cut to obtain the aggregate value.

2.3.2 *Assessment of the income-based method*

The income-based approach measures the stock of human capital by summing the total discounted values of all the future income streams that all individuals belonging to the population in question expect to earn throughout their lifetime.

This method is said to be 'forward-looking' (prospective) because it focuses on expected returns to investment, as opposed to the 'backward-looking' (retrospective) method whose focus is on the historical costs of production. While the retrospective method may include expenditures on the individual in addition to those that improve their capabilities, the prospective method seeks to value their earning power. Indeed, the income-based method values human capital at market prices, since the labour market to a certain extent account for the many factors including ability, effort, drive, and professional qualifications, as well as the institutional and technological structures of the economy in an interactive framework of human capital supply and demand (Dagum and Slottje, 2000). Also, the income-based approach does not need to assume an arbitrary rate of depreciation because depreciation is already implicitly accounted for in the model. Therefore, this method provides the most reliable results if necessary data are available. Indeed, accurate and timely life tables are readily available, and earnings and (un)employment rates by age and educational level can be easily computed from relevant surveys. The choice of a discount rate involves some subjective judgment, but this should not be a problem. Above all, since the approach based on income is forward-looking, a dynamic economy interested in evaluating its future productive capacities would be more interested in this approach than the historical cost approach (Graham and Webb, 1979).

However, this approach is not free from drawbacks, most notably, the model rests crucially on the assumption that differences in wages truly reflect differences in productivity. In fact, wages may vary for reasons other than change in productivity for example, trade unions may be able to command a premium wage for their members, or real wages may fall in economic downturns. In such circumstances, income-based measures of human capital will be biased. In addition, income-based measures of human capital are quite sensitive to the discount rate and the retirement age.[5] This requires analysts to be careful when using the results, or severe biases will result.

Whether maintenance costs should be deducted is open to debate. On the one hand, some authors argue that physical capital estimates are net figures, so to be consistent human capital should also be net of maintenance costs. De Foville (1905) and Eisner (1988), for example, criticised the income-based method by not deducting maintenance costs from gross earnings. Weisbrod (1961) attempted to account for maintenance, but he encountered many difficulties. What types of expenditures should be classified as maintenance, and how to account for economies of scale and 'public' goods when estimating per capita consumption for members in the same household are problems that are not easily resolved. Alternatively, others maintain that consumption is an end, rather than a means, of investment and production, hence gross earnings, are a more relevant variable to use when estimating human capital using a lifetime labour income approach. It is argued that net productivity is a more relevant measure of a person's value to others; whereas gross productivity is a superior estimate of his total output to the society (Graham and Webb, 1979).

Another shortcoming of the income-based method is that data on earnings are not as widely available as data on investment. This is especially the case for developing countries, where the wage rate is often not observable. In the early studies reviewed above, the major problem lies in the lack of reliable data on earnings and the unjustified assumption about the flow of future earnings.

2.3.3 The revived interest in the income-based approach to measuring human capital

Despite the merits of the income-based approach, until recently the lack of data at micro level had prevented researchers from exploring this method systematically.

Weisbrod (1961) used a modified version of Dublin and Lotka's (1930) formula to estimate human capital:

$$V_a = \sum_{x=a}^{74} \frac{Y_x W_x P_{a,x}}{(1+r)^{n-a}} \qquad (9)\text{c.f. equation (3)}$$

where V_a is the present value of expected future earnings of a person at age a, Y_x and W_x are respectively the average earnings and employment rate at age x, $P_{a,x}$ is the probability of a person of age a surviving to age x, and r is the discount rate. The retirement age in this case is set at 75, at which age earnings are nil.

While precursors only had macro data to use, Weisbrod drew on cross-sectional data for earnings, employment rates and survival probabilities. It was implicitly assumed that in n years, those currently aged x would expect to earn an income equal to what those aged $x + n$ now earn, adjusted for survival probabilities and the discount rate. A similar logic applied to employment rates and survival probabilities. The results revealed that in 1950, US males aged 0–74 had a total gross value of human capital of $1,335 billion at a discount rate of ten percent and $2,752 billion at four percent. Net of maintenance costs, the corresponding values of human capital would be $1,055 billion and $2,218 billion respectively. Apparently, even the lowest estimate value of (male) human capital exceeded the stock of non-human assets of $881 billion.

Weisbrod cautioned that the use of cross-sectional data do not account for changes in age specific values over time, which given that such changes tend to be positive mean that the estimates of human capital under static age specific conditions are likely to be an underestimation. Another source of the underestimation is the fact that median earnings of each age cohort were used, because data on mean earnings were not available. As is well-known about the distribution of earnings, the mean is often greater than the median.

Houthakker (1959) and Miller (1965) asserted that in a growing economy, every individual should benefit from an expected increase in his earning on top of the gains in experience, seniority and other factors associated with age. Also using data from the 1950 US Census, Miller demonstrated that by accounting for economic growth, estimates of lifetime income based on cohort analyses well exceeded those based on cross-sectional pattern.

Recognising the major limitation in Weisbrod (1961), Graham and Webb (1979) adjusted the framework to incorporate economic growth. They also

departed from earlier studies by including education in the model. Equation (9) is
then modified as follows:

$$PV_x^i = \sum_{x=a}^{75} \frac{Y_x^i W_x^i P_{xt}^i (1 + g_k^i)}{(1 + r_k^i)^{x-a}} \tag{10}$$

where PV_x^i is the present value of an individual aged x having a vector of
characteristics i, and r_k^i and x_k^i are respectively the interest rate and the growth
rate in earnings that apply to type i individuals at the kth year of life. So the
underlying assumption here is that an individual of age x with a certain vector of
identifying characteristics (sex, race, education, occupation, ability, of which only
education is accounted for in Graham and Webb) will base his expectation of
earnings n years from now on what those who are currently $x + n$ years old and
who possess the same basic characteristics are earning.

Applying the model to a sizeable sample of US males aged 14–75, Graham and
Webb found that education is strongly positively related to wealth at all ages.
Regardless of the level of education, lifetime wealth always has a concave parabola shape, first rising then steadily declining well into zero at retirement. Apparently, wealth always peaks well before earnings. It was also observed that higher
education does not only increase the steepness of the lifetime wealth profile but
also delays the peak in wealth. The parabola shape indicates that human capital
appreciates at younger ages followed by straight-line depreciation. In this way the
income-based framework implicitly allows for depreciation so there is no need to
assume an arbitrary depreciation rate.

In aggregate terms, the stock of capital embodied in US males aged 14–75 in
1969 ranged from \$2,910 billion at 20 percent discount rate to \$14,395 billion at
2.5 percent discount rate. According to Kendrick's (1976) cost-based method,
total human capital in 1969 was estimated to be \$3,700 billion. Taking into
account the difference in population bases, Graham and Webb claimed that
Kendrick's estimate was still comparatively lower than theirs at the highest
discount rate of 20 percent. Graham and Webb maintained that the flawed
assumption about depreciation had led Kendrick to underestimate the stock of
human capital.

2.3.4 The Jorgenson and Fraumeni approach

Graham and Webb's (1979) study was more sophisticated than earlier
approaches, however it still contained a number of methodological limitations
and covered only half the US population.

Jorgenson and Fraumeni (1989, 1992) augmented their method and presented
the most comprehensive study to date using the income-based approach to
measuring human capital. The authors proposed a new system of national
accounts for the US economy that included market and non-market economic
activities, as well as attempting to assess the impact of human capital on economic
growth. The model was applied to estimate the human capital (along with

non-human capital) for all individuals in the US population classified by the two sexes, 61 age groups, and 18 education groups[6] for a total of 2196 cohorts.

Recall the underlying assumption of Graham and Webb (1979), is that the earnings of a person aged x will receive in n years will be equal to the earnings of a person presently aged $x + n$ of the same sex and education, adjusted for real income growth and the probability of survival. An important innovation in the Jorgenson and Fraumeni's approach is that they simplified the procedure for discounting future income streams to the present value. Specifically, the authors showed that the present value of lifetime labour income for an individual of a given age is just their current annual labour income plus the present value of their lifetime income in the next period weighted by employment and survival probabilities. Thus, by backward recursion it is possible to calculate the present value of lifetime income at each age. For example, Jorgenson and Fraumeni assumed that all individuals retire when they are 75 years old, so for a 74-year-old person, the present value of lifetime labour income is just their current labour income. The lifetime labour income of a 73-year-old individual is equal to the present value of lifetime labour income of the 74-year-old plus their current labour income, etc.

Formally, the lifetime income of a certain individual with sex s, age a, education e at year y, $i_{y,s,a}$, is given by:

$$i_{y,s,a,e} = yi_{y+1,s,a} + sr_{y,s,a+1} * i_{y,s,a+1,e} * (1 + g)/(1 + i) \qquad (11)$$

where $yi_{y+1,s,a}$ is the annual earnings at year y of a person with sex s, age a and education e, and $sr_{y,s,a+1}$ is the probability that the person will survive another year.

Jorgenson and Fraumeni identified five stages of the life cycle: no school and no work (aged 0–4), school but no work (aged 5–13), school and work (aged 14–34), work but no school (aged 35–74), and no school or work (aged 75 and older). By assumption, the lifetime income for the oldest group is set to be zero, so is the annual income of those in the first stage and the second stage.

Another important contribution by Jorgenson and Fraumeni is that they incorporate the potential value created by people who are currently participating in formal education and who anticipate improved income and employment prospects as a result of that extra education. The inclusion of enrolment in the framework affects the lifetime income of those in second and third stages of the life cycle. For these people, the formula for calculating their lifetime income becomes:

$$i_{y,s,a,e} = yi_{y+1,s,a,e} + [senr_{y+1,s,a,e} * sr_{y,s,a+1} * i_{y,s,a+1,e+1}$$
$$+ (1 - senr_{y+1,s,a,e}) * sr_{y,s,a+1} * i_{y,s,a+1,e}] * (1 + g)/(1 + i) \qquad (12)$$

where *senr* indicates the school enrolment rate. Working backward from the lifetime incomes of individuals with the highest level of education enables us to obtain labour income for all individuals attending school.

Arguing that human capital is not restricted to market activities, Jorgenson and Fraumeni also imputed the value of labour compensation for non-market activities (excluding schooling). They defined full labour income as the sum of market and non-market labour compensation after taxes. The formulae above apply similarly to both market income and non-market income. How income is divided between market and non-market depends on how much time is allocated to 'maintenance'. For example, Jorgenson and Fraumeni assumed ten hours maintenance a day, so if a person works 40 hours a week for every week, they are said to have 40*52 = 2080 hours for market activities and (14*7–40)*52 = 3016 hours a year for non-market activities. Annual earnings, market and non-market, are derived from after-taxes hourly labour compensation for each sex/education/age cohort.

Jorgenson and Fraumeni (1989) obtained the value of US human capital for every year from 1948 to 1984. In 1982 constant dollars the stock of human capital almost doubled, from $92 trillion in 1949 to $171 trillion in 1984. In the later study (1992), the estimates were about 20 percent higher, due to allowance being made for school enrolment. Population growth accounted for most of the increase, as per capita human capital grew by only 15 percent, from $742 thousand in 1948 to $855 thousand in 1986. Women contributed about 40 percent in the stock of human capital and this proportion remained fairly stable over the period. The share of human capital based on market labour activities was around 30 percent. While cost-based studies found the human capital stock to be about the same size of the physical capital stock and earlier income-based studies typically observed the human capital stock to be from three to five times greater than the physical capital stock, Jorgenson and Fraumeni (1989) showed that human capital was from 12 to 16 times more than physical capital in size. For the period 1948–1969, Jorgenson and Fraumeni's (1992) estimates of US human capital were from 17.5 to 18.8 times higher than Kendrick's.

According to Jorgenson and Fraumeni, the disparity was due to the fact that their estimates include all sources of lifetime labour income, including investment in education, the value of rearing, and the lifetime incomes of individuals added to the population, prior to any investment in education or rearing. On one hand, Kendrick was criticised for underestimating human capital by over-depreciating it. On the other hand, Jorgenson and Fraumeni have been criticised for overestimating it through the treatment of non-market activities and setting the retirement age too high.

2.3.4.1 *Assessment of the Jorgenson and Fraumeni model*

The Jorgenson and Fraumeni model is subject to the general criticisms of the income-based approach discussed above and also the following.

According to Rothschild (1992), Jorgenson and Fraumeni's approach assumes that human capital raises the productivity of time spent at leisure by the same amount that it does time spent at work. Rothschild shows that the choice of hours worked is not independent of the level of human capital when the consumer gets utility from non-labour income and that full income (or the value of human capital) is not a linear function of the wage rate. Therefore, full income is not a reasonable measure of welfare.

Jorgenson and Fraumeni's way of imputing non-market activities means that unemployment matters to the division of human capital between market and non-market activities, but does not affect total human capital. As Conrad (1992) notes, there would be no change in the human capital stock if the population is fully employed or only half employed, since non-work time will be counted as non-market activities and will be fully imputed anyway. Also, average earnings estimated from workers have been used to impute the value of non-market time for non-workers and this creates a sample selection bias problem. Ahmavaara (2002) questions the validity of full imputation of non-work time, since at least some leisure time is necessary to prepare for work.

Ahlroth *et al.* (1997) and Dagum and Slottje (2000) also stress that the Jorgenson and Fraumeni model contains ability bias because it does not allow for the large variations of personal endowment due to nature and nurture among individuals of the same age, sex and education. This method equalises the returns to all types of education investments of the same length while ignoring informal schooling. It is also well-known that school years is a poor measure of productivity. These shortcomings cause biases in estimates of expected future earnings and hence human capital. Furthermore, as mentioned earlier, Jorgenson and Fraumeni set the retirement age too high (Conrad, 1992). It is clear from the framework that overvaluing people's productivity in old age results in overestimation of their lifetime labour income.

2.3.4.2 *Some applications of the Jorgenson and Fraumeni method*

Wei (2001) adopts Jorgenson and Fraumeni's framework and estimates the stock of human capital in Australia. Since his focus is on the working population, defined as all individuals aged 25–65, Wei only distinguishes two life cycle stages: *work and study* (aged 25–34) and *work only*. The author classifies education by five levels, depending on qualifications, rather than 18 levels based on years of formal schooling like in Jorgenson and Fraumeni.

Wei's results show a strong positive relationship between human capital and education. Like Graham and Webb (1979), Wei finds that lifetime labour income initially rises then falls for all education levels and that over the period examined (1981–1996) the age at which lifetime income peaked was increasing. In 1996 prices, the stock of Australia's working age human capital increased from $1.7 trillion in 1981 to $2.1 trillion in 1996, but there was a sharp drop in 1991 such that human capital in that year was the lowest. However, it was observed that the growth in human capital was accounted for by the increase in 'quality'. Even in 1991 when total human capital was decreasing, degree-qualified capital was still rising and the quality components of women's capital grew faster than men's. Women accounted for approximately 40 percent of the total stock of human capital. Even for such as small population base and based mostly on market activities, the stock of human capital was found to be larger than that of physical in all years, although this ratio has been declining, from 2:1 in 1981 to 1.6:1 in 1996.

Wei's estimates appear overstated by assuming that those who 'choose' to be out of the labour force will have the same employment and earnings pattern as those with similar characteristics to those in the labour force. Since Wei's focus is on market labour activities, the value of human capital of non-participants should not be imputed. By applying the expected lifetime labour income of the labour force to the entire working age population, the author did account for non-market effects of human capital, although not as fully as Jorgenson and Fraumeni (1989 and 1992) and Ahlroth *et al.* (1997).

Ahlroth *et al.* (1997) apply Jorgenson and Fraumeni's method to Swedish data. Interestingly, the authors show that this method is still workable with a typical micro data set of 6,000 individuals like the Swedish Level of Living Surveys. Since there are only 6,000 individuals for 2196 cohorts, most cohorts have few observations and some are even empty. Ahlroth *et al.* resolve this problem by using regression techniques to predict the values of hourly compensation, working hours, school hours, the employment rate and the school enrolment rates. It was found that even the lowest estimates of the human capital stock (after tax, excluding leisure income) were from six to ten times higher than the stock of physical capital. It should be noted that the studies by Ahlroth *et al.* (1997) and Wei (2001) are also subject to the limitations of the Jorgenson and Fraumeni method.

2.3.5 *The Mulligan and Sala-i-Martin method*

Mulligan and Sala-i-Martin (1997) develop a labour income-based measure of human capital (LIHK) which seeks to obtain an index value, rather than a monetary value, of human capital. They measure human capital for a given state in a given year as the total labour income per capita divided by the wage of the uneducated. The rationale for this method is that total labour income incorporates not only the worker's skills (human capital) but also the physical capital available to them, such that for a given level of human capital workers in regions with higher physical capital will tend to earn higher wages. Since the human and physical content of education may vary across time and space, a given level of education may attract different wage levels and thus would wrongly reflect different amounts of human capital. Therefore, the effect of aggregate physical capital on labour income should be netted out by dividing labour income by the wage of a zero-schooling worker. This model specifies that all workers with the same level of education have the same weight that is proportional to their average wage level.

This method implicitly assumes that uneducated workers have the same human capital across time and space, although they do not necessarily earn the same income always and everywhere. According to the authors, if schooling has quality and relevance that varies across states and over time, any amount of schooling will introduce inter-temporal and interregional differences in an individual's level of skills. Hence the only sensible *numeraire* is the uneducated worker. The wage rate of such a worker is estimated by the exponential of the constant term from a Mincer wage regression for each state at each year.

They observed that on the whole, the stock of human capital shrank substantially between 1940 and 1950, and then increased steadily to 1990. This pattern was quite consistent across regions. Interestingly, aggregate human capital stocks increased by 52 percent between 1980 and 1990, whereas over the four earlier decades human capital grew by only 17 percent. Mulligan and Sala-i-Martin also find that although their measure of human capital is positively correlated with other measures of human capital like average years of schooling, this correlation is not perfect. Apparently Mulligan and Sala-i-Martin's estimates of human capital grew much faster than schooling which, in the authors' view, was due to the improved quality and relevance of schooling.

Mulligan and Sala-i-Martin's LIHK clearly has some advantages. First, by netting out the effect of aggregate physical capital on labour income, this measure captures the variation in quality and relevance of schooling across time and space. Second, the elasticity of substitution across workers is allowed to vary in the model. Third, this method does not unrealistically impose equal amounts of skill on workers with equal amounts of schooling. Finally, it does not demand much data. However, like the Jorgenson and Fraumeni (1989, 1992) approach, Mulligan and Sala-i-Martin's cannot control for the fact that wages may vary for reasons other than changes in the marginal value of human capital. In addition, the model relies heavily on the assumptions that zero-schooling workers are identical always and everywhere and that workers with different levels of schooling are perfectly substitutes. These assumptions, according to Wachtel (1997), are questionable. Moreover, this method neglects the contribution to human capital by factors other than formal schooling, such as informal schooling, on-the-job training, and health. Jeong (2002) also points out that this approach is not so easy to apply to developing countries, due to the existence of a large informal sector where the wage rate is not observed.

Jeong (2002) modifies the Mulligan and Sala-i-Martin's method and applies it to measure human capital across 45 countries of diverse income levels. Jeong departs from Mulligan and Sala-i-Martin in that he uses the industrial labourer, as classified by the International Labour Office, rather than the worker with no schooling, as the *numeraire*. According to Jeong, industrial labourers, who primarily supply their physical effort with little skill, are more comparable across countries than any other types of workers. Human capital is defined in his study as the ratio of aggregate labour income to the average income of the industrial labourers in that country. Again, the underlying assumptions here are that industrial labourers have the same human capital across countries and that workers' contribution to the country's stock of human capital is proportional to their wage rates. Jeong claims that by not using schooling as a basis for comparing the workers, his method avoids the problems that are inherent in schooling based measures of human capital, namely mismeasurement of human capital that is acquired outside formal schooling, the failure to account for schooling quality, and the varied returns to a year of schooling at different levels.

Not surprisingly, it was found that poorer countries use less human capital inputs in the production process and that the richest countries have from 2.2 to 2.8 times as much human capital as the poorest countries, depending on whether outliers are included or not. However, these figures pale into insignificance in comparison with the cross-country difference in human capital measures based on years of schooling or with the output difference. Accordingly, Jeong believes that a large part of output difference between countries is due to factors other than human capital and physical capital.

In a study on Austria and Germany, Koman and Marin (1997) construct an aggregate measure of human capital stock by weighting workers of different schooling levels with their wage income. First, based on a perpetual inventory method, the number of individuals aged i whose highest level of schooling at time t is j is computed as:

$$H_{j,j,t} = H_{i-1,j,t-1} * (1 - \delta_{i,t}) + H^{+}_{i,j,t} - H^{-}_{i,j,t} \qquad (13)$$

where $H^{+}_{i,j,t}$ is the number of individuals aged i who completed the education level j at time t, $H^{-}_{i,j,t}$ is the number of individuals aged i whose highest level of schooling was j in year $t-1$ and who completed a higher educational level in year t, and $\delta_{i,t}$ is the probability that those aged $i-1$ in year $t-1$ died before reaching age i. After converting each schooling level j into years of schooling, the authors use a Cobb-Douglas aggregator to relate workers with different schooling levels to human capital:

$$\ln\left(\frac{H}{L}\right) = \sum_{s} \omega_s \ln\left(\rho(s)\right) \qquad (14)$$

where $\omega_s = e^{\gamma s}L(s)/\sum_s e^{\gamma s}L(s)$ $\rho(s) = L(s)/L$ is the share of working age individuals with s years of schooling, ω_s, defined as the share of the wage income of workers with s years of schooling in the total wage bill of the economy, is the efficiency parameter of a worker with s years of schooling, and γs the slope coefficients that capture the effect of schooling on earnings, are obtained from a Mincer-type wage regression.

Koman and Marin's estimate of human capital measures workers' productivity by their wage income. As with Mulligan and Sala-i-Martin (1997), the efficiency parameter ω_s nets out the effect of physical capital on wages (and hence on human capital). A serious limitation, however, is that one year of schooling yields the same amount of skills over time. The authors find that their measure of human capital grew faster than average years of schooling in the populace and that the time-series evidence is not consistent with a human capital augmented Solow model. Apparently, with the inclusion of human capital in the model, factor accumulation is less able to explain cross-country growth performance of Austria and Germany.

Laroche and Mérette (2000) adopt Koman and Marin's model with some modifications to suit Canada's complicated education system. Laroche and Mérette also depart from Koman and Marin by taking into account working experience in addition to formal schooling. In terms of average years of schooling, Canada's human capital per capita increased 15 percent between 1976 and 1996. The increase is even higher, by over 33 percent, when human capital is measured using Koman and Marin's income-based approach, as higher education levels command an increasing premium. Also, when experience is accounted for, Canada's average human capital increased by up to 45 percent over the period. Interestingly enough, while the two human capital measures (including and excluding experience) were virtually the same from 1976 to 1981, the two measures began to diverge since. According to Laroche and Mérette, this is because before 1981 schooling contributed more to human capital than working experience whereas after that the reverse is true. This pattern is reinforced by the fact that the Canadian population has grown older and as this greying trend is expected to persist, the difference between the two measures is likely to keep widening over time.

In aggregate terms, the Canada's stock of human capital increased in all dimensions. From 1976 to 1996, Canada's working age population grew by 33 percent and total years of education grew by a further 12 percent, however, the greatest growth was seen in labour income-based measures of human capital with and without working experience, which increased by 73 percent and 89 percent respectively. Laroche and Mérette also propose a measure of the so-called *active* human capital stock which is based on the labour force. In the authors' opinion, this measure gives better insight about the human capital stock available for market production purposes. In average terms, Canada's active human capital (measured using the labour-income based) also increased by 45 percent between 1976 and 1996, whereas the aggregate active human capital stock increased much faster, more than doubling over the same period.

2.3.6 *Other income-based measures of human capital*

Like Beach *et al.*, (1988), Macklem (1997) estimates the stock of human wealth in Canada, where human wealth is computed as the expected present value of aggregate labour income net of government expenditures based on an estimated bivariate vector autoregressive (VAR) model for the real interest rate and the growth rate of labour income net of government expenditures. Since the present value formula is non-linear, the estimated VAR is approximated as a discrete value finite-state Markov chain, which allows expectations to be calculated as a weighted sum over possible outcomes instead of an intractable integral.

Although also income-based, Macklem's measure of human wealth takes a more macro approach which, according to the author, has at least two important merits. First, it is much simpler. The macro focus requires much less onerous data, making it easily applicable to other countries. Second, this approach permits greater recognition of the joint statistical properties of innovations in income and interest rates, which improves understanding of household behaviour regarding consumption and savings. These advantages are, however, counteracted by the less disaggregated information.

Macklem finds that in per capita terms, human wealth in Canada rose steeply from 1963 to 1973, then decreased well into the mid 1980s, but has picked up since. Despite these complicated fluctuations, per capita human wealth has changed very little since the mid-1970s. First, this was due to the fact that real interest rates were very low in the mid-1970s and high in the 1980s, since a higher interest rate lowers the cumulative growth factor and thus human wealth. Second, net income in the early 1980s was lowered by both increases in government expenditures and the drop in labour income as a result of the recession in the same period. Third, in the second half of the 1980s real interest rates were falling while net income was growing strongly, reversing the earlier downward trend in human wealth. Clearly, since this human wealth (capital) measure is income-based, it has a pro-cyclical pattern with economic downturns. While human wealth fluctuated considerably like that, non-human wealth increased rather consistently over the period (1963–1994). Therefore, the ratio of human wealth to non-human wealth fell from 8 to 1 in the early 1960s to about 3 to 1 in the 1990s.

Dagum and Slottje (2000) criticise Macklem's estimation for containing large and unsubstantiated fluctuations in a period when Canada experienced steady economic growth. In the critics' view, this paradox is due to the limitations in the exogenous variables specified in the bivariate autoregressive model.

2.4 Integrated approaches to human capital measurement

Recognising that no single approach to measuring human capital is free from limitations, some authors have attempted to combine different methods in order to exploit their strengths while neutralising their weaknesses.

2.4.1 Tao and Stinson (1997)

Tao and Stinson (1997) develop an integrated approach to estimating the stock of human capital in the United States which resolves some well known problems inherent in both the cost- and income-based methods. The authors note that investments in human capital determine the human capital stock, which can be established by the cost-based method. In turn, human capital determines earnings for individuals through the income-based approach.

First, the authors specify a fundamental earning function, which establishes the relationship between human capital $h_{i,j}^s$ and earnings $E_{i,j}^s$ as:

$$E_{i,j}^s = w_t h_{i,j}^s \qquad (15)$$

where s, i, and j indicate the sex, age, and educational level respectively of an individual, and w_t is the human capital rental rate in year t. Since both of the right-hand side variables are unobservable, one of the two variables must be standardised. Tao and Stinson choose to standardise the human capital stock of the base entrants. This group is selected because they enter the labour force after leaving high school and thus no account needs to be taken of how experience, on-the-job training and the cost of training affect their human capital. In addition, the ability of these base entrants can be determined from the SAT (Scholastic Aptitude Test) scores. This test provides a consistent measure of the ability of high school graduates and SAT results are available for a number of years.[7] The human capital stock can then be identified by exploiting its relationship with human capital investments based on the cost method. The human capital stock of base entrants in this study is assumed to be equal to the accumulated real expenditures in their general education (through high school graduation). Once the human capital of these individuals is defined, the human capital rate w can then be easily estimated by applying earnings data to equation (15) above. That rental rate, which is assumed to be constant across cohorts, can then be applied together with earnings to equation (15) to derive the human capital stock for cohorts other than the base entrants.

The total human capital stock is obtained by aggregating the human capital from all cohorts in the population. It was found that the human capital stock embodied in employed individuals[8] expanded by six times between 1963 and 1988. When differences in the abilities of base entrants were considered, specifically, when the SAT scores of base entrants and entry level wages set by employers are assumed to be closely connected, the increase was less than 100 percent over the period. Effective human capital increased more for females (135 percent) than for males (75 percent), largely due to the increased participation of females in the labour force.

Tao and Stinson assert that their new framework demonstrates many advantages over existing approaches. First, by using the cost method to derive only the human capital stock of the average base entrants and estimating the human capital stock of other cohorts based on the human capital stock of this group, this method avoids the problem of what defines an investment in human capital. The authors believe that it is appropriate to consider only educational expenditures as human capital investments in base entrants. Since medical spending, for example, is already reflected in improved health and thus earnings, adding medical costs to the base entrants' human capital would be double counting. Additionally this approach does not require any assumption about depreciation or appreciation in human capital. Tao and Stinson also show that when used to estimate a Cobb-Douglas production function, their measure provides more explanatory power than hours of labour. However, a few problems persist. For example, rearing costs are classified as consumption and thus not included in human capital investments for base entrants. As discussed above, whether rearing costs should be considered consumption or investment is controversial. Another problem is more related to the income-based method. This model assumes that base entrants are paid a wage based on the abilities as measured by the SAT score, but the SAT score may not be a good measure of ability. Nevertheless, Tao and Stinson show that their measure enhances the explanatory power of the Cobb-Douglas production function for the US economy over the period studied.

2.4.2 Dagum and Slottje (2000)

Dagum and Slottje also combine various methods to develop an integrated measure of human capital. Their approach estimates personal human capital, its size distribution, the average level of human capital by age, and the average level of human capital in the population. From this a specific monetary value of the stock of human capital can be computed.

Personal human capital is construed as a dimensionless latent endogenous variable. From p indicators of human capital chosen from the sample survey database, a linear function of human capital is specified as:

$$z = L(x_1, x_2, x_l, \ldots, x_p) \qquad (16)$$

where z refers to the standardised (zero mean and unit variance) human capital latent variable, and x_1, x_2, $x_l, \ldots, x_p$ are p standardised indicators of human capital. An accounting monetary value of human capital for the ith economic unit, $h(i)$, can then be computed based on the following formula:

$$h(i) = \exp(z_i) \qquad (17)$$

Dagum and Slottje adopt an assumption that is commonly used in the income approach, namely the average human capital at age x, the average earnings of this economic unit, n years from now, is the same as the average earnings $y(x+n)$ of the economic units currently aged $x+n$, adjusted for the probability of survival and real income growth. Accordingly, the human capital of the average economic unit of age x can be estimated as:

$$h(x) = \sum_{n=0}^{70-x} \frac{y(x+n)p(x, x+n)(1+r)^n}{(1+i)^n} \qquad (18)$$

where $p(x, x+n)$ is the probability that a person aged x will survive another n years, i is the discount rate, r is the economic growth rate, and the highest working age is set at 70.

The weighted average value of the transformation in equation (17), $Av(h)$, and the weighted average of the population human capital given in equation (18), $AvHC(h)$, can be easily derived. The monetary value of the human capital of the ith sample observation is then given as:

$$HC(i) = h(i)\frac{AvHC(h)}{Av(h)}, \quad i = 1, 2, \ldots, n. \qquad (19)$$

Intuitively, the monetary value of a person's human capital is equal to the average lifetime earnings of the population, weighted by the level of human capital that he/she has relative to the average human capital of the population.

Using data from 4,103 household observations from the 1983 US Federal Reserve Board sample survey on income and wealth distributions, Dagum and Slottje estimated that in 1982 the US per capita human capital ranged from $239,000 to $365,000, depending on whether the discount rate was six percent or eight percent and whether economic growth rate was zero or positive. Their lowest estimate of US human capital was still twice Kendrick's estimate of per capita human capital in 1969 real terms. Not surprisingly, these figures are only a fraction of those obtained by Jorgenson and Fraumeni (1989, 1992) as the latter incorporates non-market human capital. Dagum and Slottje's estimates compare very unfavourably with the results for Canada in 1982 estimated by Macklem (1997). However, as discussed earlier, Dagum and Slottje question the reliability of Macklem's results.

Dagum and Slottje believe that by combining the estimation of human capital as a latent variable with a macroeconomic estimation of the average human capital of a population of economic units, their method provides a robust statistical support to the estimation of human capital. Most notably, the use of the latent variable approach is intended to remove the omitted variable bias that plagues the income-based method to measuring human capital. However, the data used in Dagum and Slottje's study does not contain any measure of intelligence, ability or any other indicators of genetic endowment, which renders the estimated $h(i)$ a less powerful indicator of human capital.

3. Some recent applications to New Zealand

Most published research on human capital in New Zealand has dealt with either changing prices – the returns to particular educational qualifications (Maani, 1999), or changing quantities, such as the compositional shift implied by the rising importance of the 'information workforce' (Engelbrecht, 2000). There are also many studies that use proxy indicators within the educational stock approach, such as Treasury (2001).

However, in New Zealand attention is now switching to directly valuing human capital. Hendy, Hyslop and Maré (2002), in work that is still in progress, examine how the value of human capital changed between 1986 and 1996. Whilst their method is also based on an expected income concept, it does not take into account enrolment in further education and survival probabilities and is not calculated on a lifetime income basis. Their study shows that the real value of the human capital of the employed New Zealand workforce rose by 11.7 percent between 1991 and 1996, after falling by one percent in the previous five years. Overall, employment growth produced 7.3 of the 10.6 percent increase in human capital over the period 1986–1996, which was then offset by a drop in productivity of 0.4 percentage points. The remaining 3.7 percentage points were attributed to relative quantity and relative price effects.

Oxley and Zhu (2002) follow the approach of Dagum and Slottje (2000) and use Census data in five-year age bands are used to estimate expected lifetime income, with different rates of productivity growth over the lifecycle. However, there is no differentiation amongst workers according to their educational attainment and the study extends only from 1986–1996. Oxley and Zhu find that in 1996, the human capital embodied in New Zealanders aged 15 and above averaged NZ\$282,000 per person. This figure reflected an increase of 7.7 percent from 1986, most of which (6.3 percent) occurred between 1986 and 1991. Some degree of catching-up by females is also evident, although women still have no more than 60 percent as much human capital as men do. These estimates can serve as a benchmark to see how much change in this stock value results when using the considerably more complex methods of our current study.

Here we present some results, derived from Le, Gibson and Oxley (2002), where full details of the model and data can be found, based upon a modified Jorgenson and Fraumeni (1989, 1992) and Wei (2001) approach. These new results place a value on the stock of human capital of the employed work force, or the *effective* human capital stock, for New Zealand.[9] We focus only on those individuals in employment, since these people are directly participating in economic production and so their human capital is arguably a better measure of the country's productive capacity.

The estimates presented below, are based on the discounted present value of expected lifetime labour market incomes. The results allow for the possibility of further educational experiences with individuals trying to move onto a higher age-earnings profile. Similar to Wei (2001), we assume that the potential working life is from age 21 to 65. A work-study phase occurs from 21–34, a work-only phase occurs from age 35. We initially followed Wei and specify five groups defined by their highest qualification: higher degree, Bachelors degree, diploma, skilled labour, and unqualified although it is apparent that in New Zealand there is not much difference between the annual labour incomes of people in the diploma group and those in the skilled labour group such that we aggregated diploma and skilled to give four categories. Extensions including a work-study phase and varying enrolment rates were used to provide for robustness analysis.

A selection of results based on data obtained from each New Zealand Census of Population from 1981 to 2001, are presented as Table 2, below. The data used were in the form of population counts within homogeneous cells defined by age, gender, educational level, employment status, and income bracket. Depending on the particular census, the number of cells approached 100,000, but for most of the analysis we formed the data into 360 cohorts defined by 45 ages (21–65), two genders, and four educational levels.[10] The last variable needed to calculate the expected value of lifetime income is survival rates, which were obtained from *New Zealand Life Tables*. Since survival rates are classified by gender and age only, we assume that the probabilities of surviving do not vary with the level of education. Survival rates were unavailable for 2001, so we use estimates for 1998–2000 from *Demographic Trends*, which are in five-year age intervals rather than by each specific age as used with the other census years.

The average per capita lifetime labour incomes (in 2001 NZ dollars) are reported in Table 2, below. These figures are weighted averages of the lifetime income profiles, where the weights are the number of people at each year of age. Consistent with the time trend for annual incomes, average lifetime incomes declined in real terms during 1981–1991 and started to increase since. Although average annual income in 2001 is nine percent higher than in 1981, average lifetime incomes grew by less than two percent over the period. The major

Table 2. Average Lifetime Labour Income Per Capita (NZ$2001).

	1981	1986	1991	1996	2001
Males					
Unqualified	500,558	479,910	456,012	480,015	455,641
Skilled	678,840	633,728	633,625	677,056	701,763
Bachelors	938,104	956,174	985,915	1,009,189	997,022
Higher	991,535	953,096	988,319	1,055,101	1,022,189
Weighted average	**588,742**	**588,451**	**596,444**	**638,471**	**631,766**
Females					
Unqualified	343,374	277,427	290,192	308,373	299,945
Skilled	478,039	399,872	422,376	448,494	470,244
Bachelors	675,291	564,624	632,443	640,275	674,362
Higher	726,225	602,110	670,562	710,553	758,011
Weighted average	**400,420**	**342,272**	**379,348**	**409,976**	**429,034**
Overall average	**527,573**	**488,791**	**503,803**	**535,607**	**537,081**
Change from last Census		−7.35%	3.07%	6.31%	0.28%

Source: Authors calculation from New Zealand Census of Population, 1981, 1986, 1991, 1996, 2001. Adjusted to 2001 dollars using the Prevailing Weekly Wage Index PWIQ.S4329 and All Salary & Wage Rates LCIQ.SA53Z9.

cause of this fall is the decrease in employment rates over the years. In particular, compared with 1981, both employment and real annual income in 1986 were lower, which explains the lower average lifetime income. Annual income rose slightly in the next inter-censual period, but employment declined dramatically, especially for the less educated, who make up the majority of the population. As a result, expected annual income and lifetime income increased only marginally. In the last ten years since 1991, both employment and real annual income have risen over time, improving average lifetime income consequently. These temporal patterns do not seem to be affected by the particular deflator used, and if anything the decline from 1981 is even greater if a price index (rather than a wage index) is used.

The contribution to the stock of New Zealand human capital by each education and gender group is presented as Table 3. The share of 'unqualified' people in the stock of human capital has declined from one-half of the male total in 1981 to just one-third in 2001, while the proportionate decline is even greater for women. By contrast, the human capital contributed by university degree holders has risen, in both relative and absolute terms. Indeed, this is to be expected, from what was observed earlier that annual incomes of these people have improved relatively the most and that their shares of the population have also expanded.

For example, in 1991, when the total human capital stock increased by a mere three percent from 1986, the capital accounted for by the university educated grew by 27 percent. While total human capital increased by half, university degree holders' capital almost quadrupled over the last twenty years. Most of the growth in total human capital comes from the additions to the labour force, since expected annual labour income in 2001 is marginally higher than in 1981.

Table 3. Aggregate Value of Human Capital in New Zealand (NZ$2001 billion).

	1981	1986	1991	1996	2001
Males					
Unqualified	215.5	181.1	144.2	163.3	177.6
Skilled	161.4	220.3	235.0	242.1	227.0
Bachelors	28.4	40.0	49.3	68.4	81.3
Higher	14.7	25.7	28.1	38.0	42.5
Subtotal	**420.0**	**467.2**	**456.6**	**511.8**	**528.4**
Females					
Unqualified	76.0	84.4	77.4	91.6	99.2
Skilled	51.0	80.6	107.7	126.8	135.6
Bachelors	7.9	12.2	20.1	33.6	53.9
Higher	2.5	7.6	11.0	17.1	25.8
Subtotal	**137.4**	**184.8**	**216.2**	**269.1**	**314.5**
Total	**557.4**	**652.1**	**672.8**	**780.8**	**842.9**
Change from last Census		**16.98**%	**3.18**%	**16.06**%	**7.95**%

Source: Authors calculation from New Zealand Census of Population, 1981, 1986, 1991, 1996, 2001.
Adjusted to 2001 dollars using the Prevailing Weekly Wage Index PWIQ.S4329 and All Salary &
Wage Rates LCIQ.SA53Z9.

4. Conclusions

In this paper we have concentrated on reviewing the cost- and income-based approaches to measuring human capital, in part, because it is a relatively neglected field in the area of human capital measurement and also due to the existence of other excellent surveys of the educational experience approach. However, the three approaches are clearly related. Inputs into the human capital production process, including, for example, the costs of rearing and educating people, form the basis for the cost-based approach to human capital valuation. The income-based approach to measuring human capital uses an individual's earnings which are assumed to be influenced by acquired skills and education. Human capital measures based upon literacy rates, school enrolment rates, and mean years of schooling, which have been widely used in their own right as educational stock-based measures of human capital, potentially form an input into such income-based measures.

It is interesting to note that there has been a radical change in the motivation behind human capital valuation. Early measures of human capital were more concerned with demonstrating the power of a nation, by estimating, in monetary terms, human loss from wars and plagues, and with developing accurate estimates of human wealth in national accounts. Now the focus has been switched to using the human capital variable as an input to explain economic growth and a potential policy instrument. Human capital is believed to play a critical role in the growth process, as well as producing positive external effects such as enhanced self-fulfilment, enjoyment and development of individual capabilities, reduction in poverty and delinquency, and increased participation in community and social and political affairs.

However, the impact of human capital on economic growth is not unambiguous. The lack of empirical consensus is, in part, due to alternative approaches to measuring human capital where each approach subject to two types of measurement error: the measure does not adequately reflect key elements of human capital, and data on the measure is of poor quality. Hence, measuring human capital remains a significant research challenge.

Acknowledgments

Support from the Royal Society of New Zealand, Marsden Fund Grant UOC108 aided completion of this work.

Notes

1. Laroche *et al.* (1999) give a detailed treatment of definition of human capital. Since our study is more concerned with measuring human capital, we do not discuss the definitions at length.
2. See, for example, Shultz (1961a, 1961b) and Shaffer (1961), who discussed the difficulties in distinguishing between consumption and investment expenditures in the formation of human capital.
3. All figures quoted in this part are net stocks of capital.
4. Many other cost-based type studies allow for human capital formation in estimating the national accounts but do not calculate the human capital stock explicitly. See Ruggles and Ruggles (1970), Nordhaus and Tobin (1972), Eisner (1978), and Zolotas (1981).
5. In New Zealand compulsory retirement ages have been abolished.
6. Education levels range from no schooling at all to 17 years of schooling.
7. The SAT data suffer from a self-selection bias, since students have the choice to take the test. Tao and Stinson have, however, corrected this problem.
8. Tao and Stinson call human capital stock of the employed *effective* human capital.
9. This term is adopted from Tao and Stinson (1997). Hendy *et al.* (2002) also focus on the same part of the population.
10. Cell counts were randomly rounded to base 3 to protect confidentiality, which could lead to errors in our results, because our data are broken down to such a detailed level. However, since the rounding is only at random, we believe that the effect it has on our results, if any, is insignificant.

References

Aghion, P. and Howitt, P. (1998) *Endogenous Growth Theory*, Boston, MIT Press.

Ahlroth, S., Bjorklund, A. and Forslund, A. (1997) The output of the Swedish education sector. *Review of Income and Wealth*, 43 (1), 89–104.

Ahmavaara, P. A. (2002) Human capital as a produced asset. Paper prepared for the 17th General Conference of the International Association for Research in Income and Wealth. Stockholm, Sweden, August 2002.

Barriol, A. (1910) La valeur sociale d'un individu. *Revue Economique Internationale*, 552–555.

Barro, R. J. and Lee, J-W. (1993) International comparisons of educational attainment. *Journal of Monetary Economics*, 32 (3), 363–394.

Barro, R. J. and Lee, J-W. (1996) International measures of schooling years and schooling quality. *American Economic Review*, 86 (2), 218–223.

Barro, R. J. and Lee, J-W. (2001) International data on educational attainment: updates and implications. *Oxford Economic Papers*, 53 (3), 541–563.

Baumol, W. (1990) Enterpreneurship: productive, unproductive, and destructive. *Journal of Political Economics*, 893–921.

Beach, C. M., Broadway, R. W. and Bruce, N. (1988) *Taxation and Savings in Canada*. Ottawa: Economic Council of Canada.

Bowles, S., Gintis, H. and Osborne, M. (2001) The determinants of earnings: A behavioural approach. *Journal of Economic Literature*, 39 (4), 1137–1176.

Bowman, M. J. (1962) Economics of Education. *HEW Bulletin* 5.

Cohen, D. and Soto, M. (2001) Growth and human capital: good data, good results. *OECD Development Centre Technical Papers* No. 179 [Online]. Available: http://www1.oecd.org/dev/publication/tp/tp179.pdf.

Conrad, K. (1992) Comment on D. W. Jorgenson and B. M. Fraumeni, 'Investment in education and U.S. economic growth'. *Scandinavian Journal of Economics*, 94 (Supplement), 71–74.

Dagum, C. and Slottje, D. J. (2000) A new method to estimate the level and distribution of household human capital with application. *Structural Change and Economic Dynamics*, 11 (2), 67–94.

De Foville, A. (1905) Ce que c'est la richesse d'un people. *Bulletin de l'Institut International de Statistique*, 14 (3), 62–74.

De la Fuente, A. and Doménech, R. (2000) Human capital in growth regressions: how much difference does data quality make? *OECD Working Paper* No. 262 [Online]. Available: http://www.oecd.org/pdf/M00002000/M00002095.pdf.

Dublin, L. I. and Lotka, A. (1930) *The Money Value of Man*. New York, N.Y.: Ronald.

Dublin, L. I. (1928) *Health and Wealth, a Survery of the Economics of World Health*. New York: Harper & Bros.

Eisner, R. (1985) The total incomes system of accounts. *Survey of Current Business*, 65 (1), 24–48.

Eisner, R. (1988) Extended accounts for national income and product. *Journal of Economic Literature*, 26 (4), 1611–1684.

Engel, E. (1883) *Der Werth des Menschen*. Berlin: Verlag von Leonhard Simion.

Engelbrecht, H-J. (2000) Towards a knowledge economy? Changes in New Zealand's information work force 1976–1996. *Prometheus*, 18 (3), 265–282.

Farr, W. (1852) Equitable taxation of property. *Journal of Royal Statistics*, 16 (March issue), 1–45.

Fisher, I. (1908) Cost of tuberculosis in the United States and its reduction. Read before the International Congress on Tuberculosis. Washington.

Graham, J. W. and Webb, R. H. (1979) Stocks and depreciation of human capital: New evidence from a present-value perspective. *Review of Income and Wealth*, 25 (2), 209–224.

Haveman, R. and Wolfe, B. (1984) Schooling and economic well-being: the role of non-markets effects. *Journal of Human Resources*, 19 (3), 377–407.

Hendy, J., Hyslop, D. and Maré, D. (2002) Qualifications, employment, and the value of human capital, 1986–1996. *Mimeo* Motu Economic and Public Policy Research, Wellington.

Houthakker, H. S. (1959) Education and income. *Review of Economics and Statistics*, 41 (1), 24–28.

Huebner, S. S. (1914) The human value in business compared with the property value. Proc. *Thirty-fifth Ann. Convention Nat. Assoc. Life* (July issue), 17–41.

Jeong, B. (2002) Measurement of human capital input across countries: a method based on the laborer's income. *Journal of Development Economics*, 67 (2), 333–349.

Jones, L. and Manuelli, R. (1990) A convex model of equilibrium growth: theory and policy implications. *Journal of Political Economy*, 98 (5), 1008–1038.

Jorgenson, D. W. and Fraumeni, B. M. (1989) The accumulation of human and non-human capital, 1948–1984. In R. E. Lipsey and H. S. Tice (Eds.), *The Measurement of Savings, Investment and Wealth* (pp. 227–282). Chicago, IL.: The University of Chicago Press.

Jorgenson, D. W. and Fraumeni, B. M. (1992) The output of the education sector. In Z. Griliches (Ed.), *Output Measurement in the Services Sector* (pp. 303–338). Chicago, IL.: The University of Chicago Press.

Kendrick, J. (1976) *The Formation and Stocks of Total Capital*. New York, N.Y.: Columbia University Press for NBER.

Kiker, B. F. (1966) The historical roots of the concept of human capital. *Journal of Political Economy*, 74 (5), 481–499.

Koman, R. and Marin, D. (1997) Human Capital and Macroeconomic Growth: Austria and Germany 1960–1997. An Update. Working Paper, Department of Economics, University of Munich.

Krueger, A. B. and Lindahl, M. (2001) Education for growth: why and for whom? *Journal of Economic Literature*, 39 (4), 1101–1136.

Laroche, M. and Mérette, M. (2000) Measuring human capital in Canada. Ministère des Finances du Canada, Division des Etudes Economiques et Analyse de Politiques.

Laroche, M., Mérette, M. and Ruggeri, G. C. (1999) On the concept and dimensions of human capital in a knowledge-based economy context. *Canadian Public Policy – Analyse de Politiques*, 25 (1), 87–100.

Le, T., Gibson, J. and Oxley, L. (2002) A forward looking measure of the stock of human capital in New Zealand, Paper presented at the NZAE conference, Wellington, July, 2002.

Lee, J-W and Barro, R. J. (2001) Schooling quality in a cross-section of countries. *Economica*, 68 (272), 465–88.

Lucas, R. E. Jr. (1988) On the mechanics of economic development. *Journal of Monetary Economics*, 22 (1), 3–42.

Maani, S. (1999) Private and public returns to investment in secondary and higher education in New Zealand over time, 1981–1996. *Treasury Working Paper* 02/99 [Online]. Available: http://www.treasury.govt.nz/workingpapers/1999/twp99–2.pdf.

Machlup, F. (1962) *The Production and Distribution of Knowledge in the United States*. Princeton, N.J.: Princeton University Press.

Machlup, F. (1984) *The Economics of Information and Human Capital*, Vol 3. Princeton, N.J.: Princeton University Press.

Macklem, R. T. (1997) Aggregate wealth in Canada. *Canadian Journal of Economics*, 30 (1), 152–168.

Miller, H. P. (1965) Lifetime income and economic growth. *American Economic Review*, 55 (4), 835–844.

Mincer, J. (1958) Investment in human capital and personal income distribution. *Journal of Political Economy*, 66 (4), 281–302.

Mincer, J. (1970) *Schooling, Experience, and Earnings*. New York, N.Y.: Columbia University Press for NBER.

Mulligan, C. B. and Sala-i-Martin, X. (1997) A labor income-based measure of the value of human capital: an application to the states of the United States. *Japan and the World Economy*, 9 (2), 159–191.

Nicholson, J. S. (1891) The living capital of the United Kingdom. *Economic Journal*, 1 (1), 95–107.

Nordhaus, W. D. and Tobin, J. (1972) *Economic Growth*. New York, N.Y.: NBER.

OECD (2001) *The Well-being of Nations: The Role of Human and Social Capital*. Paris: OECD.

Oxley, L., Greasley, D. and Zhu, S. (1999) Endogenous versus exogenous growth: the USA and New Zealand compared. *Singapore Economic Review*, 44 (1), 26–56.

Oxley, L., Greasley, D. and Zhu, S. (1999–2000) *The Role Of Human Capital In Economic Growth*. Marsden Fund Grant No. 98-UOW-015 SOC.

Oxley, L. and Zhu, W. (2002) How much human capital does New Zealand have? Presented at ESAM, Brisbane, July 2002.

Petty, W. (1690) Political Arithmetik, reprinted in C. H. Hull (1899), *The Economic Writings of Sir William Petty*. Cambridge: Cambridge University Press.

Pritchett, L. (2001) Where has all the education gone? *World Bank Economic Review*, 15 (3), 367–391.

Rebelo, S. (1991) Long Run Policy Analysis and Long Run Growth, *Journal of Political Economy*, 500–521.

Ricardo, D., *The Works and Correspondence of David Ricardo*, 11 volumes, edited by Piero Sraffa and M.H. Dobb, Cambridge: Cambridge University Press, 1951–1973.

Romer, P. (1986) Increasing returns and long run growth. *Journal of Political Economy*, 94 (5), 1002–1037.

Romer, P. M. (1989) Human capital and growth: theory and evidence. *National Bureau of Economic Research Working Paper* No. 3173.

Rothschild, M. (1992) Comment on 'Output of the education sector'. In Z. Griliches (Ed.), *Output Measurement in the Services Sector* (pp. 339–341). Chicago, IL.: The University of Chicago Press.

Ruggles, N. and Ruggles, R. (1970) *The Design of Economic Accounts*. New York, N.Y.: Columbia University Press.

Shaffer (1961) Investment in human capital. *American Economic Review*, 51 (5), 1026–1034.

Shultz, T. W. (1961a) Investment in human capital. *American Economic Review*, 51 (1), 1–17.

Shultz, T. W. (1961b) Investment in human capital. *American Economic Review*, 51 (5), 1035–1039.

Smith, A. (1776) *The Wealth of Nations*, Book 2. London: G. Routledge.

Tao, H.-L. and Stinson, T. F. (1997) An alternative measure of human capital stock. *University of Minnesota Economic Development Center Bulletin*: 97/01.

Temple, J. (2000) Growth effects of education and social capital in the OECD countries. *OECD Working Paper* No. 263 [Online]. Available: http://www.oecd.org/pdf/M00002000/M00002096.pdf.

The Treasury (2001) Human capital and the inclusive economy. *Treasury Working Paper* 01/16 Available: http://www.treasury.govt.nz/workingpapers/2001/twp01–16.pdf.

Treadgold, M. (2000) Early estimate of the value of Australia's stock of human capital. *History of Economics Review*, 32, 46–57.

Wachtel, P. (1997) A labor-income based measure of the value of human capital: an application to the states of the US: Comments. *Japan and the World Economy*, 9 (2), 193–96.

Wei, H. (2001) Measuring the stock of human capital for Australia: a lifetime labour income approach. Paper presented at the 30th Annual Conference of Economists, Perth, September 2001.

Weisbrod, B. A. (1961) The valuation of human capital. *Journal of Political Economy*, 69 (5), 425–436.

Wickens, C. H. (1924) *Human Capital*, Report of the Sixteenth Meeting of the Australasian Association for the Advancement of Science (pp. 526–554). Wellington: Government Printer. Cited in Treadgold (2000).

Wittstein, T. (1867) *Mathematische Statistik und deren Anwendung auf National-Okonomie und Versicherung-wiessenschaft*. Hanover: Han'sche Hofbuchland-lung.

Wößmann, L. (2003) Specifying human capital. *Journal of Economic Surveys*, 17 (3), 239–270.

Wolff, E. N. (2000) Human capital investment and economic growth: exploring the cross-country evidence. *Structural Change and Economic Dynamics*, 11 (4), 433–472.

Woods, E. A. and Metzger, C. B. (1927) *America's Human Wealth: Money Value of Human Life*. New York: F. S. Crofts & Co.

Zolotas, X. (1981) *Economic Growth and Declining Social Welfare*. Athens: Bank of Greece.

APPENDIX

Table 1. Summary of Studies on Measuring Human Capital Using Cost-based, Income-based, and Integrated Approaches.

Source	Method	Country, Time	Motivation	Results/Comments
Petty (1690)	Income-based	England and Wales	– Interest in public finance – To evaluate the power of England, the economic effects of migration, the loss caused by a plague or by men killed in war	Aggregate stock was about £520, or £80 per capita.
Farr (1853)	Income-based	England	Interest in public finance: taxing human capital	Per capita net human capital value was about £150.
Engel (1883)	Cost-based	Germany		
Wittstein (1867)	Income-based (Farr's approach), combined with cost-based (Engel's approach)	Germany	To determine a guide to be based on for claims for compensation from loss of life	
Nicholson (1891, 1896)	Income-based, combined with cost-based	United Kingdom (1891)		The stock of living capital was about 5 times that of conventional capital.
De Foville (1905)	Income-based (Petty's approach)	France, around 1900		
Fisher (1908)	Income-based (Farr's approach)	United States, 1907	To estimate the cost of preventable illness	The stock of human capital exceeded all other wealth.
Barriol (1910)	Income-based (Farr's approach)	France and other selected countries		
Huebner (1914)	Income-based (Farr's approach)	United States, around 1914		The stock of human capital was from 6 to 8 times that of conventional capital.
Wickens (1924)	Income-based (Farr's approach)	Australia, 1915		Human capital of £6,211 million (or £1,246 per capita, £1,923 for males and £928 for females) was about 3 times as large as the physical capital stock.

	Method	Country/Year	Purpose	Findings
Woods and Metzger (1927)	5 different methods, including – Farr's approach – Petty's approach	United States, 1920	To show the importance of the nation's population	The stock of human wealth was approximately 5 times that of material wealth.
Dublin (1928)	Unknown	United States, 1922		
Dublin and Lotka (1930)	Income-based (Improvement on Farr, 1853)		– To estimate how much life insurance a man should carry – To estimate economic costs of preventable disease and premature death	
Shultz (1961)	Cost-based	United States, 1900–1956	Economic growth, productivity	The stock of human capital grew twice as fast as that of physical capital during 1900–1956.
Weisbrod (1961)	Income-based	United States, 1950, males aged 0–74	To estimate the value of the human capital stock	– Gross: $1,335b at r = 10%, $2,752b at r = 4% – Net (of consumption): $1,055b and $2,218b respectively – Compared with non-human assets of $881b
Kendrick (1976)	Cost-based	United States, 1929–1969	To develop national wealth estimates to complement estimates of the physical stock.	The stock of human capital was often greater and grew faster than that of physical capital.
Eisner (1985)	Cost-based	United States, 1945–1981 (selected years)	As above	The stock of human capital was almost as large as that of physical capital.
Graham and Webb (1979)	Income-based	United States, 1969, males aged 14–75	As above	The stock of human capital embodied in US males aged 14–75 in 1969 ranged from $2,910 billion at 20% discount rate or $14,395 billion at 2.5% discount rate. This contrasted with an estimate of $3,700 billion obtained by Kendrick's (1976).

(continued)

Table 1. *Continued.*

Source	Method	Country, Time	Motivation	Results/Comments
Jorgenson and Fraumeni (1989, 1992)	Income-based (Improvement on Dublin and Lotka, 1930)	United States, 1948–1986	– To present a new system of national accounts for the US economy – To measure the impact of investment in education on economic growth	Stock of real human capital almost doubled, from $92 trillion in 1949 to $171 trillion in 1984. Estimates in the later study (1992), were about 20% higher, due to allowance being made for school enrolment. Per capita human capital grew by 15%, from $742,000 in 1948 to $855,000 in 1986. Women's share was around 40%. The share of human capital based on market labour activities was around 30%. Human capital was from 12 to 16 times greater than physical capital in size. For the period 1948–1969, Jorgenson and Fraumeni's (1992) estimates of US human capital was from 17.5 to 18.8 times higher than Kendrick's.
Ahlroth *et al.* (1997)	Income-based (Jorgenson and Fraumeni method)	Sweden, 1968, 1974, 1981 and 1991	To compute the aggregate measures of the output of the Swedish education sector.	Even the lowest estimates of the human capital stock (after tax, excluding leisure income) were from 6 to 10 times higher than the stock of physical capital.

Study	Method	Objective	Coverage	Findings
Wei (2001)	Income-based (Jorgenson and Fraumeni method)	To develop measures of human capital that could serve as useful counterparts to measures of physical capital	Australia, 1981–1996 quinquennially	In 1996 prices, the stock of Australia's working age human capital increased from $1.7 trillion in 1981 to $2.1 trillion in 1996, but there was a sharp drop in 1991. The stock of human capital was larger than that of physical capital, although the ratio has been declining over time.
Macklem (1997)	Income-based (macro focussed)		Canada, 1963–1994, quarterly	In per capita terms, human wealth in Canada rose steeply from 1963 to 1973, then decreased well into the mid 1980s, but has picked up since. The ratio of human wealth to non-human wealth fell from 8:1 in the early 1960s to about 3:1 in the 1990s.
Mulligan and Sala-i-Martin (1997)	Income-based		48 US continental states, 6 census years (1940, 1950, 1960, 1970, 1980, 1990)	On the whole, the stock of human capital shrank substantially between 1940 and 1950, before increasing steadily to 1990. Aggregate human capital stocks increased by 52% between 1980 and 1990.
Koman and Marin (1997)	Income-based		Austria and Germany, aged 15 and over, in 1980, 1985, 1990, and 1992	Human capital grew faster than average years of schooling in the populace and that the time-series evidence was not consistent with a human capital augmented Solow model.

(continued)

Table 1. *Continued.*

Source	Method	Country, Time	Motivation	Results/Comments
Jeong (2002)	Income-based Mulligan and Sala-i-Martin's method	45 countries	To compare human capital inputs for countries of diverse output levels	Poorer countries use less human capital inputs in the production process and the richest countries have from 2.2 to 2.8 times as much human capital as the poorest countries, depending on whether or not outliers are included. Although this figure is considerable, it is small in comparison with the cross-country difference in human capital measures based on years of schooling or with the output difference.
Laroche and Mérette (2000)	Income-based (Koman and Marin's (1997) method)	Canada, aged 15–64, 1971 to 1996		*In per capital terms: – years of schooling increased 15% between 1976 and 1996 – human capital measured using Koman and Marin's income-based approach increased by over 33%, and by 45% when working experience is accounted for. *In aggregate terms: – working age population grew by 33% – total years of education grew by a further 12% – labour income-based measures of human capital with and without working experience increased by 73% and 89% respectively.

		*For the labour force only: in average terms, Canada's active human capital (measured using the labour income-based approach) also increased by 45% between 1976 and 1996, whereas the aggregate active human capital stock increased much faster, more than doubling over the same period.
Tao and Stinson (1997)	Integrated	United States, 1963–1988, the employed	The effective human capital stock expanded by 6 times between 1963 and 1988. When differences in the abilities of base entrants were considered, the increase was less than 100% over the period. Effective human capital increased more for females (135%) than for males (75%), largely due to the increased participation of females in the labour force.
Dagum and Slotje (2000)	Integrated	United States, 1982	In 1982 the US per capita human capital was estimated to range from $239,000 to $365,000, depending on whether the discount rate was 6% or 8% and whether economic growth rate was zero or positive. The lowest figure was still twice Kendrick's estimate of per capita human capital 1969 in real terms. Not surprisingly, these figures are only a fraction of those obtained by Jorgensen and Fraumeni (1989, 1992) because the latter incorporate non-market human capital as well.

4

WHAT HAVE WE LEARNT FROM THE CONVERGENCE DEBATE?

Nazrul Islam

Emory University

1. Introduction

A central issue around which the recent growth literature has evolved is that of convergence. Whether income levels of poorer countries of the world are converging to those of richer countries is by itself a question of paramount importance for human welfare. However, interest in this question has been fueled further by the fact that it became linked with the issue of validity of alternative growth theories. It has been generally thought that convergence was an implication of the neo-classical growth theory (NCGT), while the new growth theories (NGT) did not have this implication. Accordingly, it was believed that by testing for convergence, one could test for the validity of alternative growth theories. Given this connection, it is not surprising that the convergence issue has drawn the attention of many outstanding minds of the economics profession.

This attention has however led to many different interpretations of convergence and to a wide array of empirical results, so much so that a feeling of exasperation is now not uncommon. Some have even expressed the view that the new growth literature in general and the convergence literature in particular have not produced anything new or substantive. In their surveys of the new growth literature, Durlauf and Quah (1999) and Temple (1999) try to refute this pessimistic appraisal. Both these surveys are comprehensive, and convergence is only one of the different growth topics covered. These papers therefore cannot give exclusive attention to the convergence debate. For example, Temple's survey does not include the discussion of the 'distribution approach' to convergence study. Durlauf and Quah pay considerable attention to the theoretical relationship among different growth models and relegate many details of the empirical results to a summary table. The otherwise excellent surveys by Sala-i-Martin (1996b) and De la Fuente (1997) leave out convergence studies that use the panel, time-series, and distribution approaches. Meanwhile, research on convergence continues, and new entrants to this research often do not display adequate awareness of the different ways in which convergence has already been investigated and of the connections that exist among the available results.

Presentation of new convergence results in this backdrop often adds to the confusion.

The aim of this paper is to provide a comprehensive background in the context of which future growth and convergence research can be pursued and understood. In achieving this goal, the paper builds on the previous surveys, extends and updates them, and offers some different assessments of the contribution of the convergence literature to the understanding of economic growth. An important distinction of the present survey lies in its mode of exposition. The literature on convergence has unfolded in response to perceived logical inadequacies of previous works. Understanding of the analytical points therefore requires a perusal of how this literature has evolved over time. Accordingly, the present survey uses the *historical-logical* mode of exposition and often looks at the literature from the history of thought point of view.[1] Also, the survey is presented in a fairly nontechnical fashion, so that those who are not engaged in research on growth and convergence can find it easy to follow.

The paper begins by identifying the definitions of convergence and the methodologies that have been used for their investigation. It shows that while there is some correspondence between the definitions and methodologies, this correspondence is not unique. The paper identifies the areas of overlaps and shows how the awareness about these overlaps helps in understanding the relationship among results obtained from different methodologies.

In evaluating the convergence results, the paper reexamines Barro's (1997, p. x) conclusion that the recent empirical research prompted by the advent of new growth theory has ironically helped vindicate the explanatory power of the neoclassical growth theory.[2] Temple (1999, p. 112) finds this conclusion to be only a partial characterization of the new growth evidence. Durlauf and Quah (1999) think that this conclusion is erroneous because it is based on research that uses only linear specifications of the growth-convergence equation and ignores the possibility of its non-linear specification.

Barro's conclusion derives from the general empirical finding supporting 'conditional convergence.' The present survey shows that some of the findings of the 'time series' and the 'distribution' approaches can also be interpreted as supportive of 'conditional convergence.' The paper notes the empirical difficulty in distinguishing 'club convergence' from 'conditional convergence.' However, in reflecting on the results, the survey emphasizes the metamorphosis that both the NCGT and the NGT have undergone under the impact of the convergence research. The paper shows that, as a consequence of the give and take between the NCGT and NGT, it is now possible, generally speaking, to explain both convergence and non-convergence behavior by appropriately chosen models of growth theory of both these varieties. This in some sense frustrates the original idea of using convergence as a criterion for validity of alternative growth theories. However, the fact that convergence research led both the NCGT and the NGT towards accommodation may not be a small achievement by itself.

The convergence research had other, wider ramifications. First, it has produced new stylized facts about cross-country growth regularities, such as 'persistence' and 'bi-modality.' The growth theory is now called upon to explain these facts. Second, the convergence research has brought to fore the importance of techno-logical differences across countries and has led to the development of new methodologies for quantification of these differences. The results of these quanti-fication efforts are providing a new information base for examining alternative models of technology generation and diffusion. This information base is also helpful for understanding the interaction among countries along other dimensions such as trade, migration, spread of institutions, etc. Finally, the convergence research has also provided the background for formulation of stochastic growth models. All in all, instead of proving futile, the convergence research has had impressive achievements and has opened up useful new lines of research.

The discussion of this paper is organized as follows. Section 2 discusses the link between the growth theory controversy and the issue of convergence, and it catalogues different definitions and methodological approaches used for the con-vergence research. Section 3 provides a brief description of different concepts of convergence. Section 4 reviews the initial evidence on convergence based on informal specifications of cross-section regressions. The formal, model-based growth-convergence equation that has become the mainstay of convergence research is presented in section 5. Section 6 reviews the cross-section results based on formal specifications. It also includes discussion of 'club convergence.' Section 7 reviews the panel approach to convergence study, including research on 'TFP-convergence.' Section 8 reviews the time series approach to convergence analysis. Section 9 discusses the distribution approach to convergence, including research on σ-convergence. Conclusions are drawn in section 10. The literature on convergence is too vast to make an all-inclusive survey possible. Despite efforts to be inclusive, some works are only briefly discussed here and others remain outside the purview. This however does not mean that these works are not important.

2. Growth Theory and the Issue of Convergence

The NCGT assumption of diminishing returns leads to the convergence implica-tion.[3] In the mid-eighties however a perception arose that convergence did not hold in large samples of countries. Romer (1994) identifies this perceived incon-gruity as one of the two origins of the NGT. The other origin, according to Romer, is NCGT's inability to generate long term growth from within the model. The NGT models try to solve these twin problems by avoiding diminishing returns in various ways. This lets these models avoid the convergence implication and to have endogenous long run growth. Thus we have the link between the convergence issue and the issue of validity of alternative growth theories. It is because of this link and broader significance that the convergence debate has been raging so forcefully for such a long time.

The debate has in turn led to many different interpretations of convergence. In applying NCGT to the study of cross-country growth regularities, researchers have, either explicitly or implicitly, added other assumptions (to the basic assumption of diminishing returns), and this has been the main reason for the emergence of different notions of convergence. The following, often encountered, dichotomies indicate some of the different ways in which convergence has been understood:

(a) Convergence *within* an economy vs. convergence *across* economies;
(b) Convergence in terms of *growth rate* vs. convergence in terms of income *level*;
(c) β-convergence vs. σ-convergence;
(d) *Unconditional* (absolute) convergence vs. *conditional* convergence;
(e) *Global* convergence vs. *local* or *club*-convergence;
(f) *Income*-convergence vs. *TFP* (total factor productivity)-convergence; and
(g) *Deterministic* convergence vs. *stochastic* convergence.

It is not that all these different concepts of convergence were apparent from the very beginning. Research on convergence proceeded through several stages, and it is only with time that these different definitions emerged and gained currency. Convergence research has also witnessed the use of different methodologies, which may be classified broadly as follows:

(a) Informal cross-section approach,
(b) Formal cross-section approach,
(c) Panel approach,
(d) Time-series approach, and
(e) Distribution approach.

There is some correspondence between the convergence definitions and the methodologies used. This correspondence is however not unique. For example, the informal and formal cross-section approaches, the panel approach, and the time-series approach (in part) have all studied β-convergence, either conditional or unconditional. These approaches have generally dealt with convergence *across* economies and in terms of per capita income *level*. In addition, the formal cross-section approach and the panel approach have been used to study club-convergence and TFP-convergence. The cross-section approach has even been used to study σ-convergence. The time series approach has been used to investigate convergence both *within* an economy and *across*-economies. Finally, the distribution approach has gone beyond investigating just σ-convergence and has studied the entire shape of the distribution and intra-distribution dynamics. A useful way to start reviewing the convergence literature is therefore to provide a brief introduction to these different concepts of convergence.

3. Different Concepts of Convergence

3.1. *Convergence Within vs. Convergence Across*

Robert Solow (1970), in his exposition of growth theory, starts out by relating to six stylized facts about growth put forwarded by Kaldor (1971). Coming to the fifth and sixth of these,[4] Solow pauses and makes the following comment:

"The remaining 'stylized facts' are of a different kind, and *will concern me less*, because they relate more to comparisons *between* different economies than to the course of events *within* any one economy." (p. 3; my italics.)

It is somewhat ironic that one of the recent dissatisfactions with the Solow model concerns its alleged failure to explain *between-* or *across*-country variation in growth rate and income level. Historically, the main objective of the Solow model has been to show that once factor substitution is allowed, the economy could achieve *stable* dynamic equilibrium, instead of suffering from the inherent instability that characterized the previous Harrod-Domar growth model. In NCGT, no matter whether the economy starts off from a per capita capital stock that is lower or higher than the equilibrium capital level, the substitution possibility and diminishing returns force the economy to 'converge' to the equilibrium. Hence, this is a proposition of convergence, albeit *within* the economy. Paradoxically, the concept of convergence that arose and became associated with NCGT refers to an *across*-economy process.

3.2. *Convergence in Terms of Growth Rate vs. Convergence in Terms of Income Level*

The across-economy convergence may in turn be understood in two different ways, namely 'convergence in terms of growth rate' and 'convergence in terms of income level.' Both of these require extending the NCGT conception of technology to the world level. The specification of technological progress in NCGT is based on the following assumptions: (a) no resources are needed to generate technological innovation, (b) everybody benefits equally from it, and (c) nobody pays any compensation for benefiting from it. Extended to a global setting, these assumptions imply that all countries share in the technological progress equally, and hence they all can grow at the same rate in the steady state. This yields the hypothesis of convergence in terms of *growth rate*. To this researchers often added the assumption that all countries have identical aggregate production function. This implies that steady state income *levels* of all countries are also identical. This yields convergence in terms of income level.

3.3. *β-convergence vs. σ-convergence*

Convergence in terms of both growth rate and income level requires what is called β-convergence. This follows from the assumption of diminishing returns, which imply higher marginal productivity of capital in a capital-poor country. With similar savings rates, poorer economies will therefore grow *faster*. If this scenario holds, there should be a *negative* correlation between the initial income level and the subsequent growth rate. This led to the popular methodology of investigating convergence, namely running what is now known as the *growth-initial level* regressions. The coefficient of the initial income variable in these regressions (say, β) is supposed to pick up the negative correlation. Convergence judged by the sign of β is known as the β-convergence.[5]

However, such researchers as Quah (1993a), Friedman (1994), and others have emphasized that convergence is a proposition regarding *dispersion* of the cross-sectional distribution of income (and growth rate), and a negative β from the growth-initial level regression does not necessarily imply a reduction in this dispersion.[6] According to this view, instead of judging indirectly and perhaps erroneously through the sign of β, convergence should be judged directly by looking at the dynamics of dispersion of income level and/or growth rate across countries. This gave rise to the concept of σ-convergence, where σ is the notation for standard deviation of the cross-sectional distribution of either income level or growth rate.

Despite the limitations above, researchers have continued to be interested in β-convergence, in part because it is a necessary, though not sufficient, condition of σ-convergence. The other reason is that methodologies associated with investigation of β-convergence also provide information regarding structural parameters of growth models, while research along the distribution approach usually do not provide such information, as we shall see.

3.4. *Unconditional Convergence vs. Conditional Convergence*

From a conceptual point of view, the most important distinction is probably between conditional and unconditional convergence. Proceeding from the Solow model and assuming a Cobb-Douglas production function of the type

$$Y_t = K_t^\alpha (A_t L_t)^{1-\alpha} \tag{1}$$

(where Y, K, L, and A stand for output, capital, labor, and total factor productivity, respectively), the steady state level of per capita income, y^*, is given by

$$y^* = A_0 e^{gt} [s/(n+g+\delta)]^{\alpha/(1-\alpha)}, \tag{2}$$

where s is the investment rate, g and n are the assumed exponential growth rates of A_t and L_t, respectively.[7] This shows clearly that the steady state income level of a country depends on the following six elements: A_0, s, g, n, δ, and α, which may be combined in the vector θ.[8] Unconditional convergence implies that all elements of θ are the same for the economies considered. In terms of the growth-initial level regression, this means that the sign of β should be negative even if no other variable is included on the right hand side. In contrast, the concept of conditional convergence emphasizes possible differences in the steady state and hence requires that appropriate variables be included on the right hand side of the growth-initial level regression in order to control for these differences. Which of the different elements of the vector θ should be allowed to vary and which not, continues to be an important issue, as we shall see.

3.5. *Conditional Convergence vs. Club Convergence*

The concept of conditional convergence is also related with the notion of 'club convergence.' The latter term can be traced back to Baumol (1986), but its more rigorous formulation owes to Durlauf and Johnson (1995) and Galor (1996). One property of the standard NCGT is *uniqueness* of its equilibrium, and the usual notion of convergence assumes this uniqueness. In the case of unconditional convergence, there is only one equilibrium-level to which *all* economies approach. In the case of conditional convergence, equilibrium differs by the economy, and each particular economy approaches its own but *unique* equilibrium. In contrast, the idea of club-convergence is based on models that yield *multiple* equilibrium.[9] Which of these different equilibrium an economy will reach, depends on its initial position or some other attribute. A group of countries may approach a particular equilibrium if they share the initial location or attribute corresponding to that equilibrium. This produces club-convergence.

3.6. *Income-convergence vs. TFP-convergence*

Researchers have generally dealt with convergence in terms of per capita income, i.e., with *income convergence*. However, income convergence can be the joint outcome of the twin processes of capital deepening and technological catch-up. While most researchers have focused on parameters of the capital deepening process, other researchers, such as Dowrick and Nguyen (1989), Dougherty and Jorgenson (1996, 1997), Wolff (1991), and Dollar and Wolff (1994), have directed their attention to the process of technological catch-up. Since total factor productivity (TFP) is the closest measure of technology, these researchers have investigated whether countries have come closer in terms of TFP levels. This has given rise to the concept of *TFP-convergence*. Clearly, income convergence can get either accelerated or thwarted depending on whether initial TFP-differences narrow or widen over time.

3.7. *Deterministic Convergence vs. Stochastic Convergence*

Several researchers, such as Bernard and Durlauf (1996), Carlino and Mills (1993), Evans (1996), and Evans and Karras (1996a), Qi and Papell (1999), and others have investigated convergence using time series econometric methods. As we shall see in more detail below, 'within convergence' is actually a time series concept. However, researchers have used time series analysis to examine 'across convergence' too. From this point of view, two economies, i and j, are said to converge if their per capita outputs, $y_{i,t}$ and $y_{j,t}$ satisfy the following condition:

$$\lim_{k \to \infty} E(y_{i,t+k} - a \cdot y_{j,t+k}|I_t) = 0, \qquad (3)$$

where I_t denotes the information set at time t. This definition of convergence is relatively unambiguous for a two-economy situation. This is not so when convergence is considered in a sample of more than two economies. Researchers differ on defining convergence in such multi-country situations. Some have taken deviations from a *reference economy* as the measure of convergence. In this treatment, y_{it} in equation (3) is replaced by y_{1t}, where 1 is the index for the reference country. Others have based their analysis of convergence on deviations from the *sample average*. In this treatment, y_{it} is replaced by $\bar{y}_t$, the average for time t. This difference is not innocuous, as we shall see. The time series definitions of convergence can be related with the notions of conditional and unconditional convergence too. With $a = 1$, equation (3) represents a variant of *unconditional* convergence. On the other hand, if $a \neq 1$ then equation (3) may represent a variant of *conditional* convergence. Within this framework a distinction has also been made between 'deterministic' and 'stochastic convergence.' This distinction refers to whether 'deterministic' or 'stochastic' trend is allowed in testing for unit root in the deviation series.

From a chronological point of view, the study of convergence began with the notion of 'absolute convergence' and then moved to the concept of 'conditional convergence.' Both these concepts were initially studied using the notion of 'β-convergence.' The notion of σ-convergence arose later. Alongside emerged the concepts of 'club-convergence,' 'TFP-convergence,' and the time series notions of convergence. There was also a chronological progression from the 'informal cross-section' to 'formal cross-section,' and then on to 'panel' approach to convergence study. The 'time-series' and the 'distribution' approaches developed alongside.

With this introduction to various convergence concepts, we can now proceed to follow the complex evolution of the convergence research.

4. Initial Cross-section Studies of Convergence

The specifications of 'growth-initial level regressions' used in initial studies of β-convergence were not *formally* derived from theoretical models of growth. This however does not mean that these studies did not have connection with growth models. In fact, to the extent that this connection was less formal, some of these works could derive inspiration from *several* theoretical paradigms and therefore have multiple focus. Although the concepts of unconditional and conditional convergence were not rigorously distinguished yet, the evidence of these initial works can be attributed, with hindsight, to both these notions.

4.1. *Initial Evidence of Unconditional Convergence*

The most well known initial study of unconditional convergence is by Baumol (1986). The main part of his analysis is based on a sample of 16 OECD countries for which long term data were available from Maddison (1982). Baumol obtains a significant negative coefficient on the initial income variable in a growth-initial level regression for these countries, and takes this as strong evidence of (unconditional) convergence.[10] However, prodded by Romer, Baumol also considers the relationship in an extended sample of 72 countries. In this larger sample, however, he does not find evidence of convergence.[11] Thus, Baumol's study produces evidence of both presence and absence of unconditional convergence, depending on the sample. Introspecting on the basis of the growth-initial level scatter-diagram, Baumol also coins the expression 'convergence-club.' He suggests that, while there is no convergence in the larger sample as a whole, there exist 'clubs' of countries within which evidence of convergence can be seen.[12] DeLong (1988) however shows that Baumol's finding of unconditional convergence in the 16-country OECD sample suffers from selection bias.[13] Nevertheless, Baumol's finding of absence of unconditional convergence in the larger sample of countries became an important point of departure for further discussion of convergence.

4.2. *Initial Evidence of Conditional Convergence*

While Baumol's study focuses on unconditional convergence, other studies, such as by Kormendi and Meguire (1985) and Grier and Tullock (1989), provide evidence that can be interpreted as being of conditional convergence. Reflecting research interests of an earlier period, these studies also consider other issues such as of inflation-output trade off, Philips curve relationship, etc. Regressions in these studies therefore include additional variables representing these relationships. However, the basic neoclassical paradigm is preserved through the inclusion of labor, capital, and the *initial* income variable. In a sample of about fifty countries, Kormendi and Meguire's regressions yield a negative β, which can be taken as evidence of conditional convergence. Grier and Tullock (1989) extend Kormendi and Meguire's study to a larger sample size and longer sample period. This allows them to consider the issue of parameter stability across sub-samples and sub-periods. The evidence from their study is somewhat mixed.[14]

4.3. *Initial Evidence on Convergence and the Growth Theory controversy*

Some of the initial studies of convergence, such as Baumol (1986) and Kormendi and Meguire (1985), either pre-date or are contemporaneous with pioneering NGT papers, and hence the growth theory controversy was not topical for them. The studies that are subsequent to the advent of NGT do make efforts to relate their results to the growth theory debate. However, to the extent that regression specifications of these studies are not formally linked with growth models, these efforts have to be limited and conjectural.[15] On the other hand, the absence of a formal link with growth models saves these initial studies from the *within-across tension* of the convergence concept that will soon surface.

4.4. *Convergence and Human Capital*

The convergence studies discussed above do not include human capital as an explanatory variable. Yet, as we noticed, in striving to relax the constraint of diminishing returns, many NGT models rely on human capital related processes. Hence human capital was set to become an important variable in convergence research. This begins with Barro (1991),[16] which is inspired directly by the NCGT-NGT controversy and is also one of the few studies that look at the convergence issue from the NGT perspective.[17]

Barro starts by abandoning the standard neoclassical format and, instead, emphasizes the simultaneity among growth, investment, and fertility.[18] In view of this simultaneity, he runs separate sets of regressions with growth, investment, and fertility as dependent variables.[19] His basic regressions of growth do not even include physical capital and labor as explanatory variables. Instead, the focus is now on *human capital*, which appears in all the regressions and proves important. Barro interprets the finding as vindication of the NGT-emphasis on human capital.[20]

To study convergence, Barro includes the initial income variable in his regressions. He reports absence of unconditional convergence in a broad sample of 98 countries,[21] and interprets this as supportive of the NGT.[22] However, he finds that when the initial measures of human capital are included, β turns negative and significant. This leads Barro to conclude that the data support the convergence hypothesis in a *"modified sense."*[23] To the extent that Barro's growth regressions include other control variables, his 'convergence in a modified sense' can be viewed as the germination of the concept of 'conditional convergence.' However, since investment and labour force growth rates do not appear as control variables, which are the main conditioning variables from the NCGT-point of view, there may be some ambiguity regarding this interpretation. Towards the end of the paper however Barro presents growth-initial level regression of more conventional (meaning, neoclassical) format, i.e., inclusive of investment and population growth rates as controls, [24] and finds that $\hat{\beta}$ obtained from this regression is also negative.[25]

While Barro emphasizes the role of human capital, De Long and Summers in a series of papers draw attention to the special role of equipment investment in growth. This discussion of the role of equipment investment, thought not focused on the income-convergence issue, has important bearing on the issue of TFP-convergence, as we shall see later.[26]

Meanwhile, soon after Barro (1991), the convergence research enters its 'formal specification' stage. This begins with the formulation of the neoclassical growth convergence equation, which we present in the next section.

5. The Neoclassical Equation for Convergence Study

The evolution of the 'conditional convergence' concept from its initial, inchoate stage to the subsequent, precise stage and the associated transition of the convergence regression from informal specifications to formal, model-based specifications are accomplished in Barro and Sala-i-Martin (1992), (henceforth BS) and Mankiw, Romer, and Weil (1992) (henceforth MRW). In both these works, the regression specification is derived formally from the neoclassical growth model. MRW work with the original Solow-Swan model, while BS use the Cass-Koopmans' optimal savings version of the NCGT. Since these works, the neoclassical growth-convergence equation has occupied the center stage of convergence research, and it is virtually impossible to review the literature without bringing this equation into the picture. Since its detailed derivation is available elsewhere,[27] we sketch in the following only the basic steps, primarily to introduce the notations. The exercise involves derivation of the law of motion around the steady state first and then translation of this motion into an estimable regression equation.

5.1. *Deriving the Rate of Convergence*

The dynamics of capital in the Solow model are given by

$$\dot{\hat{k}} = sf(\hat{k}) - (n + g + \delta)\hat{k}, \tag{4}$$

where, $\hat{k} = \frac{K}{AL}$ is capital per *effective* labor, $\dot{\hat{k}}$ is the time derivative of $\hat{k}$, and $f(\hat{k})$ is the production function normalized in terms of effective labour. Also, s, n, g, δ are the rates of investment, population growth, technological progress, and depreciation, respectively. First order Taylor expansion of the right hand side term around the steady state gives

$$\dot{\hat{k}} = [sf'(\hat{k}^*) - (n + g + \delta)](\hat{k} - \hat{k}^*). \tag{5}$$

Substituting for s using the steady state relationship, $sf(\hat{k}^*) = (n + g + \delta)\hat{k}^*$, gives

$$\dot{\hat{k}} = ([f'(\hat{k}^*)\hat{k}^*/f(\hat{k}^*)] - 1)(n + g + \delta)(\hat{k} - \hat{k}^*). \tag{6}$$

Under the assumption that capital earns its marginal product, $f'(\hat{k}^*)\hat{k}^*/f(\hat{k}^*)$ equals the steady state share of capital in income, α. In the Cobb-Douglas case, this will also be the exponent of capital in the production function. Using this relationship we get

$$\dot{\hat{k}} = \lambda(\hat{k}^* - \hat{k}), \text{where} \tag{7}$$
$$\lambda = (1 - \alpha)(n + g + \delta). \tag{8}$$

Evidently, λ gives the speed at which the gap between the steady state level of capital and its current level is closed and has come to be known in the literature as the *rate of convergence*. The same rate holds for convergence in terms of income per effective labor. This is because $\hat{y} = f(\hat{k})$, which upon expansion at $\hat{k}^*$ and differentiation with respect to time gives

$$\dot{\hat{y}} = f'(\hat{k}^*)\dot{\hat{k}}. \tag{9}$$

As a first order approximation, we should therefore have,

$$\hat{y}^* - \hat{y} = f'(\hat{k}^*)(\hat{k}^* - \hat{k}). \tag{10}$$

By substitution we then get,

$$\dot{\hat{y}} = \lambda(\hat{y}^* - \hat{y}), \tag{11}$$

where λ is again the rate of convergence given by equation (8).

5.2. *Deriving the Equation for Testing Convergence*

Switching to logarithms, solving this first order non-homogeneous differential equation, and rearranging, we get from (11):

$$\ln \hat{y}(t_2) - \ln \hat{y}(t_1) = (1 - e^{-\lambda \tau})(\ln \hat{y}^*(t_1) - \ln \hat{y}(t_1)), \tag{12}$$

where t_1 denote the initial period, t_2 the subsequent period, and $\tau = (t_2 - t_1)$. If we now substitute for $\hat{y}^*$ from equation (2) above, we get[28]

$$\ln \hat{y}(t_2) - \ln \hat{y}(t_1) = (1 - e^{-\lambda \tau}) \frac{\alpha}{1 - \alpha} \ln (s_{t_1})$$
$$- (1 - e^{-\lambda \tau}) \frac{\alpha}{1 - \alpha} \ln (n_{t_1} + g + \delta) - (1 - e^{-\lambda \tau}) \ln \hat{y}(t_1) \tag{13}$$

Clearly, this is again the *growth-initial level* equation, but now the coefficients are formally linked with the structural parameter of the NCGT. For example, $\beta = -(1 - e^{-\lambda \tau})$, and hence it is now possible to recover the value of λ from the estimate of β. The value of λ, in conjunction with other estimated coefficients of the equation, yields values of other structural parameters of the model such as α. The question now is how to estimate this equation.

5.3. *The Within-Across Tension in the Convergence Concept*

It may be noted that the above derivation in λ and of equation (13) is entirely on the basis of the growth process *within* an economy, and there is no reference to what is happening *across* economies. This shows that λ essentially refers to a within-economy process and is determined by the values of α, n, g, and δ of the economy concerned. It would, therefore, seem natural and proper to estimate equation (13) and λ on the basis of time series data of individual economies.

Interestingly however, researchers began estimating equation (13) using cross-section data. This is because, from the beginning, convergence arose as a concept pertaining to *across-economy* growth regularities. The question that resides in the mind of most people interested in convergence is not so much whether an individual country is closing the gap between its *own* current and steady state level of income as whether poorer countries are narrowing their gap with richer countries. From the latter point of view, cross section data is the natural place to look for evidence of convergence.

However, this introduces a tension in the interpretation of the convergence parameter λ. While according to equation (13), λ is the measure of speed at which an economy proceeds towards *its* own steady state level, the λ estimated from cross-section data is often interpreted as the speed at which poorer economies are closing their income gap with richer countries. In the case of unconditional convergence, this is not a problem, because then the steady state income levels of the currently rich and poor countries coincide, making both within and across interpretation of λ valid. However, under conditional convergence, where the steady states of the currently poor and rich countries are different, the across-

interpretation of λ is no longer valid.[29] This tension was not so apparent as long as cross-country regression specifications were informal, because in those contexts it was possible to limit to only the reduced form, cross-sectional interpretation of β.[30] Thus, the formal derivation of the neoclassical convergence equation, while being a significant step forward, has also brought to fore the within-across tension in the interpretation of the convergence rate.

6. The Formal Cross-section Approach to Convergence Study

6.1. *Cross-section Estimation of the Neoclassical Convergence Equation*

One of the most successful implementations of the formal cross section approach is MRW itself. In this influential study, two of the six elements of θ, namely s and n, are allowed to differ across countries. The values of the rest three, namely α, g, and δ, are taken to be the same for all countries. Differences in A_0 are assumed to be part of the error term, and this allows estimation of the equation by the ordinary least squares (OLS) method. MRW find that with only s and n as explanatory variables, the regression runs well, but the implied values of the rate of convergence, λ, are too low.[31] The accompanying result is that the implied values of α are too high.[32] To overcome this problem, MRW augment the Solow model by including human capital as another argument of the production function in exactly the same way as is physical capital, only with a different exponent, say ϕ. Regression on the basis of this augmented model produces more desirable results. The value of α decreases to an empirically plausible level (0.48 for the NONOIL sample), and the value of λ increases to around .02 (0.0142 for the NONOIL sample, implying a half-life of 49 years).

Similar results on conditional convergence across countries are presented in BS. These are drawn mainly from Barro (1991). However, the regressors are now clearly interpreted as determinants of the steady state. Also, the estimated regression coefficient is now traced back to yield the structural parameter λ. For a similar sample of 98 countries as MRW's NONOIL, BS report $\hat{\lambda}$ to be 0.0184.[33]

6.2. *β-Convergence across 'regions'*

The formal growth-convergence equation has been used to study convergence across regions too. In particular, whether or not convergence holds for the US states has drawn considerable attention. When it comes to regions within the same country, the assumption of identical steady states, and hence of unconditional convergence, becomes more plausible. BS make this assumption to study convergence across US states using the Cass-Koopmans version of the NCGT. This helps them avoid the difficult problem of controlling for such 'deep' behavioural parameters as inter-temporal elasticity of substitution, time discount rate, etc., for which data are difficult to get.[34] The authors find significant evidence of convergence,[35] and the estimated rate of convergence proves to be in the neighborhood of two percent per year. Holtz-Eakin (1993), on the other hand, emphasizes the possible differences in steady state even among the US states and, thereby, considers a situation of conditional convergence. He uses a human capital augmented version of the neoclassical convergence equation and implements a variant of pooled regression. Upon inclusion of variables that either represent or proxy for the determinants of steady state, Holtz-Eakin obtains higher estimates of the rate of (conditional) convergence.[36]

Regional convergence studies have been conducted in the context of other countries and continents too. Sala-i-Martin (1996b) presents a comprehensive study of convergence across regions of Japan, Germany, the UK, France, Italy, Spain, and Canada, in addition to that of the US. He generally assumes a situation of unconditional convergence, and obtains convergence rates that are close to two percent.[37] As we shall see, regional convergence has been studied using the panel and time series approaches too.

6.3. Research on Club Convergence

The formal cross-section equation has been used to study 'club convergence' too, though not that frequently. In their contribution to this line of research, Durlauf and Johnson (1995) allude to theoretical models of multiple equilibrium and observe that convergence in large samples (*global* convergence) does not hold (or proves weak) because countries belonging to different equilibrium (or 'regimes') are lumped together. The proper thing, according to them, is to identify country groups, whose members share the same equilibrium, and then to check whether convergence holds within these groups (*local* convergence). The authors use initial levels of income and literacy levels to group the countries and find the rates of convergence within the groups to be higher than that in the whole sample.[38] Also, estimated parameter values differ significantly across the groups, particularly when these groups are determined endogenously. The authors interpret the observed heterogeneity as indicative of the presence of different regimes.[39]

Despite the conceptual distinction, it is not easy to distinguish 'club convergence' from 'conditional convergence' empirically.[40] This finds reflection in the problems associated with the choice of criteria to be used to group the countries in testing for club convergence. Clearly, steady state determinants cannot be used for this purpose, because differences in them cause equilibrium to differ even under conditional convergence. On the other hand, use of time-varying characteristics, such as initial levels of income or literacy, is also not free of problems. Suppose it is postulated that countries around a higher cut-off 1960 income (say $10,000) have an equilibrium that is different from the equilibrium of the countries around a lower cut-off 1960 income (say $5,000). However, the countries of the first group also had to cross the $5,000 cut-off at some point in the past, and hence, other things being the same, the latter equilibrium should have applied to them too. This means that the initial income cut-off by itself cannot determine the equilibrium.[41] There has to be other factors. However, these other factors cannot be associated with the determinants of the steady state, because then 'conditional convergence' will subsume 'club convergence.' On the other hand, leaving these

factors unspecified (through endogenized grouping) is not satisfactory, because
the exercise then does not yield any policy guidance. The underlying theoretical
models also have to show that it is indeed these factors that determine which of
the multiple equilibrium a particular economy will approach. Finally, it needs to
be noted that if multiple equilibrium indeed depends on initial income cutoffs, the
relationship between subsequent growth and initial income will not be linear.
Appropriate non-linear specifications will have to be used to let hypothesized
'club convergence' to surface.[42]

These theoretical and empirical difficulties make the research on club convergence challenging. However, some 'stylized facts' regarding cross-country growth
regularities brought forward by the distribution approach to convergence study
indicate that further research on multiple equilibrium and 'club convergence' is
worthwhile. Desdoigts (1999) presents an important recent contribution in that
direction.

6.4. *Evaluating the Cross-section Approach*

The formal convergence equation of MRW and BS has been used to explore a
variety of other issues even within the cross-section set up. In particular, the
MRW specification has been a popular point of departure, because it does not
involve deep behavioral parameters and hence is easier to implement. Thus, Chua
(1992) and Ades and Chua (1997) use it to study external economies arising from
regional spillovers. Benhabib and Spiegel (1994) use it to study further the role of
human capital. Rodriguez-Claire and Klenow (1997) use it to examine the impact
of alternative measures of human capital on the convergence results presented in
MRW. Den Haan (1995) uses it to show that the distribution of the convergence
parameter depends on the source of variation (whether it is technology or capital
intensity) in the initial income. Nonneman and Vanhoudt (1996) augment the
MRW model further by including accumulation of technological know-how.
Tzanidakis and Kirizidis (1996) formulate an alternative way of testing the
MRW model. Temple and Johnson (1998) use the MRW specification to examine
the role of social capital in economic growth. Temple (1998b) discusses the
influence of possible measurement errors and outliers on the results of the
MRW. The research along this line continues.

However, the cross-section studies in general agree regarding the broad result
of conditional convergence. There is no consensus regarding the precise value of
either λ or α. However, the suggested values of λ are generally low and those of
capital's share in income are high. The general conclusion is that capital has to be
defined to include human capital so as to justify high values of the share of capital
and slow diminishing returns.

The cross-section approach to convergence study however soon encountered
some important limitations. These limitations often found expression in counter-
intuitive implications of some of the cross-section results. For example, Cho and
Graham (1996) draw attention to the counter-intuitive implication of the MRW
results that on average the poorer countries are approaching their steady state

from above, and the richer countries are doing so from below. Similarly, if MRW's estimated values of λ, α, and ϕ (together with their assumed values of g and δ) are used to compute the implied value of n, the results obtained are -0.001, 0.0064, and $.0028$ for the NONOIL, INTER, and OECD samples, respectively. These values are far from representative values of n in these samples, and the negative value of n for the NONOIL sample is quite problematic.

Thus while the switch from informal to formal specifications elevated the convergence discussion from one about broad presence or absence of convergence to one about *precise values* of structural parameters of the growth model, it also helped reveal some important problems. The basic limitation of the cross-section approach lies in the fact that having just one data point for a country provides a weak basis for estimation of the convergence parameter λ, which refers primarily to a within-country process. There is too much heterogeneity across countries to validate the assumption that cross-country data can be treated as multiple data of the same country. It is to overcome this basic limitation, which finds its manifestation in various ways, that the convergence research gradually moved from the cross-section to the panel approach.

7. The Panel Approach to Convergence Study

Income convergence, as noted earlier, can have two sources, namely capital deepening and technological diffusion.[43] This is reflected by the presence of the technology parameters, A_0 and g, alongside the parameters governing the capital deepening process, in the formula of the steady state income level given by equation (2). In studying convergence it is therefore necessary to take account of both these processes. However, the cross-section approach finds it difficult to do so, because it generally relies on the assumption of identical technologies across countries. This homogeneity assumption rules out any systematic process of technological diffusion, contradicting both casual observation and findings of the empirical research.[44] When neglected, these technological differences act as a confounding factor in the data and hinder correct estimation of the parameters governing the capital deepening process. We begin the discussion of the panel approach by first noting this estimation problem.

7.1. Omitted Variable Bias Problem of the Cross-section Regression

The problem can be illustrated using equation (13). Although this equation is in terms of income per *effective* labor, in actual implementation, researchers invariably work with income per capita. Expressed in terms of per capita income and rearranging, we get from equation (13) the following

$$\ln y_{t_2} = (1 - e^{-\lambda\tau})\frac{\alpha}{1 - \alpha}\ln s_{t_1} - (1 - e^{\lambda\tau})\frac{\alpha}{1 - \alpha}\ln(n_{t_1} + g + \delta) + e^{-\lambda\tau}\ln y_{t_1}$$
$$+ (1 - e^{-\lambda\tau})\ln A_0 + g(t_2 - e^{-\lambda\tau}t_1). \tag{14}$$

The A_0 term on the right hand side is the productivity shift term. MRW, for example, recognize the importance of this term and observe that, "the A_0 term reflects not just technology but resource endowments, climate, institutions, and so on; it may therefore differ across countries." (p. 410–1)[45] However, in actual estimation, they regard A_0 as part of the error term and assume it to be uncorrelated with the included variables, s and n. This assumption however contradicts the expansive definition of A_0 that MRW themselves provide. Going by that definition, it is difficult to argue that A_0 is uncorrelated with the savings and fertility behavior of a nation.

Actually, in a cross-section regression, the necessity of econometric identification forces one to relegate A_0 to the error term. This is because there are no good measures of A_0, and, even if some proxy variables are included, there still remains a part of A_0 that is unobservable or unmeasurable and yet correlated with the included variables.[46] However treating A_0 as part of the uncorrelated error term causes the well-known Omitted Variable Bias (OVB) problem.[47]

7.2. Panel Estimation of the Convergence Equation

One of the advantages of the panel approach is that it can correct the OVB problem by allowing for technological differences across countries (at least the unobservable and unmeasurable part of it) in the form of *individual (country) effects*. Using notations of the panel data literature, equation (14) can be written as

$$y_{it} = (1 + \beta)y_{i,t-1} + \beta\Psi x_{i,t-1} + \eta_t + \varepsilon_{it}, \tag{15}$$

where $y_{it} = \ln y_{t_2}$, $y_{i,t-1} = \ln y_{t_1}$, $(1 + \beta) = e^{-\lambda\tau}$, $\Psi = (-\alpha/(1 - \alpha))$, $x_{i,t-1} = (\ln s_{i,t-1} - \ln(n_{i,t-1} + g + \delta))$, $\mu_i = (1 - e^{-\lambda\tau})\ln A_0$, and $\eta_t = g(t_2 - e^{-\lambda\tau}t_1)$.[48]

In these notations, μ_i, the individual, *country effect*, represents the term A_0. There are many different ways to model and deal with μ_i. However, in view of the correlation of A_0 with s and n, it is clear that the *random effects*-specification of μ_i is not appropriate. An appropriate choice, it seems, is the *correlated effects*-model and the accompanying Minimum Distance (MD) estimator suggested by Chamberlain (1982, 1983).[49] Both Islam (1995) and Knight *et al.* (1993) use this estimator, and the results show that allowing for technological differences have a significant impact on the estimated values of the convergence parameters. The estimated values of λ now prove to be much higher,[50] and the implied values of α also now prove to be much lower and more in conformity with its commonly accepted empirical values.[51] These show that in absence of technological shifts, diminishing returns set in rather quickly; and there is not much evidence of externality associated with physical capital. The panel results also indicate that the way human capital influences output is perhaps different from the way physical capital does.[52]

Canova and Marcet (1995) also present an analysis of the European regional data and the OECD data showing the bias of the cross-section regressions. They use a Bayesian procedure to control for differences in steady state (that includes differences in A_0) and find significantly higher values of λ and lower values of α. They also show that the hypothesis of the same steady state across regions or countries is rejected.

An important by-product of the panel approach to convergence study is the estimated values of A_0, which provide indices of relative productivity or technology levels across countries. These levels are found to differ enormously. According to results of Islam (1995), in a sample of 96 countries, the highest value of A_0 is about forty times larger than the lowest. This issue of technological differences has recently drawn attention of many other researchers. For example, Hall and Jones (1996, 1997, and 1999) use a cross-section growth accounting methodology to compute TFP indices in a sample of 121 countries and conclude that TFP differences play the most important role in explaining income differences across countries.[53] Based on his analysis, Prescott (1998) declares that "savings rate differences are of minor importance. What is all important is total factor productivity (TFP)." (p. 525)[54] An important contribution of the panel approach to convergence study has been bringing to fore and provide estimates of the large differences that exist in aggregate productivity across countries. This also facilitates the analysis of the important issue of TFP convergence.

7.3. *Research on TFP-Convergence*

Originally, TFP studies were based on time series data of individual countries and were focused on computation of TFP *growth rates*. These studies did not consider the issue of convergence in TFP *levels*. International comparison of relative TFP *levels* was initiated by Jorgenson and Nishimizu (1978) and was carried forward by Christensen, Cummings, and Jorgenson (1981). Dougherty and Jorgenson (1996, 1997) have recently resumed this line of research. Wolff (1991) and Dollar and Wolff (1994) have also examined TFP-level convergence using a similar methodology, which begins with a growth-accounting exercise in a multi-country setting using time series data in order to get the TFP level indices across countries. These indices are next analyzed to check for TFP-level convergence. Employing this methodology to the G-7 countries, Dougherty and Jorgenson and Wolff all find evidence of TFP-convergence.[55] The use of this methodology to study TFP convergence in large samples of countries is however difficult, because it requires lengthy and detailed time series data, which are often not available for developing countries.

Not all researchers have adopted the time-series growth accounting methodology to study TFP-convergence. Dowrick and Nguyen (1989) for example examine TFP-convergence using a cross-section regression. The specification is similar to (13), but the authors proceed from the assumption of a common capital-output ratio for all countries of the sample. In their formulation, the initial income variable is relative to that of the USA, the most advanced country of the sample. This allows them to interpret the coefficient on the initial income variable of the equation as indicative of TFP-convergence. Their results support TFP-convergence in a sample of fifteen OECD countries. The problem with this approach is that the capital-output ratio may not be the same across countries, and labor productivity differentials may arise from differences in both technological level and capital intensity. This is particularly true for larger samples of countries.[56] This limits the applicability of the cross-section regression approach for studying TFP convergence.

By themselves, the panel studies of convergence have not yet answered the question of TFP convergence. There are inherent difficulties in separating technological change from capital deepening.[57] However, the fact that convergence-rates prove higher when panel estimation allows for technological differences in the form of country-effects indicates that these differences are either not narrowing or at least not narrowing fast enough to reinforce convergence that is resulting from diminishing returns. According to results in Islam (1995), the panel estimate of the convergence rate increases 7.2 times (relative to its OLS estimate that ignores technological differences) in the NONOIL sample, while the increase is 4.5 times in the OECD sample. This agrees with the general evidence that technological differences have narrowed much less in the larger NONOIL sample than in the OECD sample. However, further information is necessary in order to make more precise conclusions about the direction and magnitude of TFP movements in convergence.[58] In particular, this requires generation of TFP-level indices for several consecutive time periods so that the TFP dynamics can be seen more directly. The use of panel methodology can be of help in this regard.[59]

7.4. *Panel Analysis and the Extended Cross-section Regressions*

Many researchers working with cross-section data recognize the importance of technological differences across countries. However they try to control for these differences by including additional regressors in the equation. This leads to extended specifications of cross-section growth regressions. One problem with these extended specifications is that they quickly lead to unwieldy sets of explanatory variables. This is one of the reasons why growth regressions of the initial stage fell into some disrepute. Using Leamer's extreme bound analysis, Levine and Renelt (1992) try to rescue the situation by conducting a sensitivity study of a huge number of the right hand side variables that had appeared in growth regressions.

One benefit of the switch from the informal to formal specification of growth regressions is that it provides a clear guidance about the variables to be included in these regressions.[60] Recently some researchers have on occasions abandoned the strictly model-based specification and reverted back to the previous style of extended specifications. Some do this on purely conjectural grounds and do not try to link the additional variables of the regression with the variables of the growth model. Others try to maintain this link and argue that the additional variables stand for the A_0 term of the equation. This has again resulted in a swelling of

variables in growth and convergence regressions, and Sala-i-Martin (1997), following Levine and Renelt (1992)'s spirit, has responded with another effort to determine statistically the robustness of the included explanatory variables.

Durlauf and Quah (1999) provide a critique of the extended specifications of
growth-convergence equation and of Levine and Renelt (1992) and Sala-i-Martin
(1997)'s attempts to resolve the issue using mechanical statistical criterion. They
rightly argue that the guidance about which variable to include in the equation
has to come from theory. It is true that the theory does not provide specification
of A_0. But this is all the more a reason to make an essential distinction between
variables that are strictly model-determined, such as capital and labor, and
variables about which the model's guidance is less clear.[61] It may be noted that
even those researchers who justify the extended specification by linking the
additional variables to the term A_0 often do not adhere to the restrictions that
follow from such a link. For example, equation (15) suggests some clear relationships between the coefficient of the term A_0 and the coefficients of the terms
representing s and n. Also, the coefficients of variables proxying for A_0 will have
precise relationship among themselves. Second, many of these researchers frequently leave their results in the reduced form and do not trace out the implied
values of the parameters of the growth model. Even if they do, they limit
themselves to using the coefficient of the initial income variable to recover the
rate of convergence only and ignore the task of recovering other parameters of the
growth model. This shows that the claim in these studies about the link of the
included additional variables with A_0 is tenuous. Finally, to the extent that
inclusion of proxy variables still leaves a part of A_0 uncaptured, the cross-section
regressions cannot be entirely free of the omitted variable bias.

It is in view of these problems of the cross-section growth regressions that the
panel methodology for studying technological differences holds some appeal. This
methodology suggests a two-stage procedure, the first of which consists of panel
estimation based on only the strictly model based variables to produce estimates
of A_0. In the second stage, the estimated values of A_0 are analyzed to find out the
determinants of technology differences and diffusion. Since theoretical guidance
regarding specification of A_0 is lacking, the specifications at the second stage of
the analysis may again be conjectural. However, this two-stage procedure at least
preserves the primal status of the basic, strictly model-based variables such as
labour and capital, and does not relegate these variables to the same status as of
the conjectural variables. Canova and Marcet (1995) also propose a similar two-
step procedure, the first of which is devoted to estimation of the steady states.
"Once steady state estimates are obtained for each unit," the authors suggest, "we
can test, in a second step, what variables determine the cross-sectional distribution of steady states." (p. iv)

7.5. *Heterogeneity in Steady State Growth Rate*

In the panel studies discussed above, technological differences were allowed only
in the form of variation in A_0, implying variation in technology *level*. The growth

rate of technology, g, was however assumed to be common. This homogeneity assumption regarding g may be claimed to conform better to the NCGT view of technology as a public good. However, as noted earlier, the NCGT was formulated as a description of growth process *within* an economy and therefore did not automatically suggest that the public good assumption regarding technology held equally across countries. It is therefore quite possible to argue that homogeneity in g needs to be relaxed, so that even under the NCGT paradigm, countries can differ in terms of not only level but also growth rate of technology.[62]

Lee *et al.* (1997) do actually allow g to differ in their panel study of growth and convergence, and find that this leads to large increase in the estimated rate of convergence.[63] The authors do not report the corresponding values of α, the capital share. However, when worked out, these are likely to be very low, and this may indicate some problem. Binder and Pesaran (1999) also allow g to differ across countries. They compute the 'deterministic rate of technological progress' and find it to vary considerably across countries.[64] Empirical testing of heterogeneity of g is made difficult by the fact that data only give the *actual* growth rates, which are generally a combination of *steady state* and *transitional* growth rates. However, given the empirical evidence of very large differences in TFP level, the idea of g differing across countries deserves further attention.

However, it is important to note that the heterogeneity of g (in addition to A_0) leads to a virtual collapse of the convergence concept, so far as its across-dimension is concerned. This concept, which with hindsight can now be termed as the Usual (concept) of Conditional Convergence (UCC), arose to allow differences in steady state *level* of per capita income. Convergence under heterogeneity of both A_0 and g implies that the economies are converging not only to different *levels* of per capita income but also to different *growth rates*. This may be termed as the Weak (notion) of Conditional Convergence (WCC), although some may wonder whether WCC is worth calling convergence at all. Also, heterogeneity in g makes NCGT almost indistinguishable from the NGT, so far as the cross-country steady state growth pattern is concerned. Unless data pertaining to the transitional phase are available separately, it is difficult to distinguish a situation of WCC from a non-convergence situation described by many NGT models. It may be difficult to capture these finer distinctions using only cross-section data. Panel data, with its both cross-section and time-series dimensions, can be helpful in this regard.

7.6. *The Issue of Endogeneity Bias*

The use of panel data has allowed researchers to examine several other econometric problems of convergence regressions. One of these is the problem of endogeneity bias. Researchers often use contemporaneous values of investment rate and labor force growth rate as explanatory variables in growth-convergence equations. Since output-growth, investment rate, etc. in a particular period are likely to be jointly determined, the possibility of endogeneity bias in such regressions is quite obvious.[65] Caseli et al. (1996) raise this issue and try to rectify the situation by estimating a variant of equation (15) using Arellano and Bond (1991)'s GMM procedure.[66] The results lead the authors to reject the Solow-Swan model, both in its original version[67] and in its MRW augmented version.[68] The authors then abandon the strictly model-based specifications and switch to extended specifications. Based on results from the latter regressions, they suggest that the estimated value of λ is around ten percent and view that such a value is compatible with the open economy version of the Cass-Koopmans variant of the neoclassical growth theory.

The worry about potential endogeneity-bias in the convergence regressions is quite justified. However it is not clear whether use of the Arellano-Bond GMM estimator is the best strategy to rectify this bias, because Monte Carlo studies have generally found this estimator to display large small sample bias.[69] It is possible that any reduction in the endogeneity bias in Caseli et al. (1996)'s results is outweighed by the introduction of the small sample bias. (The next sub-section discusses this issue in more detail.) Their switch to extended specifications invites the issues discussed in the subsection above. For example, the authors do not work out the value of α that corresponds to their suggested value of λ. Based on their results for the original Solow model, an λ equaling ten percent would imply an α equal to 0.1258, which is too low an estimate of capital's share in output, even if capital is defined as physical capital only. Hopefully other, better ways to address the potential endogeneity bias problem of the growth-convergence equation will be found soon.

7.7. Problems of the Panel Approach

The panel approach is however not devoid of problems, a few of which are discussed below.

7.7.1 Possibility of small sample bias

The problem of small sample bias already surfaced in our discussion of the endogeneity bias above. From an econometric point of view, equation (15) represents a *dynamic* panel data model, and there exist many different estimators for such models. Indeed, a whole range of panel estimators has now been used to estimate equation (15) or its variants. These include the Least Squares with Dummy Variables (LSDV), the Minimum Distance (MD) estimator of Chamberlain, the GMM estimators of Arellano and Bond, conditional maximum likelihood estimator (MLE), etc. In addition, Nerolve (1999) uses pooled OLS, Generalized Least Squares (GLS), and unconditional maximum likelihood estimator. As noted earlier, panel estimators relying on the random-effects assumption are not appropriate for estimation of the growth-convergence equation. This implies that the GLS estimator and some variants of the maximum likelihood estimators (that treat country-effects as random) may not be suitable for estimation of equation (15). These considerations narrow down somewhat the list of possible candidate estimators.[70] However the problem remains, because theoretical properties of most of these estimators are asymptotic and similar.[71] Their small sample performance cannot therefore be ascertained without Monte Carlo studies. As already mentioned, some Monte Carlo evidence is now available. However, Monte Carlo studies are more useful when these are tailored to the equations and data sets actually used for estimation. Monte Carlo studies using Summers-Heston data set and focusing on the convergence equation (15) indicate that, in general, estimators that do not use further lagged values of the dependent variable as instruments perform better than those which do.[72] This suggests that in choosing which panel estimator to use, researchers need to pay careful attention to the possibility of small sample bias. In doing so, they may benefit from the already existing Monte Carlo evidence. In addition, they may conduct Monte Carlo studies customized to their specific data sets and specifications.

7.7.2 The issue of short frequency

Some authors have contended that panel estimation of the growth-convergence equation is not appropriate, because it throws away the cross-section variation in data and relies on the within variation only. This is not desirable, they argue, because the cross-section dimension of data contains long-run features that are more pertinent to growth study. The within dimension of data, according to this argument, is flawed because of its short frequency.[73] These concerns are genuine. However several things need to be said in clarification. First, except for LSDV, most of other panel estimators use *both* within and between variation. This is particularly true of Chamberlain's MD estimator, which is one of the more appropriate estimators for the growth-convergence equation. Second, whether or not an estimator uses *both* within and between variation cannot be the main criterion of an estimator's suitability in this case. For example, the random-effects GLS estimator uses both within and between variation, but this estimator is not suitable for estimating the convergence equation because it contradicts the correlation of the country effects with the included explanatory variables. Third, as noted earlier, the parameter λ refers to the speed at which an economy is moving to its *own* steady state. From this point of view, it may even be more appropriate to estimate the convergence equation using *within* variation. Finally, the frequency at which within variation is considered in most of the panel studies is five years. This is shorter than twenty-five years, which is often the range over which averages are computed in cross-section studies. However, it is not as short as a year, which is often the frequency at which data are considered in many convergence studies of the time-series and distribution approaches. Barro (1997) himself offers pooled regressions with data spanning over ten years. Hence, five-year spans may not be too short to study growth, particularly when several such five-year spans are combined to produce the estimates, so that the effects of cut-off years chosen to distinguish the panels are likely to get cancelled out.[74]

Overall, the panel approach has several advantages in convergence research. Convergence studies using this approach helped reveal the fact that persistent technological differences are a major cause of income dispersion in large samples of countries. The approach has its problems.[75] However, by taking advantage of the cross-section and time-series dimensions of data, it is possible to try to deal with many of these problems. It is in view of this potential that Temple (1999) concludes in his survey that, "the use of panels is often the best way forward. ..." (p. 113)

8. The Time Series Approach to Convergence Study

A progression of convergence study from the cross-section to the panel and then to the time series approach can be viewed as a natural response to the across-within tension of the convergence concept. However, many researchers early on saw the scope of application of time series methods to the study of convergence. Most of these studies proceed from standard reduced form equations of the output process. However these equations may be linked with the model-based growth-convergence equation, as illustrated below.

8.1. *The Time Series Equation for β-Convergence*

The commonly used equation for the time series analysis of convergence can be derived directly from the equation for β-convergence given by (15). This generally involves the assumption that the $x_{i,t-1}$ remains unchanged over the sample period considered. In that case, $\beta\psi x_{i,t-1}$ becomes just another time invariant term, and it can be subsumed under the term μ_i. Also, note that substituting $t_2 = t$ and $t_1 = t - 1$ in the expression for η_t, we get

$$\eta_t = g(t_2 - (1 + \beta)t_1) = g[t - (1 + \beta)(t - 1)] = (1 + \beta)g - \beta gt. \quad (16)$$

For an individual economy, $(1 + \beta)g$ is a constant, and hence can also be subsumed under μ_i, so that η_t effectively reduces to $-\beta gt$. Introducing these changes and upon rearrangement and suppressing the country subscript i, and adding an *iid* error term in an arbitrary fashion, we get from (15) the following:

$$y_t = \mu - \beta gt + (1 + \beta)y_{t-1} + \varepsilon_t. \quad (17)$$

This is the Dickey-Fuller equation with a drift and linear trend. For convergence in the usual sense, β should be negative. In other words, $(1 + \beta)$ should be less than one. The question then reduces to whether or not y_t has a unit root.[76] To the extent that the trend in equation (17) is *deterministic*, a test of unit root based on this type of equation is thought to yield a test of 'deterministic convergence.' It is clear that the deterministic trend of equation (17) is a direct result of the deterministic specification of the technology term of the growth model, whereby $A_t = A_0 e^{gt}$.

Some researchers have however allowed the trend to be *stochastic*. Unit root tests based on equations with stochastic trend are thought to yield tests of 'stochastic convergence.' A stochastic trend in equation (17) will however require a stochastic specification of A_t. So far there have been few presentations of growth models with stochastic specification of A_t. Binder and Pesaran (1999) is an important step in that direction. They provide stochastic variants of the NCGT and the *Ak* models based on explicit stochastic formulation of *A* and *L*. These authors test the cross-section implications of these stochastic growth models for the capital-output ratio and find more support for the stochastic version of the NCGT as compared with the deterministic NCGT and the *Ak* (either stochastic or deterministic) growth models. Their paper therefore can provide the theoretical basis for the concept of 'stochastic convergence.'[77]

8.2. *Time Series Analysis of Within-Convergence*

While the traditional unit root analysis has been limited mainly to output series of developed countries, under the convergence paradigm, the analysis is extended to a larger sample of countries. Lee *et al.* (1997), for example, conduct an exercise along this line and find that, out of 102 countries for which the equation is fitted, only for a few the null of unit root can be rejected.[78] Since the Dickey-Fuller unit root tests take non-stationarity as the null,[79] Lee *et al.* also use the Kiwatkowski *et al.* (1992) test, which uses stationarity as the null.[80] Using this test, Lee *et al.* find that the number of countries for which stationarity can be rejected "fell steadily with the length of the truncation parameter." When this parameter is set at eight, the number of rejections falls to only nine.

It is important to note here that the above tests are based on the assumption of $x_{i,t-1}$ being constant. However, elements of $x_{i,t-1}$ may change over time even within an economy.[81] Lee *et al.* recognize the possibility of 'once for all changes' taking the form of 'shifts or take-offs,' and observe that their finding of non-stationarity for some of the countries may be the result of not taking account of these changes.[82] There now exists a whole line of research focusing on the sensitivity of rejection of unit root with respect to allowance of 'breaks,' which is one of the forms that changes in $x_{i,t-1}$ may take. This research shows that introduction of simple trend breaks (either exogenous or endogenous) leads to large increase in the number of rejection of unit root.[83] In view of these considerations, it cannot be said that the time series analysis has produced evidence that 'within convergence' does not hold for many countries.

8.3. *Time Series Analysis of Across-Convergence*

Since convergence is primarily understood in the across-economy sense, time series studies also focus on across-economy convergence. Attention here is directed to testing of unit roots in deviations, as defined by equation (3). Notice that going by the definition of equation (3), there may be 'across-convergence' even if output processes of individual economies contain unit root and hence lack 'within-convergence.'

8.3.1 *Time series analysis of convergence across the US states*

From a chronological point of view, time series analyses of 'across-convergence' began with the analysis of convergence across regions or states of the US. For example, Carlino and Mills (1993) analyze per capita income of eight geographic regions of the US.[84] They define the deviation series as $Dy_{jt} = (\bar{y}_t - y_{jt})$, where y_{jt} is the log per capita output of the region j and $\bar{y}_t$ is the average for the USA as a whole. Application of the augmented Dickey-Fuller test on a variant of the equation (17) with y_t replaced by Dy_t yields rejection of the unit root hypothesis for a majority of the regions, thus providing evidence of convergence.[85]

In Carlino and Mills' deviation-setup above, the region specific intercept term of the equation stand for (log of) the term 'a' in equation (3) and may be interpreted as standing for *time-invariant* differences in the determinants of the steady state across regions. This is equivalent to allowing some components of $x_{i,t-1}$ to vary, albeit only in the direction of i. In addition, they feel the necessity of allowing trend break, which can be interpreted as allowing $x_{i,t-1}$ to vary in the direction of t, albeit in a very restricted way. Thus Carlino and Mill's evidence may be characterized as of 'conditional convergence.' Lowey and Papell (1996) extend this analysis further by endogenizing the timing of the break.[86] These authors conduct the analysis at a further disaggregated level by dividing the US into 22 regions instead of 6. Again, the null of unit root is rejected for majority of the regions, confirming evidence of (conditional) convergence.

While Carlino and Mills and Lowey and Papell analyze the deviation data region by region, Evans and Karras' (1996b) conduct similar analysis by *pooling* the deviation data for individual states.[87] In view of the weakness of the standard Dickey-Fuller test, Evans and Karras use a modified version of the unit root test proposed by Levine and Lin (1993) that is designed specifically for pooled data. The results show rejection of the unit root hypothesis even when trend breaks are not included. In this setup too, the *state specific* intercept term of the equation stands for (time-invariant) difference in steady state among the individual states. Hence, Evans and Karras' finding may also be interpreted as one of *conditional* convergence. In fact, the authors themselves contrast this aspect of their result with Barro and Sala-i-Martin (1992)'s result of *unconditional* convergence across US states.[88]

8.3.2 *Time Series Analysis of Convergence across Countries*

Unit Root Analysis of Pooled Data for Countries: The time series analysis has been applied to investigate convergence across countries too. In fact, Evans and Karras (1996a) conduct a similar unit root analysis of pooled *deviation* (from average) data for a sample of 56 countries. The results favor rejection of unit root and by implication favor the conditional convergence hypothesis. Analogous results are also obtained in Evans (1996) from analysis of long historical data (1870–1989) for a sample of thirteen developed countries. Earlier Quah (1990) presented an analysis of per capita income (in the form of deviations from that of the US) for

114 countries ranging from 1970 to 1985. Noting both large N and T, Quah develops and applies the inference theory appropriate for 'random field data' and rejects the null of no unit root. However, unlike other researchers mentioned above, Quah does not allow for country specific intercepts in his analysis of the deviations. Accordingly his analysis is more of the unconditional convergence hypothesis, and it is not surprising that this hypothesis is rejected. As we saw, the hypothesis of unconditional convergence in large sample of countries was rejected by other methodologies too.[89]

Vector Approach to Across-Convergence Study: In many of the studies above, the unit root analysis was conducted either on deviations of individual economies one-at-a-time. One problem with this analysis is that the source of rejection of the null of unit root is not always clear. When deviations are taken from a reference economy, such a rejection can occur because the output process of either the reference economy or the economy in question contain unit root while that of the other does not. On the other hand, the rejection may also occur because the output processes of both these economies contain unit root and they are not co-integrated. The problem remains when deviations are taken from the average of the sample. Presence of a unit root in the output process of just one of the economies of the sample will cause the average to contain unit root, and then deviations for all the economies (except for the one that has unit root) will also contain unit root. The problem persists when unit root analysis is conducted on pooled deviations for all countries. A second problem with one-at-a-time analysis of deviations from a reference economy arises when there is no agreement about which to choose as the reference economy. On the other hand, the dimension of the exercise becomes simply too large if deviations of all countries from the remaining all are to be studied one-at-a-time in a sizable sample.

An alternative approach, that albeit does not resolve all the problems above, is to conduct cointegration analysis in a vector setting.[90] Bernard and Durlauf (1995) take this route and analyze cointegration in a sample of fifteen developed countries.[91] Their goal is to check whether the per capita output series of these economies are co-integrated or not, and if they were, whether the co-integration vector is of the form $(1, -1)$ or $(1, -a)$, where a is a constant. Under the vector approach, the hypotheses can be formulated in terms of conditions on the rank of the spectral density matrix at frequency zero of ΔDY_t and ΔY_t. Here, ΔY_t is the first difference of Y_t, which, in turn, is the vector of individual (per capita) output series, y_{it}. Similarly, DY_t is the vector of Dy_{it}, the deviation of (per capita) output of country i from that of the reference country having index 1.[92]

Bernard and Durlauf use two sets of procedures to carry out the tests: one, based on Phillips and Ouliaris (1988), and the other, based on Johansen (1988). In either case, the conclusion is broadly similar: there is evidence of co-integration of the form $(1, -a)$ but not of the form $(1, -1)$. The authors interpret this result as showing that the countries 'shared common trends' but did not converge. However, as we have noted before, co-integration of the form $(1, -a)$ can also be interpreted as a manifestation of conditional convergence.[93]

Broadly therefore time series analysis supports a variant of the conditional convergence hypothesis. Viewed in this way, the results produced by the time series studies of convergence have not been all that different from those produced by studies following either the cross-section approach or the panel approach. Although we tried in the above to link the time series equation with an underlying growth model, most of the time series studies of convergence do not do so. Their analysis is limited entirely to reduced form equations, and no attempt is made to link the estimation results with parameters of the growth model. This also limits the policy relevance of these studies.

9. The Distribution Approach and σ-Convergence

While the cross-section, panel, and (in part) time-series approaches have in one way or the other investigated β-convergence, the distribution approach focuses on σ-convergence and on changes in the cross-section income distribution as a whole. However, as noted earlier, this correspondence is not that simple. The distribution approach has actually proceeded along two lines. The first maintains a relationship with β-convergence and tries to work out the precise relationship between β and σ. The second emphasizes the limitations of β-convergence and focuses on the shape of the entire distribution. We begin the review with a discussion of the first.

9.1. *Relationship between β-convergence and σ-convergence*

In order to see the relationship between β- and σ-convergence, it is worthwhile to start from the decomposition of the cross-section variance into its constituent elements. In offering this decomposition, BS for example note that if all the terms other than $y_{i,t-1}$ and ε_{it} in equation (15) are ignored, the evolution of σ_t^2, variance of y_{it}, under suitable assumptions on ε_{it}, can be described by

$$\sigma_t^2 = (1 - \beta)^2 \sigma_{t-1}^2 + \sigma_\varepsilon^2 = \tilde{\beta}^2 \sigma_{t-1}^2 + \sigma_\varepsilon^2, \tag{18}$$

where σ_ε^2 is the variance of ε, and $\tilde{\beta} = (1 + \beta)$. Iterating backwards, this yields

$$\sigma_t^2 = \frac{\sigma_\varepsilon^2}{1 - \tilde{\beta}^2} + \left(\sigma_0^2 - \frac{\sigma_\varepsilon^2}{1 - \tilde{\beta}^2} \right) \tilde{\beta}^{2t}. \tag{19}$$

As $t \to \infty$, the above approaches the steady state value $\sigma_\infty^2 = \sigma_\varepsilon^2/1 - \tilde{\beta}^2$. It is clear that σ_∞^2 increases with σ_ε^2 and decreases as β becomes more negative. What is more important is that σ_t^2 can monotonically *either increase or decrease* to σ_∞^2 depending on whether the initial variance σ_0^2 is smaller or greater than the steady state variance σ_∞^2. This algebraic result again shows that a negative β cannot guarantee falling variance. In that sense, β-convergence is not sufficient for σ-convergence. However, it also shows that an empirical finding of *increasing* cross-sectional variance is not incompatible with β-convergence.

A more extended form of the relationship between β and σ obtains if the other right hand side variables of equation (15) are not ignored. Lee *et al.* (1997) work out this relationship as shown in equation (20) below:

$$\sigma_t^2 = \tilde{\beta}^{2t}\sigma_0^2 + [1 - \tilde{\beta}^{2t}]\sigma_{*0}^2 + \left[\frac{1 - \tilde{\beta}^{2t}}{1 - \tilde{\beta}^2}\right]\sigma_\varepsilon^2 + \left[T - \frac{1 - \tilde{\beta}^{2t}}{1 - \tilde{\beta}^2}\right]\sigma_g^2, \qquad (20)$$

where σ_{*0}^2 is the cross-country variance in steady state per capita output in time 0, and σ_g^2 is variance of the steady state growth rate, g. Under the assumption of a common g, this last term drops out. Then the above expression reduces to the same as in equation (19), except that it now has the additional term involving σ_{*0}^2. As expected, the latter term now also appears in the expression for σ_∞^2:

$$\sigma_\infty^2 = \sigma_{*0}^2 + \frac{\sigma_\varepsilon^2}{1 - \tilde{\beta}^2}. \qquad (21)$$

Substituting for σ_{*0}^2 in equation (20) we get

$$\sigma_t^2 = \sigma_0^2 + [1 - \tilde{\beta}^{2t}](\sigma_\infty^2 - \sigma_0^2). \qquad (22)$$

This is now the same as equation (19) above, because σ_{*0}^2 gets subsumed under σ_∞^2. Equation (22) helps to see again that dispersion may either increase *or* decrease towards σ_∞^2, depending on whether initial dispersion, σ_0^2, is less or greater than σ_∞^2.[94]

Thus we see that β and σ^2 are algebraically related, and the value of one can be obtained from that of the other, provided some other conditions are satisfied. This implies that tests of these two concepts of convergence can also be related. This is of particular importance for σ-convergence, because, unlike β-convergence, statistical tests for σ-convergence were not readily available.

9.2. *Relationship between tests for β- and σ-convergence*

In trying to formulate a test for σ-convergence, Litchenberg (1994) for example observes that, ignoring other terms, from (15) we can also have

$$\frac{\sigma_t^2}{\sigma_{t-1}^2} = \tilde{\beta}^2 + \frac{\sigma_\varepsilon^2}{\sigma_{t-1}^2}. \qquad (22)$$

The ratio $\sigma_t^2/\sigma_{t-1}^2$ provides evidence regarding σ-convergence, because it shows whether the dispersion is increasing or decreasing over time. One can try to get information about this ratio *directly*, as do for example Miller (1995) and Lee *et al.* (1997). Lichtenberg however shows that this ratio can be estimated *indirectly* from $\tilde{\beta}$ and the R^2 of the cross section regression estimating β. Since $1 - R^2 = \sigma_\varepsilon^2/\sigma_t^2$, it follows from equation (22) that

$$\sigma_t^2/\sigma_{t-1}^2 = R^2/\tilde{\beta}^2. \tag{23}$$

This shows that a test statistic for σ-convergence can be obtained from $\hat{\tilde{\beta}}$ by adjusting it using R^2 to account for the distribution of the shock term.[95] Litchenberg suggests that the test statistic obtained from equation (23) have an F-distribution with $[n - 2, n - 2]$ degrees of freedom.[96] However, Carree and Klomp (1997) point out that Litchenberg's conclusion regarding appropriate distribution for the test statistic implied by (23) is not entirely correct. They draw attention to the fact that F-distribution is valid if σ_t^2 and σ_{t-1}^2 are independent of each other, which will not be true provided $\tilde{\beta} \neq 0$.[97] These authors try to 'salvage Litchenberg's idea of using F-distribution to test for σ-convergence by showing that if the sample is large, so that $\hat{\tilde{\beta}}$ can be thought 'close' to $\tilde{\beta}$, then $T_2 = (\hat{\sigma}_t^2/\hat{\sigma}_{t-1}^2 - \hat{\tilde{\beta}}^2)/(1 - \hat{\tilde{\beta}}^2)$ will be distributed approximately as $F(n - 2, n - 1)$.[98] Carree and Klomp (1997) suggest yet another variant of the statistic that takes into account the variability in the estimate $\hat{\tilde{\beta}}$. This is given by $T_3 = (\hat{\sigma}_t^2/\hat{\sigma}_{t-1}^2 - (\hat{\tilde{\beta}}^2 - z_\alpha\hat{\sigma}_{\tilde{\beta}})^2)/(1 - (\hat{\tilde{\beta}}^2 - z_\alpha\hat{\sigma}_{\tilde{\beta}})^2)$, where $\hat{\sigma}_{\tilde{\beta}}$ is the standard error of estimated $\tilde{\beta}$ and z_α is the adopted critical value from the standard normal distribution.[99]

Evidence regarding σ-convergence can therefore be obtained both directly and indirectly, and the evidence may or may not be formalized in the form of statistical tests. We now look at some evidence regarding σ-convergence.

9.3. Evidence regarding σ-convergence

Not unexpectedly, evidence regarding σ-convergence depends very much on the sample. For the OECD countries, data have generally favored σ-convergence. Lee et al. (1997), for example, compute variance of cross-section distribution of log of per capita income for different samples of countries for 1961 to 1989 and plot them against time. Their results show that the variance for the OECD sample has decreased over time. Miller (1995) and other researchers have produced similar results regarding the OECD sample. Going by the classification above, these are direct evidence of σ-convergence.

On the other hand, Litchenberg (1994) uses his procedure to formally test the hypothesis of σ-convergence. He runs a simple regression of ln GDP85 on ln GPD60 for the OECD countries and uses the result to compute the test statistic as per equation (23) above.[100] Application of the critical values from F-distribution results in a non-rejection of the null of non-convergence.[101] However, Carree and Klomp (1997) redo the exercise using their statistics and reverse the conclusion. For the period 1960–85, all of Carree and Klomp's three statistics report convergence.[102] In other words, the conclusion of σ-convergence for the OECD countries is upheld. Similar evidence of σ-convergence has been found for other smaller samples of countries. Evidence of σ-convergence has been reported for the US states too.[103]

However, for large, global samples of countries, the evidence generally indicates a rise in variance. For example, according to Lee *et al.* (1997)'s computation, output-variance in the sample of 102 countries increased from 0.77 to 1.24 between 1961 and 1989. Other researchers have furnished similar evidence. There are different ways in which these results can be interpreted. For example, a rising σ in the global sample may indicate that the steady state dispersion, σ_∞^2, itself has increased, which, in turn, may be the result of increased dispersion of the determinants of steady state. Alternatively, it is possible that σ_∞^2 has remained unchanged, but the initial variance, σ_0^2, was less than σ_∞^2, so that the variance increased from below towards the steady state variance.[104] In either case, the outcome is not incompatible with conditional β-convergence.

Similarly, it is not known how much of the decrease in variance in small sample of developed economies is due to negative β and how much due to reduction in other items of (20), including reduction in the dispersion of the steady state determinants. All this indicates that more knowledge is needed about the dynamics of the steady state determinants in order to understand the changes in the cross-section variance of income.

The research on σ-convergence focuses on only one feature of the cross-section distribution, namely the variance. It has been argued that attention should rather be given to evolution of the entire shape of the distribution. This line of research also goes beyond the anonymity of distribution and identifies the position of individual or groups of countries within the distribution, and it notices how these positions change over time. We now turn to a review of this line of convergence research.

9.4. *Study of the Evolution of the Cross-sectional Distribution*

The research focussing on the shape of the cross-section distribution of income has been carried forward almost single handedly by Danny Quah.[105] To capture more details about the distribution, Quah focuses on the probability mass at different quantiles. A simple plotting of the cross-section distribution of the global sample for successive years already displays two features: first, the cross-section distribution is not collapsing, and, second, this distribution is becoming more *bi-modal*. However, since it is not known whether the plotted distributions are of steady state or not, and because the plots of distribution cannot tell the position of individual countries, Quah performs a more formal analysis using the following framework involving Markov transition matrix:

$$F_{t+1} = MF_t, \tag{26}$$

where F_t is the cross-section distribution at time t, and F_{t+1} is the same at time $t+1$, and M is the transition matrix that maps F_t onto F_{t+1}. The goal is to know M, which determines the evolution of the distribution. Assuming M to be unchanged over time, we have,

$$F_{t+s} = M^s F_t, \tag{27}$$

where s is any particular length of time (number of years, say). Letting $s \to \infty$ this also allows to obtain the steady state distribution.

Quah calibrates M using actual data. Both the calibrated transition matrices and ergodic distributions obtained on their basis lead to similar conclusions. The first is 'persistence.' The values of the diagonal elements of the one-year M-matrix are in the neighborhood of 0.9, implying that most of the countries continue to remain in the same position (or range) of the distribution. Second, whatever mobility (within the distribution) exists, it works to 'thin out the middle,' and 'pile up of probability mass at the two tails.' This is Quah's result of growing 'twin-peakedness' or bi-modality of the distribution. The results do not change if higher order specifications are used. In fact, these make the bi-modal property and 'poverty piling up' even more pronounced.[106] This exercise is extended in Quah (1993a) where he lets the quantiles to evolve (instead of being fixed).[107] However, the results remain more or less intact. In fact, now the dynamics of the quantiles further confirm these results. Thus, the formal analysis using transition Markov transition matrix confirms what informal plotting of distribution of successive years already suggested.[108]

The findings of 'persistence' and 'bi-modality' are valuable additions to the known stylized facts about cross-country growth regularities. Growth theories now need to explain these facts. The Markov analysis itself does not help in the explanation. It is another type of reduced form analysis. The transition matrix M is memory-less, and no growth theory is required for its estimation; no structure is imposed on the data.[109] In fact, Quah makes it explicit that it is his intention not to be restricted by assumptions of long term growth. However, Quah has made suggestions about the directions in which explanations for the stylized facts have to be sought. One is along models of multiple equilibrium that yield 'club convergence.' At a more fundamental level, Quah (1997) suggests that the dynamics toward bi-modality can be explained by 'spatial spillovers,' which in turn are determined not so much by 'openness' of an economy as by 'who trades with whom,' i.e., the trading partners. More research will be necessary to resolve these issues. But these are useful directions for further research on growth.

10. Conclusions

Research on convergence has indeed proceeded in many directions using many different definitions and methodologies. It is therefore not unreasonable to feel somewhat dazed by the variety of results and conclusions encountered in the literature. A close review however reveals that at a broad level there is considerable agreement among the results. For example, despite differences in approach and methodology, the finding of *conditional* β-convergence has remained relatively robust. This has been true both for small samples of developed economies and for large, global samples. For developed economies, researchers have in fact often reported unconditional convergence. Similarly, once it is remembered that σ-convergence research generally focuses on *unconditional* convergence, it becomes clear that results regarding σ-convergence largely agree with those regarding β-convergence. Evidence of σ-convergence is found precisely in those small samples of developed economies for which there is also evidence of *unconditional* β-convergence. On the other hand, in large global samples, neither unconditional β-convergence nor σ-convergence holds. Finally, time series analysis of both within and across convergence has produced evidence that can be interpreted as of *conditional* convergence.

However, the convergence research has not produced consensus at more concrete levels. For example, agreement about estimated values of structural parameters of growth models, such as the rate of convergence and the elasticity of output with respect to capital, has proved elusive. In fact, not all approaches to convergence research have been equally concerned with values of structural parameters.[110] Given the differences in approach, sample, data, model, estimation technique, etc., absence of consensus regarding parameter values is not surprising. However, some generalities have emerged even in this regard. It has been observed that the more differences in the steady state of economies are controlled for (either by sample selection or by inclusion of relevant variables in the regression), the higher are the resulting convergence rates. In particular, convergence rates prove to be much higher when technological differences across countries are taken into account.

The implications of the convergence results have several dimensions. First of all, the welfare implication of the conditional convergence finding for global samples is rather limited, because it only means that poor countries are moving toward their own steady states, and knowing this may be of little solace if those steady state income levels are themselves very low. This shows that it is more important to focus on the determinants of the steady state levels. Also, improvements in steady state levels cause transitional growth, and a sequence of transitional growth brought about by intermittent improvements in steady state levels may not be that different from the 'growth effect' postulated by many NGT models.

The implications of the convergence results for the growth theory debate are more controversial. As Barro noted, the general finding of conditional convergence conforms to the basic NCGT assumption of diminishing returns to capital. The rate of conditional convergence gets extra attention because of its relation with the elasticity of output with respect to capital. A lower convergence rate is associated with a higher elasticity value, which in turn can be indicative of externality if this value proves to be much larger than that obtained from national accounts. This has some bearing on the first generation new growth models that rely on externality as the source for long run growth. However, the new growth models have themselves moved on from externality to profit motivated research as the source of growth. Hence the debate about externality via the rate of conditional convergence may not be as significant now as it was at the beginning of the growth debate.[111]

More important in this regard is to notice the metamorphosis that both NCGT and NGT have undergone as a consequence of the convergence research.

On the one hand, absence of absolute convergence in large samples of countries has forced NCGT to recognize the differences in steady state income levels across countries. Many researchers now also allow the steady state growth rates to differ across countries under NCGT, making it consistent even with 'divergent' behavior. On the other hand, the empirical finding of conditional convergence has led to the emergence of many NGT models that yield convergence implication. These NGT models have followed different routes to reach this implication.[112] However, this shows that the convergence implication can no longer be associated solely with the NCGT. As a result of this give and take between NCGT and NGT, it is now possible to explain both convergence and non-convergence behavior by appropriately chosen models of growth theory of both the varieties. This may prove disappointing from the original idea of using convergence as a test for validity of alternative growth theories. However, the fact that convergence debate forced both types of growth theories to move toward accommodation may not be a mean achievement by itself.

However, the convergence research has had other important payoffs. First, it has furnished new stylized facts regarding cross-country growth regularities, such as 'persistence' and 'bi-modality.' The growth theory faces the task of explaining these facts, and this is drawing attention anew to models of multiple equilibrium. Second, convergence research has highlighted the existence of very large productivity or technological differences across countries and has given rise to new methodologies for quantification of these differences. As a result of these quantification efforts, a new information base is emerging for the study of determinants of technology differences and diffusion. The empirical finding of large technological and institutional differences is leading to theoretical developments too. New models of technology diffusion are being proposed, along both NGT and NCGT traditions.[113] The information base furnished by the convergence research will prove helpful in discriminating among alternative models of technology diffusion.

There are several other directions in which the convergence research is leading the growth literature to develop. Most of the convergence studies so far have been conducted on the basis of closed economy growth models. In reality, however, the economies are not closed, and actual data embody the effects of interaction that occur among economies along the lines of trade, technology transfer, capital flow, labor migration, diffusion of institutions, etc. Barro, Mankiw, and Sala-i-Martin (1995), Quah (1996c), and others attempt to include capital mobility in the explanation of cross-country growth regularities. There have been recent advances in formal modeling of the impact of trade on growth too.[114] However, empirical studies embodying the insights of these theoretical developments are yet very few.

The convergence studies so far have also been based on deterministic growth models. This has limited both theoretical and policy implications of the empirical time series studies of convergence. However, researchers are now formulating stochastic growth models and deriving their implications for cross-section and time series data. These stochastic formulations shift the discussion from the usual notions of convergence to the ergodicity of variables. Future growth and convergence research has to pay special attention to the time series properties of the technology or productivity term, A.

Finally, empirical research on growth and convergence of the recent period has heavily depended on the Summer-Heston data set. While this data set has earned appreciation,[115] and is ubiquitous in terms of use, it has also been the target of considerable criticism.[116] Part of the future research effort may also be usefully directed toward improving and generating data that are necessary for better understanding of the growth and convergence issues.

Acknowledgments

I would like to thank Jesus Felipe, Joy Mazumdar, John Pencavel, Jonathan Temple, and several anonymous referees for their comments on earlier drafts of this paper. Special thanks are due to Dale Jorgenson, whose encouragement was very crucial for writing and publishing this paper. For correspondence, send e-mail to *nislam@emory.edu*.

Notes

1. This does not mean that what follows is a chronological narration *per se*. It is chronological to the extent that this is required to follow the logical progression.
2. As Barro (1997) puts it, "It is surely an irony that one of the lasting contributions of endogenous growth theory is that it stimulated empirical work that demonstrated the explanatory power of the neoclassical growth model." (p. x)
3. We include here the Inada (1963) conditions as part of the NCGT assumption of diminishing returns. This is important because, as we shall see, a particular variant of the NGT retains diminishing returns but relaxes the Inada conditions to obtain asymptotic growth.
4. The fifth of these stylized facts was that the growth rate of per capita output varied widely across countries, and the sixth was that economies with high share of profits in income had higher investment to output ratios.
5. In this paper we shall use β as the generic notation for the coefficient on the initial level variable in the growth-initial level regressions. Note that negative β can be interpreted as evidence of convergence in terms of *both* income level and growth rate.
6. They point out that a negative β can just be an example of the more general phenomenon of reversion to the mean and, by reading convergence in it, growth researchers are falling into Galton fallacy.
7. See for example Mankiw, Romer, and Weil (1992) or Barro and Sala-i-Martin (1995) for the derivation.
8. In the case of the Cass-Koopmans model, θ also has similar set of elements with s replaced by parameters for the rate of time preference and the elasticity of intertemporal substitution in consumption.
9. For models with multiple equilibria, see, for example, Azariadis and Drazen (1990).
10. The numerical magnitudes of β from different studies are not directly comparable because of the differences in regression specification.

11. The numerical results of this regression were not presented, but Baumol reported that it yielded 'slightly positive slope,' indicating a process of rather divergence.

12. One example was the OECD group, already considered. Another example, according to him, was the group of formerly centrally planned countries. According to Baumol, such clubs consisted of countries which had certain degree of homogeneity in 'product mix and education' enabling them to share in the 'public good properties of the innovations and investments of other nations.' (p. 1080) The idea of technological diffusion is also reflected here.

13. The proper criteria for sample selection for convergence study, DeLong (1988) points out, is *ex-ante* income level, and not *ex-post*. In particular, he shows that, if, guided by the ex-ante criterion, Baumol's OECD sample is modified slightly, the result of unconditional convergence no longer holds. Baumol largely accepts this criticism. See Baumol and Wolff (1988).

14. For the OECD sub-sample, they find the coefficient on the initial income variable to be negative. For the larger ROW sub-sample, this coefficient turns out to be positive. However, upon splitting ROW into (three) smaller samples, they find the sign of β to vary.

15. Grier and Tullock (1989) were themselves quite keen about this limitation. They make only the broad observation that their results are generally supportive of NCGT, and that these results may show directions for further development of NGT. For their further comment on this point, see p. 260.

16. There is an earlier tradition of cross-country growth regressions conducted by development economists that do include human capital variables. See for example Krueger (1968). These regressions are often intended to determine patterns of economic development or to ascertain determinants of growth in general. Chenery, Robinson, and Syrquin (1985) provide a useful summary of this body of work. The current wave of empirical growth research however is not that aware of and does not recognize much connection with this earlier tradition of work.

17. Also, Barro was not an outsider to this debate. He embarks on this empirical work after already making his own contribution to the development of NGT. In Barro (1990) he examines the role of government spending in the setting of an Ak-style model of endogenous growth. Becker and Barro (1988) and Barro and Becker (1989) address the issue of fertility choice. These works and his close association with the genesis of NGT, gave Barro quite a few propositions to test out, and he is quite explicit that he is doing so 'using recent theories of economic growth as a guide.' (p. 437)

18. Barro argues for this simultaneity on the basis of new theories of growth. In particular, he cites extensively the conclusions of Rebelo (1991), Barro (1990), Romer (1990), Barro and Becker (1989) and Becker, Murphy and Tamura (1990).

19. Barro's work is, thus, not limited to the convergence issue; instead it addresses a host of other issues related to growth. It therefore, to some extent, shares the characteristic of multiple focus mentioned earlier.

20. Other right hand side variables of Barro's regressions include government consumption (reflecting his earlier interest in it), an index of relative inflation, indicators of political stability and some regional and continent dummies. Although the inflation variable is interpreted as a measure of 'market distortion,' its inclusion can as well be linked to the output-inflation literature, in which Barro himself played a no small role. See for example, Barro (1976) and (1978). In fact, Barro has returned to this issue, as can be seen in Barro (1997).

21. The correlation between the average growth rate of per capita real gross domestic product between 1960 and 1985 (GR6085) and the 1960 value of real per capita GDP (GDP60) is reported to be positive 0.09.

22. As Barro (1991) puts it, "This finding accords with recent models, such as Lucas (1988) and Rebelo (1991), that assume constant returns to a broad concept of reproducible capital, which includes human capital. In these models the growth rate of per capita product is independent of the starting level of per capita product." (p. 408)

23. The inclusion of human capital causes β to be negative in the regressions with investment as dependent variable as well, and Barro interprets this too as "consistent with the convergence implication of the neoclassical growth model." (Barro 1991, p. 427). With the ratio of private investment to GDP as the dependent variable, the coefficient on the initial income is significant and ranges between $-.0093$ and $-.0098$.

24. The argumentation for the specification is, however, not neo-classical. Instead, Barro observes that NGT relationships among growth, investment, and fertility imply that residuals from the growth regression will be positively related with those from investment regression, and negatively related with residuals from fertility regression. He justifies the conventional format of the growth regression as an alternative way of checking whether the stipulated relationships among the residuals are true.

25. The coefficient is a little different in magnitude from that obtained from earlier set of growth regressions that do not include investment and fertility rates as control variables. Barro interprets this as showing that the negative effect of the initial income on growth does not work through its effects on investment or fertility. Instead, it works mainly through lower rate of return on investment. (p. 430)

26. De Long and Summers (1991) show that 'equipment investment' has strong positive effect on growth, and this effect does not depend on 'education infrastructure.' Inclusion of human capital variables, which appears in Barro's regression, does not affect the coefficient of the equipment investment variable in De Long and Summers' study. These authors interpret their regression results as showing the presence of positive externalities associated with equipment investment. De Long and Summers (1993) extend these results for developing countries. Some authors have however expressed skepticism about De Long and Summers' claim. For example, Auerbach et al. (1994) argue that countries of the De Long Summers' sample are too heterogeneous to have the same technology, so that equipment investment was also capturing impact of technological diffusion. Blomstrom, Lipsey, and Zejan (1996) argue that direction of causality runs from growth to equipment investment, rather than the other way round. Temple (1998a) and Temple and Voth (1998) return to the issue and provide some support for De Long and Summers' view. With hindsight from subsequent research, it may be said that the roles of human capital and equipment investment need not be counter-posed. While the research has confirmed human capital's important role in growth, it is not conclusive about the precise way in which this role is played. It is also not clear what the best way is to develop human capital. Equipment investment may have role both in facilitating human capital's role and in the development of human capital (through, for example, learning by doing).

27. See for example Barro and Sala-i-Martin (1995), Mankiw (1995), and Durlauf and Quah (1999).

28. An important point here concerns whether to make $\ln \hat{y}^*$ contingent on t_1 or not. If it is assumed that the determinants of the steady state income remain constant between t_1 and t_2, it does not matter whether $\ln \hat{y}^*$ is made contingent on or not. Generally, in implementation, it is assumed that such determinants of steady state income as s, n, δ, and α, remain the same between t_1 and t_2. This suggests that it is not necessary to make steady state income contingent on the initial period in considering the transitional

dynamics. This is certainly the case in the continuous time setting, where the difference between t_1 and t_2 is instantaneous. However, when dealing with steady state income per capita (as is usually the case), it is necessary to be careful. As we can see from equation (2), the formula for steady state income per capita has the term $A_0 e^{gt}$, which will differ if evaluated at t_2 instead of at t_1. In the logarithmic version of the equation, this will generally imply differences in terms involving g and may not affect the basic conclusions. However, it is worth to be aware about the issue.

29. Unfortunately, researchers do not always pay adequate attention to this within-across tension in the interpretation of the convergence rate parameter λ. Durlauf and Quah (1999) takes appropriate note of this important issue.

30. It is taken as evidence showing that, other things held constant, countries starting with lower levels of income grow faster. See for example Kormendi and Meguire (1985, p. 147). This however also meant that no information regarding the structural parameter values could be obtained.

31. For the NONOIL sample, for example, λ equals 0.00606, implying a half-life of 114 years, which is indeed very long. It needs to be mentioned that NONOIL, INTER, and OECD are three samples used in the MRW study. The NONOIL is the sample of 98 countries which include almost all the sizable countries of the Summer-Heston data set (Summers and Heston; 1988, 1991) except those for which extraction of oil was the dominating source of income. The INTER sample is a sub-sample of NONOIL consisting of 76 countries for which the quality of data is better. Finally, OECD is the sample of 22 OECD member countries. Much of the subsequent convergence literature has used these three samples.

32. MRW do not report the results of the restricted version of this regression, hence we do not have an unique estimate of α. Based on the coefficient of the s variable, its value would be 0.82, while based on the coefficient of $(n + g + \delta)$, it would be 0.68. Both of these are for the NONOIL sample and are far greater than the share of capital in the national income in the countries of this sample, computed on the basis of the national accounts data. These values agree with the estimates produced earlier by Romer (1989a) from a growth accounting exercise under similar assumptions.

33. However, it is to be noted that although BS use the neoclassical convergence equation to recover λ, they do not apply it strictly to determine the right hand side variables of the regression.

34. However, in some of their regressions BS include regional dummies and a variable proxying for output composition. Inclusion of these variables makes it a little ambiguous whether it is unconditional or conditional convergence that is investigated.

35. This was true in terms of both per capita income and product and for different time periods considered. BS left it as an unresolved puzzle why this rate proved to be similar in terms of income and product.

36. Recently, Caselli and Coleman (2001) have reexamined convergence across US states and have emphasized the role of structural transformation in the observed convergence.

37. Shioji (1995) investigates convergence across prefectures of Japan. Lusigi, Piesse, Thirtle (1998) look at converge among countries of the African continent.

38. The authors conduct two sets of exercises. In the first, the countries are grouped on the basis of arbitrarily chosen cut off levels of initial income and literacy. Apprehending selection bias in such grouping, the researchers present a second exercise in which the grouping is endogenized using the 'regression-tree' method. The results obtained from these two methods of grouping however prove to be qualitatively similar.

39. Since this instability pertains to groups classified according to both initial income and human capital levels, the authors conclude that both of these variables are important in identifying the 'regimes.'

40. Durlauf and Quah (1999) also discuss this problem in their survey.

41. The *ratio* of (initial income and literacy) levels may have better promise in this regard, because although the countries cross all the level values sooner or latter, they may not do so observing the same ratio of these levels. Durlauf and Johnson found that output dominated literacy as a criterion for group/regime identification.

42. In fact, one of Durlauf and Quah (1999)'s main arguments for rejection of Barro's conclusion regarding convergence research is that this research has so far limited itself to use of linear specifications only.

43. Some authors refer to other sources of convergence, such as changes in sectoral composition (alternatively expressed as structural transformation). Changes in sectoral composition usually find reflection in changes in capital intensity, so that the latter may subsume the former. Also, one-sector models, that have been the basis of most of the convergence studies, do not allow changes in sectoral composition to surface directly.

44. For recent empirical evidence on R&D spillovers see for example Coe and Helpman (1995), Coe, Helpman, and Hoffmaister (1997), and Bayomi, Coe, and Helpman (1999). For earlier historical discussion of technological diffusion see in particular Gerschenkron (1953), who coined the expression 'advantages of backwardness.'

45. Durlauf and Johnson (1995) also note the issue of potential differences across countries in aggregate production function. Observing wide variation in the estimated parameter values across groups, they observe that, "aggregate production function differs substantially across countries." In particular, large differences in the intercept term – which is related with A_0 of equation (14) – lead them to conclude that, "different economies have access to different aggregate technologies." (p. 375) Hence, they express the view that "...the Solow growth model should be supplemented with a theory of aggregate production function differences in order to fully explain international growth patterns." See also Bernard and Jones (1996b)

46. The exercise by De la Fuente (1996) shows that even after accounting for A_0 by carefully constructed variables, a part remains that prove significant in the regressions.

47. There are other possible sources of bias for the cross-section regression as well. See Lee *et al.* (1997) and Evans and Karras (1996a) on this point. Lee *et al.* (1997), for example, draw attention to another possible bias of the cross section growth regression. They start with an equation similar to (13) and assume t and t-1 to be one year apart. Since the cross-section regression generally considers growth over a long (say, 25 year) period, they try to have the equation correspond to that one by assuming initial $t = 0$, and iterating it forward to T. This gives rise to, among others, a composite error term $\xi_{iT} = \sum_{j=0}^{T-1} \beta^j \varepsilon_{i,T-j}$. Thus, possible serial correlation in ε now acts as a source of bias. So does possible across-country variation in A_0 and g. See Lee *et al.* (1997, Appendix A) for details.

48. Recall the earlier discussion about whether the variables representing determinants of steady state should be made contingent on the initial period or not. The formulation in equation (14) and (15) is on the basis of such contingent $\hat{y}^*$. However under the assumption that s and n remain constant between t and t-1, we can replace $x_{i,t-1}$ in the equation above by x_{it}.

49. Instead of hiding or sidetracking, the correlated effects model allows the correlation between μ_i and x_{it}'s to come to fore and play out its role in the estimation process.

50. The estimated values of λ for the NONOIL, INTER and OECD samples in Islam (1995) prove to be 0.0434, 0.0417, and 0.0670, respectively. Knight *et al.* report an even higher value, 0.0652, for the NONOIL sample.

51. The estimated values of α in Islam (1995) for the three samples above are 0.4397, 0.4245 and 0.2972, respectively. The value of α reported for NONOIL sample in Knight *et al.* (1993) is even lower, 0.335.

52. Incorporation of human capital in the panel analysis leads to 'anomalous' results, with the coefficient of the human capital variable turning out to be negative and generally insignificant. This agrees with earlier results regarding human capital obtained from pooled regressions (see for example Gregorio (1992)) and also the results obtained by Benhabib and Spiegel (1994). To the extent that the human capital data are weak, there may be some data issues related with this result. The schooling data used for construction of human capital variable are yet to be adjusted for quality differences. Also, many processes of human capital formation that occur outside of formal schooling are not included in this variable. Nevertheless, panel results indicate that the channel of influence of human capital on output may be more complicated than suggested by MRW though their proposal of multiplicative inclusion of human capital in the aggregate production function, alongside physical capital. Benhabib and Spiegel (1994) also find support for multiple and more complex channels of influence of human capital on output. Panel results in Islam (1995) show very strong positive correlation between measures of human capital and estimated values of A_0. This provides a basis for the suggestion that the route along which human capital influences output may run through A_0. In particular, it seems that human capital impacts output largely through its influence on the overall technological level.

53. Islam (1999) provides a recent review of international comparison of TFP levels across countries.

54. The finding of large total factor productivity differences across countries also helps explain the issue of capital flows that Lucas (1990) and others discuss. Bernard and Jones (1996a) also provide evidence on productivity differences. Maddison (1987) and Fagerberg (1994) provide excellent discussions of productivity differences across countries.

55. Dougherty and Jorgenson's second step analysis is limited to graphical treatment. Wolff, on the other hand, runs regression of subsequent TFP growth on initial TFP level.

56. Dowrick and Nguyen try to distinguish between these two sources by including an interaction term in the regression. The interaction is between initial income variable and the average investment rate over the period. They conclude in favor of technological diffusion. The procedure, however, involves several simplifying assumptions.

57. There is a large body of literature emphasizing this issue. See for example Abramovitz (1956) and Abramovitz and David (1973). Recently, Wolff (1991) has also drawn attention to this issue. Also related to this issue is the literature on the 'embodiment' hypothesis.

58. De la Fuente (1996) presents an interesting decomposition of income-convergence among Spanish regions into its two sources, namely technological diffusion and capital deepening.

59. The indices produced by the panel method contain ordinal as well as cardinal information, which can both be helpful in answering questions regarding TFP-convergence.

60. For example, the specification based on the original version of the NCGT allows for only two variables, namely the investment rate and the labor force growth rate,

assuming that g and δ are the same across countries. The specification based on the MRW augmented version of the NCGT allows for three variables.

61. The discussion here is in the context of the NCGT model and the growth-convergence equation that is derived from that model. That does not mean that all growth-convergence equations have to proceed from this model. The general point is that no matter what model is used, the inclusion of variables needs to be decided by the model, and not on mechanical statistical grounds.

62. Regarding heterogeneity of g see for example Romer's comment on Mankiw's paper in Mankiw (1995).

63. For NONOIL, INTER, and OECD samples respectively the estimated value of this rate turns out to be 0.1845, 0.1521, and 0.1495, respectively. The correspondence between Lee et al.'s samples and MRW's NONOIL, INTER, and OECD samples is approximate.

64. According to their Table 1, the coefficient of variation in this rate is 0.85, 0.66, and 0.36 for the 'Full,' 'Intermediate,' and 'OECD' samples respectively. These samples consist of 72, 58, and 20 countries, respectively.

65. It may be noted that by itself, equation (15) does not pose a problem of endogeneity, because in this specification the right hand side variables are pre-determined. However, Chamberlain's MD estimation procedure uses both past and *future* values of x to substitute out μ_i (and y_{i0}) and hence requires strict exogeneity of x_{it}'s for the validity of estimation.

66. This procedure eliminates μ_i by first differencing and then uses lagged values of y_{it}'s and x_{it}'s as instruments.

67. This is because the results do not support the restriction that the coefficients of the s and n variable should be equal in magnitude but opposite in sign.

68. This is because the estimated coefficient of the human capital variable turns out to be negative.

69. See for example Alonso-Borrego and Arellano (1999), Kiviet (1995), Harris and Matyas (1996), Islam (2000), Jusdon and Owen (1997), and Ziliak (1997). However, it needs to be mentioned that the instrument set used for the Arellano and Bond (1991) estimator in the Monte Carlo study is not exactly the same that Caseli et al. seems to have used.

70. Also the pooled OLS is not strictly a panel estimator, because it ignores the individual effect. Only those estimators that explicitly allow for individual effects and account for these effects in the estimation process can be properly called panel estimators. Sometimes, researchers have called their regressions as *panel* when, in fact, these are *pooled* regressions. Barro (1997) for example divides up the 1960–90 period into decades. He then pools the data and uses OLS. This is a pooled OLS, and not really an exercise in panel estimation. A pooled regression may also be conducted in a SURE multi-equation framework with the equations distinguished by the time period. This involves some specification of the error covariance matrix and therefore has some semblance to the (GLS) estimation under random-effects assumption. However, the error covariance structures in these two cases are not the same. Hence the SURE method that applies to data stacked by time periods and ignores the individual effect does not actually represent panel estimation.

71. Note that the asymptotic properties of panel estimators can be considered in the direction of $N \to \infty$ or $T \to \infty$ or both N and T going to infinity. Further, N and T can go to infinity either at the same rate or different rates. In fact, properties of panel estimators may differ depending on the direction in which asymptotics are considered.

For example, Amemiya (1967, 1971) shows that, although LSDV is biased in the direction of $N \to \infty$, it is consistent in the direction of $T \to \infty$.

72. See for example Islam (2000). The dynamic panel data estimators considered in this study include: LSDV, two instrumental variable estimators by Anderson and Hsiao (1981, 1982), two GMM estimators by Arellano and Bond (1991), 2SLS, 3SLS, generalized 3SLS and Minimum Distance estimators by Chamberlain (1982, 1983). The Arellano-Bond GMM estimator, which depends heavily on lagged y's as instruments, displayed large bias.

73. Barro (1997) and Durlauf and Quah (1998) have made these arguments.

74. This was shown in Islam (1995) by comparing the single cross-section results from a 25-year span and pooled OLS results obtained from five 5-year spans constituting the same 25-year period. The difference in results was negligible.

75. Some researchers have felt other problems than the ones discussed above. For example, Barro (1997) expresses concern about presence of auto-correlation induced by measurement errors. This problem can however be dealt with through use of such estimators as Chamberlain's MD estimator, which uses a heteroskedasticity and auto-correlation consistent variance-covariance matrix of the error term.

76. If we cannot reject the $H_0 : (1 + \beta) = 1$, then by implication we cannot reject the null $\beta = 0$, i.e., we cannot reject the hypothesis that there is no convergence.

77. Li and Papell (1999) offer a different definition of 'deterministic' and 'stochastic' convergence.

78. The exact number of rejections depends on the particular specification and variant of the Dickey-Fuller test. The simple DF test yields three rejections at 5 percent significance level. Noting that standard Dickey-Fuller tests have low power, Lee *et al.* also use a test proposed by Im, Pesaran and Shin (1995), referred to as the t-bar test, which is based on the average value of the DF statistics obtained across countries. The results remain basically unchanged. To account for potential serial correlation, they also adopt the augmented Dickey-Fuller specification with the number of lags determined by use of the SBC information criterion. This, however, does not change the results that much. Based on the ADF t-statistics, the number of rejections of the unit root null ranges between 3 and 14, depending on the number of lags and whether data were demeaned or not. Lee *et al.* refer to allowing for 'common time specific effects.' (p. 21) It is unclear what is meant because apparently the procedure works on individual time series separately. The use of an analogous *t*-bar statistic for the ADF set-up, as proposed in Im *et al.*, does not affect these results by that much.

79. A non-rejection of the null therefore leaves a wide range of other non-unit root alternatives still compatible with the evidence.

80. With this test however the outcome depends on the degree of truncation.

81. The presence of $x_{i,t-1}$ in equation (15) is linked to the notion of *conditional* convergence when considered in an across-country setting. However, the notions of 'unconditional' and 'conditional' convergence have some relevance in the within economy context too. Equation (2) shows that the steady state of a particular economy can change over time if its determinants change over time. The term $x_{i,t-1}$ in equation (15) basically stands for these determinants, and the time subscript indicates the possibility of such changes. An analysis of 'within convergence' that allows for changes in the steady state over time can be thought to be an analysis of 'conditional convergence.' On the other hand if the analysis constrains $x_{i,t-1}$ to be time-invariant, then it may be termed as analysis of 'unconditional convergence.' Whether or not taking into account of changes in $x_{i,t-1}$

will affect the outcome of the unit root tests depends on the nature of changes and the time series properties of $x_{i,t-1}$ itself.

82. Lee *et al.* (1997) observe that Solow model does not have *internal explanation* for such changes. However, that does not mean that the model does not allow for the *possibility* of such changes.

83. For details, see Ben-David and Papell (1995, 1997), Ben-David, Lumsdaine, and Papell (1997), Lumsdaine and Papell (1997), and Zivot and Andrews (1992).

84. The regions are: New England, Mideast, Great Lakes, Plains, Southeast, Southwest, Rocky Mountains, and Far West.

85. They also impose a time series structure on the error term ε_t.

86. Carlino and Mills set the trend break exogenously for the year 1946.

87. This makes their results directly comparable with Barro and Sala-i-Martin (1992)'s analogous results obtained from the cross-section approach.

88. However, as we noted earlier, Barro and Sala-i-Martin also include regional dummies and an index of composition of output in part of their analysis. Hence, it is a moot point whether their result is entirely of unconditional convergence.

89. For further discussion of issues involved with tests of unit root in panel data, see for example, Hall, Robertson, and Wickens (1993) and Hall and Urga (1995).

90. It is clear that unit root analysis of deviations is a type of cointegration analysis. This is obvious when deviations are taken from a reference country. When the deviations are taken sample average, the interpretation is not clear, as we noticed earlier.

91. They also consider two sub-samples: the first consisting of 11 European countries, and, the second, consisting of 6 European countries that show a high degree of 'pairwise cointegration.'

92. The basic idea, from Engle and Granger (1987), is that if the number of distinct stochastic trends in Y_t is less than n (which would imply co-integration), then the spectral density matrix at frequency zero of ΔY_t, i.e., of $f_{\Delta Y}(0)$, is not of full rank. If all n countries are converging in per capita output, then $f_{\Delta DY}(0)_i = 0, \forall i$, or equivalently, the rank of $f_{\Delta DY}(0)$ is zero. So, in operational terms, the task is to look at the spectral density matrix at frequency zero of ΔDY and ΔY, and check for the rank conditions (more concretely, number of co-integrating vectors). For the 15-country sample, the US is the reference country. For the European sub-samples, the reference country is France.

93. Bernard and Durlauf were inclined to interpret the shared common trends as indicative of club convergence. However, this is not clear. We have noted earlier the difficulty in distinguishing evidence of club convergence from that of conditional convergence in general.

94. Drawing attention to this result, Lee *et al.* (1997) note that σ-convergence is not an implication of the Solow model.

95. Short of this adjustment, hypothesis of absence of σ-convergence will be rejected too often.

96. Note that the above relationships are based on a host of simplifying assumptions and ignoring, in particular, differences in the steady state. Litchenberg thinks that similar relationships hold even when differences in steady state are allowed. However, there are a few issues here. First, the relationship involves, apart from conditioning on the left-hand side, both σ_u^2 and σ_ε^2 on the right hand. Second, it is derived on the assumption that the steady state is not time-contingent, so that $\hat{y}_{it}^*$ is the same as $\hat{y}_{i,t-1}^*$. Third, the relationship above is in terms of income per effective worker; it will be more complicated when transformed in terms of income per capita. However, the basic ideas are evident from this algebra.

97. They also point out that the correct degrees of freedom is [(n-1), (n-1)] instead of [(n-2), (n-2)]

98. They denote original Litchenberg statistic by T_1.

99. The adjustment will cause a type-I error that is lower than the significance level. One feature of these tests is that the comparison of variance is limited to that of first and last period only. In order to make use of the information in between, Carree and Klomp, proceeding from simplified version of equation (15), iterating backwards, and making use of the independence assumption, derive the following expression for the first difference of cross-section variance,

$$\Delta \sigma_t^2 = \tilde{\beta}^{2(t-1)}[(\tilde{\beta}^2 - 1)\sigma_0^2 + \sigma_\varepsilon^2]. \tag{24}$$

Under the null of no convergence, $(\tilde{\beta}^2 - 1) = 0$. Hence the equation above can be used to test this null by regressing $\Delta \sigma_t^2$ on $\tilde{\beta}^{2(t-1)}$ and using the $t(T\text{-}2)$ distribution, if $\tilde{\beta}$ is known. In practice, one has only an estimate of $\tilde{\beta}$ and the distribution will hold only approximately. This is their statistic, T_4.

100. He obtains a slope coefficient of 0.715 and $R^2 = 0.802$. This gave $R^2/\hat{\beta}^2 = 1.57$ which is equal to $var(ln\ GDP85)/var(ln\ GDP60)$, the test statistic.

101. The probability value is 0.31.

102. When a later sample period of 1972–94 is considered, they however find that convergence does not hold any more. This, in their view, shows that while during initial years there has been significant reduction in variance, in the more recent years σ_t^2 has become close to σ_ε^2 and hence no further pronounced tendency for it to decrease is found. In other words, as the countries get closer to the steady states, the transition-component of the dynamics recede, and idiosyncratic shocks take over, which then displays no systematic tendency to decrease.

103. See for example, Sala-i-Martin (1996), Miller (1995).

104. Lee *et al.* (1997) point out that increased variance may also be the result of increasing dispersion in g.

105. Quah has produced a series articles based on this line of research. These include Quah (1993b, 1996a, 1996b)

106. Quah also allows the one year transition matrix to be iterated 23 times and compares the resulting matrix (which he calls 'stationary estimate') with the 23-year transition matrix that is obtained from actual calibration of the data. He finds that the long run matrix shows stronger persistence than found in the 'stationary estimate.'

107. He fits a VAR model to forecast the quantiles, $Q(t)$, and then takes the convolution with M raised to the appropriate power to get the dynamic evolution of the sequence of distributions.

107. For example, the results are contingent on the arbitrary grid that is used to discretize the point in time empirical distributions. However, as Quah notes, inappropriate discretization may destroy the Markov property of an otherwise well behaved first order Markov process. Also, conclusions regarding piling up of probability mass are contingent on the choice of discretizing grid and may not be robust. (See Quah 1993a, p. 437.) Finally, Quah observes that the VAR models are estimated on the basis of only about 20 data points and hence are not that precise

108. Quah notes certain technical shortcomings of this analysis. For example, the results are contingent on the arbitrary grid that is used to discretize the empirical distributions. Quah notes that inappropriate discretization may destroy the Markov property of an otherwise well-behaved first order Markov process. Also, conclusions regarding

piling up of probability mass is contingent on the choice of discretizing grid and may not be robust. (Quah 1993a, p. 437) Similarly, Quah observes that the VAR models are estimated on the basis of only twenty data points and hence are not that precise.

109. This contrasts with research on conditional β-convergence, which imposes structure and uses growth theory to decide on specification, choice of right hand side variables, etc. De la Fuente (1996) also draws attention to this feature of Quah's analysis.

110. From this point of view, convergence studies can be classified into two broad groups. One group, comprised mainly of the cross-section and the panel approach, imposes theoretical structure (derived from formal growth models) on the data and produces estimates of structural parameters of growth models. The other group, comprised mainly of the time series and the distribution approach, tends to avoid structure and thus resembles to reduced-form analysis of the output data.

111. Also as Solow (1994) notes, the externality-based NGT models suffer from the 'generalized Domar problem' requiring the social or aggregate elasticity of output with respect to capital to be exactly equal to one. While the estimated rates of conditional convergence have differed, the implied values of this elasticity have generally remained well short of being equal to one. As Chad Jones (1995a, 1995b) has shown, there are other ways to test for the validity of the new variants of the NGT.

112. For example, Jones and Manueli (1990) relax the Inada conditions while preserving diminishing returns so that there can be both convergence and asymptotic growth. Ventura (1997), Duffy and Papageorgiou (2000), and others use the CES production function and show that for a certain range of the value of the elasticity of substitution between capital and labor, there can be long run growth. Tamura (1991) allows the strength of externality to depend on the level of human capital accumulation, and this leads to the convergence implication. Barro and Sala-i-Martin (1995) and Basu and Weil (1998) show how convergence can occur via technological diffusion. Ortigueira and Santos (1997) compare rates of convergence under alternative NGT models. Kocherlakota and Yi (1995) also discuss the problem of distinguishing between NCGT and NGT on the basis of convergence regressions.

113. Recent models of technological diffusion include Grossman and Helpman (1991), Parente and Prescott (1994a, 1994b), Barro and Sala-i-Martin (1997), Basu and Weil (1998), and Howitt (2000). As noted earlier, development economists and economic historians were aware all along about technological differences across countries, and many of them provided descriptive account of the technological diffusion process. Nelson (1968) provides an early formal model of technology diffusion. He notices that "the result that there are significant unexplained productivity differences across countries has been largely unnoticed," (p. 1223) and that "there are no reasons why (the assumption of) a common linear homogeneous production function...should be held sacrosanct." (p. 1229) In an earlier paper, Nelson and Phelps (1966) emphasized the role of human capital in technological diffusion. Many of the ideas currently used by the NGT models of technological diffusion can be found in these earlier works.

114. NGT models that allow role of trade in growth include Krugman (1990) and Grossman and Helpman (1991). For discussion of the role of trade in growth under the NCGT paradigm see Richard Baldwin (1993) and Mazumdar (1996). For an early discussion of the subject, see Robert Baldwin (1966). Ventura (1997) provides a recent elaborate integration of trade and growth. The issue of institutions has also gained importance. McGuire and Olson (1996) offer a model of interaction between institution and growth. There has been significant development in collection of data on institutional quality across countries too, and these data have been employed to

establish the importance of institutions in explaining cross-country growth regularities. See for example Knack and Keefer (1995).

115. The *American Economic Association (AEA)* has awarded prize to Alan Heston and
Robert Summers for their work in putting together this data set.

116. See for example, Bardhan (1995).

References

Abramovitz, Moses (1956) Resource and Output Trends in the US since 1870. *American
Economic Review* 46, 5–23.

Abramovitz, Moses and Paul David (1973) Reinterpreting American Economic Growth:
Parables and Realities. *American Economic Review* 63, 428–437.

Ades, Alberto and Hak B. Chua (1997) Thy Neighbor's Curse: Regional Instability and
Economic Growth. *Journal of Economic Growth* 2, 279–304.

Alonso-Borrengo, Cesar and Manuel Arellano (1999) Symmetrically Normalized Instru-
mental-Variable Estimation Using Panel Data. *Journal of Business & and Economic
Statistics* 17, 36–49.

Amemiya, T. (1967) A Note on the Estimation of Balestra-Nerlove Models, Technical
Report No. 4, Institute for Mathematical Studies in Social Sciences, Stanford University.

Amemiya, T. (1971) The Estimation of the Variance in a Variance-Component Model.
International Economic Review 12, 1–13.

Anderson, T. W. and C. Hsiao (1981) Estimation of Dynamic Models with Error Components. *Journal of American Statistical Association* 76, 598–606.

Anderson, T.W. and C. Hsiao (1982) Formulation and Estimation of Dynamic Models
Using Panel Data. *Journal of Econometrics* 18, 47–82.

Arellano, Manuel and Stephen Bond (1991) Some Tests of Specification for Panel Data:
Monte Carlo Evidence and an Application to Employment Equations. *Review of
Economic Studies* 58, 277–297.

Azariadis Costas and Allan Drazen (1990) Threshold Externalities in Economic Development. *Quarterly Journal of Economics* 105, 501–526.

Auerbach, Alan J., Kevin A. Hassett, and Stephen D. Oliner (1994) Reassessing
the Social Returns to Equipment Investment. *Quarterly Journal of Economics* 109,
789–802.

Baldwin, Robert (1966) The Role of Capital-Goods in the Theory of International Trade.
American Economic Review 56, 841–848.

Baldwin, Richard E. (1992) Measurable Dynamic Gains from Trade. *Journal of Political
Economy* 100, 162–74.

Bardhan, Pranab (1995) The Contribution of Endogenous Growth Theory to the Analysis of
Development Problems: An Assessment, in *Handbook of Development Economics*, Vol. III,
edited by J. Behrman and T. N. Srinivasan, New York, Elsevier Science, pp. 2984–2998.

Barro, Robert J. (1976) Rational Expectations and the Role of Monetary Policy. *Journal of
Monetary Economics* 2, 1–32.

Barro, Robert J. (1978) Unanticipated Money, Output, and the Price Level in the United
States. *Journal of Political Economy* 86, 549–580.

Barro, Robert J. (1990) Government Spending in a Simple Model of Endogenous Growth.
Journal of Political Economy 98, 5, part II, S103-S125.

Barro, Robert J. (1991) Economic Growth in a Cross Section of Countries. *Quarterly
Journal of Economics* 106, 407–443.

Barro, Robert J. (1997) *Determinants of Economic Growth*, Cambridge, MIT Press.

Barro, Robert J. and Gary Becker (1989) Fertility Choice in a Model of Endogenous Growth. *Econometrica* 57, 481–501.

Barro, Robert J. and Jong-Wha Lee (1993) International Comparisons of Educational Attainment. *Journal of Monetary Economics* 32, 363–94.

Barro, Robert J., N. Gregory Mankiw and Xavier Sala-i-Martin (1995) Capital Mobility in Neoclassical Models of Growth. *American Economic Review* 85, 103–115.

Barro, Robert J. and Xavier Sala-i-Martin (1992) Convergence. *Journal of Political Economy* 100, 223–51.

Barro, Robert J. and Xavier Sala-i-Martin (1995) *Economic Growth*, McGraw Hill, New York, 1995.

Barro, Robert J. and Xavier Sala-i-Martin (1997) Technological Diffusion, Convergence, and Growth. *Journal of Economic Growth* 2, 1–27.

Basu, Susanto and David N. Weil (1998) Appropriate Technology and Growth. *Quarterly Journal of Economics* 113, 1024–1054.

Baumol, William J. (1986) Productivity Growth, Convergence and Welfare: What the Long Run Data Show? *American Economic Review* 76, 1072–85.

Baumol, William J. and Edward N. Wolff (1988) Productivity Growth, Convergence and Welfare: Reply. *American Economic Review* 78, 1155–1159.

Bayomi, Tamim, David Coe, and Elhanan Helpman (1999) R&D Spillovers and Global Growth. *Journal of International Economics* 42, 399–428.

Becker, Gary and Robert J. Barro (1988) A Reformulation of the Economic Theory of Fertility. *Quarterly Journal of Economics* 103, 1–25.

Becker, Gary, Kevin M. Murphy and Robert Tamura (1990) Human Capital, Fertility and Economic Growth. *Journal of Political Economy* 98, S12–S37.

Ben-David, Dan and David H. Papell (1995) The Great Wars, the Great Crash, and Steady State Growth: Some New Evidence about an Old Stylized Fact. *Journal of Monetary Economics* 36, 453–475.

Ben-David, Dan and David H. Papell (1997) Slowdowns and Meltdowns: Post-War Growth Evidence from 74 Countries. *Review of Economics and Statistics* 80, 561–71.

Ben-David, Dan, Robin Lumsdaine and David Papell (1997) Unit Roots, Postwar Slow-downs, and Long-Run Growth: Evidence from Two Structural Breaks, Department of Economics, University of Houston, mimeo.

Benhabib, Jess and Mark M. Spiegel (1994) The Role of Human Capital in Economic Development: Evidence from Aggregate Cross-Country Data. *Journal of Monetary Economics* 34, 143–173.

Bernard, Andrew and Steven N. Durlauf (1996) Interpreting Tests of the Convergence Hypothesis. *Journal of Econometrics* 71, 161–173.

Bernard, Andrew and Steven N. Durlauf (1995) Convergence in International Output. *Journal of Applied Econometrics* 10, 97–108.

Bernard, Andrew and Charles I. Jones (1996) Technology and Convergence. *Economic Journal* 106, 1037–1044.

Binder, Michael and M. Hashem Pesaran (1999) Stochastic Growth Models and Their Econometric Implications. *Journal of Economic Growth* 4, 139–183.

Blomstrom, Magnus, Robert E. Lipsey and Mario Zejan (1996) Is Fixed Investment the Key to Economic Growth? *Quarterly Journal of Economics* 111, 269–276.

Canova, Fabio and Albert Marcet (1995) The Poor Stay Poor: Non-convergence across Countries and Regions, Discussion Paper No. 1265, Center for Economic Policy Research (CEPR), London.

Carlino, G. A. and L. O. Mills (1993) Are the US Regional Incomes Converging? A Time Series Analysis. *Journal of Monetary Economics* 32, 335–346.

Carree Martin and Luuk Klomp (1995) Testing the Convergence Hypothesis: A Comment. *Review of Economics and Statistics* 79, 683–86.

Caselli, Francesco, Gerardo Esquivel and Fernando Lefort (1996) Reopening the Convergence Debate: A New Look at Cross Country Growth Empirics. *Journal of Economic Growth* 1, 363–89.

Caselli, Francesco and Wilbur John Coleman II (2001) The US Structural Transformation and Regional Convergence: A Reinterpretation. *Journal of Political Economy* 109, 584–616.

Cass, David (1965) Optimum Growth in an Aggregative Model of Capital Accumulation. *Review of Economic Studies* 32, 233–40.

Chamberlain, Gary (1982) Multivariate Regression Models for Panel Data. *Journal of Econometrics* 18, 5–46.

Chamberlain, Gary (1983) Panel Data, in *Handbook of Econometrics*, edited by Zvi Griliches and Michael Intriligator, Amsterdam: North Holland, pp. 1247–1318.

Chenery, Hollis, Sherman Robinson and Moshe Sirquin (1985) *Industrialization and Growth: A Comparative Study*, New York, Oxford University Press.

Cho, Dongchul and Stephen Graham (1996) The Other Side of Conditional Convergence. *Economics Letters* 50, 285–290.

Christensen, Lauritis R., Dianne Cummings and Dale W. Jorgenson (1981) Relative Productivity Levels, 1947–1973: An International Comparison. *European Economic Review* 16, 61–74.

Chua, Hak B. (1992) Regional Spillovers and Economic Growth, Department of Economics, Harvard University, 1992.

Coe, David T. and Elhanan Helpman (1995) International R&D Spillovers. *European Economic Review* 39, 859–887.

Coe, David T., Elhanan Helpman and Alexander W. Hoffmaister (1997) North-South and R&D Spillovers. *Economic Journal* 107, 134–149.

De Gregorio, Jose (1992) Economic Growth in Latin America. *Journal of Development Economics* 39, 59–84.

De Long, Bradford J. (1988) Productivity Growth, Convergence, and Welfare: A Comment. *American Economic Review* 78, 1138–54.

De Long, Bradford J. and Lawrence Summers (1991) Equipment Investment and Economic Growth. *Quarterly Journal of Economics* 106, 445–502.

De Long, Bradford J. and Lawrence Summers (1993) How Strongly Do Developing Economies Benefit from Equipment Investment? *Journal of Monetary Economics* 32, 395–415.

De Long, Bradford J. and Lawrence H. Summers (1994) Equipment Investment and Economic Growth: Reply. *Quarterly Journal of Economics* 109, 803–807.

De la Fuente, Angel (1996) On the Sources of Convergence: A Close Look at the Spanish Regions, Discussion Paper No. 1543, Center for Economic Policy Research (CEPR), London.

De la Fuente, Angel (1997) The Empirics of Growth and Convergence: A Selective Review. *Journal of Economic Dynamics and Control* 21, 23–73.

Den Haan, Wouter J. (1995) Convergence in Stochastic Growth Models: The Importance of Understanding Why Income Levels Differ. *Journal of Monetary Economics* 35, 65–82.

Desdoigts, Alain (1999) Patterns of Economic Development and the Formation of Clubs. *Journal of Economic Growth* 4, 305–330.

Dickey, D. and W. Fuller (1979) Distribution of the Estimators for Autoregressive Series with a Unit Root. *Journal of the American Statistical Association* 74, 427–431.

Dickey, D. and W. Fuller (1981) Likelihood Ratio Tests for Autoregressive Time Series with a Unit Root. *Econometrica* 49, 1057–1072.

Dollar, David and Edward Wolff (1994) Capital Intensity and TFP Convergence in Manufacturing, 1963–1985, in William J. Baumol, Richard R. Nelson, and Edward N. Wolff, *Convergence of Productivity: Cross National Studies and Historical Evidence.* New York, Oxford University Press.

Domar, Evsey (1946) Capital Expansion, Rate of Growth and Employment. *Econometrica* 14, 137–147.

Dougherty, Chrys and Dale W. Jorgenson (1996) International Comparison of Sources of Growth. *American Economic Review* 86, 25–29.

Dougherty, Chrys and Dale W. Jorgenson (1997) There is No Silver Bullet: Investment and Growth in the G7. *National Institute Economic Review* 162, 57–74.

Dowrick, Steve and Duc-Tho Nguyen (1989) OECD Comparative Economic Growth 1950–85: Catch-Up and Convergence. *American Economic Review* 79, 1010–30.

Duffy, John and Chris Papageorgiou (2000) A Cross-country Empirical Investigation of the Aggregate Production Function Specification. *Journal of Economic Growth* 5, 87–120.

Durlauf, Steven N. and Danny T. Quah (1999) The New Empirics of Economic Growth, in John Taylor and Michael Woodford (eds.), *Handbook of Macroeconomics*, Vol. 1A, Amsterdam, North-Holland.

Durlauf, Steven. and Paul A. Johnson (1995) Multiple Regimes and Cross-Country Growth Behavior. *Journal of Applied Econometrics* 10, 365–384.

Engle, Robert and Clive Granger (1987) Cointegration and Error Correction Model. *Econometrica* 55, 251–76.

Evans, Paul (1996) Using Cross-country Variances to Evaluate Growth Theories. *Journal of Economic Dynamics and Control* 20, 1027–1049.

Evans, Paul and Georgios Karras (1996a) Convergence Revisited. *Journal of Monetary Economics* 37, 249–265.

Evans, Paul and Georgios Karras (1996b) Do Economies Converge? Evidence from a Panel of US States. *Review of Economics and Statistics* 78, 384–388.

Fagerberg, Jan (1994) Technology and International Differences in Growth Rates. *Journal of Economic Literature* 32, 1147–1175.

Friedman, Milton (1994) Do Old Fallacies Ever Die? *Journal of Economic Literature* 30, 2129–2132.

Galor, Oded (1996) Convergence? Inference from Theoretical Models. *Economic Journal* 106, 1056–1069.

Gerschenkron, Alexander (1953) Economic Backwardness in Historical Perspective, in Bert F. Hoselitz (ed.) *The Progress in Underdeveloped Areas*, Chicago, Chicago University Press.

Gregorio, Jose De (1992) Economic Growth in Latin America. *Journal of Development Economics* 39, 59–84.

Grier, Kevin B. and Gordon Tullock (1989) An Empirical Analysis of Cross-National Economic Growth, 1951–1980. *Journal of Monetary Economics* 24, 259–276.

Grossman, Gene M. and Elhanan Helpman (1991) *Innovation and Growth in the Global Economy*. Cambridge, MIT Press.

Hall, Robert E. and Charles I. Jones (1996) The Productivity of Nations, NBER Working Paper No. 5812, Cambridge, MA.

Hall, Robert E. and Charles I. Jones (1997) Levels of Economic Activity across Countries. *American Economic Review* 87, 173–177.

Hall, Robert E. and Charles I. Jones (1999) Why Do Some Countries Produce So Much More Output Than Others? *Quarterly Journal of Economics* 114, 83–116.

Hall, Stephen and Giovanna Urga (1995) Stochastic Common Trends and Long-Run Relationships in Heterogeneous Panels, Discussion Paper No. 27–95, Center for Economic Forecasting, London Business School.

Hall, Stephen, Donald Robertson and Michael Wickens (1993) How to Measure Convergence with an Application to the EC Economies, Discussion Paper No. 19–93, Center for Economic Forecasting, London Business School.

Harris, Mark N. and Laszlo Matyas (1996) A Comparative Analysis of Different Estimators for Dynamic Panel Data Models, Department of Economics, Monash University.

Harrod, Roy (1993) An Essay in Dynamic Theory. *The Economic Journal* 49, 14–33.

Holtz-Eakin, Douglas (1993) Solow and the States: Capital Accumulation, Productivity, and Economic Growth. *National Tax Journal* 46, 425–439.

Howitt, Peter (2000) Endogenous Growth and Cross-country Income Differences. *American Economic Review* 90, 829–846.

Im, Pesaran, and Shin (1995) Testing for Unit Roots in Heterogeneous Panels, Working Paper, Amalgamated Series 9526, Department of Applied Economics, University of Cambridge.

Inada, Ken-Ichi (1963) On a Two-sector Model of Economic Growth: Comments and Generalization. *Review of Economic Studies* 30, 119–127.

Islam, Nazrul (1995) Growth Empirics: A Panel Data Approach. *Quarterly Journal of Economics* 110, 1127–1170.

Islam, Nazrul (1999) International Comparison of Total Factor Productivity: A Review. *Review of Income and Wealth* 45, 493–518.

Islam, Nazrul (2000) Small Sample Performance of Dynamic Panel Data Estimators in Estimating the Growth-Convergence Equation: A Monte Carlo Study. *Advances in Econometrics* 15, 317–339.

Johansen S. (1988) Statistical Analysis of Co-integration Vectors. *Journal of Economic Dynamics and Control* 12, 231–54.

Jones, Larry E. and Rodolfo Manuelli (1990) A Convex Model of Equilibrium Growth: Theory and Policy Implications. *Journal of Political Economy* 98, 1008–1038.

Jones, Charles I. (1995a) Time Series Tests of Endogenous Growth Models. *Quarterly Journal of Economics* 110, 495–525.

Jones, Charles I. (1995b) R&D-Based Models of Economic Growth. *Journal of Political Economy* 103, 759–784.

Jorgenson, Dale W. and M. Nishimizu (1978) US and Japanese Economic Growth, 1952–1974. *Economic Journal* 88, 707–726.

Judson, Ruth A. and Ann L. Owen (1997) Estimating Dynamic Panel Data Models: A Practical Guide for Macroeconomists, Finance and Economic Series No. 3, Federal Reserve Bank, Washington, D.C.

Kaldor, Nicholas (1971) Capital Accumulation and Economic Growth, in F. A. Lutz and D. C. Hague (eds.) *Theory of Capital*, New York: St. Martin's Press.

Kelly, Morgan (1992) On Endogenous Growth with Productivity Shocks. *Journal of Monetary Economics* 30, 47–56.

Kiviet, Jan F. (1995) On Bias, Inconsistency, and Efficiency of Various Estimators in Dynamic Panel Data Models. *Journal of Econometrics* 68, 53–78.

Klenow, Peter J. and Andres Rodriguez-Clare (1997) *NBER Macroeconomics Annual 1997*, pp. 73–103, Cambridge and London: MIT Press.

Knight Malcolm, Norman Loyaza and Delano Villanueva (1993) Testing for Neoclassical Theory of Economic Growth. *IMF Staff Papers* 40, 512–541.

Knack, Stephen and Philip Keefer (1995) Institutions and Economic Performance: Cross-country Tests Using Alternative Institutional Measures. *Economics and Politics* 7, 207–227.

Kocherlakota, Narayana R. and Kei-Mu Yi (1995) Can Convergence Regressions Distinguish between Exogenous and Endogenous Growth Models? *Economics Letters* 49, 211–215.

Koopmans T.C. (1965) On the Concept of Optimal Economic Growth, in *The Economic Approach to Development Planning*, Pontifical Academy of Sciences, Amsterdam: North-Holland.

Kormendi, Roger C. and Philip G. Meguire (1985) Macroeconomic Determinants of Growth: Cross-country Evidence. *Journal of Monetary Economics* 16, 141–163.

Krueger, Anne O. (1968) Factor Endowments and Per Capita Income Differences among Countries. *Economic Journal* 78, 641–659.

Krugman, Paul (1990) *Rethinking International Trade*, Cambridge: MIT Press.

Kwiatkowski, Denis, Peter P. C. Phillips, Peter Schmidt and Yongcheol Shin (1992) Testing the Null Hypothesis of Stationarity against the Alternative of Unit Root. *Journal of Econometrics* 54, 159–178.

Lee, Kevin, M. Hashem Pesaran and Ron Smith (1997) Growth and Convergence: A Multicountry Empirical Analysis of the Solow Growth Model. *Journal of Applied Econometrics* 12, 357–392.

Levin, Andrew and Chien-Fu Lin (1993) Unit Root Tests in Panel Data, Dept. of Economics, University of California-San Diego.

Levine, Ross and David Renelt (1992) A Sensitivity Analysis of Cross Country Growth Regressions. *American Economic Review* 82, 4, 942–963.

Litchenberg, Frank R. (1994) Testing the Convergence Hypothesis. *Review of Economics and Statistics* 76, 576–579.

Lowey, Michael B. and David H. Papell (1996) Are US Regional Incomes Converging? Some Further Evidence. *Journal of Monetary Economics* 38, 587–598.

Lucas, Robert E. Jr. (1988) On the Mechanics of Economic Development. *Journal of Monetary Economics* 22, 3–42.

Lucas, Robert E. Jr. (1990) Why Doesn't Capital Flow from Rich to Poor Countries? *American Economic Review* 80, 92–6.

Lucas, Robert E. Jr. (1993) Making a Miracle. *Econometrica* 61, 251–272.

Lusigi, Angela, Jenifer Piesse and Colin Thirtle (1998) Convergence of Per Capita Incomes and Agricultural Productivity in Africa. *Journal of International Development* 10, 105–115.

Lumbsdine, Robin and David Papell (1997) Multiple Trend Breaks and the Unit Root Hypothesis. *Review of Economics and Statistics* 79, 212–218.

Maddison, Angus (1982) *Phases of Capitalist Development*, Oxford University Press, Oxford.

Maddison, Angus (1987) Growth and Slowdown in Advanced Capitalist Economies: Techniques of Quantitative Assessment. *Journal of Economic Literature* 25, 649–698.

Miller, Ronald I. (1995) Time Series Estimation of Convergence Rates, Department of Economics, University of Columbia, 1995 (typescript).

Mankiw, N. Gregory, David Romer and David Weil (1992) A contribution to the Empirics of Economic Growth. *Quarterly Journal of Economics* 107, 407–37.

Mankiw, N. Gregory (1995) The Growth of Nations. 4 *Brookings Papers on Economic Activity* No. 1, 275–325.

Mazumdar, Joy (1996) Do Static Gains from Trade Lead to Medium-Run Growth? *Journal of Political Economy* 104, 1328–1337.

McGuire, Martin and Mancur Olson (1996) The Economics of Autocracy and Majority Rule: The Invisible Hand and the Use of Force. *Journal of Economic Literature* 34, 72–96.

Nelson, Richard R. (1968) A Diffusion Model of International Productivity Differences in Manufacturing Industry. *American Economic Review* 58, 1219–1248.

Nelson, Richard R. and Edmund S. Phelps (1966) Investment in Humans, Technological Diffusion, and Economic Growth. *American Economic Review* 56, 69–75.

Nerlove, Marc (1999) Properties of Alternative Estimators of Dynamic Models: An Empirical Analysis of Cross-country Data for the Study of Economic Growth, in Cheng Hsiao, Kajal Lahiri, Lung-Fei Lee, and Hashem Pesaran (eds.), *Analysis of Panels and Limited Dependent Variable Models*, Cambridge: Cambridge University Press.

Nonneman, Walter and Patrick Vanhoudt (1996) A Further Augmentation of the Solow Model and the Empirics of Economic Growth for OECD Countries. *Quarterly Journal of Economics* 111, 943–53.

Ortigueira, Salvador and Manuel S. Santos (1997) On the Speed of Convergence in Endogenous Growth Models. *American Economic Review* 87, 383–399.

Parente, Stephen L. and Edward C. Prescott (1994a) Barriers to Technology Adoption and Development. *Journal of Political Economy* 102, 298–321.

Parente, Stephen L. and Edward C. Prescott (1994b) Changes in Wealth of Nations, *Quarterly Review*, Federal Reserve Bank of Minneapolis, Spring, 3–16.

Phillips, P. C. B. and S. Ouliaris (1988) Testing for Co-integration Using Principal Components Method. *Journal of Economic Dynamics and Control* 12, 205–230.

Prescott, Edward C. (1998) Needed: A Theory of Total Factor Productivity. *International Economic Review* 39, 525–551.

Li, Qing and David Papell (1999) Convergence of International Output: Time Series Evidence for 16 OECD Countries. *International Review of Economics and Finance* 8, 267–80.

Quah, Danny (1990) International Patterns of Economic Growth: I. Persistence in Cross-country Disparities, Department of Economics, MIT, Cambridge.

Quah, Danny (1993a) Galton's Fallacy and Tests of the Convergence Hypothesis. *Scandinavian Journal of Economics* 95, 427–443.

Quah, Danny (1993b) Empirical Cross-Section Dynamics in Economic Growth. *European Economic Review* 37, 426–434.

Quah, Danny (1996a) Empirics for Economic Growth and Convergence. *European Economic Review* 40, 1353–75.

Quah, Danny (1996b) Twin Peaks: Growth and Convergence in Models of Distribution Dynamics. *Economic Journal* 106, 1045–1055.

Quah, Danny (1996c) Convergence Empirics Across Economies with (Some) Capital Mobility. *Journal of Economic Growth* 1, 95–124.

Rebelo, Sergio (1991) Long Run Policy Analysis and Long Run Growth. *Journal of Political Economy* 99, 500–21.

Romer, Paul (1986) Increasing Returns and Long Run Growth. *Journal of Political Economy* 94, 1002–1036.

Romer, Paul (1989a) Crazy Explanations for Productivity Slowdown, *Brookings Papers on Economic Activity*, Washington D. C., 163–202.

Romer, Paul (1989b) Capital Accumulation in the Theory of Long Run Growth, in *Modern Business Cycle Theory*, Robert J. Barro (ed.), Harvard University Press, Cambridge MA.

Romer, Paul (1990) Endogenous Technological Change. *Journal of Political Economy* 98, S71–S102.

Romer, Paul (1994) Origins of Endogeneous Growth. *Journal of Economic Perspectives* 8, 3–22.

Sala-i-Martin, Xavier (1996a) The Classical Approach to Convergence Analysis. *Economic Journal* 106, 1019–1036.

Sala-i-Martin, Xavier (1996b) Regional Cohesion: Evidence and Theories of Regional Growth and Convergence. *European Economic Review* 40, 1325–1352.

Sala-i-Martin, Xavier (1997) I Just Ran Two Million Regressions. *American Economic Review* 87, 178–183.

Shioji, Etsuro (1996) Regional Growth in Japan, Discussion Paper No. 1425, Center for Economic Policy Research.

Solow, Robert M. (1956) A Contribution to the Theory of Economic Growth. *Quarterly Journal of Economics* 70, 65–94.

Solow, Robert M. (1970) *Growth Theory: An Exposition*, Cambridge University Press, London.

Solow, Robert M. (1994) Perspectives on Growth Theory. *Journal of Economic Perspectives* 8, 45–54.

Summers, Robert and Alan Heston (1988) A New Set of International Comparisons of Real Product and Price Levels Estimates for 130 Countries. 1950–85. *Review of Income and Wealth* 34, 1–26.

Summers, Robert and Alan Heston (1991) The Penn World Table (Mark 5): An Expanded Set of International Comparisons, 1950–1988. *Quarterly Journal of Economics* 106, 327–368.

Swan, Trevor W. (1956) Economic Growth and Capital Accumulation. *Economic Record* 32, 334–361.

Tamura, Robert (1991) Income Convergence in an Endgenous Growth Model. *Journal of Political Economy* 99, 522–540.

Temple, Jonathan (1998) Equipment Investment and the Solow Model. *Oxford Economic Papers* 50, 39–60.

Temple, Jonathan (1998) Robustness Tests of the Augmented Solow Model. *Journal of Applied Econometrics* 13, 361–75.

Temple, Jonathan (1999) The New Growth Evidence. *Journal of Economic Literature* 37, 112–156.

Temple, Jonathan and Paul A. Johnson (1998) Social Capability and Economic Growth. *Quarterly Journal of Economics* 113, 965–90.

Temple, Jonathan and Hans-Joachim Voth (1998) Human Capital, Equipment Investment, and Industrialization. *European Economic Review* 42, 1343–1362.

Tzanidakis, George and Theo Kirizidis (1995) A Test of a Modern Version of the Solow Model. *Economics Letters* 3, 587–590.

Verspagen, Bart (1992) Endogenous Innovation in Neo-classical Growth Models: A Survey. *Journal of Macroeconomics* 14, 631–662.

Ventura, Jaume (1997) Growth and Interdependence. *Quarterly Journal of Economics* 112, 57–84.

Wolff, E. N. (1991) Capital Fromation and Productivity Convergence. *American Economic Review* 81, 565–579.

Young, Alwyn (1995) The Tyranny of Numbers: Confronting the Statistical Realities of the East Asian Growth Experience. *Quarterly Journal of Economics* 110, 641–680.

Zivot, Eric and Donald Andrews (1992) Further Evidence on the Great Crash, the Oil Price Shock, and the Unit Root Hypothesis. *Journal of Business and Economic Statistics* 10, 251–270.

5

HOW LARGE IS INTERNATIONAL TRADE'S EFFECT ON ECONOMIC GROWTH?

Joshua J. Lewer

West Texas, A & M University

Hendrik Van den Berg

University of Nebraska

1. Introduction

Most economists would agree with Harry Johnson that 'The proposition that freedom of trade is on the whole economically more beneficial than protection is one of the most fundamental propositions economic theory has to offer.'[1] Of course, consensus does not imply that a truth has been discovered. In fact, as Irwin (1996) so well documents, skeptics have repeatedly questioned mainstream economists' pro-trade conclusions, and that questioning continues today. There are still a number of serious challenges that have not been turned back by the meticulously-developed theory of international trade. For example, Leontief's (1953) paradox has not yet been fully solved. More recently, Trefler (1995), Helpman (1999), and Davis and Weinstein (2001), among others, have brought up other cases where textbook trade models do a poor job of describing the trade patterns that we observe in the world.

One of the most serious challenges to the theory of international trade are the disappointing estimates of the size of the welfare gains from free trade predicted by the theory.[2] Studies on the gains from trade based on the standard partial and general equilibrium models have seldom found the welfare gains to be larger than one percent of GDP. These results raise a serious question: If free trade raises per capita GDP by one percent, how can economists so fervently promote free trade as a priority policy for closing the 1,000-plus percent differences in per capita incomes between developed and less developed economies?

Economists have increasingly shifted their attention to the dynamic relationships between international trade and economic growth and away from the traditional static models of trade on which the empirical estimates of the gains from trade have been based. Over the past four decades, economists have produced an extensive set of empirical evidence confirming that international trade and economic growth are positively, and significantly, related. Even though many authors have questioned the methods and conclusions of individual empirical studies, the statistical evidence suggesting that trade and growth are positively related is today widely accepted. T. N. Srinivasan (1997) echoed the sentiments of many authors who have surveyed this empirical literature when he concluded that '...the fact that a number of studies using different data sets, countries and methodologies happened to arrive at similar conclusions...suggests that they deserve serious consideration, with due allowances being made for their conceptual and statistical deficiencies.'[3] The relationship between trade and growth has even gained the status of 'stylized fact' in the growth literature.[4]

Of course, not everyone agrees that the empirical evidence on the relationship between trade and growth is robust. For example, Rodriguez and Rodrik (2001) and Rodrik, Subramanian, and Trebbi (2002) have argued that international trade policy is closely correlated with many other economic policies, and that therefore it is difficult to differentiate between the effects of trade and those other policies on economic growth.[5] The purpose of this survey, however, is not to revisit the debate about whether or not the vast empirical literature convincingly establishes that there is a positive relationship between trade and growth. Rather, this survey has the more modest, but necessary, purpose of re-examining the empirical literature on trade and growth in order to assess whether the trade-growth nexus is *quantitatively* important. In light of the disappointing estimates of the static gains from international trade, we should be careful about jumping to the conclusion that the statistically significant and positive relationship between trade and growth is also an *economically significant* relationship. This survey's search for a number to go along with the sign of the trade-growth relationship reveals that the growth effects of international trade are large and, with several exceptions detailed below, fairly consistent across the many different empirical studies.

2. The Econometric Analysis of International Trade and Economic Growth

The empirical literature on the relationship between international trade and economic growth has grown to huge proportions over the past four decades. Before attempting to extract a consensus estimate, a brief review of the evolution of this broad and varied literature is in order. Most of the earliest empirical studies of international trade and growth supplemented more detailed studies of the protectionist import substitution policies by the governments of most developing economies after World War II.[6] In one such study, Michaely (1977) used simple correlation analysis and found a strong positive correlation between trade and growth for 41 developing economies, which led him to conclude that the protectionist import substitution policies had been ill advised. Balassa (1978) applied regression analysis for a sample of 10 countries in order to test the relationship between trade and growth, which he found to be positive and statistically significant.

As computing power grew, regression analysis became the standard econometric tool for empirical studies of trade and growth. Linear regression analyses of the relationship between foreign trade and economic growth most often specified linear econometric models of the form:

$$G_{\text{GDP}} = a_0 + a_1 G_K + a_2 G_L + a_3 \text{TRADE} + a_4 Z + u, \qquad (1)$$

where G_{GDP}, G_K, and G_L are the growth rates of real gross domestic product, capital stock, and labor force, respectively, TRADE is a measure of international trade (usually the growth of exports), Z is a set of other variables believed to explain economic growth, and u is the error term. This specification is convenient because data to proxy the model's variables are readily available from national accounts and several large data bases such as the Penn World Table and Angus Maddison's (1995, 2001) historical time series.[7] The specification can also be theoretically justified. Model (1) can be derived from the neoclassical production function. For example, suppose that output, Y, is a function of the stock of capital, K, the labor force, L, and the growth of technology at the rate p as given by the Cobb-Douglas production function $Y = e^{pt} K^\alpha L^{1-\alpha}$. Converting to logarithms and differentiating with respect to time then yields the well-known *sources of growth equation*:

$$G_Y = G_{\text{TFP}} + \alpha G_K + (1 - \alpha) G_L + u, \qquad (2)$$

In equation (2) the variables G_Y, G_K, G_L, and G_{TFP} are the growth rates of total output, capital, labor, and total factor productivity, respectively, and α and $(1 - \alpha)$ are the relative income shares of capital and labor. The addition of variables such as TRADE and Z in equation (1) in effect helps to 'explain' the constant in equation (1), which in the growth literature is often referred to as the total factor productivity growth residual. This puts the model in accord with Feder (1982), Holmes and Schmitz (1995), Parente and Prescott (2000), Rivera Batiz and Romer (1991), and many others who who have provided theoretical arguments suggesting that an open economy achieves more rapid productivity growth. Clerides, Lach, and Tybout (1998) and Bernard and Jensen (1999) focused specifically on exports as a source of productivity gains, while Dertouzos, Lester, and Solow (1990) and McDonald (1994) showed that import competition enhances productivity growth.

Trade's influence on economic growth is also likely to operate through the other explanatory variables on the right-hand side of the sources of growth equation (1). Levine and Renelt (1992) and Wacziarg (2001) showed that international trade influences growth through investment (factor accumulation). Frankel and Romer (1999) specifically found trade to influence growth through human capital accumulation.

Many other regression models have been used to test the relationship between international trade and economic growth. For example, some of the early empirical tests used simple linear regression models with the growth of trade as the only regressor; such models are essentially a restricted version of equation (1) in which the coefficients for the growth of factors are constrained to equal zero. Other researchers put the Cobb-Douglas equation into per capita terms. Defining the lower-case letter on a per person or per worker basis, so that $y = Y/L$ for example, and dividing the Cobb-Douglas production function $Y = e^{pt} K^\alpha L^{1-\alpha}$ by L leaves $Y/L = e^{pt}(K/L)^\alpha$ Again taking logarithms and differentiating with respect to time yields what we call the *per capita growth equation*:

$$G_{Y/L} = G_{TFP} + \alpha G_K - \alpha G_L \tag{3}$$

An added trade variable helps to explain the unknown growth of total factor productivity and factor accumulation, just as in equation (1). Adding a trade variable to the explanatory variables performs the same task as in the sources of growth equation (1). We will discuss the results of the simple and per capita regression models along with the results from the sources of growth regression model shown in Equation (1).

Another popular regression specification was pioneered by Feder (1982), who split the economy into an export sector and a non-export sector under the assumption that exports have external effects on the rest of the economy. He specified production functions of the export, X, and non-export sectors, N, as:

$$N = f(K, L, X) \quad \text{and} \quad X = g(K, L), \tag{4}$$

respectively. Feder also assumed that the export sector is more productive than the non-export sector, so that the growth of the export sector as a percentage of overall output enhances the economy's rate of growth. Feder shows that under a number of assumptions about marginal products in the two sectors of the economy, the following regression equation can be derived:

$$G_Y = \alpha/Y) + \beta G_L + \delta/Y)G_X + \theta G_X, \tag{5}$$

in which the coefficient δ captures the growth effect of the export sector's higher relative productivity and θ captures the externalities of export production on the rest of the economy. Quite a few studies have used Feder's regression model despite its strong assumptions.

There has always been concern that the relationship between trade and growth is bi-directional and that, therefore, estimates using single equation models were biased. Some researchers have used simultaneous equations models to deal with this problem. These models usually contained one of the above-mentioned regression equations along with other equations intended to capture various interrelationships among the variables. Instrumental variables (IV) regressions have also been used by researchers who were concerned about simultaneity bias.

There are, in fact, many econometric problems that researchers have addressed. Multicollinearity, simultaneity, omitted variable bias, nonstationary intertemporal processes, and measurement errors are just a few of the well-known problems that can lead to inconsistent results. Statisticians have found new procedures that mitigate some of these problems, and many of the empirical studies of trade and growth over the past three decades were motivated by the newer econometric methods and better data sets that promised to correct the statistical problems of earlier studies. An important question addressed in this survey is whether the many econometric improvements have improved our understanding of how trade is related to economic growth.

Researchers have also differed in how they defined international trade. Most studies simply inserted actual measures of exports, imports, total trade volume, trade as a share of GDP, or most often, the growth rates of exports. However, some of the most frequently-quoted studies of trade and growth used qualitative measures of 'openness' to international trade in place of direct measures of exports and imports. These 'openness' studies really test the association between trade liberalization and economic growth rather than the actual growth of trade and economic growth. For at least a decade after its publication, proponents of free trade policies for developing economies used a World Bank study reported in World Bank (1987) to support their position.[8] The World Bank subjectively classified countries as either 'strongly outward-oriented,' 'moderately outward-oriented,' 'moderately inward-oriented,' or 'strongly inward-oriented' on the basis of information on tariff levels, non-tariff barriers, black market premiums, etc. The study found that 'strongly outward-oriented' economies grew fastest, and economic growth rates were successively lower across the remaining three groups. Two other popular 'openness' studies are Dollar (1992) and Sachs and Warner (1995). The three often-referenced studies suggest that, on average, economies classified as being 'open' grew somewhere between 2 and 3 percent faster than economies classified as 'closed.'[9]

A common criticism of the openness studies has been that the openness indexes were often subjectively arrived at. Edwards (1998) tested the robustness of openness indexes; he found that the statistical results were relatively invariant to the manner in which the openness index was constructed. Nevertheless, the fact remains that the classification of countries into open and closed economies was not purely data-driven and usually involved some judgement. Rodrigues and Rodrik's (2001) criticism that trade and openness are closely correlated with other important policy variables was primarily directed at the openness studies. In fact, among the many openness indices used in empirical studies were policy variables borrowed from data sets such as Pritchett's (1996) *Tariff Restrictions and Non-Tariff Barriers*, Heitger's (1986) *Index of Effective Rates of Protection*, Harrison and Hanson's (1999) *Marketing Board Dummy*, Harrison and Hanson's (1999) *Socialist Dummy*, and Kornai's (1992) *Socialist Variable*.

Another frequently-used statistical method was causality analysis that used either single-equation Granger regressions or multi-equation vector autoregressions (VARs). Giles and Williams (2000a,b) and Ahmad (2001) provide thorough summaries of causality and VAR studies used to measure the effect of international trade on economic growth. Leamer (1985) provides a well-known critique of causality analysis. In general, these studies have not been very successful in proving that trade 'causes' economic growth.

There have also been a number of studies that have specified regressions in which all variables are in levels rather than growth rates. In their recent study, Frankel and Romer (1999) took this approach, claiming that the larger differences among the levels variables permits more accurate regression estimates.

This survey focuses on the large number of empirical regression studies that directly estimate the quantitative relationship between the growth of international trade, almost always specified as the growth of real exports, and economic growth. We leave out the openness studies, since their estimated coefficients are not immediately comparable to the coefficients from regressions like equation (1). We also omit the causality studies because they do not relate contemporaneous variables. Also, many causality studies report only significance levels, not coefficient values. And, we also leave out of our survey those regressions that were estimated with variables in levels rather than growth rates. There have been hundreds of sources of growth regressions and other specifications that generate compatible coefficient estimates, such as per capita regressions, single-equation regressions, and regressions using the Feder two-sector model, to give us a very large and robust set of results to analyze. At the end of this survey, we will offer some comparisons of our findings about the effects of trade on economic growth with the principal openness, causality, and levels regressions.

This survey groups the growth-trade regressions into eight categories: (1) cross-section regressions models using the basic sources of growth equation discussed above or some variation, (2) time-series regressions using a sources of growth equation, (3) cross-section regressions using the per capita version of the sources of growth equation, (4) time-series regressions using the per capita sources of growth equation, (5) cross-section regressions using the Feder two-sector model, (6) time-series regressions using the Feder two-sector model, (7) cross-section regressions using simultaneous equations models that contain some version of the sources of growth equation, and (8) time-series regressions using a simultaneous equations model. Each of these different sets of regressions generate, on average, similar estimates of the size of the relationship between international trade and economic growth. Some exceptions will be noted, however.

3. Cross-Section Regressions Using the 'Sources of Growth' Model

Regression analyses of the relationship between economic growth and the growth of international trade have applied cross-section data covering many different sets of countries. Frequently, researchers used observations consisting of average values for five- or ten-year periods in order to avoid the 'noise' of cyclical disturbances. Table 1 summarizes the results of the cross-section studies using regression models similar to the sources of growth equation (1) and TRADE specified as the growth rate of exports. We found 34 such studies that were carried out between 1973 and 2001, and they included a total of 196 different regressions. The mean of the 196 coefficients of the growth of real exports variable is 0.22. That is, on average and all other things equal, for every percentage point increase in the rate of growth of international trade, the rate of growth of the economy increased by a little over one-fifth of one percentage point. On average, the statistical significance of the coefficient estimates exceeds the 99 percent level, and the average t-value is equal to 3.46. For the entire set of 196 cross-section regressions, 111 (57 percent) of the coefficients fall between 0.15 and 0.45.

To supplement the averages in Table 1, we present a scatter diagram in Figure 1 of the estimated regression coefficients for the growth of exports from each of the 196 cross-section regressions, listed from left to right in order of publication date. The great majority of cross-section studies have found a positive relationship

Table 1. Cross-Section Coefficients: Regressing the Growth of Real GDP on the Growth of Real Exports.

	All Coefficients[1] (n = 196)
Average Coefficient Value	0.220
Median Coefficient Value	0.189
Average t-Statistic	3.460[**]
Maximum Coefficient Value	1.851
Minimum Coefficient Value	−1.433
Average Standard Error	0.021
Average 95% Confidence Interval[2]	± 0.042
Average Kurtosis Distribution	11.502
Average Skewness	−0.134

Notes: **Significant at the 95% level. *Significant at 90% level.
[1] The selected cross-sectional articles that contain the growth of exports on growth of output include: Lubitz (1973), Michalopoulos and Jay (1973), Balassa (1978), Krueger (1978), Tyler (1981), Feder (1982), Kavoussi (1984), Ram (1985), Rana (1986), Goncalves and Richtering (1987), Ram (1987), Rana (1988), Kohli and Singh (1989), Mbaku (1989), Moschos (1989), Fosu (1990), Sheehey (1990), Alam (1991), Esfahani (1991), Moore (1992), Sheehey (1992), Sprout and Weaver (1993), Coppin (1994), Hotchkiss *et al.* (1994), Van den Berg and Schmidt (1994), Yaghmaian (1994), Amirkhalkhali and Dar (1995), Song and Chen (1995), Yaghmaian and Ghorashi (1995), Balasubramanyam *et al.* (1996), Burney (1996), Fosu (1996), Park and Prime (1997), Sun and Parikh (2001).
[2] The mean of all of the 95 percent confidence intervals in the set of regressions included in the column.

between international trade and economic growth. Figure 2 shows the 95 percent confidence intervals of the point estimates shown in Figure 1. On average, 91 percent of the coefficient values covered by the confidence intervals are positive values. The coefficient estimates or their confidence intervals do not become noticeably larger or smaller over time, which suggests that the more sophisticated econometric methods of the more recent studies have not changed the empirical results. The most recent cross-section studies largely confirm the quantitative relationship between trade and growth revealed in earlier studies.

4. Time-Series Regressions Using the 'Sources of Growth' Model

Time-series analysis became popular in the 1990s after statisticians learned to avoid the 'spurious' relationships that standard OLS estimates are likely to report when variables are nonstationary.[10] Time-series regressions offer some advantages over cross-section analysis. Cross-section regressions effectively assume that the underlying production functions and regression parameters are constant across countries, and they generate results that do not clearly apply to any individual country and do not translate into country-specific conclusions. Time-series analysis permits researchers to analyze the importance of growth factors for individual countries. Presumably, institutions and production functions vary less over time than they do across countries, and time-series analysis may therefore be less vulnerable to Rodrigues and Rodrik's (2001) critique that the trade variable mistakenly captures the effects of other institutional and structural factors that

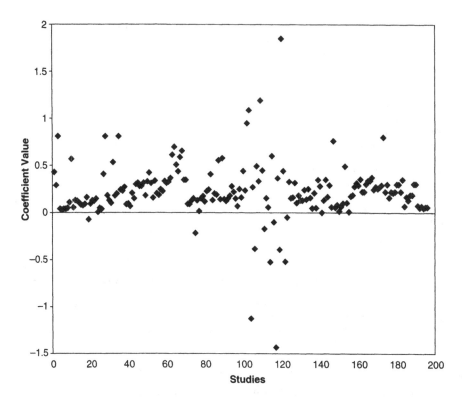

Figure 1. The Scatter of Coefficient Estimates for Cross-Section Regression from Table 1.

Regression observations 1–3 refer to Lubitz (1973), 4–5 to Michalopoulos and Jay (1973), 6–8 to Balassa (1978), 9 to Krueger (1978), 10–11 to Tyler (1981), 12–13 to Feder (1982), 14–19 to Kavoussi (1984), 20–23 to Ram (1985), 24–28 to Rana (1986), 29–32 to Goncalves and Richtering (1987), 33–62 to Ram (1987), 63–70 to Rana (1988), 71–78 to Kohli and Singh (1989), 79–84 to Mbaku (1989), 85–90 to Moschos (1989), 91–92 to Fosu (1990), 93 to Sheehey (1990), 94–99 to Alam (1991), 100–123 to Esfahani (1991), 123–125 to Moore (1992), 126 to Sheehey (1992), 127–129 to Sprout and Weaver (1993), 130–134 to Coppin (1994), 135–138 to Hotchkiss *et al.* (1994), 139–142 to Van den Berg and Schmidt (1994), 143–145 to Yaghmaian (1994), 146–155 to Amirkhalkhali and Dar (1995), 156–171 to Song and Chen (1995), 172–173 to Yaghmaian and Ghorashi (1995), 174–183 to Balasubramanyam *et al.* (1996), 184–186 to Burney (1996), 187–190 to Fosu (1996), 191–193 to Park and Prime (1997), and 194–196 to Sun and Parikh (2001).

vary across countries. Time-series analysis for individual countries also has the added benefit of permitting researchers to compare country results and to explicitly analyze the potential causes of those different outcomes.

Table 2 summarizes the coefficient values for the 402 time-series regressions from 19 different studies that specified regression equations similar to the sources of growth equation (1) with trade specified as the growth of exports. The average value of the 402 coefficients for the growth of real exports variable is 0.22, nearly identical to the average cross-section results. Thus, the time-series studies suggest

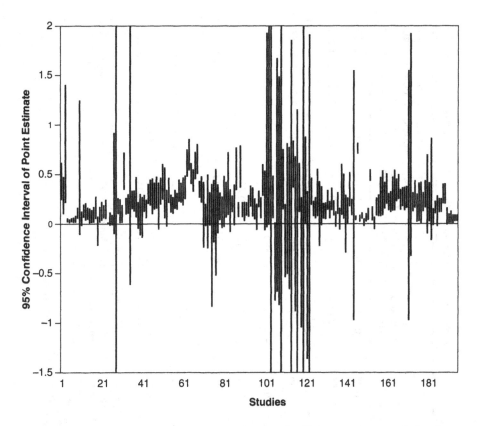

Figure 2. The 95 Percent Confidence Intervals for Coefficient Estimates of the Cross-Section Regression from Table 1.

Regression observations 1–3 refer to Lubitz (1973), 4–5 to Michalopoulos and Jay (1973), 6–8 to Balassa (1978), 9 to Krueger (1978) 10–11 to Tyler (1981), 12–13 to Feder (1982), 14–19 to Kavoussi (1984), 20–23 to Ram (1985), 24–28 to Rana (1986), 29–32 to Goncalves and Richtering (1987), 33–62 to Ram (1987), 63–70 to Rana (1988), 71–78 to Kohli and Singh (1989), 79–84 to Mbaku (1989), 85–90 to Moschos (1989), 91–92 to Fosu (1990), 93 to Sheehey (1990), 94–99 to Alam (1991), 100–123 to Esfahani (1991), 124–125 to Moore (1992), 126 to Sheehey (1992), 127–129 to Sprout and Weaver (1993), 130–134 to Coppin (1994), 135–138 to Hotchkiss *et al.* (1994), 139–142 to Van den Berg and Schmidt (1994), 143–145 to Yaghmaian (1994), 146–155 to Amirkhalkhali and Dar (1995), 156–171 to Songand Chen (1995), 172–173 to Yaghmaian and Ghorashi (1995), 174–183 to Balasubramanyam *et al.* (1996), 184–186 to Burney (1996), 187–190 to Fosu (1996), 191–193 to Park and Prime (1997), and 194–196 to Sun and Parikh (2001).

that, on average and all other things equal, for every one percentage point increase in the rate of growth of international trade, the rate of growth of the economy increases by a little over one-fifth of one percentage point. Figure 3 presents the scatter of estimated coefficients of the time-series studies listed from left to right in chronological order by date of publication, and Figure 4 shows the

Table 2. Time-Series Coefficients: Regressing the Growth of Real GDP on the Growth of Real Exports.

	All Coefficients[1] (n=402)	Simple Regression (n=100)	Multiple Regression (n=302)	No Unit Root Test (n=299)	Unit Root Test (n=103)	Open Classification[2] (n=91)	Closed Classification[2] (n=311)	Low Income[3] (n=147)	Lower Middle Income (n=141)	Upper Middle Income (n=85)	High Income (n=29)
Average Coefficient Value	0.215	0.200	0.219	0.261	0.081	0.309	0.187	0.206	0.217	0.154	0.429
Median Coefficient Value	0.119	0.138	0.113	0.167	0.059	0.230	0.096	0.113	0.123	0.073	0.365
Average t-Statistic	3.641**	3.277**	3.771**	4.172**	2.126**	4.533**	3.389**	3.212**	4.178**	2.350**	7.085**
Maximum Coefficient Value	1.386	1.386	1.301	1.386	0.463	1.386	1.301	1.301	1.285	1.301	1.386
Minimum Coefficient Value	−0.652	−0.590	−0.652	−0.652	−0.417	−0.652	−0.590	−0.138	−0.417	−0.590	−0.652
Average Standard Error	0.014	0.029	0.016	0.018	0.012	0.035	0.015	0.022	0.022	0.027	0.081
Average 95% Confidence Interval[4]	± 0.028	± 0.058	± 0.032	± 0.035	± 0.023	± 0.070	± 0.029	± 0.044	± 0.043	± 0.054	± 0.166
Average Kurtosis Distribution	3.048	4.695	2.558	1.844	4.335	1.337	4.098	2.724	3.293	7.871	0.464
Average Skewness	1.549	1.818	1.466	1.257	0.548	0.957	1.784	1.714	1.649	2.093	0.056

Notes: **Significant at the 95% level. *Significant at 90% level.
[1] Time-series articles that contain the growth of real exports on growth of real GDP include: Darrat (1987), Ram (1987), Grabowski (1988), Serletis (1992), Dodaro (1993), Khan and Saqib (1993), Atesoglu (1994), Sengupta and Espana (1994), Van den Berg and Schmidt (1994), Yaghmaian (1994), Amirkhalkhali and Dar (1995), Kwan *et al.* (1996), Van den Berg (1996a, 1996b), Al-Yousif (1997), Dhananjayan and Devi (1997), Van den Berg (1997), Amin Gutierrez de Pineres and Ferrantino (1999), Vohra (2001).
[2] We follow the Sachs and Warner (1995) criterion to classify trade regimes.
[3] Income groups are based on World Bank classification, see *World Development Reports*.
[4] The mean of all of the 95 percent confidence intervals in the set of regressions included in the column.

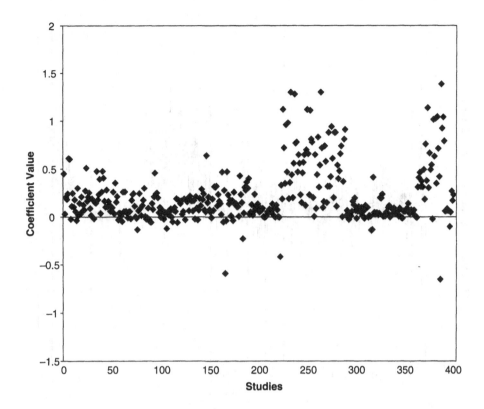

Figure 3. The Scatter of Coefficient Estimates for Time-Series Regression from Table 2.

Regression observations 1–4 refer to Darrat (1987), 5–92 to Ram (1987), 93–94 to Grabowski (1988), 95–98 to Serletis (1992), 99–185 to Dodaro (1993), 186–188 to Khan and Saqib (1993), 189–190 Atesoglu (1994), 191 to Senguta and Espana (1994), 192–255 to Van den Berg and Schmidt (1994), 226–290 to Yaghmaian (1994), 291–313 to Amirkhalkhali and Dar (1995), 314–316 to Kwan *et al.* (1996), 317–346 to Van den Berg (1996a), 347–364 to Van den Berg (1996b), 365–368 to Al-Yousif (1997), 369–392 to Dhananjayan and Devi (1997), 393–395 to Van den Berg (1997), 396–397 to Amin Gutrierrez de Pineres and Ferrantino (1999), and 398–402 to Vohra (2001).

95 percent confidence intervals of those point estimates in chronological order. In Figure 4, 84 percent of the confidence intervals for the 402 regressions cover positive values, which is slightly lower than the 91 percent of the confidence intervals that exceeded zero for the cross-section regressions using the same model.

The scatter of point estimates in Figure 3 and the intervals in Figure 4 do not appear to show any clear trends over time, suggesting that earlier time-series results have been confirmed by the more recent, and econometrically-superior, studies. Further analysis suggests that we should be careful about drawing such a conclusion, however. In order to explain the variation across regressions in Figure 3, Table 2 also reports the average estimate values for four sub-groupings: the 402 regressions are

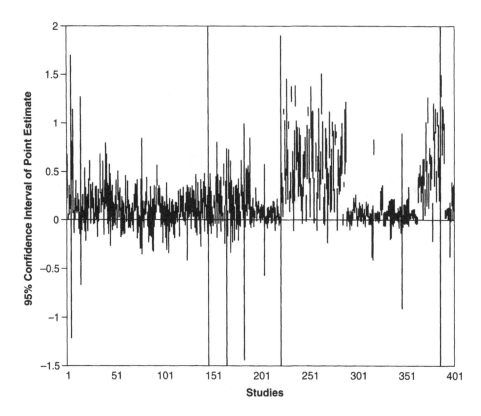

Figure 4. The 95 percent Confidence Intervals for Coefficient Estimates of Time-Series Regressions from Table 2.

Regression observations 1–4 refer to Darrat (1987), 5–92 to Ram (1987), 93–94 to Grabowski (1988), 95–98to Serietis (1992), 99–185 to Dodaro (1993), 186–188 to Khan and Saqib (1993), 189–190 to Atesoglu (1994), 191 to Sengupta and Espana (1994), 192–225 to Van den Berg and Schmidt (1994), 226–290 to Yaghmaian (1994), 291–313 to Amirkhalkhali and Dar (1995), 314–316 to Kwan *et al.* (1996), 317–346 to Van den Berg (1996a), 347–364 to Van den Berg (1996b), 365–368 to Al-Yousif (1997), 369–392 to Dhananyaan and Devi (1997), 393–395 to Van den Berg (1997), 396–397 to Amin Gutierrez de Pineres and Ferrantino (1999), 398–402 to Vohra (2001).

alternatively grouped by (1) whether they used simple or multiple regression models, (2) whether unit root tests were or were not performed and used, (3) the level of openness of the economy, and (4) the level of development of the economy.

The average of the 100 simple regression time-series estimates have a mean that is slightly smaller, 0.20, than the average of the remaining 302 multiple regression estimates, 0.22. The proportion of the confidence intervals covering positive coefficient values is 82 percent for simple regression estimates and 85 percent for multiple regression estimates.

The average value of the 299 coefficients from time-series regressions for which no unit root tests were performed is 0.26. This average point estimate is over three times as large as the average value of the growth of trade coefficient from 103 time-series regressions for which time-series estimation procedures were adjusted in accordance with unit root test results, which is just 0.08. The proportion of the 95 percent confidence intervals falling in the range of positive values is almost exactly the same for both subsets of time-series regressions, 85 percent for the former versus 82 percent for the latter. Thus, modern time-series methods do not weaken the statistical significance of trade's effect on economic growth, but they sharply reduce the size of the effect. Figures 5, 6, 7, and 8 present the scatters of coefficient estimates and intervals of time-series regressions that were not adjusted for potential unit roots and those that were adjusted for unit

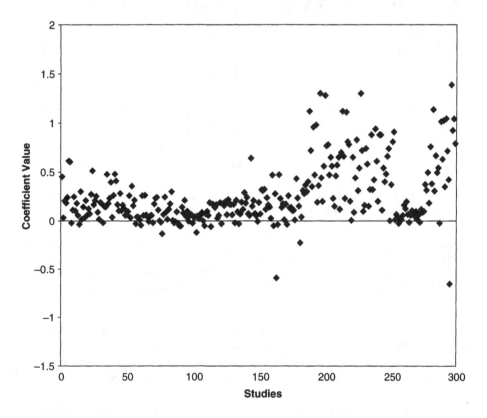

Figure 5. The Scatter of Coefficient Estimates for Time-Series Regressions with no Correction for Unit Roots from Table 2.

Regression observations 1–4 refer to Darrat (1987), 5–92 to Ram (1987), 93–94 to Grabowski (1988), 95–81 to Dodaro (1993), 182–184 to Khan and Saqib (1993), 185–186 to Atesoglu (1994), 187 to Sengupta and Espana (1994), 188–252 to Yaghamaian (1994), 253–275 to Amirkhalkhali and Dar (1995), 276–299 to Dhananjayan and Devi (1997).

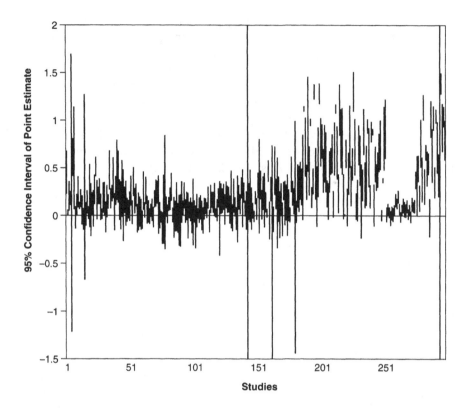

Figure 6. The 95 percent Confidence Intervals for Coefficient Estimates of Time-Series
Regression with no Correction for Unit Roots from Table 2.

Regression observations 1–4 refer to Darrat (1987), 5–92 to Ram (1987), 93–94 to
Grabowski (1988), 95–181 to Dodaro (1993), 182–184 to Khan and Saqib (1993), 185–186
to Atesoglu (1994), 187 to Sengupta ad Espana (1994), 188–252 to Yaghmaian (1994),
253–275 to Amirkhalkhali and Dar (1995), 276–299 to Dhananjayan and Devi (1997).

roots, respectively. It appears that spurious regression results have biased the
average coefficient estimate of 0.22 reported in column one of Table 2. Further
time-series analysis is clearly called for; panel regressions that combine the
advantages of cross-section and time-series methods may be an attractive
approach for future research.

 The set of time-series regressions was also split according to whether countries
were 'open' or 'closed' using Sachs and Warner's (1995) classification. Table 2
shows that the effect of international trade on growth is much greater in open
economies than in closed economies. The coefficient estimates for economies
classified as open is 0.31 compared to 0.19 for the closed economies. Moreover,
the percentage of the confidence intervals that cover positive values is greater for
economies classified as open, 92 percent, than those classified as closed,

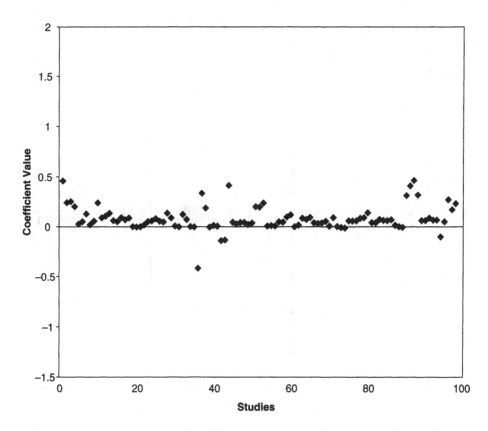

Figure 7. The Scatter of Coefficient Estimates for Time-Series Regressions Corrected for
Unit Roots from Table 2.

Regression Observations 1–4 refer to Serletis (1992), 5–38 to Van den Berg and Schmidt
(1994), 39–41 to Kwan *et al.* (1996), 42–71 to Van den Berg (1996a), 72–89 to Van den Berg
(1996b), 90–93 to Al-Yousif (1997), 94–96 to Van den Berg (1997), 97–98 to Amin
Gutierrez de Pineres and Ferrantino (1999), and 99–103 to Vohra (2001).

81 percent. Since Sachs and Warner used institutional and policy variables to
classify countries as open or closed, these differences in regressions results for
open and closed countries suggests, like Rodrigues and Rodrik (2001), that the
empirical analyses have been ignoring other important influences on economic
growth. In past regressions, the trade variable may have erroneously captured the
effects of cross-country differences in institutions, structures, and policies in
cross-section studies or the effects of year-to-year changes in those other influences in time-series studies.

The final disaggregation is based on per capita income. We classify countries
according to the World Bank's (2000) classification of low, lower-middle, upper-
middle, or high income countries. As with the cross-section results, time-series
estimates confirm that countries with higher income have larger trade-growth

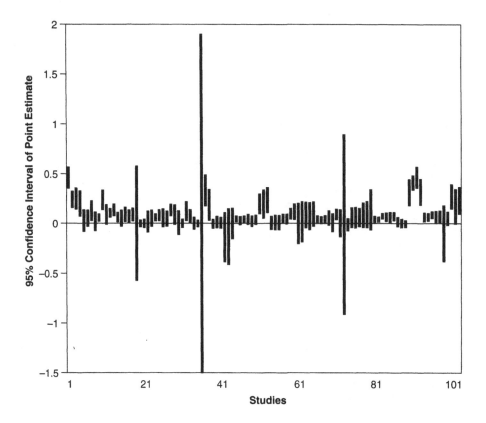

Figure 8. The 95 percent Confidence Intervals for Coefficient Estimates of Time-Series Regressions Corrected for Unit Roots from Table 2.

Regression observations 1–4 refer to Serletis (1992), 5–38 to Van den Berg and Schmidt (1994), 39–41 to Kwan *et al.* (1996), 42–71 to Van den Berg (1996a), 72–89 to Van den Berg (1996b), 90–93 to Al-Yousif (1997), 94–96 to Van den Berg (1997), 97–98 to Amin Gutierrez de Pineres and Ferrantino (1999), and 99–103 to Vohra (2001).

coefficients. The average coefficient on export growth for high income countries is 0.43, 0.15 for upper-middle, 0.22 for lower-middle, and 0.21 for low income. The fraction of the 95 percent confidence intervals covering the range of positive coefficient values is 93, 83, 88, and 80 percent for high, upper-middle, lower-middle, and low income low countries, respectively.

Many researchers have found evidence suggesting that trade generates more growth in developed economies than in developing countries. Among the empirical studies reviewed here, Tyler (1981), Kavoussi (1984), Moschos (1989), and Burney (1996) have found differences in coefficient values between high income and low income countries. The different growth rates may be due to developing countries' lower capacity to 'absorb' the foreign technology that accompanies trade, as suggested by Everson and Singh (1997) and Coe, Helpman, and Hoffmaister (1997).

5. The Per Capita Income and Feder Models

A number of studies have used the per capita income variant of the sources of growth regression model, as described earlier. Table 3 summarizes the average results for the cross-section and time-series regressions that specified per capita income as the dependent variable, as in Equation (3). The average cross-sectional coefficient value is 0.20 and the average time-series coefficient value is 0.21. These values are very close to the 0.22 average value for the earlier summary results. Figures 9 and 11 present the coefficient scatters and Figures 10 and 12 show the 95 percent confidence intervals for the cross-section and time-series per capita income regressions, respectively. The intervals fall predominantly in the positive region; on average, 92 percent of the cross-section intervals lie above zero, and 80 percent of the time-series intervals lie above zero, proportions that are similar to the results for the broad-based average cross-section and time-series results reported above.

Many researchers have used the Feder model, described earlier, to estimate the effects of trade on economic growth. The average coefficients from the 99 cross-section and 116 time-series regressions using the Feder model are about twice as large as the coefficients estimates using either the total income or per capita income sources of growth models. The average coefficient values of over 0.40 are comparable to those found by Feder in his own study. He claimed his high coefficient estimates reflected the fact that his model captures trade's effect on growth through two separate channels: (1) that the export sector of the economy is more productive and (2) that trade generates externalities that increase growth in other parts of the economy. The confidence intervals fall predominantly in the positive region; on average, 91 percent of the confidence intervals for the

Table 3. Regressions of the Growth of Real GDP per capita on the Growth of Real Exports.

	Cross-Section Coefficients[1] (n = 37)	Times-Series Coefficients[2] (n = 57)
Average Coefficient Value	0.199	0.211
Median Coefficient Value	0.140	0.101
Average t-Statistic	4.045**	2.118**
Maximum Coefficient Value	0.450	2.373
Minimum Coefficient Value	−0.122	−0.170
Average Standard Error	0.027	0.056
Average 95% Confidence Interval[3]	± 0.054	± 0.113
Average Kurtosis Distribution	−1.381	16.109
Average Skewness5	0.054	3.759

Notes: **Significant at the 95% level. *Significant at 90% level.
[1] The cross-section 37 regressions are from: Emery (1967), Syron and Walsh (1968), Salvatore (1983), Otani and Villaneuva (1990), Salvatore and Hatcher (1991), Greenaway and Sapsford (1994b).
[2] The 57 time-series regressions are from: Salvatore and Hatcher (1991), Greenaway and Sapsford (1994a), Rashid (1995), Greenaway, Morgan, and Wright (1997), Lin (2000).
[3] The mean of all of the 95 percent confidence intervals in the set of regressions included in the column.

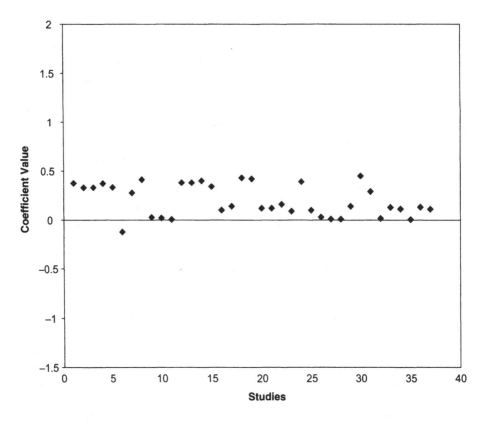

Figure 9. The Scatter of Coefficient Estimates of the Per Capita Income Cross-Section
Regression from Table 3.

Regression observations 1–2 refer to Emery (1967), 3–8 to Syron and Walsh (1968), 9–11 to
Salvatore (1983), 12–19 to Otani and Villaneuva (1990), 20–31 Salvatore and Hatcher
(1991), and 32–37 to Greenway and Sapsford (1994b).

cross-section regressions of Feder's model lie above zero, and 79 percent of the
95 percent confidence intervals for the time-series regressions lie above zero.
The higher average coefficient value from estimating Feder's model suggests
that the sources of growth regressions surveyed above may not account for all
of the growth effects of trade. Perhaps the average coefficient values of 0.22
reported for the sources of growth regressions are too low.

6. Dealing with Simultaneity

The relationship between international trade and economic growth is likely to be
bi-directional. International trade not only affects an economy's rate of economic
growth, but international trade is itself affected by the growth in an economy's
capacity to produce and generate income. Hence, it is not clear whether the

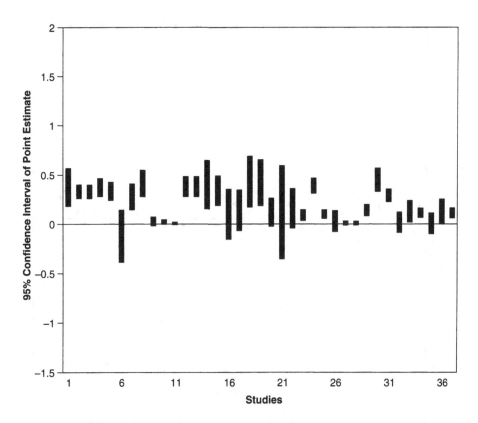

Figure 10. The 95 Percent Confidence Intervals for Coefficient Estimates of the Per-Capita Income Cross-Section Regressions from Table 3.

Regression observations 1–2 refer to Emery (1967), 3–8 to Syron and Walsh (1968), 9–11 to Salvatore (1983), 12–19 to Otani and Villaneuva (1990), 20–31 Salvatore and Hatcher (1991), and 32–37 to Greenaway and Sapsford (1994b).

coefficient in a regression model such as equation (1) reflects the effect of trade on growth or growth's effect on trade.

Sheehey (1990, 1992) used instrumental variables to replace direct measures of trade in his cross-section regressions. Another common approach for addressing simultaneity bias has been to specify simultaneous equations models and use 2SLS or 3SLS estimation methods. Esfanani (1991) used cross-section data in a three-equation model whose first equation is essentially equation (1) with trade represented by two variables, the growth of exports and the growth of imports. The model's second and third equations explain exports and imports, respectively. The growth of output serves as an explanatory variable in the second and third equations to capture the bi-directional influences. Sprout and Weaver (1993) used cross-section data in a three-equation model that endogenized output, investment, and exports. Van den Berg (1996a, 1996b) built on Esfahani and Sprout and

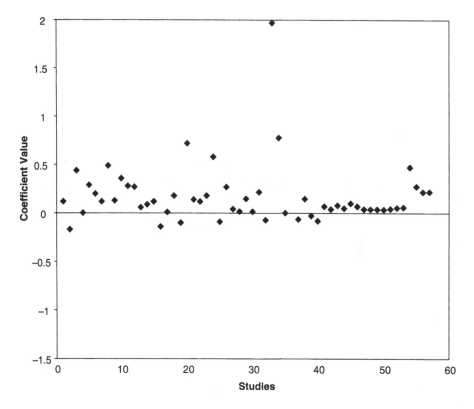

Figure 11. The Scatter of Coefficient Estimates of the Per Capita Income Time-Series Regressions from Table 3.

Regression observations 1–26 refer to Salvatore and Hatcher (1991), 27–40 to Greenaway and Sapsford (1994a), 41–48 to Rashid (1995), 49–54 to Greenaway, Morgan, and Wright (1997), and 55–57 to Lin (2000).

Weaver, using time-series data in a four-equation simultaneous-equations model that explicitly explains exports, imports, and investment. In two articles, he estimated and compared regression results from both single-equation and simultaneous equations systems for Asia and Latin America, respectively. His results suggest that simultaneity did not bias single-equation estimates toward confirming a positive relationship between trade and growth: more often than not, the coefficients for the growth of exports were larger and more significant in the simultaneous equation regressions than in single-equation regressions. Esfahani similarly found that his cross-section simultaneous equations regression estimates exceed his comparable single-equation coefficient estimates.

The average results for the set of cross-section and time-series studies that both use a standard growth equation such as equation (1) *and* adjust for potential simultaneity by using a simultaneous-equations regression model are summarized in Table 5. The average coefficient value for the 14 cross-section regressions is

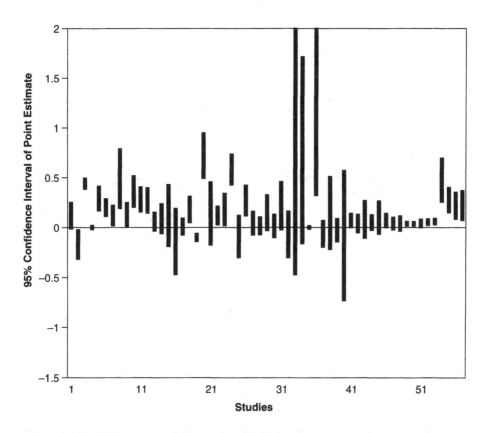

Figure 12. The 95 Percent Confidence Intervals for Coefficient Estimates of the Per Capita Income Time-Series Regressions from Table 3.

Regression observations 1–26 refers to Salvatore and Hatcher (1991), 27–40 to Greenaway and Sapsford (1994a), 41–48 to Rashid (1995), 49–54 to Greenaway, Morgan, and Wright (1997), and 55–57 to Lin (2000).

0.29. The average coefficient value for the 21 time-series regressions is 0.19. The 95 percent confidence intervals fall predominantly in the positive region, as before; 73 percent of the cross-section intervals and 91 percent of the time-series intervals lie in positive territory.[11] These estimates are comparable to the average coefficient values of the regressions reported earlier. Among the reasons suggested for the counter-intuitive result that the coefficients from simultaneous-equations regressions are not smaller than estimates from specifications that do not take bi-directional influences into account include sampling error and measurement bias. Frankel and Romer (1999) suggest that measurement error is caused by the fact that exports are an imperfect measure for the many international economic transactions that trade creates, which biases OLS results downward and potentially outweighs endogeneity bias. In any case, these results suggest that simultaneity did not bias the many single equation

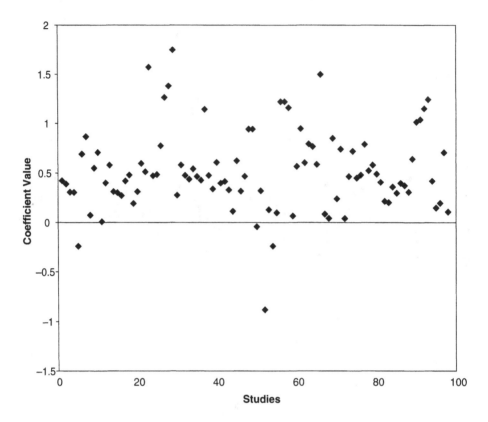

Figure 13. The Scatter of Coefficient Estimates of the Feder Cross-Section Regressions
from Table 4.

Regression observations 1–5 refer to Feder (1982), 6–11 to Balassa (1985), 12–20 to Rana
(1986), 21–42 to Ram (1987), 43–64 to Kohli and Singh (1989), 65–68 to Rana (1988), 69 to
Sheehey (1990), 70–73 to Moore (1992), 74–79 to Hotchkiss *et al.* (1994), 80–85 to Song
and Chen (1995), 86–88 to Park and Prime (1997), 89–93 to McNab and Moore (1998), and
94–98 to Sun and Parikh (2001).

regressions discussed earlier toward finding a positive relationship between growth
and trade.

7. Comparisons With Openness, Causality, and Levels Regressions

The cross-section and time-series regressions' average coefficient values of 0.22
seem small compared to the results for the qualitative 'openness' regressions
mentioned earlier in Section 2. Recall that several of the most popular openness
studies reported that economies classified as being 'open' grew between 2 and 3
percent faster than economies classified as 'closed.' However, upon some reflection, these large differences in annual growth rates between open and closed

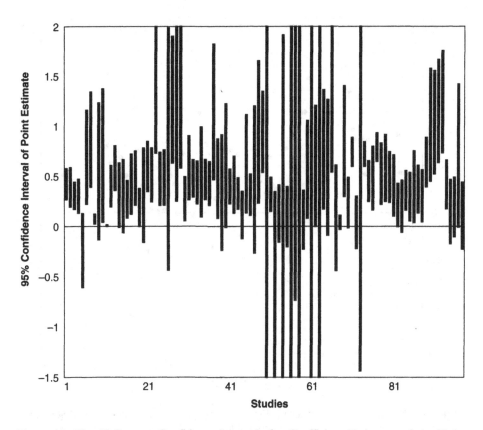

Figure 14. The 95 Percent Confidence Intervals for Coefficient Estimates of the Feder Cross-Section Regressions from Table 4.

Regression observatin 1–5 refer to Feder (1982), 6–11 to Balassa (1985), 12–20 to Rana (1986), 21–42 to Ram (1987), 43–64 to Kohli and Singh (1989), 65–68 to Rana (1988), 69 to Sheehey (1990), 70–73 to Moore (1992) 74–79 to Hotchkiss *et al.* (1994), 80–85 to Song and Chen (1995), 86–88 to Park and Prime (1997), 89–93 to McNab and Moore (1998), and 94–98 to Sun and Parikh (2001).

countries are not incompatible with the average results of cross-section and time-series regressions. A 0.22 percentage point increase in economic growth for every 1 percentage point increase in the growth of trade implies that for an economy to grow 2.5 percentage points faster than another economy it must expand trade between 11 and 12 percentage points faster. Some of the fast-growing export-oriented developing economies, such as Taiwan, South Korea, Singapore, Hong Kong or, more recently, China, actually expanded their exports at annual rates that were 10 percentage points faster than most economies in South Asia, Africa, and Latin America.[12] On average, during the 1980s all East Asian economies, most of which would be classified as 'open,' increased exports by 11.1 percent per year, while Sub-Saharan Africa and its mostly 'closed' economies increased its

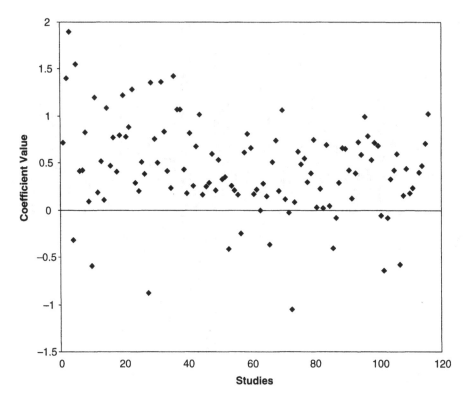

Figure 15. The Scatter of Coefficient Estimates of the Feder Time-Series Regression from Table 4.

Regression observations 1–88 refer to Ram (1987), 89 to Grabowski (1988), 90–93 to Sengupta (1993), 94 to Hansen (1994), 95–98 to Al-Yousif (1997), 99–11 to Ibrahim and MacPhee (1997), and 112–116 to Vohra (2001).

exports by just 2.4 percent per year, a difference of nearly 10 percentage points. During the 1990s, the growth rates of exports for the two regions were 12.6 percent and 4.4 percent, respectively.[13] Thus, the Sachs and Warner's (1995) findings using levels regressions are not out of line with the average coefficient values of the cross-section and time-series studies covered in this survey.

Causality studies use Granger regressions or VARs, which regress current economic growth on lagged trade and other lagged explanatory variables. It is difficult to interpret such an intertemporal relationship. And, because they lack a firm theoretical structure, many causality studies report only the statistical significance levels of the overall Granger regressions or VARs, not individual regression coefficients. An examination of 14 Granger causality regressions studies that did report coefficient values from regressing current economic growth on past trade growth reveals an average coefficient value of 0.17, a number not very different from the average of 0.22 for the many sources of growth regressions that we surveyed.[14]

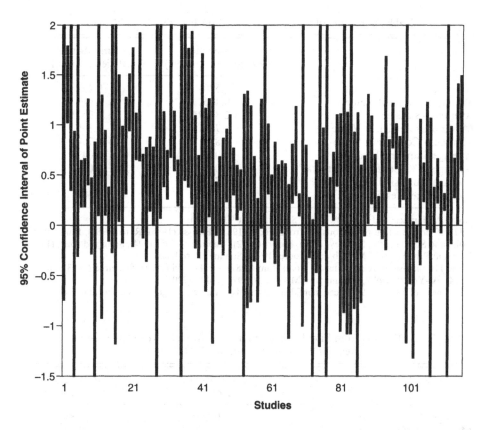

Figure 16. The 95 Percent Confidence Intervals for Coefficient Estimates of the Feder
Time-Series Regression from Table 4.

Regression observations 1–88 refer to Ram (1987), 89 to Grabowski (1988), 90–93 to
Sengupta (1993), 94 to Hansen (1994), 95–98 to Al-Yousif (1997), 99–11 to Ibrahim and
MacPhee (1997), and 112–116 to Vohra (2001).

Frankel and Romer (1999) regressed the level of per capita GDP on the share of
trade in GDP, and they found 'that, on average, a one percentage point increase
in the trade share raises income per person by 2.0 percent.'[15] Frankel and Romer's
results are compatible with the results of the sources of growth regressions that
relate economic growth and the growth of trade. International trade accounted
for about 12 percent of GDP in the world during the 1980s, a period covered by
Frankel and Romer and the majority of the cross-section and time-series studies
of trade and growth.[16] That means that, during that decade, a 1 percentage point
increase in the growth rate of trade was equivalent to an absolute increase in trade
of about 0.12 percent of GDP. Since Frankel and Romer estimated that a 1
percent increase in trade's share of GDP increased GDP by 2 percent, they
effectively found that an increase in trade of 0.12 percent of GDP leads to a

Table 4. Results of Regressions Based on Feder's (1982) Model.

	Cross-Section Coefficients[1] (n = 99)	Times-Series Coefficients[2] (n = 116)
Average Coefficient Value	0.520	0.421
Median Coefficient Value	0.466	0.419
Average t-Statistic	2.844**	1.953**
Maximum Coefficient Value	1.747	1.899
Minimum Coefficient Value	−0.880	−1.780
Average Standard Error	0.041	0.049
Average 95% Confidence Interval[3]	± 0.082	± 0.098
Average Kurtosis Distribution	1.560	2.559
Average Skewness5	0.378	−0.604

Notes: **Significant at the 95% level. *Significant at 90% level.
[1] The 99 cross-section regressions are from: Feder (1982), Balassa (1985), Rana (1986), Rana (1988), Kohli and Singh (1989), Sheehey (1990), Moore (1992), Hotchkiss *et al.* (1994), Song and Chen (1995), Park and Prime (1997), McNab and Moore (1998), Sun and Parikh (2001).
[2] The 116 time-series regressions are from: Ram (1987), Grabowski (1988), Sengupta (1993), Hansen (1994), Al-Yousif (1997), Ibrahim and MacPhee (1997), Vohra (2001).
[3] The mean of all of the 95 percent confidence intervals in the set of regressions included in the column.

Table 5. Coefficients from Simultaneous-Equations Models: Regressing the Growth of Real GDP on the Growth of Real Exports.

	Cross-Section Coefficients[1] (n = 14)	Times-Series Coefficients[2] (n = 21)
Average Coefficient Value	0.286	0.185
Median Coefficient Value	0.246	0.093
Average t-Statistic	1.261	2.613**
Maximum Coefficient Value	1.851	0.904
Minimum Coefficient Value	−0.518	−0.006
Average Standard Error	0.153	0.046
Average 95% Confidence Interval[3]	± 0.329	± 0.097
Average Kurtosis Distribution4	3.874	5.759
Average Skewness	1.437	2.133

Notes: **Significant at the 95% level. *Significant at 90% level.
[1] The selected cross-section articles that use a simultaneous equations model to correct for potential measurement errors include: Esfahani (1991) and Sprout and Weaver (1993). We have not included the 1960–1973 negative outlier from Esfahani in the summary.
[2] The selected time-series articles that use a simultaneous equations model to correct for potential measurement errors include: Grabowski (1988), Khan and Saqub (1993), Atesoglu (1994), Van den Berg (1996a,1996b), Van den Berg (1997), Amin Gutierrez de Pineres and Ferrantino (1999).
[3] The mean of all of the 95 percent confidence intervals in the set of regressions included in the column.

0.24 percent growth of GDP, which is very close to the 0.22 percentage point averaged by the sources of growth regressions reported in this survey.

In summary, the average coefficient of 0.22 that we find across the very large number of cross-section and time-series sources of growth regressions is not incompatible with the results of other popular regression models that tested the relationship between trade and growth. The exceptions to this conclusion are the Feder model regressions, which find a much stronger effect of trade on growth, and the modern time-series regressions that made adjustments for unit root variables, which found a much lower average coefficient for trade in the sources of growth model.

8. Conclusions: What We Know and What We Do Not Yet Know About Trade and Growth

There have been many statistical studies of the relationship between international trade and growth, and the results have been predominantly positive and statistically significant. This survey has focused on the *size* of the relationship between trade and growth to see whether this statistically-significant relationship is also economically-significant. The quantitative relationship is robust across many samples, data sets, and regression models. Explicit corrections for obvious econometric problems such as omitted variable bias and simultaneity bias do not seem to greatly alter the average quantitative result, which is that for every percentage point increase in the growth of trade, the rate of economic growth defined as either an increase in real GDP or real per capita GDP rises by slightly more than one-fifth of a percentage point.

These results suggest that a country whose exports grow by 12 percent per year, as in the case of East Asia during the 1980s, will grow by about 2.5 percentage points faster than a country whose trade grows by 2 percent per year, as was the average rate of export growth in Sub-Saharan Africa during the same decade. The power of compounding implies that such a 2.5 percent difference in growth rates will give the faster-growing country a GDP that is 12 times as great as the slower-growing country after just one century, a difference that is about equal to the income differences between today's most developed economies and the average developing country. Therefore, the average estimates for the coefficients of the growth of trade variables in the cross-section and time-series growth regressions suggest that the growth effects of trade are quite substantial. These results suggest that economists are indeed quite justified in promoting free trade policies as a good for economic growth and human welfare.

These important statistical results do not imply that economists' work is done, however. Quite to the contrary, there are many questions still to be answered. The large quantitative results only underscore the importance of addressing the many remaining questions. A serious weakness of the many statistical studies is that they have not yet shed much light on *why* the statistical relationship between trade and growth holds so robustly. Several recent studies have tried to distinguish the channels of influence through which trade enhances economic growth, but the results so far are merely suggestive.

For example, the Frankel and Romer (1999) study discussed earlier in this survey decomposed per capita real output into capital deepening, human capital investment, and overall labor productivity and then regressed each component of total output against a constant, the trade share, population, and area. They found that 'a one-percentage point increase in the trade share raises the contributions of both physical capital depth and schooling by about one-half of a percentage point, and the contribution of technology to per capita output by about two percentage points.'[17] Their finding suggests that it may indeed be appropriate to model international trade using the sources of growth equation (1), in which the TRADE variable helps to explain the growth of total factor productivity as well as factor accumulation.

An ambitious attempt to distinguish the channels through which international trade influences economic growth is by Wacziarg (2001). He hypothesized that trade effects economic growth through six potential channels: (1) macroeconomic policy quality, (2) government size, (3) price distortions or black market premium, (4) investment share of GDP, (5) technology, and (6) foreign direct investment. He specifies a simultaneous equations model consisting of an extended growth equation, an equation to capture the simultaneity between growth and trade, plus six channel equations in which an openness index is one of the explanatory variables. Wacziarg's results show that the most important channel through which trade influences economic growth is investment, accounting for 63 percent of trade's total growth effect. The technology channel (22.5 percent of trade's total growth effect), and stabilizing macroeconomic policy (18 percent of trade's total growth effect) account for nearly all of the remainder of trade's positive influence on growth.[18] These results reinforce Levine and Renelt's (1992) finding that international trade acts through investment to influence economic growth.

More time-series regressions need to be performed in order to clarify why the regressions that adjusted for unit roots gave a much lower, albeit equally significant, average estimate of international trade's influence on economic growth. Also, Rodriguez and Rodrik's critique that trade merely serves as a proxy for a myriad of other important policy variables cannot be easily rejected. Omitted variable bias and simultaneous relationships undoubtedly still plague even the most sophisticated statistical models, and we cannot yet feel confident that robust results have been achieved.

The greatest task for economists is to develop a consistent body of theory that explains the relationship between trade and growth. Unlike the traditional body of static trade theory, in which the major intellectual battles were fought using logical reasoning rather than empirical analysis, the intellectual battles over the relationship between trade and growth have, so far, been predominantly econometric. A widely accepted body of theory to link trade and growth has not yet emerged. Fortunately, growth theory has progressed rapidly over the past decade. The challenge for trade economists is therefore to combine what is known about economic growth, the incentives that guide human behavior, and how international trade affects those incentives into models that firmly establish the logic of *how* international trade influences economic growth. Until we agree on a logical explanation why trade and growth go together, it is not likely that we will agree that the statistical results have robustly settled the matter. Romer (1990), Rivera-Batiz and Romer (1991), Grossman and Helpman (1991), Baldwin (1992), Holmes and Schmitz (1995), Devereux (1997), among many other contributors to the growth literature, have pointed out some the directions that our theoretical work should pursue. This survey suggests that we proceed with urgency. The impact of trade on economic growth appears to be very important for human welfare.

Acknowledgments

We would like to thank the editors and two anonymous referees for their very helpful comments on an earlier draft of this paper. The authors of course remain fully responsible for all content.

Notes

1. Johnson (1971), p. 187. Blendon, *et al.* (1997) reported that nine out of ten economists favored further international agreements to liberalize trade.
2. See for example Feenstra (1992), Hufbauer and Elliott (1994), Sazanami, Urata, and Kawai (1995), Wall (2000), and Messerlin (2001), among many others.
3. Srinivasan (1997), p. 38.
4. For example, see Charles I. Jones (2002).
5. Even Srinivasan has since backtracked somewhat and called for more detailed country studies to supplement the many statistical studies; see T. N. Srinivasan and Jagdish Bhagwati (1999).
6. For an interesting summary of this literature, see Anne O. Krueger (1997).
7. For a description of the Penn World Table, see Summers and Heston (1991).
8. The study's results are summarized in Figure 5.1 on p. 83 of World Bank (1987).
9. Rodriguez and Rodrik (2001), op. cit., tabulate how often individual empirical studies were cited in the economics literature; the World Bank (1987, Dollar (1992), and Sachs and Warner (1995) studies were the three most-often referenced openness studies.
10. See Granger and Newbold (1974) for an extensive study on the spurious regression problem.
11. The usual scatter and interval diagrams are not shown for these cases; they look very similar to earlier diagrams and add no new insights.
12. See Maddison (2001), Tables F-2, F-4, and F-5.
13. World Bank (2000), *World Development Report 2000/2001*, New York: Oxford University Press, Table 11, pp. 294–295.
14. These regressions are from Hsiao (1987), Sung-Shen, Biswas, and Tribedy (1900), Supo Alege (1993), Holman and Graves (1995), Amin Gutierrez de Pineres and Ferrantino (1997), Shan and Sun (1998), and Amin Gutierrez de Pineres and Ferrantino (1999).
15. Frankel and Romer (1999), op. cit., p. 387.
16. See Angus Maddison (2001)., *The World Economy, A Millennial Perspective*, Paris: OECD, Tables F-3 and F-5, and Table C5-b.
17. Frankel and Romer (1999), op. cit., pp. 390.
18. The channels shares to not add up to one because Wacziarg found some channels to have negative effects on growth.

References

Ahmad, J., (2001) Causality between exports and economic growth: what do the econometric studies tell us? *Pacific Economic Review* 6, 147–167.
Alam, M.S., (1991) Trade orientation and macroeconomic performance in LDCs: an empirical study. *Economic Development and Cultural Change* 39, 839–848.

Al-Yousif, Y.K., (1997) Exports and economic growth: some empirical evidence from the Arab gulf countries. *Applied Economics* 29, 263–267.

Amin Gutierrez de Pineres, S., Ferrantino, M., (1997) Export diversification and structural dynamics in the growth process: the case of Chile. *Journal of Development Economics* 52, 375–391.

Amin Gutierrez de Pineres, S., Ferrantino, M., (1999) Export sector dynamics and domestic growth: the case of Colombia. *Review of Development Economics* 3, 268–280.

Amirkhalkhali, S., Dar, A., (1995) A varying-coefficients model of export expansion, factor accumulation and economic growth: evidence from cross-country, time series data. *Economic Modeling* 12, 435–441.

Atesoglu, H.S., (1994) An application of a Kaldorain export-led model of growth to the United States. *Applied Economics* 26, 479–483.

Balassa, B., (1978) Exports and economic growth: further evidence. *Journal of Development Economics* 5, 181–189.

Balassa, B., (1985) Exports, policy choices, and economic growth in developing countries after the 1973 oil shock. *Journal of Development Economics* 18, 23–35.

Balasubramanyam, V.N., Salisu, M., Sapsford, D., (1996) Foreign direct investment and growth in EP and IS countries. *Economic Journal* 26, 92–105.

Baldwin, R.E., (1992) Measurable dynamic gains from trade. *Journal of Political Economy* 100, 162–174.

Bernard, J. and Jensen, J. B., (1999) Exceptional exporter performance: cause, effect, or both? *Journal of International Economics* 47, 1–25.

Blendon, Robert J., Benscn, J., Brodie, M., Morin, R., Altman, D., Gitterman, D., Brossard, M., James, M., (1997) Bridging the gap between the public's and economists' views of the economy. *Journal of Economic Perspectives* 11, 105–18.

Burney, N.A., (1996) Exports and economic growth: evidence from cross country analysis. *Applied Economic Letters* 3, 369–373.

Clerides, S., Lach, S., Tybout, J., (1998) Is learning by exporting important? Microdynamic evidence from Colombia, Mexico, and Morocco. *Quarterly Journal of Economics* 113, 903–947.

Coe, D.T., Helpman, E, Hoffmaister, A.W., (1997) North-south r&d spillovers. *Economic Journal* 107, 134–149.

Coppin, A., (1994) Determinants of LDC output growth during the 1980s. *Journal of Developing Areas* 28, 219–228.

Darrat, A.F., (1987) Are exports an engine of growth? Another look at the evidence. *Applied Economics* 19, 277–283.

Davis, D.R., Weinstein, D. E., (2001) What role for empirics in international trade? *NBER Working Paper* No. 8543.

Dertouzos, M., Lester, R., Solow, R., (1990) *Made in America: Regaining the Competitive Edge*, MIT Press, Cambridge, Massachusetts.

Devereux, M. B., (1997) Growth, specialization, and trade liberalization. *International Economic Review* 38, 565–585.

Dhananjayan, R.S., Devi, S.N., (1997) Exports and economic growth: a study of select nations in Asia and Europe during 1980–81 to 1993–94. *Indian Journal of Applied Economics* 6, 41–63.

Dodaro, S., (1993) Exports and growth: a reconsideration of causality. *Journal of Developing Areas* 27, 227–244.

Dollar, D., (1992) Outward-oriented developing economies really do grow more rapidly: evidence from 95 LDCs, 1976–1985. *Economic Development and Cultural Change* 40, 523–544.

Edwards, S., (1998) Openness, productivity and growth: what do we really know? *Economic Journal* 108, 383–398.

Esfahani, H.S., (1991) Exports, imports, and economic growth in semi-industrialized countries. *Journal of Development Economics* 35, 93–116.

Emery, R.F., (1967) The relation of exports and economic growth. *Kyklos* 20, 470–486.

Evenson, R.E., Singh, L., (1997) Economic growth, international technology spillovers and public policy: theory and empirical evidence from Asia. Discussion paper 777, Economic Growth Center, Yale University.

Feder, G., (1982) On exports and economic growth. *Journal of Development Economics* 12, 59–72.

Feenstra, R.C., (1992) How costly is protectionism? *Journal of Economic Perspectives* 6, 159–178.

Fosu, A.K., (1990) Exports and economic growth: the African case. *World Development* 18, 831–835.

Fosu, A. K., (1996) Primary exports and economic growth in developing countries. *World Economy* 19, 465–475.

Frankel, J.A., Romer, D., (1999) Does trade cause growth? *American Economic Review* 89, 379–399.

Giles, J.A., Williams, C.L., (2000a) Export-led growth: a survey of the empirical literature and some non-causality results: part 1. *Journal of International Trade and Economic Development* 9, 261–337.

Giles, J.A., Williams, C.L., (2000b) Export-led growth: a survey of the empirical literature and some non-causality results: part 2. *Journal of International Trade and Economic Development* 9, 445–470.

Goncalves, R., Richtering, J., (1987) Intercountry comparison of export performance and output growth. *The Developing Economies* 25, 3–18.

Grabowski, R., (1988) Early Japanese development: the role of trade, 1885–1940. *Quarterly Journal of Business and Economics* 27, 104–129.

Granger, C.W.J., Newbold, P., (1974) Spurious regressions in econometrics. *Journal of Econometrics* 2, 419–35.

Greenaway, D., and Sapsford, D., (1994a) What does liberalization do for exports and growth. *Weltwirschaftliches Archiv* 130, 152–174.

Greenaway, D., and Sapsford, D., (1994b) Exports, growth, and liberalization: an evaluation. *Journal of Policy Modelling* 16, 165–186.

Greenaway, D., Morgan, W., Wright, P., (1997) Trade liberalization and growth in developing countries: some new evidence. *World Development* 25, 1885–1892.

Grossman, G. M., Helpman, E., (1991) *Innovation and Growth in the Global Economy*. MIT Press, Cambridge.

Hansen, P., (1994) The government, exporters and economic growth in New Zealand. *New Zealand Economic Papers* 28, 133–142.

Harrison, A., Hanson, G., (1999) Who gains from trade reform? Some remaining puzzles. *Journal of Development Economics* 59, 125–154.

Heitger, B., (1986) Import protection and export performance: their impact on economic growth. *Weltwirschaftliches Archiv* 260, 1–17.

Helpman, E., (1999) The structure of foreign trade. *Journal of Economic Perspectives* 13, 121–144.

Holman, J.A., Graves, P.E., (1995) Korean exports economic growth: an econometric reassessment. *Journal of Economic Development* 20, 45–56.

Holmes, T.J., Schmitz, J.A., (1995) Resistence to new technology and trade between areas. *Federal Reserve Bank of Minneapolis Quarterly Review* 19, 2–17.

Hotchkiss, J.L., Moore, R.E., Rockel, M., (1994) Export expansion and growth at different stages of development. *Journal of Economic Development* 19, 87–105.

Hsiao, M-C. W., (1987) Tests of causality and exogeneity between exports and economic growth: the case of Asian NICs. *Journal of Economic Development* 12, 143–159.

Hufbauer, C., Elliott, K., (1994) Measuring the Costs of Protection in the United States. *Institute for International Economics*, Washington, D.C.

Ibrahim, I., MacPhee, C.R., (1997) Export externalities and economic growth. *University of Nebraska Working Paper*, May.

Irwin, D.A., (1996) *Against the Tide*. Princeton University Press, Princeton, New Jersey .

Johnson, H.G., (1971) *Aspects of the Theory of Tariffs*. Harvard University Press, Cambridge.

Jones, C.I., (2002) *Introduction to Economic Growth*. Second Edition. W.W Norton & Company, New York.

Kavoussi, R.M., (1984) Export expansion and economic growth: further empirical evidence. *Journal of Development Economics* 14, 241–250.

Khan, A.H., Saqib, N., (1993) Exports and economic growth: the Pakistan experience. *International Economic Journal* 7, 53–64.

Kohli, I., Singh, N., (1989) Exports and growth: critical minimum effort and diminishing returns. *Journal of Monetary Economics* 30, 391–400.

Kornai. J., (1992) *The Socialist System: The Political Economy of Communism*. Princeton University Press, Princeton, New Jersey.

Krueger, A. O., (1978) *Foreign Trade Regimes and Economic Development: Liberalization Attempts and Consequences*. Ballinger Publishing Company for NBER, Cambridge.

Krueger, A.O., (1997) Trade policy and economic development: how we learn. *American Economic Review* 87, 1–22.

Kwan, A.C.C., Cotsomitis, J.A., Kwok, B., (1996) Exports, economic growth and exogeneity: Taiwan 1953–88. *Applied Economics* 28, 467–471.

Leamer, E.E., (1985) Vector autoregresstions for causal inference, in Brunner, K., Meltzer, A.H. (Eds.), *Carnegie-Rochester Conference Series on Public Policy: Understanding Monetary Regimes* 22, McGraw-Hill, New York, 255–304.

Leontief, W. W., (1953) Domestic production and foreign trade: the American capital position re-examined. *Proceedings of the American Philosophical Society* 97, 332–349.

Levine R., Renelt, D., (1992) A sensitivity analysis of cross-country growth. *American Economic Review* 82, 942–963.

Lin, S., (2000) Foreign trade and China's economic development: a time-series analysis. *Journal of Economic Development* 25, 145–153.

Lubitz, R., (1973) Export-led growth in industrialized economies. *Kyklos* 26, 307–320.

MacDonald, J., (1994) Does import competition force efficient production? *The Review of Economics and Statistics* 74, 721–727.

Maddison, A., (1995) *Monitoring the World Economy 1820–1992*, OECD, Paris.

Maddison, A., (2001) *The World Economy, A Millennial Perspective*, OECD, Paris.

Mbaku, J.M., (1989) Export growth and economic performance in developing countries: further evidence from Africa. *Journal of Economic Development* 14, 127–142.

McNab, R.M., Moore, R.E., (1998) Trade policy, export expansion, human capital and growth. *Journal of International Trade and Economic Development* 7, 237–256.

Messerlin, P.A., (2001) *Measuring the Costs of Protection in Europe: European Commercial Policy in the 2000s*, The Institute for International Economics, Washington, D.C.

Michaely, M., (1977) Exports and growth: an empirical investigation. *Journal of Development Economics* 4, 49–53.

Michalopoulos, C., Jay, K., (1973) Growth of exports and income in the developing world: a neoclassical view. *AID Discussion Paper* No. 28, 1–26.

Moore, R.E., (1992) The level of development and GSP treatment: an empirical investigation into the differential impacts of export expansion. *Journal of World Trade* 26, 19–30.

Moschos, D., (1989) Export expansion, growth and the level of economic development: an empirical analysis. *Journal of Development Economics* 30, 93–102.

Otani, I., Villaneuva, D., (1990) Long-term growth in developing countries and its determinants: an empirical analysis. *World Development* 18, 769–783.

Parente, S., Prescott, E. (2000) *Barriers to Riches*, MIT Press, Cambridge, Massachusetts.

Park, J.H., Prime, P.B., (1997) Export performance and growth in China: a cross-provincial analysis. *Applied Economics* 29, 1353–1363.

Pritchett, L., (1996) Measuring outward orientation: can it be done? *Journal of Development Economics* 49, 51–61.

Ram, R., (1985) Exports and economic growth: some additional evidence. *Economic Development and Cultural Change* 33, 415–425.

Ram, R., (1987) Exports and economic growth in developing countries: evidence from time-series and cross-section data. *Economic Development and Cultural Change* 36, 51–72.

Rana, P.B., (1986) Exports and economic growth: further evidence from Asian LDCs. *Pakistan Journal of Applied Economics* 5, 163–178.

Rana, P.B., (1988) Exports, policy changes, and economic growth in developing countries after the 1973 oil shock. *Journal of Development Economics* 28, 261–264.

Rashid, A.I., (1995) Trade, growth, and liberalization: the Indian experience, 1977–1989. *The Journal of Developing Areas* 29, 355–370.

Rivera-Batiz, L., Romer, P.M., (1991) Economic integration and endogenous growth. *Quarterly Journal of Economics* 56, 531–555.

Rodriguez, F., Rodrik, D., (2001) Trade policy and economic growth: a skeptics guide to the cross-national evidence. In Bernanke, B., Rogoff, K. S. (Eds.), *NBER Macroeconomics Annual 2000*, MIT Press, Cambridge, Massachusetts.

Rodrik, D., Subramanian, A., Trebbi, F., (2002) Institutions rule: the primacy of institutions over geography and integration in economic development. *NBER working paper* w9305, November.

Romer, P.M., (1990) Endogenous technological change. *Journal of Political Economy* 95, S71–S102.

Sachs, J.D., Warner, A., (1995) Economic reforms and the process of global integration. *Brookings Papers on Economic Activity* 1, 1–118.

Salvatore, D., (1983) A simultaneous equations model of trade and development with dynamic policy simulations. *Kyklos* 36, 66–90.

Salvatore, D., Hatcher, T., (1991) Inward and outward oriented trade strategies. *Journal of Development Studies* 27, 7–25.

Sazanami, Y., Shujiro U., Hiroki K., (1995) *Measuring the Costs of Protection in Japan*. Institute for International Economics, Washington, D.C.

Sengupta, J.K., (1993) Growth in NICs in Asia: some tests of new growth theory. *Journal of Development Studies* 29, 342–357.

Sengupta, J.K., Espana, J.R., (1994) Exports and economic growth in Asian NICs: an econometric analysis for Korea. *Applied Economics* 26, 45–51.

Serletis, A., (1992) Export growth and Canadian economic development. *Journal of Development Economics* 38, 133–145.

Shan, J., Sun, F., (1998) On the export-led growth hypothesis for the little dragons: an empirical reinvestigation. *Atlantic Economic Journal* 26, 353–371.

Sheehey, E.J., (1990) Exports and growth: a flawed framework. *Journal of Development Studies* 27, 111–116.

Sheehey, E.J., (1992) Exports and growth: additional evidence. *Journal of Development Studies* 28, 730–734.

Song, L., Chen, T., (1995) On exports and economic growth: further evidence. *Pacific Economic Papers* 242, 1–23.

Sprout, R.V.A., Weaver, J.H., (1993) Exports and economic growth in a simultaneous equations model. *Journal of Developing Areas* 28, 289–306.

Srinivasan, T. N., (1997) As the century turns: analytics, empirics, and politics of development. Working Paper, Economic Growth Center, Yale University, December.

Srinivasan, T. N., Bhagwati, J., (1999) Outward-orientation and development: are revisionists right? Working Paper, September 17.

Summers, R., Heston, A., (1991) The Penn World Table (Mark 5): an expanded set of international comparisons, 1950–1988. *Quarterly Journal of Economics* 106, 327–368.

Sun, H., Parikh, A., (2001) Exports, inward foreign direct investment (FDI) and regional economic growth in China. *Regional Studies* 35, 187–196.

Sung-Shen, N., Biswas, B., Tribedy, G., (1990) Causality between exports and economic growth: an empirical study. *Journal of Economic Development* 15, 47–61.

Supo Alege, P., (1993) Export and growth in the Nigerian economy: a causality test. *Indian Journal of Economics* 73, 397–416.

Syron, R., Walsh, B., (1968) The relation of exports and economic growth. *Kyklos* 21, 541–545.

Trefler, D., (1995) The case of the missing trade and other HOV mysteries. *American Economic Review* 85, 1029–1047.

Tyler, W.G., (1981) Growth and export expansion in developing countries: some empirical evidence. *Journal of Development Economics* 9, 121–130.

Van den Berg, H., (1996a) Trade as the engine of growth in Asia: what the econometric evidence reveals. *Journal of Economic Integration* 11, 510–538.

Van den Berg, H., (1996b) Libre comercio y crecimiento: la evidence econometrica para America Latina. *Comercio Exterior* 46, 364–373.

Van den Berg, H., (1997) The relationship between international trade and economic growth in Mexico. *North American Journal of Economics and Finance* 8, 1–21.

Van den Berg, H., Schmidt, J.R., (1994) Foreign trade and economic growth: time series evidence from Latin America. *The Journal of International Trade and Economic Development* 27, 249–268.

Vohra, R., (2001) Export and economic growth: further time series evidence from less-developed countries. *International Advances in Economic Research* 7, 345–350.

Wall, H.J., (2000) Using the gravity model to estimate the costs of protection, *St. Louis Federal Reserve Bank Review* 81, 33–40.

Wacziarg, R., (2001) Measuring the dynamic gains from trade. *World Bank Economic Review* 15, 393–429.

World Bank, (1987) *The World Bank World Development Report.* The World Bank, New York.

World Bank, (2000) *World Development Report 2000/2001.* Oxford University Press, New York.

Yaghmaian, B., (1994) An empirical investigation of exports, development and growth in developing countries: challenging the neo-classical theory of export-led growth. *World Development* 22, 1977–1995.

Yaghmaian, B., Ghorashi, R., (1995) Export performance and economic development: an empirical analysis. *The American Economist* 39, 37–45.

6

FISCAL POLICY AND ECONOMIC GROWTH

Martin Zagler

Vienna University of Economics & Business Administration and Free University of Bozen - Bolzano

Georg Dürnecker

Vienna University of Economics & Business Administration

1. Introduction

In recent years, a vast literature has emerged on the relationship between fiscal policy and long-run economic growth. In order to give an overview of the recent discussion and establish a point of departure for future research, this survey attempts to provide a creative synthesis of existing research in the field.

Fiscal policy, in essence, is a short-run issue. In the debate on economic policy, fiscal policy is predominantly viewed as an instrument to mitigate short-run fluctuations of output and employment. By a variation in government spending or taxation, fiscal policy aims at altering aggregate demand in order to move the economy closer to potential output. Hence the quality of fiscal policy should be evaluated by its capability to dampen output fluctuations. Nonetheless, we cannot and should not ignore the long-run implications of short run policy instruments in taxation and government expenditure.

On the expenditure side, several fiscal policy instruments are known to exhibit long-run effects. For instance, early models of endogenous growth have introduced public expenditure categories as the engine of economic growth. In his seminal paper on endogenous growth, Robert Lucas (1988) argues that investment into education increases the level of human capital. This increases the resource base of the economy, and thus output. If the returns to education do not decline over time due to non-decreasing returns to scale in reproducible factors of production, education expenditure can be seen as the main source of long-run economic growth. Given credit market imperfections and human capital externalities, private agents have only partial incentives, and not enough means, to finance their own education. For this reason, publicly provided education can reduce or eliminate the externalities in the human capital accumulation process. Thus any changes in the public provision of educational services, induced by a short-run change in fiscal policy, will alter the process of human capital accumulation and thus long-run economic growth. Even in the absence of credit market imperfections there is room for public education policy, if education is subject to congestion (Keuschnigg and Fisher, 2002). Other examples for the influence of government expenditure on economic growth are public infrastructure (Barro, 1990), research and development expenditures (Romer, 1990), and health expenditures (Bloom *et al.*, 2001).

On the revenue side, taxes are known to distort private agents' decisions with respect to factor accumulation and supply. Insofar as distortionary taxes interfere in the private decision to save and invest, they may very well change the accumulation process of capital, and thus alter the growth rate of the economy (Milesi-Feretti and Roubini, 1998). Given that endogenous growth models intrinsically contain externalities, either in the accumulation of physical or human capital or in the innovation process, distortionary taxation can internalize the effect of the externality in private decision rules, and thus induce the efficient allocation (Turnovsky, 1996).

Finally, fiscal policy in the short-run is considered expansionary (contractionary), when public expenditures exceed (fall short of) public revenues. The resulting deficit can be interpreted as a means to finance additional government expenditures. If these expenditures are growth enhancing, then a government deficit exhibits an indirect effect on long-run economic growth. In a Ricardian world, where agents view the deficit simply as taxes delayed, there should, however, be no difference between tax and deficit finance of government expenditures, unless the tax structure will be different in the future from today (Ludvigson, 1996). If the economy is non-Ricardian, e.g. due to credit imperfections or overlapping generations, then public debt can change the private incentives to accumulation and thus directly influence the rate of growth in the economy (Zagler, 1999, 46ff).

After this introduction, the next section of this survey establishes a unifying framework for the analysis of the impact of fiscal policy instruments on economic growth, in order to provide a creative synthesis of the recent literature on growth and fiscal policy. Thereafter we discuss relevant literature on public expenditure and economic growth, where we separate between productive and unproductive expenditure. Focusing on productive expenditure, we further separate between public infrastructure, education and health expenditures, and research and development activities. After this discussion of public expenditure, we analyse public revenues, where we first focus on labour and profit taxation, then capital and consumption taxation, before finally investigating the growth implications of public debt.

2. A unifying framework

This section presents a simple model of innovation driven endogenous growth. Several public expenditure categories and tax rates will be included in order to investigate the impact of fiscal policy on the growth rate of the economy. This approach includes subsidies, as we can think of a subsidy simply as a negative tax.

The stylized model economy comprises a competitive sector for final goods Y_t. These are produced using labour L_t, specialized intermediate input goods X_t, which closely resemble physical capital, and publicly provided infrastructure G_t, according to the following Cobb-Douglas technology,

$$Y_t = X_t^\alpha G_t^\beta L_t^{1-\alpha}, \tag{1}$$

which comprises the Solow model (1956) as a special case with $X_t = K_t$ and $\beta = 0$ and the Barro model (1990) with $X_t = K_t$ and $\alpha + \beta = 1$. The inclusion of public infrastructure or, more general, public capital in the private production function has important implications for private sector productivity. An increase in government spending directly raises marginal productivity of private input factors, which encourages their accumulation and hence may induce output growth (Aschauer, 1989). X_t is a composite intermediate input, composed of a variety of specialized input goods $x_{i,t}$, that are all imperfect substitutes, according to the following CES function,

$$X_t^\alpha = \sum_{i=1}^n x_{i,t}^\alpha, \tag{2}$$

where n is the number of currently available differentiated intermediate inputs. The competitive firm minimizes costs of production, C_t, subject to technology as indicated in equations (1) and (2), where costs are defined as,

$$C_t = (1 + \tau_L)w_t L_t + \sum_{i=1}^n (1 + \tau_{xi})p_{i,t}x_{i,t} = (1 + \tau_L)w_t L_t + (1 + \tau_X)P_t X_t, \tag{3}$$

where the net wage w_t is taxed with the wage tax τ_L, and a tax of τ_{xi} is levied on the net price $p_{i,t}$ of each individual intermediate input good. As a thought experiment, we could also think of tax-exempt wholesalers to purchase all intermediate inputs and sell bundles X_t to producers of final goods at the hypothetical net price P_t. Then for any tax on the intermediate input bundle τ_X, there exits a price P_t where final good producers are indifferent between purchasing the intermediate input bundle or each intermediate input separately. A perfectly competitive final good manufacturer sets marginal costs equal to marginal revenues, where we normalize the price of output to unity and assume that a tax τ_Y is levied on output, yielding the following first order conditions,

$$\frac{\partial Y_t}{\partial X_t} = \alpha(1 - \tau_Y)X_t^{\alpha-1}G_t^\beta L_t^{1-\alpha} = \alpha(1 - \tau_Y)Y_t/X_t = (1 + \tau_X)P_t, \tag{4}$$

$$\frac{\partial Y_t}{\partial x_{i,t}} = \alpha(1 - \tau_Y)x_{i,t}^{\alpha-1}G_t^\beta L_t^{1-\alpha} = \alpha(1 - \tau_Y)(Y_t/X_t)(x_{i,t}/X_t)^{\alpha-1} = (1 + \tau_{xi})p_{i,t}, \tag{5}$$

$$\frac{\partial Y_t}{\partial L_t} = (1 - \alpha)(1 - \tau_Y)X_t^\alpha G_t^\beta L_t^{-\alpha} = (1 - \alpha)(1 - \tau_Y)Y_t/L_t = (1 + \tau_L)w_t. \tag{6}$$

Rearranging the first order conditions with respect to the intermediate input bundle (4) and labour (6), and adding both sides, we find that net revenues equal expenditure on both factors,

$$(1 - \tau_Y)Y_t = (1 + \tau_X)P_tX_t + (1 + \tau_L)w_tL_t, \tag{7}$$

or that profits are zero for the competitive final good producer. Dividing equation (5) by equation (4), taking everything to the power of $\alpha/(\alpha - 1)$ and summing over all n differentiated input varieties, we obtain an index for the net price of the intermediate input bundle,

$$(1 + \tau_X)P_{i,t} = \left[\sum_{i=1}^{n} [(1 + \tau_{xi})P_{i,t}]^{\frac{\alpha}{\alpha-1}} \right]^{\frac{\alpha-1}{\alpha}}. \tag{8}$$

Dividing equation (5) by equation (4) again, and rearranging terms, we obtain a demand function for intermediate inputs,

$$x_{i,t} = \left[\frac{(1 + \tau_{xi})p_{i,t}}{(1 + \tau_X)P_t} \right]^{\frac{1}{\alpha-1}} X_t. \tag{9}$$

An increase in the relative gross price of a particular input i reduces demand with elasticity $1/(1 - \alpha)$. An increase in aggregate demand in intermediate inputs X_t increases demand for a particular input proportionally.

Each intermediate input is provided by a single monopoly supplier, who produces one unit of a specific intermediate input i using one unit of the final good and her (private) knowledge on how to transform the final good into an intermediate good i. The normalisation that one unit of the output good produces one unit of the input good is similar to the conventional concept that an output good can be used both as a consumption and an investment good in a single good economy. Intermediate input providers maximise profits subject to demand (9) resulting in a conventional mark-up pricing equation,

$$p_{i,t} = 1/\alpha. \tag{10}$$

Given that α is less than unity, we find that intermediate input providers charge a price above marginal costs, which is the price of the final product and has been normalized to unity. Here we have assumed that there are no taxes levied either on the revenue or the cost side of intermediate input providers. The reason is that we already tax the intermediate inputs in the final goods sector, which is equivalent to a tax on intermediate input providers. Moreover, a tax on the costs of intermediate input providers would give strong incentives for every intermediate input provider to set up a final good production unit in order to avoid double taxation. However we do introduce a tax τ_π on profits, which are neutral with respect to the input choice. As the price for every input i is identical (10), we can solve for the aggregate price index (9), which, assuming that all taxes on intermediate inputs are identical, reads,

$$P_t = \frac{1}{\alpha}\frac{1 + \tau_{xi}}{1 + \tau_X} n^{\frac{\alpha-1}{\alpha}}.\tag{11}$$

An increase in the number of available intermediate inputs n reduces the cost of the intermediate input bundle P_t. This is due to the fact that an increase in variety renders the intermediate input bundle X_t more efficient. With prices defined in (9), subtracting revenues from costs, we find that net profits of the intermediate input providers equal,

$$(1 - \tau_{\pi,i})\pi_{i,t} = \frac{1 - \alpha}{\alpha}(1 - \tau_{\pi,i})x_{i,t}.\tag{12}$$

We can define physical capital in this economy as the sum of all intermediate inputs, which, using the demand function (9), solves for

$$K_t \equiv \sum_{i=1}^{n} x_{i,t} = n^{\frac{\alpha-1}{\alpha}}X_t.\tag{13}$$

The first part of this equation states that one unit of any intermediate input increases the capital stock proportionally. In contrast to a true investment good, our intermediate inputs face complete instantaneous depreciation. In all other respects, however, we can treat them as capital goods. The capital stock K_t differs from the intermediate input bundle X_t by a factor $n^{(\alpha-1)/\alpha}$. As the number of differentiated inputs increases, this scale effect implies that there will be more intermediate inputs X_t per unit of capital K_t, as the capital inputs will be more efficient. Substituting for the intermediate input in technology (1) yields,

$$Y_t = K_t^{\alpha}G_t^{\beta}(nL_t)^{1-\alpha}.\tag{14}$$

This is a transformed production function in four arguments, the physical capital stock, government infrastructure expenditure, labour, and the number of available intermediate inputs. We can interpret the number of intermediate inputs as the level of technology. The output elasticity of the number of intermediate inputs n is identical to the output elasticity of labour, hence we can think of technology as labour-augmenting, in line with empirical evidence (Kaldor, 1961). The gross price of capital $(1 + \tau_K)q_t$ should equal the marginal product of capital,

$$\frac{\partial Y_t}{\partial K_t} = \alpha(1 - \tau_Y)K_t^{\alpha-1}G_t^{\beta}(nL_t)^{1-\alpha} = \alpha(1 - \tau_Y)Y_t/K_t = (1 + \tau_K)q_t.\tag{15}$$

We can solve for the user cost of capital by substituting (15) into (13) and (4), which yields,

$$q_t = \frac{1 + \tau_{xi}}{1 + \tau_K}\frac{1}{\alpha}.\tag{16}$$

q_t is the shadow price of capital where agents are indifferent between purchasing a particular input with tax τ_{xi} and raw capital with a tax τ_K. Hence any changes in τ_K

alter the shadow price of capital. As one unit of the final output good produces one unit of intermediate input, the gross price of capital should be equal to the gross price of the final good, which due to our normalization is equal to $1/(1 - \tau_Y)$. However, in the absence of taxation, the price of capital equals $1/\alpha$, which is due to the monopoly rents incurred by suppliers of intermediate inputs. In order to eliminate this externality, the optimal tax on intermediate inputs should be set to $\alpha(1 - \tau_Y) - 1$, implying that intermediate inputs should be subsidized.

The capital stock can at most be equal to output, as one unit of the final good produces one unit of the intermediate composite capital good, which would leave nothing for consumption. From the first order condition with respect to capital (15) and our definition of the user cost of capital (16), we find that the capital stock in the economy equals,

$$K_t = \alpha^2 \left(\frac{1 - \tau_Y}{1 + \tau_{xi}} \right) Y_t, \qquad (17)$$

which is strictly less than output. Substituting the capital stock into the transformed production function (14), and taking time derivatives, we find that the growth rate of the economy is given by,

$$\hat{Y}_t = \frac{\beta}{1 - \alpha} \hat{G}_t + \hat{n}_t + \hat{L}_t, \qquad (18)$$

where we have assumed that tax rates do not change over time. This implies that output growth is driven by an increase in the manufacturing sector labour force L_t, the growth rate of public infrastructure spending, and the growth rate of available intermediate inputs. A change in the number of available intermediate inputs is called an innovation. An innovation occurs when someone invests time and effort into research and development activities. As the cost for an innovation usually have to be paid up front, whilst the revenues will only follow thereafter, R&D is the only activity in this economy which has an investive character, and requires funds to finance its projects. We use the old fashioned approach that agents save a constant proportion s of their disposable income Y^D, and that R&D firms use these funds to finance projects,

$$(1 - \tau_s)s Y_t^D = (1 + \tau_{RD})w_t E_t, \qquad (19)$$

where the only cost in research and development is employment cost, given by $w_t E_t$. A tax on both savings and R&D expenditures is levied. As we funnel all savings to the R&D sector, if negative, the tax on savings should better be interpreted as an investment subsidy or even better a subsidy for venture capital market investments (cf. Keuschnigg and Nielsen, 2002). We refrain from modelling the consumption-saving trade-off using intertemporal optimization, as we are interested in growth and not welfare implications of fiscal policy. And, as Robert Solow (1994) has argued, we "see no redeeming social value in using this construction [...] It adds little or nothing to the story anyway, while encumbering it with unnecessary implausibilities and complexities."

The R&D sector is perfectly competitive, so there are no dividends, and workers receive all revenues. Disposable income in the economy is then defined as income from employment in manufacturing, $w_t L_t$, income from employment in research and development, $w_t E_t$, and net profit income from intermediate input providers, $\pi_{i,t}$,

$$Y_t^D = w_t L_t + w_t E_t + \sum_{1=1}^{n} (1 - \tau_{\pi i}) \pi_{i,t}$$

$$= w_t E_t + (1 - \alpha)(1 - \tau_Y) Y_t \left[\alpha \frac{(1 - \tau_\pi)}{(1 - \tau_{xi})} + 1/(1 + \tau_L) \right]. \qquad (20)$$

The labour market is assumed to be in equilibrium, total labour supply N_t will equal labour demand from manufacturing, L_t, and labour demand from research and development, E_t. Given savings decisions modelled in (19), we find that R&D employment is proportional to total employment according to,

$$E_t = \frac{s(1 - \tau_s) + \alpha s(1 - \tau_s)(1 + \tau_L)(1 - \tau_\pi)/(1 + \tau_{xi})}{1 + \tau_{RD} + \alpha s(1 - \tau_s)(1 + \tau_L)(1 - \tau_\pi)/(1 + \tau_{xi})} N_t$$

$$\approx \frac{s + \alpha s(1 + \tau_L)(1 - \tau_\pi - \tau_{xi})}{1 + \tau_{RD} + \tau_s + \alpha s(1 + \tau_L)(1 - \tau_\pi - \tau_{xi})} N_t, \qquad (21)$$

where the approximation holds when the tax or subsidy on R&D and savings are small. As employment in research and development is proportional to the total labour force, both grow at the same rate. Evidently, an increase in the saving rate fosters R&D employment, as does an increase in the share of intermediate inputs α, if R&D and saving subsidies are not too large. An increase in the R&D and saving tax evidently reduces R&D employment, as it allocates less funds to the R&D sector. An increase in the taxation of profits and intermediate input goods, and equivalently a reduction in the labour taxation, reduces R&D employment, as in these cases profits in the intermediate input sector decline, thus reducing revenues for financing research and development activities. This result is of second order importance only. If the denominator is close to one, and we can ignore all products of two tax rates as they are close to zero, hence equation (21) reduces to $E_t = [s(1 - \tau_s) - \tau_{RD}]N_t$.

Innovation takes time, effort and knowledge. The latter is provided by the (public) education system, implying an arrival rate for new innovations according to,

$$\hat{n}_t = \phi h_t E_t, \qquad (22)$$

where ϕ is productivity in R&D and h_t is the average level of human capital per R&D worker. Evidently, human capital is important in production, but even more so in research and development (Romer, 1986). In our framework, which focuses explicitly on government expenditure and taxation, workers acquire human capital only during public education for the sake of simplicity. Dividing both sides by the number of available products n, and substituting the total labour force for R&D employment (21), we can solve for the per capita growth rate of the economy (18) in terms of exogenous and policy parameters only,

$$\hat{Y}_t - \hat{N}_t = \frac{\beta}{1-\alpha}\hat{G}_t + \phi\frac{s + \alpha s(1 + \tau_L)(1 - \tau_\pi - \tau_{xi})}{1 + \tau_{RD} + \tau_s + \alpha s(1 + \tau_L)(1 - \tau_\pi - \tau_{xi})}\frac{h_t N_t}{n_t}. \quad (23)$$

This equation has several important implications. First, the literature on fiscal policy and economic growth has so far only focused on the first part of this equation, ignoring the second part, which has only been discussed in theoretical work (Romer, 1990, Grossman and Helpman, 1991, and Aghion and Howitt, 1992). Looking at the first part only, we observe that taxation has only an indirect effect on economic growth, by financing the required level of government infrastructure. Early works (Barro, 1990) assume a proportional tax on output, thus implying that the growth rate of public infrastructure is identical to the growth of output. Solving for output using this rule, we find that output growth is less than population growth by a factor $(1 - \alpha)/(1 - \alpha - \beta)$, implying that per capita output will grow less than population by a factor $\beta/(1 - \alpha - \beta)$. As population grows, a larger number of manufacturing workers use a given public infrastructure. As the output elasticity of public infrastructure β declines, the growth rate of output approaches the growth rate of population. Public infrastructure is therefore subject to full congestion. Models with partial congestions have been discussed by Turnovsky (1996) and Glomm and Ravikumar (1994). However, if and only if the output elasticity of public infrastructure β equals $1 - \alpha$, we have nondecreasing returns with respect to reproducible factors of production (1), and cannot solve for the above equation (23), but obtain long-run economic growth, as postulated by Barro (1990).

The second part of the above equation contains several taxes explicitly. Note that a tax on output Y_t has no direct effect on the growth rate of the economy. It does, however, have an impact on the current level of output. The last term in the previous equation is the economy-wide level of human capital per innovation. As the blueprints for intermediate inputs are the only marketable knowledge in this economy, this ratio postulates that the growth rate of the economy will increase (decline) if the growth in the level of human capital exceeds (falls short of) the growth rate of innovations. Note that output grows faster than the innovation rate (22) by $\beta/(1 - \alpha)$ times the growth rate of public infrastructure. Thus, in a growing economy, we can ensure that the growth rate of human capital exceeds the growth rate of innovation even for constant tax rates. Alternatively, we can allow for the financing of other government activities, such as subsidies or public infrastructure investment. The choice set of government is bound by the government budget constraint, which is assumed to be balanced for the sake of simplicity,

$$\Gamma(G_t) + \Phi(h_t N_t) + C_t^G = \tau + \tau_Y Y_t + \tau_s s Y_t^D + \tau_L w_t N_t + \tau_X P_t X_t$$
$$+ \tau_{RD} w_t E_t + \tau_K q_t K_t + \tau_\pi \pi_t, \tag{24}$$

where $\Gamma(G_t)$ is the cost function for the provision of public infrastructure, $\Phi(h_t N_t)$ is the cost function for the provision of public education, τ is a lump sum tax, and C_t^G is government consumption. A more detailed analysis of government consumption can be found in Zagler and Ragacs (1999). Thus the model knows twelve policy parameters, three categories of government expenditure and nine tax rates.

3. Government expenditure

In order to examine the effects of government expenditure policy on long term economic growth, it is useful to disaggregate the total volume of expenditure into several categories and analyse them separately. A widely used approach has been to divide it into government consumption and investment. The former is in general considered to hamper and the latter to foster economic growth. It seems obvious that this classification is no longer sufficient, since certain categories of government consumption expenditures are expected to support growth, such as infrastructure, education, and health expenditures. In contrast, not well targeted investment projects could create distortions which result in a welfare loss for the economy. Following Devarajan *et al.* (1996), we divide public expenditure into productive (or growth-enhancing) and unproductive (or purely consumptive) expenditure. The unifying framework discussed in the previous chapter is well equipped in analyzing different government expenditure categories, which are depicted on the left hand side of equation (24). Note that both government infrastructure investment and education expenditures exhibit a direct impact on the growth rate of the economy (Glomm and Ravikumar 1997). Whilst only a change in the growth rate of public infrastructure influences the growth rate, it is the level of public education which influences the rate of growth. In particular, whenever the level of education exceeds (falls short of) the level of knowledge or innovation, we obtain a positive (negative) impact on economic growth. Other public expenditures, however, do not directly alter the growth rate as described in equation (23), but may reduce the growth rate if they are financed through growth reducing taxation. Whilst consumptive public expenditures C_t^G do not directly affect the long-run performance of the economy, they may very well exhibit positive welfare implications (Turnovsky 1996). These welfare implications, however, are not the focus of this paper.

A central aim of government spending in order to raise the growth rate is to improve the marginal productivity of the private sector's physical capital and labour (cf. equation 1). Accordingly public expenditure would typically include the provision of a basic social and economic infrastructure. Aschauer (2000) discusses in detail the impact of public capital on economic growth. Physical infrastructure (roads and railways) and communication as well as information systems (phone, internet) are typical examples for publicly provided goods which enter, in a productivity enhancing way, directly into the private production function (Feehan and Matsumoto, 2002). Although investment in this sort of infrastructure might not be profitable from the single firm's point of view (as private costs exceed private returns), the whole economy would nevertheless benefit enormously, which justifies public provision. Odedokun (1997) finds evidence for 48 developing countries that public infrastructure investment facilitates private investment and promotes growth.

As argued previously, this public capital is well represented in our public infrastructure, G_t. From the first-order conditions (4), (5), (6), and (15), we note that an increase in public infrastructure expenditure will ceteris paribus raise the demand for the intermediate input bundle X_t, the demand for every particular input $x_{i,t}$, demand for labour L_t, and the demand for raw capital K_t. Any public good, which is in a similar fashion capable of interfering with private allocation decisions, falls into this category of a productive public good.

However, there is widespread belief that, if government expenditure replaces private output beyond mitigating certain market failures, any additional spending is expected to reduce at least the level of output, if not economic growth (Morales 2001). The optimal level of government infrastructure provision is given when the marginal product of public infrastructure equals marginal costs,

$$\frac{\partial Y_t}{\partial G_t} = \beta(1 - \tau_Y)X_t^\alpha G_t^{\beta-1}L_t^{1-\alpha} = \beta(1 - \tau_Y)Y_t/G_t = \Gamma'(G) \qquad (25)$$

Any public infrastructure beyond that point could crowd out private investment, and thus indeed reduces the level of output.

Beyond its influence on allocation decision in the final goods sector, public spending affects the labour productivity mainly through two fairly obvious channels, knowledge accumulation and health care. Both, in the case of education and health care, the market allocation leads to sub-optimal solutions. This is mainly due to the occurrence of market imperfections such as externalities and non-excludability. Due to the existence of imperfect credit markets (which may raise difficulties for individuals to borrow in order to finance education) and asymmetric information, individuals are often not able to acquire basic as well as advanced education. But since the average stock of human capital plays a decisive role in determining the long run growth rate of an economy, a reduced access to education is likely to have a negative growth implication. Publicly provided education through public schools and universities therefore ensures a continuous human capital accumulation process. In their work Bils and Klenow (2000) find a positive correlation between schooling and economic growth. Barham et al. (1995) show that imperfect capital markets force individuals to borrow from their parents to finance schooling. But if parents savings are insufficient, a sub-optimal level of education is likely to exist. In our unifying framework presented in the previous chapter, there is an explicit role for public education expenditures, if only in the research and development sector. If the level of education remains

constant, for any given level of R&D employment, the number of new innovations will remain constant as well (cf. equation 22), thus implying that the growth
rate of innovations, and ultimately the innovation driven growth rate of the
economy, will come to a halt. If the level of education grows at least at the rate
of innovation, the economy will exhibit long-run innovation driven economic
growth (23). In the model presented in the previous chapter, we consider education to matter only in research and development. The idea is that the knowledge
of existing innovations facilitates the future innovation process. This is, by the
way, the underlying reason why the level of education must grow with the rate of
innovation. We assume, however, that education plays no role in manufacturing
(1). The intuition behind this assumption is that the production of the same final
output good does not require knowledge of existing innovations. However,
manufacturing labour uses all the differentiated inputs i generated by the innovation sector, and knowledge of the innovations may very well increase their
productivity. We could capture this effect by considering L_t as units of efficient
labour, growing at the rate of population and innovation.

Similar to the effect of education on labour efficiency units, public spending
can also affect the volume of labour supplied through its impact on the state of
health. Expenditures on the health care system (which are not simply replacing
private expenditures, but increasing the total amount of "the good health" consumed by individuals) are expected to reduce illness and absenteeism leading to an
increase in the quantity of labour. Of course health also affects the quality of
labour. Good health tends to increase workers ability to acquire new knowledge
and skills. Bloom et al. (2001) took up this idea in their study and they found that
health has a positive and statistically significant effect on economic growth. They
claim that a one year improvement in population life expectancy leads to a 4
percent increase in output. In terms of the model in the previous chapter, we can
think of health care as an increase in N_t beyond population growth. Given that a
change in N_t increases output by a factor $(1 - \alpha)/(1 - \alpha - \beta)$, we obtain a direct
effect of health care on economic growth through the first part of the growth
equation (23).

As we have seen in the previous chapter, research and development expenditures provided by the public sector are expected to increase the growth rate of
innovation (22) and hence may stimulate output growth. Although this fact has
been a well researched area in growth theory, the existing literature is divided
concerning the impact of public expenditures on R&D. Early works of Romer
(1990), Segerstrom et al. (1990) and Grossman and Helpman (1991) emphasise the
importance of R&D subsidies in order to promote long run growth. Aghion and
Howitt (1992) follow the Schumpeterian approach and employ a model of creative destruction, where they find that subsidies have an unambiguously positive
effect on output growth. In contrast to this view, Jones (1995) argues that the
scale effects of research and development, which are assumed to be the main
engine of growth in the above cited models, are not consistent with empirical
findings. He investigates a modified version of the Romer model and finds that
R&D expenditures only affect the relative size of the R&D sector, but have no

consequences for long run growth. Interestingly Segerstrom (1998), who adopts a related approach, obtains similar results. However, Howitt (1999) who takes into account the non scale effects in R&D mentioned by Jones rejects the assumption that R&D expenditures have no long run growth impact. Morales (2001) examines the effects of different types of research policies on economic growth. She finds that while basic research, performed at public institutions has positive effects, applied public research (which could also be done by private firms) has negative growth effects.

The unifying framework introduced above can accommodate these implications from the reviewed literature on public R&D policy. First, an increase in the quality of education (h_t) due to public schooling increases the quality of research employees, thus fostering the rate of innovation (22). Second, an increase in R&D subsidies (a decline in τ_{RD}) reduces the unit costs of the R&D sector (19), thus fostering R&D activities. Equivalently, a reduction in the tax on R&D funding (τ_s), increases the funds allocated to the R&D sector, and by the same token increases research and development activities. Both of these taxes (subsidies) exhibit a direct negative (positive) impact on the growth rate of the economy (23). We may even go as far as arguing that because of their direct positive impact on output, R&D subsidies can be considered a productive public good, following Devarajan et al. (1996).

4. Taxation

All kinds of publicly provided goods and services, including the ones discussed above, need to be financed by revenues raised either by taxing private sector activities like income and consumption taxes or issuing debt. For ease of exposition we leave aside the possibility of monetary financing. Similar to government spending, the level and structure of taxation of an economy can influence its long run growth rate through numerous channels. Based on the assumption that all taxes apart from lump-sum taxes are non-neutral, tax induced distortions tend to alter private agents' allocative decisions with regard to factor accumulation and supply and hence may affect the growth rate.

In this section of the paper, we attempt to shed light on the relationship between taxation as a short run fiscal policy instrument and long run growth. Rather than providing a detailed analysis of each possible tax, we aim to survey the theoretical links of some in practice widely used taxes and economic growth. We can distinguish between two types of taxes. One group of taxes, in particular taxes on savings, R&D, profits, raw capital and labour, have a direct impact on the growth rate of the economy (23), whilst all others do not. All the taxes introduced in our model can exhibit an indirect effect on economic growth, as they may finance growth enhancing government expenditures. Therefore the overall effect on economic growth of all taxes can be considered as the difference between the negative effects caused by distortions and the positive effect from productive government expenditures.

Several of the twelve policy instruments summarised by equation 24 are super-fluous. First, neither the government consumption good (G_t^C) nor a lump sum tax interfere with any economic decision. Hence the impact of a public consumption good is equivalent to a negative lump sum tax. This implicitly assumes that the public consumption good can be as efficiently provided as private consumption goods. As already mentioned above, a tax on research and development (τ_{RD}) exhibits the same influence as a tax on savings (τ_s). Next, if all taxes on particular inputs (τ_{xi}) are identical, the tax on particular inputs is economically equivalent to a tax on raw capital (τ_K).

Dividing equation (7) by $1 - \tau_Y$, we find that an increase in the tax on final products (τ_Y) is equivalent to an increase in both the tax on the intermediate input bundle (τ_X) and tax on labour income (τ_L). Finally, a tax on the intermediate input bundle is economically and fiscally identical to a tax on intermediate inputs if equation (11) holds, and revenues from a tax on intermediate inputs are identical to revenues from a tax on the intermediate input bundle. We find that this is the case whenever $\tau_Y = \alpha\tau_{xi}/[1 + (1 - \alpha)\tau_{xi}]$. With these five restrictions and the government budget constraint (24), there remain six degrees of freedom to set fiscal policy.

Note that there are two distinct tax bases for our nine different tax rates. The tax on output as well as the tax on labour, the tax on raw capital, the tax on profit income, the intermediate inputs, the taxes on savings and research and develop-ment expenditures all have total output either directly or indirectly as their tax base, hence an increase in growth will proportionally increase revenues from these sources. By contrast, the base for the tax on intermediate input, bundle is $n^{(1-\alpha)/\alpha}Y_t$, which follows from equation (13). Tax revenues from the latter cate-gory of taxes grow faster than revenues from taxes that have output as its tax base, and in particular grow faster than output growth. In a dynamic sense this implies that the prior category of taxation is more fruitful.

4.1 *Taxation of labour and profits*

It may come as a great surprise that taxes on labour income exhibit a direct effect on economic growth, and even more that this impact is positive. In our model we tax labour only in manufacturing (6) but not in research and development (19). In this respect we may interpret the tax on research and development expenditures (τ_{RD}) as a tax on labour in the research and development sector. Changes in these tax rates have an impact on the division of labour between the manufacturing and the research and development sector (21). Whilst a tax on labour increases labour costs in manufacturing and shifts employment to the growth enhancing research and development sector, a tax on R&D employment has the opposite effect.

In one respect the model in the previous sector may be over simplistic. We consider labour supply in any period of time as given, thus ignoring substitution and income effects from changing wages. According to the widely accepted assumption of an upward sloping labour supply curve, individuals extend the amount of labour supplied to the economy up to the point where the marginal benefit of an additional hour worked (which is the after tax wage they receive) equals the marginal cost (the marginal opportunity cost of the last unit of leisure just given up). It is straightforward to see that an increase in the labour income tax rate lowers the marginal benefit of a unit of labour supply, but the opportunity cost remains unchanged, which induces individuals to substitute leisure for work time. This effect, commonly referred to as the substitution effect, tends to decrease the total volume of labour supplied to the economy, with the corresponding negative impact on output growth. Simultaneously an increase in the labour income tax rate generates an income effect, which works precisely in the opposite way. A reduction of real income of private agents, due to a higher tax rate combined with the assumption of leisure acting like a normal good, implies that individuals now substitute labour for leisure leading to an increase in the total volume of labour supplied. So the overall effect of a tax on labour income is ambiguous.

Since the endogenous growth theory driven by fundamental works of Romer (1986) and Lucas (1988) stressed the importance of human capital as main engine of long run growth, all kinds of taxation which affects not only the existing stock but also the accumulation of human capital play an important role in determining the growth rate of an economy.

Apart from quantity implications, labour income taxation additionally influences the quality of labour through altering the stock of knowledge. The acquisition of new knowledge and skills is driven by the workers' incentive to gain higher future wages. They will extend their additional schooling up to the point where the marginal benefits (the higher future wages) equal the marginal costs (the tuition fees and wages foregone). An increase in the labour income tax rate now alters both benefits as well as costs. But since the tuition costs of schooling remain unchanged after the tax increase, which seems intuitively obvious, the benefit side experiences a higher reduction which as a result induces the individuals to cut their schooling efforts leading to a decline of the average quality of the workforce and ceteris paribus of growth.

Several studies concerning the effect of labour income taxation on human capital accumulation have emerged in recent time. Trostel (1993) argued that a fall in the utilisation of existing human capital arises due to a tax wedge between gross and net wage rates and thus reduces the volume of labour, which discourages further investment in human capital. Lin (1998) demonstrated that the impact of labour taxation on human capital accumulation depends on the relationship between the labour tax rate and private savings (through the real interest rate). In his analysis an increase in the labour income tax rate is expected to increase (decrease) the real interest rate and reduce (increase) the level of human capital if private savings are negatively (positively) related to the tax rate.

A tax on profit income reduces the disposable income in the economy and thereby reduces savings. Similar to a tax on labour in manufacturing, it interferes with the division of labour between the manufacturing and the research and development sector, thus altering the growth rate of the economy (23). In contrast to a tax on labour, it does not interfere in the allocation of resources within the manufacturing sector and should therefore be less distortive.

4.2 *Taxation of capital and consumption*

In order to examine the effects of a capital income tax on output growth, we trace three different but related channels concerning the impact on the accumulation of physical capital. Following conventional wisdom, a capital income tax reduces the net rate of return of investing in physical capital (15), therefore increases the relative price of future consumption and consequently encourages current consumption. Thus, distorting the household's consumption-saving choice, a capital income tax acts as a disincentive to accumulate physical capital and as a result harms economic growth (Engen and Skinner 1996, Boadway and Wildasin 1994).

Normally households use their disposable income either for consumption or saving (19). The decision which fraction of income is used for saving is at least partly determined by the amount of interest income which can be gained as a compensation for postponing current consumption. Endogenous growth theory found that the volume of savings is a crucial factor in determining the long run growth rate of an economy, hence all kinds of taxation which distort the consumption-saving decision also affect the accumulation of physical capital and hence the growth rate.

The second channel is based on the assumption that a reduced rate of return not necessarily implies a substitution towards current consumption as just discussed. A lower rate of return encourages under certain circumstances instead the accumulation of human capital which after the taxation of physical capital income possibly is the relative better investment (Trostel, 1993). The tax induced disincentive to accumulate physical capital is therefore at least partly offset by intensified investment in human capital. The impact on growth depends in the end on the specification of the production function and in particular which sort of capital (physical or human) acts as decisive factor to generate growth.

The third channel uses the fact that the volume of households saving is positively related to the amount of their disposable income (which implies that saving acts like a normal good – the marginal propensity to save rises with increasing income). It is straightforward to see that when total income (which consists of labour and capital income) is reduced due to a capital income tax, also savings, and thus capital accumulation and long run growth, decline.

Our unifying framework knows different types of capital taxation. On the one hand there is a tax on raw capital, either τ_K or τ_{xi}, and on the other hand there is a tax on productive capital or the intermediate input bundle τ_X.

In our framework, consumption is the residual. We can therefore not directly model taxes on consumption. However, we can simulate the consumption tax with a tax on output τ_Y and a negative tax on savings τ_s, with $\tau_Y = -\tau_s$. Since a consumption tax levied uniformly on all products available to households (like a value added tax) changes all current and future prices proportionally, it does not alter the relative price of current compared with future consumption and has as a result no impact on the household's consumption – saving decision choice and therefore on the rate of output growth. We do however find, however, that it distorts the labour leisure decision.

Of more relevance for long run growth implications is a consumption tax levied not uniformly (but only on specific goods and services), which tends to alter the relative prices of taxed and untaxed goods. This induces consumers to substitute away from taxed (and now more expensive) goods to cheaper alternatives which, as a result, it affects firstly the profitability of certain industries and secondly the growth rate if the "substitution firms" have a higher growth potential.

Studies discussing growth effects of consumption and capital income taxation have been published for instance by Milesi-Ferretti and Roubini (1998) who examine the macroeconomic effects of consumption and factor income taxation on factor accumulation and economic growth. Razin and Yuen (1996) find that under free capital mobility and endogenous population, taxation of capital income has also large effects on long term growth. Turnovsky (1996) employs an endogenous growth model in order to analyse the role of a consumption tax in fostering growth. His major finding is that a second fiscal instrument (e.g. an income tax) is needed to obtain the first best optimum. In contrast Uhlig and Yanagawa (1996) doubt the view that a capital income tax harms growth. They employ an overlapping generation model where a higher capital income tax means a lower labour income tax (due to a fixed fraction of government expenditure) which leaves the young generation more net income of which to save. However Mendoza *et al.* (1997) provide theoretical and empirical evidence in favour of the view of Harberger (1964), that tax policy is an ineffective instrument in altering the growth rate of an economy. Turnovsky (2000) rightly criticises the treatment of labour supply in recent studies which analyses growth effects of various taxes. When labour supply is accordingly assumed to be inelastic, taxes on consumption and labour income operate simply as non distorting lump sum taxes.

4.3 *Structure of the tax system*

So far we have viewed taxes as necessary instruments to raise revenue in order to finance all kinds of government expenditure. But since taxes create various distortions and thus affect output growth in a non negligible negative way, it is a major goal of policymakers to minimise tax induced reductions in the long run growth rate of an economy.

But the non-neutrality of taxes can deliberately be used to influence consumers' (and/or producers') behaviour in order to mitigate certain market failures, in particular negative external effects. When the marginal social cost of a certain economic activity exceeds its marginal private cost, then the total amount of output (or the use of economic resources) would exceed its social optimum, resulting in a welfare loss. Taxes which attempt to internalise such externalities (often called corrective or Pigouvian taxes) induce the agent to reduce her activity to social optimum. In the case of publicly provided goods which are at least partly subject to congestion, taxes could be implemented as corrective measures to reduce possible excessive demand.

The model presented here exhibits four externalities. First, final good manufactures do not take the effect of a change in government infrastructure expenditures into account. Second, the R&D sector does not reward the impact of the quality of education on the innovation rate of the economy. Third, due to monopolistic competition in the provision of intermediate goods (10), raw capital does not earn its marginal product (16). Finally, the savings behaviour is modelled exogenously, therefore we can not be sure that the level of consumption is optimized. Fiscal policy should be able to internalize all four externalities with four of the six available policy instruments, leaving two degrees of freedom for short run policy objectives. Thus we can achieve both short run and long run goals without the use of lump sum taxation.

In addition to growth effects caused by singular taxes, also the structure of the entire tax system has broad significance. Due to the fact that a consumption tax distorts only the labour leisure decision, but acts neutral with regard to the consumption saving choice, a shift from income to consumption taxation would encourage capital accumulation and therefore foster growth. In contrast, an income tax distorts the labour leisure as well as the consumption saving choice. A comprehensive discussion concerning growth effects of consumption tax systems compared with those of income tax systems has been provided by Krusell *et al.* (1996).

The impact of the entire tax structure on economic growth has been a well researched area. A recent study concerning this point has been provided for instance by Ortigueira (1998), who studies the effects of labour and capital income taxes on the transitional dynamics to the balanced growth path. Fiaschi (1999) presents a model which exhibits a positive (negative) correlation between growth and the tax rate on labour (capital) income. Peretto (2001) claims that taxes on consumption, labour and corporate income have level but no steady state growth effects. Only a tax on asset income has growth effects because it affects households saving. Using a panel data set for 22 OECD countries, Kneller *et al.* (1999) find that the structure of taxation (and expenditure) can have important growth implications.

5. Public Debt

Thus far we have assumed that the tax revenue raised by the government in a certain period of time exactly equals the total amount of public spending in the corresponding period. We shall now relax this fairly strict assumption of a balanced budget and allow the government to run a deficit. Similar to taxation and public expenditure, the total stock and the repayment of public debt can have a significant impact on the long term growth rate of an economy.

One link is built on the identity of national saving as sum of private and public saving. We consider the case where the government holds the tax revenue constant and increases spending, thereby it creates a budget deficit. For further analysis it is now a crucial criterion how the private sector responds to this decrease in public saving.

The opinion under economists concerning this issue is twofold. One predicts that households will rise their savings exactly as much as public savings fall (= public dissaving is neutralised). This view, commonly referred as the Ricardian equivalence, states that households regard public debt simply as taxes delayed and therefore increase their saving in order to pay higher future taxes. For a comprehensive and systematic analysis of the Ricardian equivalence see Elmendorf and Mankiw (1998). Since its recent revival which is usually awarded to Barro (1974), this view has been of much and controversial debate among economists. For an insight into the controversy see e.g. Barro (1989), Bernheim (1987) and Zagler (2002). If Ricardian equivalence is violated due to overlapping generations, then public debt can change the private incentives to accumulation and thus directly influence the rate of growth in the economy (Zagler, 1999, 46ff).

With the assumption of a constant savings rate, we adopt the conventional view of a private sector's behavioural response to budget deficits. According to this view, an increase in private savings by less than the decline in public savings, leads to a decline in national saving which in turn implies reduced total (private and public) investment with implications for the level of output and maybe growth.

Running a deficit induces the government to absorb additional resources from the private sector, which could have been used instead for the accumulation of private physical capital. And if the revenue, so raised, is spent in a less productive way than it would be by the private sector, the overall growth effect would be negative. Works by Araujo and Martins (1999) confirm this view. In their analysis they find that public debt hampers growth because it competes with private physical capital for individual savings. However Lin (2000) claims that public debt does not necessarily reduce growth. He finds that government debt will increase the growth rate of per capita output if the growth rate is greater than the real interest rate.

Public debt can of course be seen as an alternative instrument to finance government expenditure. In general, the introduction of (or increase in) public debt, which is not accompanied by a corresponding increase in government spending, typically replaces existing taxes. Since taxes create various sorts of growth reducing distortions, a debt financed tax cut is expected to stimulate growth. However the opposite effect arises when the stock of accumulated debt needs to be repaid by higher taxes. The work by Ludvigson (1996) fully supports this view. But according to his analysis two key parameters are expected to influence the results, the elasticity of labour supply and the degree of persistence in government debt. Interestingly Dotsey (1994), who assumes labour supply to be inelastic, obtains the reverse results, debt financed income tax cuts will reduce growth.

6. Conclusion

This paper has surveyed the literature on fiscal policy and economic growth. Fiscal policy is a short run issue. It was therefore not our aim to evaluate fiscal policy by long run implications, as it should be exclusively judged by its achievements of its short run targets. We have therefore refrained from conducting a welfare analysis, and have in contrast investigated the non-normative question of the impact of fiscal policy on the long run behaviour of the economy.

We have presented a unifying framework for the analysis of long run growth implications of government expenditures and revenues. We can divide government expenditure into productive and unproductive expenditures, where the latter have an impact on the growth rate of the economy. We find that the level of education expenditures and the growth rate of public infrastructure investment both exhibit a positive impact on the growth rate of the economy. Similarly we find that several tax rates, such as taxes on savings, on intermediate input goods, on research and development expenditures, a tax on profit income and a tax on manufacturing labour directly influence the division of labour between the manufacturing sector and the research and development sector, and thereby alter the innovation driven growth rate.

In a creative synthesis we have assigned the relevant literature to policy variables as introduced in the model framework. On the expenditure side, the literature can be segregated between works that discuss public infrastructure investment, public health care, public education, and public research and development policy. On the revenue side we have first investigated taxes that interfere with the division of labour, namely taxes on labour and profit income. Thereafter we have summarized the vast literature on capital income taxation and consumption taxation. Finally we have discussed public debt as a means to finance productive government expenditures.

We can broadly separate the future research agenda into two categories. On the one hand, we find that little or no work on the effects of fiscal policy on innovation driven economic growth has so far been conducted. Research in this area seems particularly fruitful as we obtain level effects of education expenditures on the growth rate of the economy, and no longer require non decreasing returns with respect to reproducible factors of production to explain long run economic growth. On the other hand empirical research, if conducted at all, has so far only focused on particular tax rates or expenditure categories, and has investigated only part of the growth equation presented in this survey. Future empirical work should focus on the implications of the entire tax system on economic growth, and more thoroughly analyse the growth implications of fiscal policy regimes.

References

Aghion, P. and Howitt, P., (1992) A Model of Growth through Creative Destruction, *Econometrica* 60, 323–351.

Araujo, J. T. and Martins, M. A. C., (1999) Economic Growth with Finite Lifetimes, *Economics Letters* 62, 377–381.

Aschauer, D. A., (1989) Is Public Expenditure Productive?, *Journal of Monetary Economics* 23, 177–200.

Aschauer, D. A., (2000) Do States Optimize? Public Capital and Economic Growth, *Annals of Regional Science* 34, 343–363.

Barham, V., Boadway, R., Marchand, M., Pestieau, P., (1995) Education and the Poverty Trap, *European Economic Review* 39, 1257–1275.

Barro, R. J., (1974) Are Government Bonds Net Wealth?, *Journal of Political Economy* 82, 1095–1117.

Barro, R. J., (1989) The Ricardian Approach to Budget Deficits, *Journal of Economic Perspectives* 3 (2), 37–54.

Barro, R. J., (1990) Government Spending in a Simple Model of Endogenous Growth, *Journal of Political Economy* 98 (5).

Bernheim, D. B., (1987) Ricardian Equivalence: An Evaluation of Theory and Evidence. In Stanley Fisher ed. *NBER Macroeconomics Annual 1987* (pp. 263–304), The MIT Press, Cambridge Massachusetts.

Bils, M. and Klenow, P. J., (2000) Does Schooling Cause Growth?, *American Economic Review* 90 (5).

Bloom, D. E., Canning, D., Sevilla, J., (2001) The Effect of Health on Economic Growth: Theory and Evidence, *National Bureau of Economic Research*, Working Paper no.: 8587.

Boadway, R. and Wildasin, D, (1994) Taxation and Savings, *Fiscal Studies* Vol. 15 (3), 19–63.

Devarajan, S., Swaroop, V., Zou, H., (1996) The Composition of Public Expenditure and Economic Growth, *Journal of Monetary Economics* 37, 313–344.

Dotsey, M., (1994) Some Unpleasant Supply Side Arithmetic, *Journal of Monetary Economics* 33, 507–524.

Elmendorf, D. W. and Mankiw, G., (1998) Government Debt, *National Bureau of Economic Research*, Working Paper no.: 6470.

Engen, E. M. and Skinner, J., (1996) Taxation and Economic Growth, *National Bureau of Economic Research*, Working Paper no.: 5826.

Feehan, P. J. and Matsumoto, M., (2002) Distortionary Taxation and Optimal Public Spending on Productive Activities, *Economic Inquiry* 40 (1), 60–68.

Fiaschi, D., (1999) Growth and Inequality in an Endogenous Fiscal Policy Model with Taxes on Labour and Capital, *European Journal of Political Economy* 15, 727–746.

Glomm, G. and Ravikumar, B., (1994) Public Investment in Infrastructure in a Simple Growth Model, *Journal of Economic Dynamics and Control* 18 (6), 1173–1187.

Glomm, G. and Ravikumar, B., (1997) Productive Government Expenditures and Long-Run Growth, *Journal of Economic Dynamics and Control* 21, 183–204.

Grossman, G. M. and Helpman, E., (1991) Quality Ladders in the Theory of Growth, *Review of Economic Studies* 58, 43–61.

Harberger, A. C., (1964) Taxation, Resource Allocation and Welfare, in *The Role of Direct and Indirect Taxes in the Federal Revenue System*, NBER and the Brookings Institution (eds), Princeton University Press.

Howitt, P., (1999) Steady Endogenous Growth with Population and R&D Inputs Growing, *Journal of Political Economy* 107, 715–730.

Jones, C., (1995) R&D-Based Models of Economic Growth, *Journal of Political Economy* 103, 759–784.

Kaldor, N., (1961) Capital Accumulation and Economic Growth, in: *The Theory of Capital*, ed. by Friedrich A. Lutz and Douglas C. Hague (New York: St. Martin's Press), 177–222.

Keuschnigg, C. and Nielsen, S. B., (2001) *Tax Policy, Venture Capital, and Entrepreneurship*, NBER DP 7976.

Keuschnigg, C. and Fisher, W. H., (2002) *Public Policy for Efficient Education*, University of St. Gallen, 1–33.

Kneller, R., Bleaney, M. F., Gemmell, N., (1999) Fiscal Policy and Growth: Evidence from OECD Countries, *Journal of Public Economics* 74, 171–190.

Krusell, P., Quadrini, V., Ríos-Rull, J. V., (1996) Are Consumption Taxes Really Better Than Income Taxes?, *Journal of Monetary Economics* 37, 475–503.

Lin, S., (1998) Labor Income Taxation and Human Capital Accumulation, *Journal of Public Economics* 68, 291–302.

Lin, S., (2000) Government Debt and Economic Growth in an Overlapping Generations Model, *Southern Economic Journal* 66 (3), 754–763.

Lucas, R. E., Jr (1988) On the Mechanics of Economic Development, *Journal of Monetary Economics* 22 (1), 3–42.

Ludvigson, S., (1996) The Macroeconomic Effects of Government Debt in a Stochastic Growth Model, *Journal of Monetary Economics* 38, 25–45.

Mendoza, E. G., Milesi-Ferretti, G. M., Asea, P., (1997) On the Ineffectiveness of Tax Policy in Altering Long Run Growth: Harbergers Superneutrality Conjecture, *Journal of Public Economics* 66, 99–126.

Milesi-Ferretti, G. M. and Roubini, N., (1998) Growth Effects of Income and Consumption Taxes, *Journal of Money, Credit and Banking* 30 (4).

Morales, M. F., (2001) Research Policy and Endogenous Growth, Universitat Autònoma de Barcelona and Universitat de Murcia.

Odedokun, M. O., (1997) Relative Effects of Public versus Private Investment Spending on Economic Efficiency and Growth in Developing Countries, *Applied Economics* 29, 1325–1336.

Ortigueira, S. (1998) Fiscal Policy in an Endogenous Growth Model with Human Capital Accumulation, *Journal of Monetary Economics* 42, 323–355.

Peretto, P. F., (2001) Fiscal Policy and Endogenous Growth: A Superneutrality Result for R&D based Models, Department of Economics, Duke University.

Razin, A. and Yuen, C. W., (1996) Capital Income Taxation and Long Run Growth: New Perspectives, *Journal of Public Economics* 59, 239–263.

Romer, P. M., (1986) Increasing Returns and Long Run Growth, *Journal of Political Economy* 94, 1002–1037.

Romer, P. M., (1990) Endogenous Technological Change, *Journal of Political Economy*, 98 (5), 71–102.

Segerstrom, P., (1998) Endogenous Growth without Scale Effects, *American Economic Review* 88, 1290–1310.

Segerstrom, P., Anant, T. and Dinopoulos, E., (1990) A Schumpeterian Model of the Product Life Cycle, *American Economic Review* 80, 1077–1092.

Solow, R. M., (1956) A Contribution to the Theory of Economic Growth, *Quarterly Journal of Economics*, 70, 65–94.

Solow, R. M., (1994) Perspectives on Growth Theory, *Journal of Economic Perspectives*, 8 (1), 45–54.

Trostel, P. A., (1993) The Effect of Taxation on Human Capital, *Journal of Political Economy* 101 (21).

Turnovsky, S. J., (1996) Optimal Tax, Dept and Expenditures Policies in a Growing Economy, *Journal of Public Economics* 60, 21–44.

Turnovsky, S. J., (2000) Fiscal Policy, Elastic Labour Supply, and Endogenous Growth, *Journal of Monetary Economics* 45, 185–210.

Uhlig, H. and Yanagawa, N., (1996) Increasing the Capital Income Tax may lead to Faster Growth, *European Economic Review* 40, 1521–1540.

Zagler, M. and Ragacs, C., (1999) Endogenous Growth, Division of Labor and Fiscal Policy, In: Zagler, M., *Endogenous Growth, Market Failures, and Economic Policy*, Macmillan, Basingstoke.

Zagler, M., (1999) *Endogenous Growth, Market Failures, and Economic Policy*, Macmillan, Basingstoke.

Zagler, M., (2002) Öffentliche Verschuldung, Budgetdefizite und Budgetkonsolidierung, In: Theurl, E., Sausgruber, R., Winner, H. (Eds.), *Kompendium der österreichischen Finanzpolitik*, Springer, Heidelberg, 481–508.

7

GROWTH AND UNEMPLOYMENT: TOWARDS A THEORETICAL INTEGRATION

Fabio Aricó

University of Pavia

1. Introduction

Economic growth and labour economics have been regarded so far as two separate fields of investigation, dealing with different issues and developed through different tools. In spite of this general statement it recently seems that a theoretical integration between growth and unemployment might be considered something possible and even desirable.

The revolution of endogenous growth theory, started at the end of the '80s, has not yet exhausted its potentialities in producing new contributions. Departing from the Solow-Ramsey paradigm this process of diffusion generated a heterogeneous set of models. These models allowed to produce a fertile ground to grow new ideas and to develop new tools for the economic analysis.

A similar story can be told about developments in labour economics. The debates amongst Monetarist and Keynesian views of unemployment, as well as the new contributions of Lucas' approach and New Keynesian Economics, have generally assumed a static perspective in respect of the productive capacity of the system. It is obvious that, under this assumption, there was no reason to account for growth in a model of unemployment. A significant innovation occurred with Pissarides' (1990) formulation of an unemployment theory in equilibrium. He formalized in a unique framework many previous attempts to study the labour market in a dynamic perspective, providing useful tools to analyse both long run and short run unemployment. Pissarides also introduced a first link between long run unemployment and growth (see Pissarides, 1990, Ch. II), matching his model with the neoclassical framework of economic growth. The main result founded by Pissarides is a positive correlation between growth and unemployment based on a 'capitalization effect.' When the labour market is not frictionless this effect relies on the fact that firms are much more willing to invest in new vacancies during periods of high growth.

An alternative view was suggested by Aghion and Howitt (1994). They presented a model based on the Schumpeterian idea of 'creative destruction,' to show that the relation among growth and unemployment is actually much more complex than in Pissarides' framework. Their general statement claims that, because of the interplay of competing effects, the sign of the relation between growth and unemployment can be either positive or negative. Their model consistently predicts that high rates of growth are negatively correlated with unemployment, while low rates of growth are positively correlated with unemployment.

In a different contribution, based on strategical interaction among agents, Acemoglu (1997) suggests a third way to explain the presence of unemployment in a model of technological change, which relies on the concept of strategic complementarities and co-ordination failure.

The literature about growth and unemployment formalized in a dynamic general equilibrium environment is still based on very few contributions. This just seems to be the very beginning of an interesting and important debate. The persistence of unemployment as a long run phenomenon still represents (especially for European countries) a core issue that needs to be solved through a convincing explanation and an opportune set of remedies. Actually the need for further studies is self-evident.

This survey means to present the most important contributions about the presence of unemployment in a growing economy, suggesting further alternative and possible explanations for this phenomenon. For this reason the article can be ideally divided in two parts. In the first part we will introduce the recent literature about the topic of growth and unemployment, which will be summarized in Section 2. In the second part we will provide a classification of some early contributions in the field of growth theory, which seem able to generate a fertile ground for further research. In Section 3 we will focus on the characteristics of the labour supply and on the heterogeneous distribution of skills among different workers. In Section 4 we will stress the relevance of complementarities of factors, processes and strategies as a possible cause of unemployment. The main results and observations will be summarized in Section 5.

2. Technological change, growth and unemployment

Research about the topic of growth and unemployment took place in the middle of the last century, thanks to the seminal works of Harrod (1939) and Domar (1947). These were important but isolated contributions in growth theory since they have not been followed by any relevant debate in the literature. The affirmation of Solow's (1956) model and of its Ramsey-Cass-Koopmans formulation was based, in spite of earlier descriptions of the growth process, on substitutability among factors, flexible coefficients of the production function and inelastic supply of inputs. These core assumptions of the Neoclassical paradigm led growth theorists to focus on models based on a balanced path with efficient allocation of resources.

Technological progress was introduced as exogenous variable and the steady state of the model was often determined independently in respect to the degree of 'embodiment' of technological progress. This fact displaced any concern about heterogeneity inside the economy, allowing to build aggregate models without loss of generality.

These common features clarify the reason why long run unemployment was totally ruled out by Neoclassical growth models, which have represented for a long period the leading, if not unique, tool to investigate economic expansion.

For the reasons explained above the literature about growth and unemployment is new and not extensive. After almost fifty years it seems that the issues raised by the Harrod-Domar model returned back to the economists' attention. The introduction of dynamic tools for the analysis of the labour market and the diffusion of the endogenous growth research programme represented two basic steps that allowed establishing a first link between these two fields.

At the end of the 1980s endogenous growth models started to develop increasing interest about the specific features of the cumulative factors, showing that the steady state may be neither unique, not efficient. At the same time labour economics abandoned its static, short run perspective, in order to redefine concepts and tools apt to investigate the persistence of unemployment in the long run. The concurring effects of these two processes generated fertile ground to develop further studies about the presence of unemployment in a growing economy, starting a process which is just at the very beginning, but that displays high potentialities for producing more fruitful results in the future.

We can identify two main sets of contributions about the topic of growth and unemployment. In the first set the issue is developed devoting much more attention to the institutional context of the economy, building models that are definitely more policy-oriented. In the second set of contributions, we observe models that are more specifically concerned with technological processes and with the interplay of multiple heterogeneous factors. In our opinion these models are still characterized by a descriptive attitude, rather than suggestions about policy-making. On the other side, they are better micro-founded and flexible for developing further studies.

Belonging to the first set of contributions we remark on the work by Gordon (1995), who meant to provide a common explanation to the productivity slowdown and high employment of the US and the relatively high growth, high employment of European countries. Gordon claims that the trade-off between growth and unemployment may occur in the short run, generated by structural shocks, like wage shocks. The trade-off disappears in the long run, through to a process of dynamic adjustment.

Another famous contribution dealing with the effect of fiscal policy in a growing economy was provided by Daveri and Tabellini (2000). The authors present a theoretical model supported by a wide set of empirical evidence, in order to investigate the relation between growth, unemployment and taxation in the industrialized countries. Daveri and Tabellini claim that if the wage-setting mechanism is affected by any form of rigidities, such as the presence of a monopolistic union, the role of fiscal policy is determinant for the identification of a trade off between growth and unemployment. The main idea relies on the fact that, when wages are protected by a monopolistic union, taxing labour income determines an increase in the real wage rate. An increase in the cost of labour gives incentive to firms to substitute capital for labour, lowering the marginal productivity of capital. That displaces investments, thus slowing down economic growth. The empirical evidence provided by Daveri and Tabellini shows that the tax-effect on the level of unemployment can be permanent even when the effect on the wage rate is just temporary.

In another interesting contribution, Cahuc and Michel (1996) investigate about the role of minimum wage in a model of endogenous growth. Like Daveri and Tabellini (2000) they develop a model of overlapping generations. In their model the labour force is composed of a group of skilled workers and a group of unskilled workers. The technology displays constant return to scale and it is influenced by the presence of a social externality generated by the process of human capital accumulation, following Lucas (1988). The presence of a minimum wage plays an important role in this model, determining a high relative demand for skilled labour. Since a higher relative price for unskilled labour increases the demand for skilled labour, rational workers find an incentive to invest in human capital in order to avoid unemployment. This enhances the positive effect of the social externality, supporting both growth and employment.

As a last example we report the presence in literature of a contribution by Van Schaick and De Groot (1998). The authors match growth and unemployment through a re-interpretation of Solow's condition in a model of endogenous growth with efficiency-wages[1]. The modified version of Solow's condition interprets the level of labour efficiency as the result of R&D activities performed in a high-tech sector, determining a link between the invention activity and the unemployment equilibrium determined in the labour market.

In all the previous examples the role of the institutions is determinant to identify the link between economic expansion and the labour market. We will now turn to the second set of models of growth and unemployment. Removing all of the considerations concerned with the structure of taxation and the rigidity of wages, it is in our intention to show that one can still identify many other different links between growth and unemployment. These links are intimately related with the characteristics of the accumulation process and with the strategic behaviour of agents. We will focus our attention in deeper detail about these issues.

We will depart from the theory of job-search, developed by Pissarides (1990) in his seminal work, and we will subsequently consider some of the developments and contributions that followed this approach, which is the closest to the neo-classical tradition. We will then analyse the neo-Schumpeterian approach of Aghion and Howitt (1994) and their attempt to provide some micro-foundations of labour market dynamics, related with the effect of creative destruction emerging from the invention process. We will finally consider a third approach by Acemoglu (1997), which will be completely based on strategic interaction between firms and workers.

2.1 *Pissarides and the job-search theory*

2.1.1 *The basic framework*

The seminal work by Charles Pissarides (1990) represents a first and complete collection of job-search models[2]. Chapter II of his book is dedicated to job-search and growth and consists of one of the first attempts to explain the presence of unemployment in a growing economy. The model adopted is an extension of the Neoclassical growth model with exogenous technological progress. At this first stage there is no aim to endogenize changes in technology.

Search-theory assumes that activity in the labour market is uncoordinated, time-consuming and costly. A proper matching function represents the result of this activity as the number of matches in function of the number $U = uN$ of unemployed workers and the number $V = vN$ of vacancies available in the economy at a certain point in time.

$$mN = m(uN, vN) \qquad [2.1.1]$$

The function m is concave, homogeneous of degree one and increasing in both arguments. Concavity is assumed in order to represent a congestion externality that takes place in the labour market. The more vacancies opened by the firms, the shorter the search-effort of unemployed workers; the more unemployed workers on-search in the labour market, the faster the match available for each firm. Defining $\theta = v/u$, we can express: $q(\theta) = m(uN, vN)/vN = m(v/u, 1)$ as the rate of recruitment by the firms.

Workers' flows move *out of* and *into* unemployment. Job-specific shocks occur according with a Poisson process of rate λ and determine the end of a match with a firm. We can write the dynamic evolution of unemployment in the following form:

$$\dot{u} = \lambda(1 - u) - \theta q(\theta)u \qquad [2.1.2]$$

On the right side of equation [2.1.2] the first term represents the flow of workers *into* unemployment and the second term the flow of workers *out of* unemployment. In steady state we can express the rate of unemployment as a function of the parameter λ and of the labour market tightness θ.

$$u = \lambda/[\lambda + \theta q(\theta)] \qquad [2.1.3]$$

Equation [2.1.3] is the Beveridge-curve, usually represented as a convex to the origin and downward-sloping relation on the (U, V) space of the labour market. Pissarides assumes that firms produce the final good using capital and labour through a constant return to scale (CRS) technology, concave and increasing in both factors:

$$y_i = F(K_i, AL_i) \qquad [2.1.4]$$

Equation [2.1.4] can be expressed in its intensive form: $y = f(k)$. We assume at first that each firm can open only one vacancy. The firm engages a research activity for matching his vacancy with a worker affording a hiring cost per unit of labour denoted by z. When the vacancy is matched, the firm rents capital at rate r and produces output y. Firms evaluate the present-discounted revenue of a vacant job W and the present discounted revenue of a matched job J, in order to satisfy the Bellman equation:

$$rW = -z + q(\theta)(J - W)$$ [2.1.5]

On the left side it expressed the capital cost, where r indicates the interest rate. On the right side the value of the rate of return is obtained by summing the hiring cost and the expected net revenue in the occurrence of a job match. In equilibrium there are no rents for vacant jobs, so that if $W = 0$:

$$J = z/q(\theta)$$ [2.1.6]

The 'job-creation equation' [2.1.6], expresses that the profit belonging to a new job is equal to the expected cost of hiring a worker. A similar evaluation is performed for each matched job, by using the Bellman equation:

$$r(J + k) = f(k) - \delta k - w - \lambda J$$ [2.1.7]

The left side represents the asset value of a matched vacancy plus the value of rented capital. The right side expresses the profit emerging from a filled job, where w is the cost of labour and δ is the rate of depreciation of capital.

Substituting equation [2.1.6] in equation [2.1.7] we obtain[3]:

$$f(k) - (r + \delta) - w - z(r + \lambda)/q(\theta) = 0$$ [2.1.8]

In order to derive a complete specification of the steady state, a description of the wage-setting mechanism is required. Pissarides observes that in a labour market described as an uncoordinated and costly activity, the sum of expected returns of a searching firm and expected returns of a searching worker is strictly inferior to the returns emerging from a job match. There are rents, generated by each matched job, that are to be shared between profits and wages. The solution suggested is the adoption of a Nash-bargain mechanism, which leads to the following result:

$$w = \pi z + (1 - \pi)[f(k) - (r + \delta)k + \theta z]$$ [2.1.9]

The equilibrium wage equation expressed in [2.1.9] is the solution of the bargaining problem. It is a weighted average between the unemployment benefit b and the marginal productivity of labour, augmented by the average hiring cost θz. Parameter π indicates the profit share. The congestion externality in the labour market displays its linear effects on the equilibrium wage through parameter θ. Equations [2.1.3], [2.1.8], [2.1.9] determine the steady state configuration for (u, θ, w).

This basic model can now be extended in order to obtain exogenous growth.

Exogenous disembodied technological progress can occur, assuming that the productivity parameter A in equation [2.1.4] increases over the time and for all the firms in a classical labour-augmenting fashion.

$$A_t = A_0 e^{\gamma} \qquad \qquad [2.1.10]$$

Each firm can now open a wider number of vacancies, denoted by V_i. It is assumed that the number of firms is large enough to eliminate uncertainty about labour flows. The wage setting mechanism follows the same Nash-bargaining mechanism described by equation [2.1.9]. This assumption about wage-setting mechanism is consistent with results if a market for capital does exist and there are no long-term contracts. In fact each firm decides how many jobs are to be created by anticipating the correct wage, but the same firm assumes the wage as given when the number of jobs is actually stated. The stream of firm i's expected profits is expressed by:

$$\prod_i = \int_0^{\infty} e^{-rt}[F(K_i, AL_i) - wL_i - zAV_i - \dot{K}_i - \delta K_i]dt \qquad [2.1.11]$$

The dynamics of the labour force for each firm is described by:

$$\dot{L}_i = q(\theta)V_i - \lambda L_i \qquad \qquad [2.1.12]$$

Profits are maximized in respect to capital and number of vacancies opened, subject to the constraint expressed by [2.1.12]. For given paths of A and θ, Euler's conditions guarantee the existence of an optimal path for K_i and L_i. The steady state is obtained setting to zero equation [2.1.12], when:

$$V_i = \lambda L_t / q(\theta) \qquad \qquad [2.1.13]$$

To obtain consistency in steady state, we assume that the unemployment benefit b and the hiring cost z are both indexed with the level of wages: $b = b_0 w$, $z = z_0 w$. The new wage-equation turns into the following expression:

$$w = \{(1 - \pi)/[1 - \pi z_0 - (1 - \pi)b_0\theta]\}A[f(k) - (r + \delta)k] \qquad [2.1.14]$$

Solving the intertemporal optimisation problem for equation [2.1.12], conditions for the steady state are derived. As long as $F(K_i, AL_i)$ is homogeneous of degree one, we can express these conditions in terms of units of efficient labour, through the use of the intensive form:

$$f'(k) = r + \delta \qquad \qquad [2.1.15]$$

$$A[f(k) - kf'(k)] = w + [(r + \lambda - \gamma)/q(\theta)]z_0 w \qquad [2.1.16]$$

The marginal productivity of labour equals the wage paid to the workers, plus a term which accounts for the frictions of the labour market. Substituting equation

[2.1.16] in equation [2.1.14] we identify a final condition for the labour market tightness θ:

$$\pi b_0 - (1 - \pi)z_0\theta - [(r + \lambda - \gamma)/q(\theta)](1 - \pi)z_0 = 0 \qquad [2.1.17]$$

From equation [2.1.17] we find that γ and θ are, *ceteris paribus*, positively related. That is due to the dynamics which lie behind the firm's profit maximization process. Considering Euler's conditions for maximizing equation [2.1.11], it can be shown that each firm is supposed to afford hiring costs today for the stream of profits it will earn tomorrow. We assumed that profits and hiring costs both grow at the same rate in steady state so, with higher growth rates, firms will find rational to open more vacancies today in order to save hiring costs of tomorrow, thus obtaining an increase in the stream of profits. This identifies the 'capitalization effect' which is based on the forward-looking behaviour of firms that are supposed to maximize their profits. A change in the rate of growth determines a change in the optimal choice of firms about the number of vacancies to be opened, reflecting its effects on the labour market.

The model still lacks the means to determine the rate of interest, which is identified by the demand-side of the economy. Pissarides follows a traditional dynamic IS-LM approach. The law of accumulation of capital is defined from:

$$\dot{K}_t = Y_t - \delta K_t - C_t \qquad [2.1.18]$$

The aggregate consumption is defined as a fixed amount β of the disposable income:

$$C_t = \beta(Y_t - \delta K_t + (\mu - \dot{p})M_t/P_t) \qquad [2.1.19]$$

Where: μ is the rate of growth for money, $\dot{p}$ is the rate of inflation and M/P expresses the real balances. The LM balance condition closes the model:

$$M_t/P_t = g(r + \dot{p})Y_t \quad g' < 0 \qquad [2.1.20]$$

From the demand-side set of equation one can derive the following steady-state condition:

$$[1 - \beta - \beta\gamma g(r + \mu - \gamma)]f(k) - [(1 - \beta)\delta + \gamma]k = 0 \qquad [2.1.21]$$

Equation [2.1.21], together with equation [2.1.15], determines r and k in steady-state.

We have already observed that the rate of growth is negatively related with the rate of unemployment from the perspective of the supply side. From equation [2.1.21] we note that an increase in the growth rate lowers the capital ratio per unit of efficient labour, determining an increase in the rate of interest r. Through equation [2.1.17] this affects the labour market tightness and the effect can be either positive or negative, depending on the sign of the difference r-γ. While the supply-side of the model determines a unequivocal relation among growth and unemployment, the final effect can be either positive or negative when one considers the demand-side dynamics.

2.1.2 *Endogenous growth and unemployment: Neoclassical and Keynesian features*

Bean and Pissarides (1993) presented further developments of the basic model of job-search. They built an overlapping generation model where both growth and unemployment are endogenous variables: this allows us to analyse another kind of feedback effect that unemployment generates on growth. Their framework is based on an extension of the basic overlapping generation model by Diamond (1965), where they introduce a technology that displays decreasing returns to capital at the firm level, but constant returns at the aggregate level, following Romer (1986). As a second assumption, the authors introduce a costly process of matching between workers and firms. In a first phase, the model simply displays in steady state endogenous growth with positive rate of unemployment. In a second phase, Keynesian features are introduced inside the model, assuming imperfect competition in the goods market. The model is enriched with many different parameters that can account for policy intervention.

The authors are particularly focused on the effect of changes in aggregate savings. They argue that unemployment can reduce the pool of savings and, subsequently, the investments necessary to enhance accumulation of capital. Departing from this observation, they use their model to investigate how different kinds of policy intervention can affect the endogenous variable through the mechanism described above[4].

In the model a reduction of the hiring costs determines an increase in the number of vacancies created by firms. This enhances employment and generates an increase in the pool of savings, which stimulates accumulation of capital and growth. In this case an intervention oriented to the labour market determines positive effects for both growth and unemployment. When the intervention is directed to increase the workers' bargaining power, the results are much more ambiguous. A higher wage discourages firms from opening new vacancies, increasing unemployment. On the other side higher income for workers turns into an increase in the pool of savings, which could stimulate growth. The net effect on the pool of savings cannot be determined *a priori*.

In the extended version of the model, Bean and Pissarides introduce two sectors (consumption and investment goods), assuming imperfect competition in the goods market. When entry-costs in the goods market are sufficiently large and the mark-up margin is high, one observes that an increase in the marginal propensity to consume can increase the pool of savings and stimulate growth despite what could be predicted under classical assumptions. The authors assume that hiring costs are valued in terms of consumption. In this way increasing demand for final goods lowers the price, diminishing hiring costs and reducing unemployment.

This new framework by Bean and Pissarides (1993) can turn into an useful tool to investigate the impact of different policies on both the endogenous variables. The model is based on a wider set of assumptions, such as expressing all the costs in terms of consumption and assuming standard conditions for determinacy of the steady state in the overlapping generation model. The results become more precise, but less robust.

2.1.3 *Endogenous consumer's behaviour*

Pissarides (1990) defines the aggregate consumption as a fixed amount of disposable income. Eriksson (1997) presents a slightly different version of the model, developing the demand-side along the lines of the Ramsey model. This modification can turn into an interesting tool to investigate the feedback impact generated by the labour market on the rate of growth of the economy. Assuming that each consumer displays a constant intertemporal elasticity of substitution (CIES) instantaneous utility function:

$$U_j = \left(C_j^{1-\sigma} - 1\right)/(1 - \sigma) \qquad\qquad [2.1.22]$$

The household's budget constraint is defined by:

$$\dot{K}_j = (1 - \tau)rK_j + w(1 - u)L_j + b_o wuL_j - C_j + VI_j \qquad [2.1.23]$$

Households are all identical. Each household accounts for the time spent in production $(1 - u)L_j$ and the time spent in unemployment uL_j as well as it needs to consider the rental income derived from putting out vacancies VI_j. The parameter τ represents the tax rate on capital income.

Re-expressing the consumption in unit of efficient labour and solving the intertemporal optimisation problem for the households one finds that:

$$\dot{c} = \sigma^{-1}(f'(k) - \rho - \sigma\gamma)c \qquad\qquad [2.1.24]$$

From equations [2.1.15], [2.2.24] and [2.2.23], expressed in efficiency units, one can determine the responsiveness of k, c and the new endogenous variable r in respect of the parameters of the model. The rate of interest becomes positively varying in respect of the tax rate τ, the elasticity of substitution σ, the rate of intertemporal substitution ρ and of the rate of growth γ.

Computing the effect of a variation of the growth rate on the market tightness and of a variation of the market tightness on unemployment, Eriksson determines a positive relation between growth and unemployment (under the assumption that the elasticity of intertemporal substitution is small enough). Technically, Eriksson showes that $dr/d\gamma = \sigma/(1 - \tau)$, so that if $\sigma < 1 - \tau$, then an increase in γ decreases the difference $(r - \gamma)$. From equation [2.1.17] this turns into a lower level of the market tightness and a subsequent increase in unemployment. Since all the parameters of the model display a positive relation with the rate of interest, one can even focus on the demand side of the model, concluding that if either σ or ρ increase, the rate of interest increases, stressing the trade-off between growth and unemployment.

Eriksson shows how an apparently slight change of the original model determines an opposite result in respect to what was obtained by Pissarides (1990). Endogenizing the rate of interest allows us to explore in detail the interplay of the labour market with the mechanics of growth. The rate of interest assumes a key role in Eriksson's specification of the model. Every kind of intervention which is meant to lower the rate of interest determines higher employment.

A similar result is obtained when the rate of growth is endogenously determined by some cumulative factor which sustains the fall of the productivity of capital in equation [2.2.24]. The rate of growth becomes much more responsive to a change of the parameters, and the trade-off between growth and unemployment can be still identified.

2.1.4 *Workers on active search*

In the basic framework of the job-search model only firms are assumed to incur in a cost to match workers with their opened vacancies. Workers are just supposed to be passively waiting for a match, comparing their prospective income with the opportunity cost of being unemployed. King and Welling (1995), on the contrary, assume that workers need to bear a direct cost when they decide to actively search for a new job, while firms can create vacancies without any cost.

The authors develop a model where firms belonging to different spatial locations can receive different location-specific shocks. The firms are also affected by economy-wide exogenous technological progress. Under the rational expectation hypothesis, workers find an incentive to move to high-productivity districts since they can increase their expected income in terms of wage. In steady state one finds that, in the presence of active cost of search for workers, the rate of search is an increasing function of the growth rate and total unemployment is a decreasing function of the growth rate.

This result allows us to show a different mechanism of determination of equilibrium unemployment. In both Pissarides (1990) and King and Welling (1995) there is a negative correlation between growth and unemployment, but in Pissarides (1990) the amount of search is decreasing with the size of innovations, since more vacancies are opened through the capitalization effect. In King and Welling (1995) the rate of search is increasing since workers try to move to more productive districts.

In the model the concept of 'waiting-time unemployment' it is also introduced, and this occurs when the worker does not move, but just waits for an improvement of the condition of her/his own district. 'Waiting-time unemployment', as well as total unemployment, is a decreasing function of the rate of growth.

The key assumption on which King and Welling (1995) derived their results is based on the presence of a direct cost for active search for workers that does not seem to find much support in literature. Nevertheless King and Welling (1995) show that the presence of asymmetry between the rational choice of workers and firms is a basic assumption for the result derived about the rate of search.

More, we find interesting the idea of developing the presence of spatially distinct locations affected by different shocks. The authors claim that this assumption can be even interpreted as the presence in the economy of different productive opportunities, to be matched with specific types of human capital by heterogeneous workers. The positive relation between the rate of search and the rate of growth could be interpreted as an incentive for workers to devote much time to human capital accumulation when innovations are larger. This would imply that in periods of expansion there is less search within a profession and more switching between professions. We will develop this issue in the next sections.

2.2 The neo-Schumpeterian approach to growth and unemployment

Aghion and Howitt (1994) presented one first interesting reply to Pissarides' (1990) attempts to consider growth and unemployment in a joint way. They extended their basic model of creative destruction to take into account the problem of labour reallocation across firms. A few years later further extensions have been brought to this model in their contribution on endogenous growth theory (see Aghion and Howitt, 1998).

Aghion's and Howitt's (1994) model is based on an economy constituted by a continuum of infinitely lived agents, indexed on the space [0,1]. Each household is endowed with a flow of one unit of labour service that s/he supplies to firms. S/he is also endowed with a stock of h units of human capital. All the households display the same preferences and the same intertemporal utility function over the final good y:

$$U(c) = E_0 \int_0^\infty c_t(y_t)e^{-\rho}dt \qquad [2.2.1]$$

The number of firms is endogenously determined in steady state. Aghion and Howitt define the firm as: '[...] an 'institutional embodiment of knowledge', in other words [...] a research facilities for producing new knowledge, for generating new ideas.' [Aghion and Howitt (1994), p.479].

Setting up a new plant requires a sunk cost D_t, which rises at the steady state growth rate: $D_t = D_0 e^\gamma$. Once settled, each plant produces a stream of innovations, following a Poisson process of rate λ.

Production of the final good is performed combining a machine that embodies a specific technology, an appropriate worker to be matched with the machine and a variable amount of human capital:

$$y_t = A_t f(h_t - h_{\min}) \qquad [2.2.2]$$

The function $f(\cdot)$ displays all the neoclassical features and Inada conditions are assumed as well. In the basic framework the productivity parameter A_t is exogenously determined and following the standard exponential rule: $A_t = A_0 e^{\gamma t}$. The Poisson process describes the flow of innovations for the firm. If a firm decides to convert the innovation project in new technology, it will afford an implementation cost C_t and the new process will be available at time t.

Unemployment is generated in the model by labour-reallocation across firms. In fact, as long as a firm does not innovate, it will not be able to cover its fixed cost and it will be forced to close, forcing the worker into unemployment. The worker will start looking for a new match with another firm. The matching process is deterministic and it is described following a matching function of the type adopted by Diamond and Blanchard (1989) and Pissarides (1990). The matching function is assumed to display all the neoclassical standard features.

The recruitment rate $q(V)$ for a firm searching a new worker will be a decreasing function of the number of vacancies in the economy. For each worker looking for a new match the job-finding rate v will be an increasing function of the whole number of vacancies. Assume that the duration of each match takes S unit of time. A worker forced into unemployment will wait $1/v(V)$ units of time before finding a new job. On the other side a firm trying to associate a worker with a new machine, will wait $1/q(V)$ units of time before obtaining a proper match. Aghion and Howitt identify a situation of 'involuntary unemployment' if workers spend more time looking for a job than working: $1/v(V) > S$. Denoting by u the rate of unemployment we can state the equilibrium condition for flows *out of* and *into* unemployment:

$$(1 - u)(1/S) = v(V) \qquad [2.2.3]$$

If we assume S constant and technologically determined, equation [2.2.3] can be re-written as:

$$u = 1 - Sv(V) \qquad [2.2.4]$$

This is a Beveridge curve, representing the typical negative relation between vacancies and unemployment. Aghion's and Howitt's main purpose consists on expressing the Beveridge curve in function of technological change. Through a progressive process of specification they nest growth generated by innovation into the labour market's steady state condition expressed by [2.2.4].

Whenever a firm decides to innovate, say at time t_0, it starts looking for a specialized worker. A match is obtained at time $t_0 + 1/q(V)$ and the production process can begin.

The maximization condition for each firm is:

$$\max_{h \geq h_{\min}} \{A_t f(h - h_{\min}) - p_t h\} = A_t \Pi(p_t/A_t) \qquad [2.2.5]$$

The price for human capital grows, as well as the other prices and costs, at the steady state rate: $p_t = p_0 e^{\gamma t}$. It follows that the firm needs to innovate to survive in the long-run. In fact, if the level of A_t does not grow, the profit will decrease and finally falls to zero at time $t_0 + S$, forcing the worker into unemployment.

If no innovations are introduced, at time $t_0 + S$ human capital reaches a trigger value p^{max} which determines null profits for the firm. We can express the duration of a match in the following way:

$$p_{t_0+S}/A_t = (p_{t_0}/A_t)e^{\gamma S} = p^{max} \qquad [2.2.6]$$

$$S = \Gamma/\gamma \quad \Gamma = \log(p^{max}) - \log(p_{t_0}/A_t) > 0 \qquad [2.2.7]$$

Substituting equation [2.2.7] into equation [2.2.4] we obtain:

$$u = 1 - (\Gamma v(V)/\gamma) \qquad [2.2.8]$$

This shows that growth generates a direct 'creative destruction' effect on unemployment, acting through a reduction of the duration of the job match. Aghion and Howitt denote that other competing effects of growth on unemployment are to be taken into account. These effects work indirectly through the dynamic mechanism of entrance of new firms into the economy and through the clearing equation in the human capital market.

Consider the flow of discounted expected profits for a firm that is going to enter into the market:

$$W_t = WA_t = E_{\varepsilon \geq 0}[(V_{t+\varepsilon} + W_{t+\varepsilon})e^{-r\varepsilon}] \qquad [2.2.9]$$

Where $t + \varepsilon$ denotes the date of the first innovation for the firm which enters at t and $V_{t+\varepsilon} = VA_{t+\varepsilon}$ is the present value of the stream of profits generated by the innovation that occurred at $t + \varepsilon$. Solving equation [2.2.9] one obtains that:

$$W = \lambda V/(r - \gamma) \qquad [2.2.10]$$

Denoting by d the sunk cost the firm has to afford, the free-entry condition will be:

$$d = \lambda V/(r - \gamma) \qquad [2.2.11]$$

Equation [2.2.5] represents the stream of profits that an innovation provides during the match $[t_0, t_0 + S]$. As in Pissarides (1990), firms and market set the wage through a bargaining mechanism. Firms obtain a profit-share π: $0 \leq \pi \leq 1$. Each match requires an implementation cost, denoted by $Z_t = zA_t$.

An innovation introduced at time t, starts to generate profits at time $1 + 1/q(V)$, when an appropriate match with a worker occurs. At this time the implementation cost is paid and the firm obtains a stream of profits lasting at time $1 + 1/q(V) + S$. Considering what stated with equations [2.2.5], [2.2.6] and [2.2.7] we can finally express the discounted stream of profits generated by a firm:

$$V = \exp(-r/\tau)\left\{ \pi \int_0^{\Gamma/\gamma} \exp(-r/s)\Pi[p^{max}\exp(\gamma s - \Gamma)]ds - z \right\} \qquad [2.2.12]$$

obtaining a definitive formulation for the free-entry condition:

$$d = [\lambda/(r-\gamma)]\exp(-r/\tau)\left\{\pi \int_0^{\Gamma/\gamma} \exp(-r/s)\Pi[p^{\max}\exp(\gamma s - \Gamma)]ds - z\right\} \quad [2.2.13]$$

If the growth rate γ increases two competing effects will emerge:

- It will decrease the net rate at which the stream of profits is discounted. For each firm the entry will result less costly. More vacancies will be created, reducing the unemployment rate (capitalization effect).
- It will reduce the life-time of each firm (see equation [2.2.8]), by increasing the price for human capital. Each innovation will generate fewer vacancies than before. That will be reflected in an increase of the rate of unemployment (indirect creative destruction effect).

Considering equation [2.2.8] we can observe that creative destruction determines a direct negative effect on unemployment through the duration of each match and the parameter Γ. It also determines an indirect effect through the reduction of V, which lowers the job-finding rate $v(V)$.

To close the model we finally consider the clearing condition for the human capital market:

$$H = (1-u)(1/\Gamma)\int_0^\Gamma h[p^{\max}\exp(\chi - \Gamma)]d\chi \quad [2.2.14]$$

The left side represents the aggregate supply of human capital in the economy. The right side is the demand side, obtained by multiplying the labour force by the demand of human capital of each firm, where $\chi = \gamma s : \chi \in [0,\Gamma]$ is the technological age of the plant. From equation [2.2.14] we can deduce that Γ, maximum technological age for a plant is an increasing function of the rate of unemployment and a decreasing function of the aggregate stock of human capital in the economy.

The steady state for the system is a configuration (u^*, V^*, Γ^*) that guarantees: clearing of the human capital market, a constant unemployment rate, a constant number of vacancies, fixed at the level that sets to zero the profitability on the free-entry condition.

Differently parameterized simulations for the model reflected only two possible results: a reverse U-shaped relation between growth and unemployment or a monotone increasing relation between growth and unemployment. The presence of many parameters drives to a complex explanation of the effects of growth on unemployment, but simulations seemed to fit what happens in reality.

Aghion and Howitt extended their framework to account for flexible rate of interest, endogenous growth, and learning by doing. Endogenous growth was introduced adopting the results presented in Aghion and Howitt (1992). Learning by doing effects seem to be the most interesting feature of these new extensions.

Suppose introducing a learning mechanism, which depends on the level of workers employed in production:

$$\gamma = \gamma_0 + \alpha(1 - u) \quad \alpha > 0, \gamma > 0 \qquad [2.2.15]$$

The new definition for the rate of growth affects the free-entry condition expressed in [2.2.13]. The productivity of each match will depend on the constant rate of growth γ_0 and on the share of growth based upon the learning process. The final effect turns to be ambiguous.

An increase in unemployment determines an increase of the technological age of each machine Γ, as seen in the human capital market clearing equation. That increases the number of vacancies V with a positive effect, reducing future unemployment. An increase in unemployment also determines an increase in the discount rate for the stream of expected profits and a reduction of learning-by-doing on each match. The latter effect occurs as long as less workers in the active labour force generate less aggregate learning spillovers.

The authors assume that learning is a process that involves all the productive units, so that it does not generate creative destruction effects. An increase in the learning performance of households will not determine reallocation, but only unemployment reduction. On the other hand the learning process generates a feedback effect that might also determine strategic complementarities in the sense of Cooper and John (1988) (see Section 4.2) and then multiple equilibria. The economy could be trapped in a situation of low growth, low learning and high-unemployment. The intervention of a planner would be required to move the system on a Pareto-preferred equilibrium.

In the earliest version of the model (see Aghion and Howitt, 1998a) the perfect substitutability hypothesis among intermediate good has been removed[5] but nothing was said about the demand of final goods. The demand side of the model is reduced to a very simple problem of utility maximization, where the utility function is assumed to be linear. Consumers do not perform consumption-smoothing. More, households can be either employed or unemployed, but they are assumed to consume the same amount of good in each period. That is less likely to be true, as long as the same feedback effect that was presented for learning-by-doing can be experimented regarding the demand for the final good. Introducing a demand-side into the model could lead us to conclude that as long as less workers are in the active labour force, there will be less consumption and that will reduce the incentive to firms to enter and create new vacancies. Even in this case strategic complementarities could arise.

2.3 Coordination failures, growth and unemployment

Acemoglu (1997) criticizes the recent literature about the problem of growth and unemployment, pointing out that none of the contributions presented considers the problem of labour supply. Labour is carefully described in terms of demand, but not many considerations are spent regarding worker skills in relation to specific technologies. Acemoglu focuses on this aspect, presenting a model with two competing technologies and potential heterogeneity among workers endowed with different skills.

The first existing technology requires a fixed cost, normalized to 0, while the second technology requires a new machine at the fixed cost $d > 0$. The new machine needs to be matched with a skilled worker to produce a stream of productivity $y + \alpha$. Both the first technology and the second, if not properly matched with a skilled worker, produce a stream of productivity equal to y.

Suppose that the labour market allocation mechanism is described by a standard random matching function. If the proportion of skilled workers in the unemployment pool is u_{skill}, the probability that a skilled worker will be matched with a vacancy will also be u_{skill}. Job-specific shocks occur at the exogenous rate λ, and determine the end of a match.

Assume that the system is in steady state when the new technology becomes available. At any point in time each firm may decide about opening a new vacancy at flow cost c, adopting the new technology for production. Investing in the new technology, the firm may also choose whether to train an unskilled worker at cost χ. Assuming that θ represents the tightness on the labour market, the steady state condition at time $t = 0$ is expressed by equation [2.1.3]. The value of a firm adopting a new technology with a filled job is denoted by J^N. The value is denoted V^N, when the vacancy is still available. Values J^0 and V^0 will denote the same quantities when the firm has not adopted the new technology. Let us now consider the following set of Bellman equations:

$$rJ^N - \dot{J}^N = y + \alpha - w^N + \lambda(V^N - J^N)$$

$$rV^N - \dot{V}^N = -c + q(\theta) \left[\begin{array}{l} (1 - u_{skill}) \max\{J^N - V^N - \chi; J^{ON} - V^N, 0\} + \\ + u_{skill}(J^N - V^N) \end{array} \right] \qquad [2.3.1]$$

Where r is the fixed interest rate, the first equation states that the period value of a firm with a filled job is equal to the instantaneous capital gain $\dot{J}^N$, plus the net product $y + \alpha - w^N$, plus the opportunity cost of the stream of profit obtained in the case a job-specific shock occurs, expressed by λ. The second equation states that the period value of a firm with an open vacancy is equal to the instantaneous capital gain, minus the cost of opening a vacancy and plus a weighted average of the different profits the firm can earn if filling the vacancy at probability $q(\theta)$. The worker matched with the firm can be skilled and so able to generate the stream of profits: $J^N - V^N$. In the case that the worker is unskilled, the firm will decide whether it is worthy to train him/her, at cost χ, leaving him/her unskilled obtaining the stream of profits $J^{ON} - J^N$, or leaving the vacancy unfilled with a null profit.

A second set of Bellman equations describes similar conditions for a firm that does not adopt the new technology:

$$rJ^0 - \dot{J}^1 = y + \alpha - w^0 + \lambda(V^0 - J^0)$$

$$rV^0 - \dot{V}^0 = -c + q(\theta) \begin{bmatrix} (1 - u_{\text{skill}}) \max\{J^0 - V^0; J^N - V^0 - d - \chi\}+ \\ + u_{\text{skill}} \max\{J^{N0} - V^0; J^N - V^0 - d; 0\} \end{bmatrix} \qquad [2.3.2]$$

Assume that: m denotes the number of firms adopting the new technology, n^0_{skill} the number of skilled workers employed in firms adopting the traditional technology, n^1_{unskill} the number of unskilled workers employed in firms adopting the new technology. Acemoglu derives the dynamics for the pool of unemployed skilled workers, obtaining the following differential equation:

$$\dot{u}_{\text{skill}} = \theta q(\theta)[m(1 - n^1_{\text{unskill}}) + (1 - m)n^0_{\text{skill}} - u_{\text{skill}}] \qquad [2.3.3]$$

Quantities m and n^1_{unskill} are determined by equations [2.3.1] and [2.3.2] and they consequently determine the flow of skilled workers *into* and *out of* unemployment.

Wages are setted through a Nash-bargain game, where workers are assumed to display a bargain power of $(1 - \pi)$. No-arbitrage conditions are also assumed for equilibrium: $V^0 = 0$, $V^N = \delta$. Under the above assumptions from equation [2.3.1] and [2.3.2] we can obtain the following results:

$$J^N(t) = [(1 - \pi)(y + \alpha) + \lambda d]/[r + \lambda]$$
$$J^0(t) = [(1 - \pi)y]/[r + \lambda] \qquad [2.3.4]$$

A new technology is adopted when: $J^N \geq J^0 + d + \chi$. This condition depends on the market tightness θ and can be re-written as:

$$\alpha \geq \alpha'(\theta_0) \equiv [rd + (r + \lambda)\chi]/(1 - \beta) \qquad [2.3.5]$$

If the condition expressed in equation [2.3.5] holds, Acemoglu shows that the system will move towards an equilibrium where the new technology will be adopted progressively by all the firms and where firms will decide to train all workers. The dynamics are determined through the market tightness θ, which shifts from an initial value θ_0 to a final value θ_1, where $u(\theta_0) \geq u(\theta_1)$.

Acemoglu observes that a coordination failure could arise if we assume that each firm expects that no other firms will adopt the new technology. In this case one of the two no-arbitrage conditions does not hold any more ($V^N \neq d$). Firms that lose their workers because of a random shock will not be able to sell the machine embodying the new technology. They will also expect no possibilities in finding a new skilled worker ($u_{\text{skill}} = 0$), since all the workers will be still unskilled in the labour market. The new condition to invest in the innovative technology will be:

$$\alpha \geq \alpha^0(\theta_0), \quad \text{where} : \alpha^0(\theta_0) \geq \alpha^1(\theta_0) \qquad [2.3.6]$$

The effective cost for investing in the new technology will be higher in respect of the case expressed by condition [2.3.5]. The author demonstrates that if $\alpha \in \left(\alpha^1(\theta_0), \alpha^0(\theta_0)\right)$ there will exist two pure strategy symmetric equilibria for this game between firms. In one equilibrium there will be no innovation and high unemployment, in the other equilibrium there will be innovation and lower unemployment.

Expectations about the technology adopted by firms determines a kind of strategic complementarity which influences the actual rate of unemployment. This result is achieved within an intertemporal horizon model, where the relative frequency of skilled workers in the unemployment pool is dynamically upgraded over the time by equation [2.3.3]. This seems to suggest a way to introduce the static concept of Nash-equilibrium in a dynamic environment.

3. The role of human capital

In the previous section we presented some results already obtained to model unemployment in a growing economy. We now mean to explore alternative solutions to the problem, referring to the recent existing literature about growth. It is our purpose to show that some of the models and mechanisms adopted to describe the growth process display uncovered potentialities to provide an explanation for the persistence of unemployment in the economy.

We noted that the models based on Pissarides' framework are much more linked with the neoclassical conception of physical capital interpreted as the basic accumulating factor. A slightly different and interesting interpretation about the presence of heterogeneous skills can be found in the spatial model by King and Welling (1995), even if not deeply developed. The neo-Schumpeterian approach, on the other hand, assumes the presence of heterogeneous workers to be matched with different technologies, but the attention is focused on the decisional algorithm of the entrepreneur, leaving the workers to be passively waiting for a match. The process of match is hidden inside the 'black box', represented by the matching function. In Acemoglu's (1997) framework, explicit consideration about the heterogeneity of the labour supply does not rely on a matching function, but the dynamics of the distribution of skills is still analysed as an aggregative result. The leading role is still assigned to firms that, in this case, strategically interact in the economy.

In this section we mean to focus on the role of human capital, devoting particular attention to the distribution of skills across the pool of workers. In our opinion, modelling this kind of heterogeneity among agents can turn into an interesting tool to analyse the relationship between growth and unemployment. The endogenous growth revolution that occurred at the end of 19080s, gave a determinant contribution in this sense. In the Neoclassical framework capital stock has traditionally been considered the most important cumulative factor. In spite of that a large number of endogenous growth models emphasized the features of the labour force.

3.1 *Education and human capital*

Following Lucas' (1988) re-exposition of human capital theory, some models have introduced new and more complex definitions of labour as a productive factor, finding that it could be assigned the leading role in the accumulation process. This fact can be very useful for our analysis if heterogeneity of the labour force can lead to a better explanation for the persistence of unemployment in a growing economy.

Lucas (1988) attributed to the workers a personal identity through the different endowment of human capital that they decide to cumulate before entering the process of production. This idea was not developed any further in his model and all the significant results were derived at the aggregative level.

Stokey (1991) followed Lucas' contribution, introducing a relation between heterogeneity of workers and heterogeneity of goods. Heterogeneity of workers is defined by Stokey in terms of different levels of human capital which they decide to cumulate before entering the process of production. Each agent sets the quantity of time to dedicate to education. The agent compares this investment with the opportunity cost of a higher wage during the time devoted to production. Investing time in education the agent unconsciously determines an increase of the aggregate stock of knowledge into the system. S/he is not able to take into account the external effect reflected in the whole economy, which is determinant to generate growth. Heterogeneity of goods is defined by their technological intensities. Goods providing a higher number of Lancasterian characteristics are goods which require more specialized workers to be produced. The technology adopted consists of a CRS neoclassical production function, unchanging over time. Technological progress is defined in this framework as dropping lower-intensity goods and adding higher-intensity goods in the production set of the economy (see also Stokey[6], 1988). This process is generated by the external effect that allows improving technological skills and expanding the upper bound of the production set. Stokey's main goal is providing an explanation for the leading role of international trade in determining different patterns of human capital specialization and goods production. To achieve this goal, Stokey removes the classical hypothesis of perfect substitutability among skilled and unskilled labour: skilled labour performs higher-quality services to produce technology-intensive goods displaying more characteristics.

Even if the main aim of Stokey's work is dealing with path dependence and international trade, we can underline some interesting features about the composition of the labour force. The paper explicitly considers the problem of allocating heterogeneous workers over production of different goods. Removing the hypothesis of perfect substitutability among different workers we could infer a first cause of unemployment, which may arise in a context of growth. We can even think about this feature in a dynamic way. If international trade has strong influence on labour specialisation and production it might happen that the distribution of workers across different lines of goods could be locked-in by international market mechanisms.

Let us suppose that one country displays a high share of its output composition totally devoted to export. If an external shock affects the demand for the main set of goods produced by that country, unemployment could rise. In fact production could not be easily switched to different and more profitable goods as long as the distribution of workers is locked-in. The conclusions presented are just conjectures, derived by a simple framework built with different purposes, but they stress the importance of core assumptions, (like labour imperfect substitutability and labour and goods heterogeneity) that may be introduced to think about unemployment in a growing economy.

3.2 Learning-by-doing and human capital

The examples presented above interpret human capital as the result of investment in education. We will now consider another model developed by Lucas (1993). This framework collects Stokey's contributions about lock-in mechanisms and it matches them with a different formulation of sustained growth depending on allocation of labour across different lines of production[7]. In this case the main mechanism is not based on education, but on learning-by-doing.

Lucas defines an economy with a continuum of goods x, indexed by s, such that $s \in [0, S]$.

$$x_{s,t} = A_s L_{s,t} h_{s,t}^{\alpha} \qquad [3.2.1]$$

Skilled labour hL is the only factor of production. The level of accumulated skill is represented by h, where α expresses the effect of previously accumulated skill on the actual level of production. A is a productivity parameter. Learning-by-doing is the leading process that allows cumulating skills over the time:

$$\dot{h}_{s,t} = L_{s,t} h_{s,t}^{\alpha} \qquad [3.2.2]$$

At any point in time, the actual level of ability in producing the good s depends on a starting level of knowledge referred to time t_0 and on the flow of workers who previously gave their contribution to the production of good s:

$$h_{s,t} = \left[h_{s,t_0}^{1-\alpha} + (1 - \alpha) \int_0^1 L_s(v_s) dv_s \right]^{\frac{1}{1-\alpha}} \qquad [3.2.3]$$

At first we consider the learning process as developing independently over goods of different vintage. All the goods x, jointly considered, determine the aggregate production y for the system:

$$y = \int_0^{S_t} e^{\mu s} x_s ds \qquad [3.2.4]$$

S defines the upper bound of the production set, while $e^{\mu s}$ represent the price coefficient for good s. Equations [3.2.1] and [3.2.3] imply:

$$x_{s,t} = A_s L_s \left[h_{s,t_0}^{1-\alpha} + (1-\alpha)L_s(t-t_0) \right]^{\frac{\alpha}{1-\alpha}} \qquad [3.2.5]$$

At time t, the production of good s depends on a preliminary level of knowledge and on the previous history in producing that good. To obtain sustained growth, Lucas assumes, at first, that the upper bound of the production set is exogenously augmented, following a Poisson process of rate λ:

$$S_t = \lambda t \qquad [3.2.6]$$

At this stage not many differences arise between Lucas' (1993) model and Stokey's (1991) model.

Stokey endogenizes the rate λ, assuming it dependent on average knowledge previously cumulated. Lucas (1993) still considers agents' heterogeneity, assuming that φ is a density function with cdf ϕ. This describes the distribution of workers across production of goods of different vintages. It follows that: $\forall s \in [0, \lambda t]$, $L_{s,t} = \varphi(t - s/\lambda)$, where $L_{s,t}$ defines the number of workers devoted to produce goods of age $(t - s/\lambda)$. The remaining $1 - \phi(t)$ workers produce a good over which no learning occurs. The same initial productivity is assumed for all goods and it is fixed at level: $h(s/\lambda, s) = \xi \geq 1$. One can now remove the hypothesis of independence of learning across goods and assume that $h_{s,t}$ denotes the experience accumulated in the whole economy for $s < S_t$. If the production of a good $s \geq S_t$ is started at time $\tau_s = s/\lambda$ (with $\tau_s = t$) we can assume that its starting level is proportional (in reason of θ) in respect of the average skills previously accumulated:

$$h_{s,\tau_s} = \theta \delta \int_0^s \exp[-\delta(s-v)] h_{v,\tau_s} dv \qquad [3.2.7]$$

We can eventually infer that the ability required to produce the most sophisticated good at time t follows a similar rule, such that:

$$h_{S,t} = h(\theta, \delta, \varphi(v), \alpha) \qquad [3.2.8]$$

Assume that a new good will be effectively produced every time the previously accumulated ability reaches the trigger value $\xi \geq 1$. We can re-write equation [3.2.8] in the following ways:

$$\xi = h(\underline{\theta}, \underline{\delta}\lambda, \varphi(v), \underline{\alpha}) \qquad [3.2.9]$$

$$\lambda = \lambda(\underset{+}{\theta}, \underset{+}{\alpha}, \underset{+}{\varphi(v)}) \qquad [3.2.10]$$

Equation [3.2.9] shows the relation that links the technological parameters of the model with the distribution of labour across different sectors. The trigger value of knowledge required for the introduction of a new good will be negatively related to the spillover parameter θ, and with the learning parameter α. If spillover and learning effects are high, it will be necessary that there exist a lower level of knowledge to start producing a new good. It is actually possible to change the perspective (see equation [3.2.10]) and regard λ as the endogenous variable. The rate of introduction of new goods is increasing in respect of both the spillover and the learning parameters. It is also increased when the distribution of workers displays much of its density over the most sophisticated goods.

The relationship among these parameters and variables is pretty complex. Lucas assumes that the distribution of workers is steady and focuses his consideration to explain how 'growth miracles' can happen, adopting a technology with learning-by-doing mechanism and continuous innovations. This kind of model is very interesting because it emphasizes the role of labour and human capital accumulation by learning-effects that generate dynamic returns to scale. New goods are introduced into the system. The mechanism which generates this process emerges by a self-feeding interaction between sectors (where α and θ are the parameters of interest) and the macroeconomic level, where λ, ξ and $\varphi(v)$ determine the pattern of growth.

For our main purposes we have to emphasize the fact that Lucas explicitly attributes an important role to the distribution of labour over the production of goods of different vintages. Considering the result derived in equations [3.2.9] and [3.2.10] we can infer that a good policy to obtain a higher growth rate in such a framework is giving incentives to concentrate the labour force on the production of more sophisticated goods. That would increase both learning effect and spillovers on λ. It would give acceleration to the system, lowering the trigger rate for introduction of more new goods. These considerations find a good justification especially dealing with international trade and lock-in mechanisms. But there is a risk which must be taken into account. If the policy-maker tries to specialise the process of production on goods of higher vintage, workers will be more and more specialised and less able to switch to different lines of production. If an external shock lowers the demand for high quality goods, the distribution of workers will be locked-in. This could determine a possible explanation for unemployment. In this case we might identify a trade-off between higher and faster growth with unbalanced distribution of labour and lower growth with balanced distribution of labour. Balancing the distribution of labour among sectors could be regarded as an irrational policy to achieve a Pareto-improvement for the growth path. In spite of that, the decision could be regarded as a good insurance against the risk of external shocks that can affect the foreign demand for higher quality goods. Moreover, this framework can represent an alternative way to model heterogeneity among workers.

3.3 *The distribution of human capital supply*

Galor and Tsiddon (1997) present a deeper analysis of human capital distribution, even formalized in its dynamic transition. They use an overlapping generation model defined in discrete time to show that human capital dynamics can evolve non-monotonically, determining path dependence.

In the model, agents produce a single good. In each period the good is used to be consumed, saved or invested in human capital. Production technology is described by a neoclassical CRS function:

$$y_t = \lambda_t h_t f(k_t) \qquad [3.3.1]$$

The production function displays two inputs: human capital h and physical capital k. The parameter λ denotes the state of technology. In this framework technological progress is assumed to be labour augmenting. Production is performed in a competitive market and function $f(k)$ satisfies all the boundary conditions for an internal solution of the profit-maximizing problem. Denoted with w and r the wage rate and rate of return of capital respectively, first order conditions for the producer are:

$$r_t = f'(k_t)$$
$$w_t = \lambda_t[f(k_t) - f'(k_t)k_t] \equiv \lambda_t w(k_t) \qquad [3.3.2]$$

Assume that the world rental rate is a constant given: $r_t = r^*$, so that wage rate depends only on technological progress. At time $t + 1$ the level of technology depends on the average level of human capital h_t^a of the previous generation:

$$\lambda_{t+1} = \max[\lambda(h_t^a), \lambda_t] \qquad [3.3.3]$$

The function $\lambda(h_t^a)$ is non-decreasing monotone and concave in the average level of human capital of the whole economy. In the first period of their life, agents invest an amount of real resources in human capital that will be devoted to production in the second period. Formally: an agent who was born at time t to a parent belonging by dynasty i inherits human capital h_t^i. S/he will invest x_t^i units of real resource and one unit of labour in order to obtain h_{t+1}^i of human capital.

$$h_{t+1}^i = \phi(h_t^i, x_t^i) \qquad [3.3.4]$$

Equation [3.3.4] represents the technology that generates human capital. Function $\phi(\cdot)$ displays properties that determine the foundation of the theory:

1. Each individual's level of human capital is an increasing function of the parental level of human capital and of the investment in real resources devoted to its production.
2. There is complementarity between the two inputs of human capital production function.
3. There are diminishing returns on both inputs in the production of human capital.

Function ϕ captures the so called 'home environment externality', as long as it states a link between the level of human capital of parents and children.

Parents also affect their children's level of human capital in an indirect way, through a 'technological externality'. This effect is registered by the function $\lambda(h_t^a)$. Through the labour augmenting technological progress, parents' average level of human capital affects the rate of return on investment in human capital for the child's generation. In this way parents stimulate further investment in human capital for the next generation.

Under proper assumptions for the function ϕ, Galor and Tsiddon show that from equation [3.3.4]:

$$x_t^i = \xi(h_t^i, \lambda_{t+1}) \qquad\qquad [3.3.5]$$

Investment in producing human capital is positively related to the parental level of the previous generation. From equation [3.3.3] we can also infer that investment in real resources is related with the average level of human capital of the previous generation. This double mechanism generates path dependence due to a 'local home' externality.

Equations [3.3.4] and [3.3.5] jointly describe the evolution of human capital within a dynasty:

$$h_{t+1}^i = \phi(h_t^i, \xi(h_t^i, \lambda_{t+1})) \equiv \psi(h_t^i, \lambda_{t+1}) \qquad\qquad [3.3.6]$$

While function ϕ displays the typical neoclassical behaviour, ψ is a non-linear differential equation that may display a behaviour that is convex, concave one or even both. This result may lead to an interesting conclusion. In fact, even if the economy is described in a competitive environment and the ability is identically distributed across individuals, we register the presence of multiple steady states. In the long run polarization phenomena can arise in the distribution of human capital, allowing the existence of a steady state with different dynasties endowed with different levels of human capital. At this stage we have just focused on 'local home externality' and we still suppose the technological progress to be steady. If we consider interaction between dynasties, the 'global technology externality' should be taken into account as well. The authors consider the average level of human capital as a source to generate labour augmenting technological progress. Technological progress can be regarded as an upward shift of the function $\psi(\cdot)$. In the long run it eliminates the presence of a multiple steady state (see Figure 1). In this steady state the distribution of human capital across dynasties converges to a unique level of equilibrium. Transitional dynamics are led by the technology bias of the wage rate, which induces an increase in the optimal quantity of human capital to be accumulated by the agents.

Galor's and Tsiddon's model was basically built to investigate the selection of the growth path as the result of human capital distribution. As a matter of fact, the authors devote special attention to the characteristics of the labour supply through a parental mechanism of transmission and technological change. This

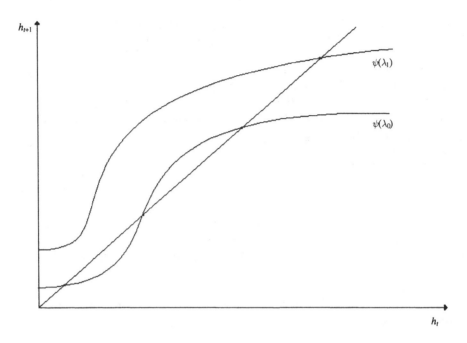

Figure 1. The effect of technological progress in Galor and Tsiddon (1997).

kind of approach is not very common in the literature. Nevertheless, it can be related with the intuition that the process of job-matching can be influenced by endogenous determination of the labour supply. This might be an answer to the models presented in the previous section where the characteristics of the labour supply were substantially neglected.

4. The role of complementarities

4.1 *Complementarities amongst inputs and amongst processes*

Endogenous growth theory emphasized the importance of definitions of factors that are involved in the process of growth. Descriptions of the production process became more complex, involving deeper degrees of microeconomic foundation, leaving the aggregative approach used in the past contributions. All these facts reflected on more accuracy devoted to the definition of the inputs. They also reflected on the description of a wider range of alternative ways to combine these inputs through technology. For the purpose of our search, this also means that we can actually dispose of a larger set of alternative and not mutually exclusive explanations and intuitions for the presence of mismatches of factors and, therefore, of unemployment.

   For example, we have already noticed that capital has been considered in a broad definition and used as proxy for the level of social knowledge. Lucas (1988) distinguished skilled from unskilled labour. Stokey (1991) removed the substitutability in order to introduce some degree of heterogeneity among workers and subsequently among goods. In a more recent work, (see Stokey (1993)) she also presented a framework in which physical capital and unskilled labour are substitutes, while physical capital and skilled labour are complements. Goldin and Katz (1996) developed Stokey's contribution, building a model in which there are three competing technologies adopting three different factors (skilled labour, unskilled labour and capital). In their model it emerges that complementarity among capital and skilled labour is always present within the same technology, while this effect can be hidden in the first stage of transition from one technology to another. In phases of transition, the first impact of the new technology into the system generates an increase of demand for unskilled labour at the very beginning. When the new production process finally diffuses, it is followed by a subsequent increment in the demand for skilled labour.

Chari and Hopenayin (1991) consider the presence of complementarities developing a model of diffusion where human capital is specific to different technologies. The marginal product of the investment in a specific technology is assumed to be increasing in respect of the existing stock of human capital specific to that technology. In this way, old and new technologies are characterized by complementarities. The model is based on an infinite-horizon overlapping generations framework. Workers live two periods and they are unskilled in the first period of their life. Each agent acquires specific skills, through a process of learning-by-doing that induces a distribution of heterogeneous skills across different technologies for the next period. The distribution of human capital is endogenously determined by the choices of agents who invest in the first period of their life to earn benefits in the second period. The investment is irreversible, since the skill is specific for each vintage. The authors find that in steady state (when the distribution of human capital is time-invariant), an increase in the exogenous rate of technological change shifts the distribution of skilled workers on the production of the most recent vintages. Chari and Hopenayin (1991) derive another interesting result, much more related with the purpose of our survey. They find that an increase in the rate of technological change not only speeds up the process of diffusion of new technologies, but it also lowers the amount of employees demanded by firms.

We introduce here another contribution by Young (1993a) which relies on the issue of complementarities and the dynamic allocation of labour. In his work he shows that the presence of complementarities can rise not only among factors, but also as the result of interaction among simultaneous processes, of invention and learning-by-doing.

Young observes that models led by learning-by-doing generally assume that the productivity's growing path is unbounded, as in Lucas (1988). This fact implies that technological progress should be regarded as a linear phenomenon, ignoring that history always displays cycles with intermittent phases of stagnation and growth. On the other hand R&D models commonly assume that each occurring innovation drives all the previous technologies into obsolescence. Romer (1990), Grossman and Helpman (1991), Aghion and Howitt (1992) and many other contributions introduce that hypothesis.

Even in this case Young moves an objection based upon historical considerations. In his opinion, technologies follow a more complicated cycle. When a new technology is introduced into the system setting-up costs are high and uncertainty about perspective results is also high: new ideas are unknown and not yet diffused. At the very beginning there are no facilities to help the diffusion of the innovating process and there are no experienced workers able to use the new technology without a proper training. In this early stage phenomena of complementarities between new and old technologies arise. It takes time to wait for the diffusion of the new technology to be sufficiently large. It is also necessary that enough workers can be matched with the new production process. Only at that point substitutability with the previous technology takes place.

To maintain a deeper degree of realism, Young (1993a) considers a framework where innovation and learning-by-doing are both present and binding each other.

More formally, he assumes that different goods are produced. Goods are indexed on the linear space $[0, N(t)]$, where $N(t)$ denotes the most sophisticated good. Labour is the only input to production. Letting s denote the quality of a good and t the time of production of that good, he defines the demand for labour $a(s, t)$ necessary to produce one unit of good:

$$a(s, t) = \bar{a}e^{-s} \qquad \forall s \in [0, T(t)]$$
$$a(s, t) = \bar{a}e^{-T(t)}e^{s-T(t)} \quad \forall s \in [T(t), N(t)] \qquad [4.1.1]$$

The term $\bar{a}$ denotes the upper bound for productivity's increments. That means that a certain level of labour will always be required to produce good s and that also means that the learning process will extinguish at a certain point of time. The learning process occurs only on more sophisticated goods, as long as with the less sophisticated ones it has already been extinguished. The learning process also generates spillovers[8] across sectors. This kind of phenomenon is a source of knowledge and improves the know-how to produce more efficiently. The variable $T(t)$ represents the dynamic bound for the learning frontier and it summarizes the social knowledge generated by the learning process. Assume that the function $L(s, t)$ accounts how many workers are employed at time t over production of good s. We can define the following dynamic rule for index $T(t)$:

$$\dot{T}(t) = \int_{T(t)}^{N(t)} \psi L(s, t) ds \qquad [4.1.2]$$

where ψ is the rate of learning for each worker. The stronger learning effect, the faster the index $T(t)$ will run towards more sophisticated goods.

The system can even introduce new and more sophisticated goods through its R&D sector. The R&D sector is characterized by free entry conditions and monopolistic competition. Firms own an infinitely lived patent for each new good they invent. Denote by L_r the number of workers employed and by λ the productivity of the R&D sector. The expansion of the production set can be expressed by the following rule:

$$\dot{N}(t) = L_r/\lambda \qquad\qquad [4.1.3]$$

Different processes are actually inserted into the same framework. If it happens that $\dot{T}(t) = \dot{N}(t)$ the labour demand will be monotone downward sloping and the model will behave as if it was driven by a pure learning-by-doing process. On the other hand, if $\dot{T}(t) = 0$, technological change will be generated by R&D sector only. Any intermediate case generates a situation in which learning-by-doing and R&D are mutually interconnected (see Figure 2). In this case the labour demand is downward sloping on the space $[0, \ T(t)]$ and upward sloping on the space $[T(t), N(t)]$. That is because with the most sophisticated goods, the learning process has just started and costs are high. This also reflects the fact that new technologies are generally less profitable in respect of older ones, in spite of the hypothesis of a linear obsolescence process. When the learning process generates enough knowledge, costs start to decrease and labour demand switches from upward sloping to downward sloping until it reaches its lowest bound $\bar{a}e^{-s}$.

The connection between invention and learning-by-doing generates a particular shape for the labour demand. Even in this case, mismatches on the labour market could occur depending on the distribution of skills across the labour force.

4.2 *Strategic complementarities*

We noted that in section 2, one Acemoglu (1997), as well as one of the extensions of Aghion's and Howitt's (1994) model refer to the concepts of strategic

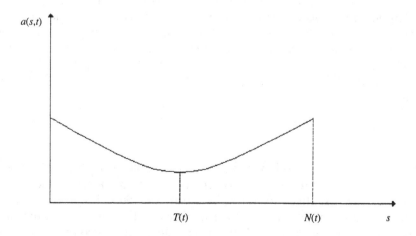

Figure 2. Labour demand over goods in Young (1993).

complementarities and co-ordination failure. This approach registered increasing interest in the most recent literature.

The main results about the theory of strategic complementarities and co-ordination failure were presented by Cooper and John (1988). In their seminal work the authors claim that the role of expectations allows the identification of the causes of Pareto-inefficiency in the system. They formalize a flexible general Nash-equilibrium environment where agents interact strategically. A strategic complementarity is identified in this framework when an increment in strategy for a player i determines an increment in the optimal strategy for a player $j \neq i$.

The main results derived by Cooper and John (1988) claim that the presence of strategic complementarities generates multiple equilibria in the system. Multiplicity of equilibria in itself is a sufficient condition for the presence of multiplier-effects. Cooper and John assume that 'multiplier effects' are present when a change in one of the parameters of the model determines an aggregate response which exceeds the individual response. More formally, indicated with s_j^* the optimal strategy for agent j. Multiplier effects are present when the following inequality holds:

$$d\Sigma s_j^*/d\theta_i > ds_i^*/d\theta_i > \partial s_i^*/d\theta_i \text{ for any } i,j \text{ such that: } i \neq j$$

The identification of a multiplier-effect represents the microeconomic explanation of a macroeconomic co-ordination failure, that can assume the form of an externality.

For this reason, this tool developed by Cooper and John has to be regarded as a powerful link between macroeconomic and microeconomic analysis. Often the identification of multiplier-effects in a contest of strategical interaction is still formalized in a static perspective. Its application in the field of growth theory is not widely diffused.

Several contributions started to consider the role of expectations as another source of multiplicity of equilibria in models of growth. Path dependence does not only depend on the role of history, but it can be generated by interaction of the agents. (See for example Krugman, 1991 and Adesrà and Ray, 1998). Developments in a dynamic environment and benchmark models about the role of complementarities in macroeconomics can be found in Cooper (1999). More related with the topic of our survey we refer to Acemoglu (1994, 1996) and Redding (1996).

5. Discussion

We found that the main models of growth and unemployment display four basic features able to generate a link between the labour market and the growth mechanism. The first effect, identified by Pissarides (1990), is due to capitalisation. If the labour market is uncoordinated and costly to access competitive firms settled in a growing economy will try to maximize their discounted stream of profits, creating more vacancies each time the rate of growth increases in order to save higher hiring costs for the future. The second effect, introduced by Aghion and Howitt (1994), relies on Schumpeter's concept of creative destruction. It assumes that innovations introduce new technologies and drop old ones from the system, leading to labour re-allocations across the firms. If each job-match requires specific human capital for a specific vacancy, persistent unemployment may arise. The faster the rate of introduction of new technology, the shorter the duration for each match.

In Pissarides (1990) and Aghion and Howitt (1994), the rate of growth was introduced as an exogenous variable, while in Bean and Pissarides (1993) and Eriksson (1997) both growth and unemployment are considered as endogenous variables. In these models the authors identify a third mechanism able to generate a link between growth and unemployment, which relies on the role of consumption.

The fourth effect, mentioned in Aghion and Howitt (1994), is emphasized by Acemoglu (1997) and deals with the concept of strategic complementarities in the sense of Cooper and John (1988). This last mechanism describes the interaction among firms that mutually influence their decisions about investing in new technology and accumulating human capital. Multiple equilibria may arise in this kind of framework and may possibly lead to unemployment stagnation traps.

Starting from these considerations we try to summarize some of the basic features of the explanation of unemployment in a growing economy, explicitly referring to the models and contributions we presented in the previous sections.

5.1 Externalities, strategic complementarities and feedbacks

In the models mentioned above the mechanisms described easily generate any sort of feedback, crossing externalities with agents' beliefs. The arrow of the growth-unemployment relation can be oriented in both directions and also generate recursive effects. Pissarides' models are focused on unemployment, introducing growth factors into the main framework of the job-search theory. Following Bean and Pissarides (1993), an example of feedback mechanism is due to a modification in the pool of savings. Unemployment generates a decrease in the size of the pool of savings that may slow down growth in a perfectly competitive environment. A totally opposite effect may be obtained in the New Keynesian version of this framework, introducing the presence of an intermediate good sold in an imperfectly competitive market. In this set of models the arrow basically runs from unemployment to growth.

On the contrary, the neo-Schumpeterian analysis re-interprets the Beveridge relation, stressing the microfoundation of the determinants of growth, leading the arrow to run from growth to unemployment. Aghion and Howitt (1994), however, consider the presence of feedbacks occurring as the result of learning-by-doing. In this case they assume that the process of introduction of new technologies is sustained by learning-by-doing mechanisms. If unemployment rises, the fraction of active labour force that is actually on-learning gets smaller. The authors denote that feedbacks are not only sustained by externalities but that the role of expectations can generate other kinds of feedback. Aghion and Howitt (1994), as well as Acemoglu (1997), introduce them explicitly, referring to the concept of strategic complementarities. This fact means that when unemployment is high entrepreneurs do not expect the average skill of workers to increase, so they neither innovate nor hire. In this way, unemployment rises and expectations of the agents are self-fulfilled.

Expectations can play a leading role in determining the pattern of growth. The authors mentioned above seem to suggest that a good explanation for the presence of unemployment in a growing economy can emerge combining many different kinds of inefficiency. Inefficiencies can emerge from technology changes not registered by the agents, but they can also emerge by co-ordination failures in the market, whenever agents take decisions simultaneously and their strategies generate multiplier effects at the macro-level. In this way one can compare different Pareto-ranked Nash-equilibria.

Dynamic contribution within this kind of approach, based on expectations and interaction, are still very few though. We consider the stream of articles by Acemoglu (1994, 1996, 1997) as an interesting contribution about that topic. Acemoglu (1997) eliminates the problem of a static approach based on Nash equilibrium and suggests adopting a system of Bellman equations to represent the behaviour of heterogeneous agents over the time.

5.2 *Micro foundations of growth and unemployment*

We have already had opportunity to note that the neo-Schumpeterian approach displays a deeper degree of microeconomic foundation. Pissarides assumes that the outcomes of the matching function are a useful aggregate expression of what is generated at the microeconomic level by the mechanism of interaction among firms and workers. Starting from this observation, Pissarides claims that there is no need to introduce heterogeneity into the model, when a macroeconomic tool like the matching function works so well and is empirically corroborated. The fact is that each event of separation from job, which contributes to composing the stream of workers *out of* unemployment, is explained by the job-search theory as due to 'firm-specific shocks'. These shocks are generated by changes in technology and tastes, but they are not explained in detail. On the contrary Aghion and Howitt (1994) base their explanation for unemployment on differences among firms and among workers. Each worker is identified by her/his own skills and each firm is identified by its own technology. On the labour market the demand is determined by the technological level of firms and the supply is characterized by workers' level of human capital. In a normative perspective we find this kind of micro-foundation of the Beveridge curve very useful. The Schumpeterian approach is based on the leading role of the entrepreneur in the process of growth. An accurate analysis of the entrepreneur's decision algorithm allows us to show that job/vacancy mismatches can be determined by causes which lay far away from the labour market. In this environment growth and unemployment are completely integrated and there is no point to think about policies for growth in the long run and policies for unemployment in the short run. We finally need to consider that when creative destruction and other kinds of feedback effects are present inside the system, a policy maker has to choose carefully the best way to enhance growth and lower unemployment, avoiding ambiguous results. A deeper degree of investigation represents a safer way to identify the right incentive which does not stimulate creative destruction and other negative feedbacks.

5.3 *Human capital and labour supply*

The majority of growth models usually consider labour supply inelastic or given. Attempts to endogenize the supply side of the labour market have been developed introducing a leisure-wage trade-off into workers' utility functions. We had opportunity to note that in various frameworks of endogenous growth labour supply can even be considered from a skill-technology perspective.

In our analysis of the neo-Schumpeterian approach we focused on the central role played by human capital, but we observe that while demand for skilled labour is analytically formalized, human capital supply is often treated in an aggregative way, like in Aghion and Howitt (1994, 1998). That is typical of the neo-Schumpeterian perspective, which follows the definition of human capital introduced by Nelson and Phelps (1966).

In our opinion the heterogeneous distribution of skills in the labour force, which characterizes the most recent models of growth, can represent one missing piece among the possible explanations for unemployment in a growing economy. For this reason we devoted more attention to different definitions of human capital and the way they are accumulated. We believe that the contributions of Lucas (1993) and Stokey (1991) about labour allocation among sectors and over products of different vintages, may suggest some different and interesting developments about that issue. Galor and Tsiddon (1997) showed how the dynamics of human capital distribution across generations can determine different patterns of growth. This can represent another interesting way to extend previous results involving the problem of unemployment.

5.4 *Complementarities among factors, among processes and strategies*

Young (1993a) criticized another shortcoming of the neo-Schumpeterian approach. Young (1993a) removes the hypothesis of immediate substitutability among old and new technologies, developing a framework in which learning by doing and R&D are concurrent engines of growth. Production of goods with different qualities is characterized by dynamic returns to scale that generates a U-shaped demand for labour. In a context of persistent unemployment this fact could represent another source of reflection about possible ways to co-ordinate demand and supply on the labour market. In this case the slope of labour demand and its wideness over the production of different lines of goods depends on both the rate of learning and the rate of introduction of new goods.

Dealing with different and concurrent engines of growth still confirms that the causes for the persistence of unemployment in a growing economy can be identified by analysing different issues in the economic system that may lie far away from the labour market. The interplay of complementarity of factors, processes and strategies of the agents suggests a wide range of, not mutually exclusive, explanations for unemployment in a growing economy.

6. Conclusions

We have presented in this paper part of the most recent literature about the persistence of unemployment in a growing economy. We have also tried to provide a first classification of the contributions which seem able to promote further studies about this issue. In this last decade the evolution of economic research allowed us to interpret the dynamics of the labour market, as well as growth, in a new perspective.

The renewed interest about the role of externalities, feedbacks, strategic complementarities and the interplay of different processes of accumulation (such as human capital and R&D) led to drop assumptions like a neutral and disembodied technological progress. On the other side, the new tools that have been developed for the analysis of the labour market allowed us to explain long run unemployment in terms of differences among flows *out of* and *into* the active labour force. This approach requires an increasing degree of microeconomic foundation for models. Very often it obtains the determination of multiple patterns of growth as a final result. If dynamic equilibria can be Pareto-ranked, the policy maker should try to select the best one, by running appropriate policies.

In this context the assumption of full employment may be more easily dropped from models of growth, in order to obtain a joint explanation of both growth and unemployment. By the contributions considered in this paper it may be inferred that when growth and unemployment are matched in a unique framework, the causes of unemployment can be found far from the labour market. If we consider Aghion and Howitt's (1994) model, we can find that policies for enhancing employment should be addressed to the firm. More attention should be dedicated to the role of the entrepreneur, trying to increase the 'capitalisation' effect of growth and trying to avoid the consequences of 'creative destruction'. Acemoglu (1997) shows us the relevance of interaction among heterogeneous agents and the interplay of a strategical behaviour which can lead to inefficient results and unemployment. Even in this case it emerges that different policies should be co-ordinated and addressed to both growth and unemployment at the same time.

Acknowledgments

The author is indebted to Marina Murat for the early discussions about the topic of the survey and her continuous support. Special thanks to Guido Ascari, Carluccio Bianchi, Nicolò De Vecchi and two anonymous referees for their helpful suggestions about the structure of the survey and the revision process. The author is also grateful to David Tumback for his language support. Financial support from the University of Studies of Pavia is gratefully acknowledged.

Notes

1. For an introduction about the literature on efficiency-wages consider in example: Stiglitz (1976), Shapiro and Stiglitz (1984), Akerlof and Yellen (1986).
2. See also Pissarides (2000). The new edition presents some developments about the basic issues introduced in Pissarides (1990) and collects an extensive bibliography of the most recent works related to job-search.
3. Equation [2.1.8] can be regarded as a labour demand relation, which is downward sloping in the space (w,θ), even when the productivity of labour is constant.
4. We are referring here to Caballero's comments on Bean and Pissarides (1993). At the end of their paper, Caballero summarizes the main results and presents some first considerations about the empirical evidence of the link between growth and unemployment.
5. Introducing imperfect substitutability in the production of final goods, allows emphasizing the role of the capitalization effect. In fact, in a system with low degree of substitutability among intermediate goods, an innovation that occurs in one sector will reflect positive effects in many other sectors, and employment will rise. The creative destruction effect will be lower.
6. In Stokey (1988) it is presented a formalization of this process, by which upper and lower bounds over the horizon of characteristics increase over time. The bounds move as a function of the level of knowledge previously cumulated inside the system.
7. For another similar example, developed within a dynamic interpretation of the 'big-push' mechanism of growth, see also Temple and Voth (1998).
8. In this kind of formulation we are assuming symmetric spillovers across sectors.

References

Acemoglu D., (1994) Search in the Labour Market, Incomplete Contracts and Growth, CEPR Discussion Paper, no. 1026.
——, (1996) A Microfoundation for Increasing Returns in Human Capital Accumulation, *Quarterly Journal of Economics*, 111, 779–804.
——, (1997) Technology, Unemployment and Efficiency, *European Economic Review*, 41, 525–533.
Adserà A., Ray D., (1998) History and Coordination Failure, *Journal of Economic Growth*, 3, 267–276.
Aghion P., Howitt P., (1998a) *Endogenous Growth Theory*, London, MIT press.
——, (1998b) Capital Accumulation and Innovation as Complementary Factors in Long-Run Growth, *Journal of Economic Growth*, 3, 111–30.
——, (1994) Growth and Unemployment, *Review of Economic Studies*, 61, 477–94.
——, (1992) A Model of Growth Through Creative Destruction, *Econometrica*, 60, 323–51.
Akerlof G.A., Yellen J.L., (1986) *Efficiency Wage Models of the Labour Market*, Cambridge, Cambridge University Press.
Arrow K., (1962) The Economic Implications of Learning by Doing, *Review of Economic Studies*, 29, 155–73.
Ashenfelter O.C., Layard R., (1986) *Handbook of Labour Economics*, Amsterdam, North-Holland.
Barro R.J., Sala-i-Martin X., (1995) *Economic Growth*, New York, Mc Graw-Hill.

Bean C.R., (1994) European Unemployment: A Survey, *Journal of Economic Literature*, 32, 573–619.

———, Pissarides C., (1993) Unemployment Consumption and Growth, *European Economic Review*, 37, 837–859.

Blanchard O., Diamond P., (1989) The Beveridge Curve, *Brookings Papers on Economic Activity*, 1, 1–76.

Cahuc P., Michel, P., (1996) Minimum Wage Unemployment and Growth, *European Economic Review*, 40, 1463–1482.

Chari V., Hopenhayn H., (1991) Vintage Human Capital, Growth, and the Diffusion of New Technology, *Journal of Political Economy*, 99, 6, 1142–1165.

———, (1986) Vintage Human Capital, Growth and Strucutral Unemployment, Working Paper no. 326, Federal Reserve Bank of Minneapolis, Minneapolis, MN.

Cooper R., (1999) *Coordination Games: complementarities and macroeconomics*, Cambridge, Cambridge University Press.

———, John A., (1988) Coordinating Coordination Failures in Keynesian Models, *Quarterly Journal of Economics*, 53, 441–63.

Daveri F., Tabellini G., (2000) Unemployment, Growth and Taxation in Industrial Countries, *Economic Policy*, 30, 47–88.

Diamond P., (1965) National Debt in a Neo-classical Growth Model, *American Economic Review*, 55, 1126–1150.

Domar E.D., (1947) Expansion and Employment, *American Economic Review*, 37, 1, 343–55, in: Domar E.D., (1957) *Essays in the Theory of Economic Growth*, Oxford, Oxford University Press, 83–108.

Dunne T., Haltiwanger J., Troske K.R., (1996) Technology and Jobs: Secular Changes and Cyclical Dynamics, *NBER Working Papers Series, n. 5656*.

Eriksson C., (1997) Is there a Trade-off Between Employment and Growth?, *Oxford Economic Papers*, 49, 1, 77–88.

Galor O., Tsiddon D., (1997) The Distribution of Human Capital and Economic Growth, *Journal of Economic Growth*, 2, 93–124.

Goldin C., Katz L.C., (1996) The Origins of Technology-Skill Complementarity, *NBER Working Paper Series, n. 5657*.

Gordon R., (1995) Is There a Tradeoff Between Unemployment and Productivity Growth?, *NBER Working Paper Series, n. 5081*.

Grossman G.M., Helpman H, (1994) Endogenous Innovation in the Theory of Growth, *Journal of Economic Perspectives*, 8, 1, 23–44.

Harrod R.F., (1939) An Essay in Dynamic Theory, *Economic Journal*, in: Harrod R.F., (1972) *Economic Essays*, London, MacMillan Economic Press, 256.

Jones C.I., Manuelli, R.E., (1997) The Sources of Growth, *Journal of Economic Dynamics and Control*, 21,1, 75–114.

———, (1998) *Introduction to Economic Growth*, London, W.W. Northon & Co.

King. I, Welling L., (1995) Search, Unemployment and Growth, *Journal of Monetary Economics*, 35, 499–507.

Krugman P., (1993) Toward a Counter-Counterrevolution in Development Theory, *Proceedings of the World Bank Annual Conference on Development Economics 1992*.

———, (1991) History versus Expectations, *The Quarterly Journal of Economics*, 651–667.

Layard P.R., Nickell S.J., Jackman R., (1991) *Unemployment: Macroeconomic Performance and the Labour Market*, Oxford, Oxford University Press.

Lucas R.E.Jr., (1993) Making a Miracle, *Econometrica*, 61, 2, 251–272.

———, (1988) On the Mechanics of Economic Development, *Journal of Monetary Economics*, 22, 3–42.

Nelson R., Winter S., (1982) *An Evolutionary Theory of Economic Change*, Cambridge Mass.: Belknap.

Nickell S., (1997) Unemployment and Labor Market Rigidities: Europe versus North America, *Journal of Economic Perspectives*, 11, 55–74.

Pissarides C.A., (2000) *Equilibrium Unemployment Theory*, Oxford, Blackwell.

——, (1990) *Equilibrium Unemployment Theory*, Oxford, Blackwell.

Pugno M., (1998) Crescita Economica e Disoccupazione: alcuni recenti sviluppi teorici, *Economia Politica*, 15, 1, 119–65.

Redding S., (1996) The Low Skill, Low-Quality Trap: Strategic Complementarities Between Human Capital and R&D, *Economic Journal*, 106, 458–70.

Romer P., (1990) Endogenous Technological Change, *Journal of Political Economy*, 98, 71–102.

——, (1987) Crazy Explanations for the Productivity Slowdown, *NBER Macroeconomics Annual*, Cambridge MIT Press, 163–202.

——, (1986) Increasing Returns and Long-Run Growth, *Journal of Political Economy*, 94, 1002–37.

Shapiro C., Stiglitz J.E., (1984) Equilibrium Unemployment as a Worker Discipline Device, *The American Economic Review*, 74, 433–444.

Siebert H., (1997) Labor Market Rigidities: at the Root of Unemployment in Europe, *Journal of Economic Perspectives*, 11, 37–54.

Solow R.M., (1994) Perspectives on Growth Theory, *Journal of Economic Perspectives*, 1, 8, 45–54.

——, (1969) Investment and Technical Progress in: Arrow K.J., Karlin S., Suppes P. (eds.), *Mathematical Methods in the Social Sciences*, Stanford University Press.

——, (1956) A Contribution to the Theory of Economic Growth, *Quarterly Journal of Economics*, 70, 65–94.

Stiglitz J.E., (1976) The Efficiency Wage Hypothesis, Surplus Labour, and the Distribution of Income in L.D.C.s., *Oxford Economic Papers*, 28, 185–207.

Stokey N.L., (1996) Free Trade, Factor Returns, and Factor Accumulation, *Journal of Economic Growth*, 1, 421–49.

——, (1991) Human Capital, Product Quality, and Growth, *Quarterly Journal of Economics*, 587–616.

——, (1988) Learning by Doing and the Introduction of New Goods, *Journal of Political Economy*, 96, 4, 701–717.

Temple J., Voth H.J., (1998) Human Capital, Equipment Investment, and Industrialization, *Journal of Economic Dynamics and Control*, 42, 1343–1362.

Van Schaik A.B.T.M., De Groot H.L.F., (1998) Unemployment and Endogenous Growth, *Labour*, 12, 2, 189–219.

Young A., (1993a) Invention and Bounded Learning by Doing, *Journal of Political Economy*, 101, 3, 443–472.

——, (1993b) Substitution and Complementarity in Endogenous Innovation, *Quarterly Journal of Economics*, 108, 775–807.

Zagler M., (2001) *Endogenous Growth and Equilibrium Unemployment*, Vienna, Habilitationsschrift.

8

PRODUCTIVITY, TECHNOLOGY AND ECONOMIC GROWTH: WHAT IS THE RELATIONSHIP?

Kenneth I. Carlaw

University of Canterbury, New Zealand

Richard G. Lipsey

Simon Fraser University, Canada

1. Introduction

What does total factor productivity (TFP) measure? This question is our starting point and we answer it by presenting a brief review of the literature on total factor productivity, including its definition and method of measurement. We then argue that the correct interpretation of the measure (at least under ideal circumstances) is neither technological change nor longer term prospects for increases in output but contemporary returns that are in excess of the normal rate of return on investing in known technology. The part of these returns that are obtained by third parties are correctly identified as 'free lunches' or externalities; but the part that is appropriated by the initial entrepreneur is correctly seen as a return for undertaking the uncertainty associated with technological change (and would only be a free lunch in a static world of perfect competition where there would in any case be no uncertain activity in making technological change.) We then go beyond this question to consider the relationship between productivity, technological change and economic growth, drawing on a body of work that models the relationship between technological change (particularly general purpose technologies (GPTs)) and economic growth.[1] Finally we make some headway on Prescott's (1998) call for a theory of TFP by presenting TFP calculations on simulated data from a model of GPT-driven sustained growth, showing how to relate changes in the underlying data generating process to different measurement methodologies.[2]

One of our purposes is to direct attention to alternatives to TFP for measuring the technological change that drives long term economic growth. However, we must pay attention to TFP because it is often interpreted by economists to measure technological change and this interpretation has influenced the debate within policy circles about what TFP measurements imply about the appropriateness of policies designed to induce economic growth. Another of our purposes is to argue against the view that TFP is a lever for policy makers to use in the process of encouraging economic growth. One of the major problems with this view is identified by Hulten (2000). 'The various factors of TFP are not measured directly, but lumped together as a residual 'left over' factor (hence the name). They cannot be sorted out within the pure TFP framework, and this is the famous epithet 'measure of our ignorance.' (61) An additional problem is that TFP, whatever it measures, is an outcome not a cause of anything and, therefore, not a lever for policy makers to use to affect growth rates. As is the case with all measures, TFP may be an indicator but it is certainly not a policy instrument.

Many economists whose insights have been honed on the aggregate production function in which technological change must raise TFP deny that there is a New Economy. (See, for example, Gordon 2000.) In spite of a growing literature pointing out that productivity change is not an index of technological change (e.g., Hulton) most commentators have argued one of two positions. The first extreme position is that there has been no New Economy because there has been no increase in TFP growth. The second, less extreme, but in our opinion no less misguided, position is that there is a paradox in the apparent evidence of a technological transformation and the lack of major TFP gains. In contrast, we have argued in a number of publications that there is no necessary relation between the rate of technological transformation of the economy on the one hand and the rate of productivity growth on the other hand.[3]

2. Productivity is not a measure of technological change

The identification of changes in TFP as a measure of technological change originates in Solow's seminal 1956 and 1957 articles. An aggregate production function is used to relate measured indexes of inputs to a measured index of output. Growth in output that is not associated with the growth in inputs is interpreted to be the result of changes in technology (and some other causes such as scale economies).[4]

A major problem with TFP is that it has several mutually incompatible interpretations among economists, only one of which is that it measures technological change. We distil these views into three categories; the TFP is technological change view (group 1), the TFP is free lunches view (group 2) and the TFP is ignorance view (group 3). The following quotations, which we list in descending order of the scope that they give to TFP, illustrate some of the different interpretations of TFP that are current in the literature.[5]

(1) 'A growth-accounting exercise [conducted by Alwyn Young] produces the startling result that Singapore showed no technical progress at all.' Krugman (1996, p.55) 'Singapore will only be able to sustain further growth by reorienting its policies from factor accumulation toward the considerably more subtle issue of technological change.' Young (1992, p.50) (**Group 1**)

(2) 'Improvements in technology – the invention of the internal combustion engine, the introduction of electricity, of semiconductors – clearly increase total factor productivity.' Law (2000, pp.6–7) **(Group 1)**

(3) 'Technological progress *or* the growth of total factor productivity is estimated as a residual from *the* production function.... Total factor productivity is thus the best expression of the efficiency of economic production *and the prospects for longer term increases in output.*' Statistics Canada, (1998, pp. 50–51, italics added) **(Group 1)**

(4) 'Growth accounting provides a breakdown of observed economic growth into components associated with changes in factor inputs and a residual that reflects technological progress and other elements.' Barro (1999, p. 119) **(Group 1)**

(5) 'The defining characteristic of [total factor] productivity as a source of economic growth is that the incomes generated by higher productivity are external to the economic activities that generate growth. These benefits 'spill over' to income recipients not involved in these activities, severing the connection between the creation of growth and the incomes that result.' Jorgenson (1995, p. xvii.) 'That part of any alteration in the pattern of productive activity that is 'costless' from the point of view of market transactions is attributed to change in total factor productivity.' Jorgenson and Griliches (1967), reprinted in Jorgenson (1995, p.54) **(Group 2)**

(6) 'The residual should not be equated with technical change, although it often is. To the extent that productivity is affected by innovation, it is the costless part of technical change that it captures. This 'Manna from Heaven' may reflect spillover externalities thrown of by research projects, or it may simply reflect inspiration and ingenuity.'[6] Hulten (2000, p. 61) **(Group 2)**

(7) 'The central organising concept...[is] the division of observed growth in output per worker into two independent and additive elements: capital-labour substitution, reflected in movements around the production function; and increased efficiencies of resource use, as reflected by shifts in this function. To maintain additivity, ... the analysis ... could not be applied cumulatively without introducing an interaction term between capital substitution and increased efficiency ... [The residual debate] never did attempt to answer the question, of what is the residual composed. This remains the dominant question.' Metcalfe (1987, p. 619–20) **(Group 3)**

(8) 'Is there something possibly wrong with the way we ask the productivity question, with the analytical framework into which we force the available data? I think so. I would focus on the treatment of disequilibria and the measurement of knowledge and other externalities.' Griliches (1994) **(Group 3)**

(9) 'All of the pioneers of this subject were quite clear about the tenuousness of such calculations and that it may be misleading to identify the results as 'pure' measures of technical progress. Abramovitz labelled the resulting

index 'a measure of our ignorance'.' Griliches (1995, pp.5–6) quoting
Abramovitz (1956, p.8) (**Group 3**)

Surely it must be a cause of major concern that a measurement that is relied on
for so many purposes in theory, applied work, and policy assessment is so
variously interpreted.

3. An overview of Total Factor Productivity

Although initially the most common method of calculating TFP was growth
accounting, both index number and distance function methods for calculating
TFP are becoming more common. We describe each of these methods briefly
before moving onto our discussion of what TFP actually measures.[7]

3.1. *Growth accounting*

Growth accounting calculations of TFP require the specification of a production
function that is both stable across time (regardless of changes in technology) and
valid at whatever level of aggregation the calculations are to be made.[8] Our
discussion of such a function simplifies broader concepts of the aggregate
production variously provided by Jorgenson and Griliches (1967), Jorgenson
(2001) and Barro (1999) which include research and development among the
lines of production in the aggregate function. Jorgenson and Griliches (1967)
and Jorgenson (2001) treat all lines of production activities, including R&D, as
having constant returns to scale, which implies that the part of technological
change that involves costly R&D is not measured by TFP. In contrast, Barro
(1999) uses production functions that allow R&D to generate increasing returns
to the intermediate R&D inputs to production. In Barro's case, TFP measures the
exogenous (Hicks neutral, 'Manna from heaven') component of technological
change and the endogenous technological change generated from costly R&D.
However Barro's endogenous component has the same the free lunch characteristics of the un-paid for 'manna from heaven' benefits that are in the Jorgenson
and Griliches model. This is because the endogenous component results from
increasing returns to all lines of production activities. All of this leaves open the
questions about the meta or all encompassing notion of aggregate production and
about the appropriate formulation of R&D and knowledge production in that
framework.

Let the production function at some level of aggregation be:

$$Y = AF(K, H, L) = AK^\alpha L^\beta \quad \alpha \in [0, 1), \beta \in [0, 1), \text{ and } \alpha + \beta = 1 \qquad (\text{I.1})$$

where Y is output, K is physical capital and L labour.[9] The specification of the
function is often a constant returns to scale Cobb-Douglas.

Total factor productivity is calculated either as a geometric index in levels:

$$TFP = Y/(L^\alpha K^\beta) = A. \qquad (I.2)$$

or as an arithmetic index in rates of change:

$$\frac{\dot{A}}{A} = \frac{\dot{Y}}{Y} - \alpha\frac{\dot{L}}{L} - \beta\frac{\dot{K}}{K} = \Delta TFP \qquad (I.3)$$

and α and β are equated to their share weights in income. Equation (I.3) defines total factor productivity as the difference between the proportional change in output and the proportional change in a Divisia index of inputs.[10]

The use of such a production function, or the broader conceptual ones used by Jorgenson and Griliches or Barro, pose several problems that are pointed out by Lipsey and Carlaw (2003).

First, there is the strong assumption that we can meaningfully measure the inputs of factors over these long periods, and across very different technologies. For example, in what units do we compare the amount of capital invested in an office communication network based on electric telephones and paper based type written message and to a system based on computer, email local area networks and the internet? (Jorgenson, Gollop and Fraumeni (1987) attempt to control for some of these problems by specifically accounting for changes in such things as input quality, legal forms of organizations, capital asset classes and sectoral substitution.)

Second, to calculate TFP over long periods of time, we must assume that this production function remains stable with productivity-increasing changes in technology being registered solely by changes in the productivity factor, A. This is a very strong assumption when a general purpose technology (GPT) is evolving through its many new uses such as occurred with the electronic computer over the last half of the 20th century; it is positively heroic when it is extended over the life times of several GPTs, such as when electricity replaced steam or when mechanical power replaced horse power in myriad applications throughout the entire economy.[11]

Third, the aggregation from the production functions for individual products to the function used to calculate TFP is only possible under the standard assumptions that treat competition among firms as the *end state* that is the perfectly competitive equilibrium. Even in this situation there are, as we will see later, serious aggregation problems when technological changes require a lagged movement of resources out of one sector into another. More serious, probably insurmountable, problems arise if we take the contrasting Austrian view of inter-firm competition as a dynamic *process* that takes place in real time and that a major tool of inter-firm competition is the introduction of new technologies, which must take place under conditions of uncertainty not just risk.[12] There is no known way in which we can obtain a macro production function (either industry or economy wide) by aggregating from a set of firms that are in process competition, even if they are all price takers.

Fourth, aggregation is also impossible when the markets contain the mixture of monopoly, oligopoly, monopolistic and perfect competition that characterizes real-world industrial structures, even if all firms were in end state equilibrium.

3.2. *Index number approach*

The index number approach can be viewed as an extension of, and complement to, growth accounting. The two approaches are similar. Both use indexes and both suffer from similar problems. The main difference is that the index number approach does not necessarily require an aggregate production function, although one way of selecting the appropriate index is via the economic approach where a production function is specified. Index number theory provides explanations for what is and is not possible in aggregation and it acts as a check on some measurement problems in accounting. In the economic approach to index number theory discussed by Diewert and Lawrence (1999), particular aggregate production functional forms can be explicitly linked to particular indexes. As Diewert and Lawrence point out, index number theory can also use an axiomatic approach where the type of index to be used is shown to meet criteria of having 'desirable properties.' We say more about this below.

The index number approach divides an output index by an input index as follows:[13]

$$A_t = \frac{Y_t}{I_t}$$

where A_t is a level measure of total factor productivity, Y_t is an index of real output and I_t is an index of the factor quantities used in production. This is a straight forward calculation, given the indexes of output and input. It is the selection and calculation of the indexes that presents the major problem for this approach.

One critical issue is selecting the appropriate index. While in the growth accounting approach, we start with an aggregate production function (APF) and in the index number approach we start with index numbers, the one implies the other in the sense that to measure TFP from an APF, we need index numbers, while if we start with a specific index number, an APF is implied. Different indexes relate to different underlying assumptions about the aggregate production function and the calculation varies with the different indexes. We have just seen, for example, that the Cobb-Douglas production function is explicitly related to the Divisia index for calculating TFP when the model is in continuous time (and to the Tornquist index when the model is in discrete time). The many different index numbers that can be used in his type of measurement are surveyed by Diewert (1987) and Deiwert and Lawrence (1999).

Another problem is how to add up the various outputs and inputs into single scalars. Index numbers avoid the 'adding apples and oranges' problem by using prices (or output shares to weight the various different kinds of output). This is also the approach that must be taken when constructing input indexes for human and physical capital.

There are four main index numbers used to measure TFP; the Laspeyre's, the Paasche, the Fisher and the Tornqvist. The Layspeyre's index is the value of period 1 output measured using period 0 prices divided by the value of period 0 output measured using period 0 prices. The Paasche index measures the value of output in the two periods using period 1 prices. The Fisher index is the average of the Laspeyre's and Paasche indexes. The Tornqvist index geometrically weights the output of the two periods using and average of the two period share weights. The mathematical representations of these indexes are provided in appendix A.

Two approaches, the economic and the axiomatic, are commonly used for selecting which index number to calculate. 'The economic approach selects index number formulation on the basis of an assumed underlying production function and assumed price taking profit maximizing behaviour on the part of producers. For example, the Tornqvist index used extensively in past TFP studies can be derived assuming the underlying production function has the translog form and assuming producers are price taking revenue maximizers and price taking cost minimizers' (Diewert and Lawrence, 1999, p9). As we have already discussed, these assumptions are based on the abstract and unreal world of end-state stationary general equilibrium and have no counterpart in the reality of process competition with path dependent and uncertain technological change.

The axiomatic approach compares the properties of the index number formulations with 'desirable properties' and the index number that has the largest number of desirable properties is then used to calculate TFP. Of the four index numbers listed here, only the Fisher index has all of the desirable properties outlined in the axiomatic approach.[14] Thus, selecting an index such as the Tornqvist for its economic properties may result in the introduction of some undesirable properties and thus not meet the criteria of the axiomatic approach.

Further problems with index numbers are discussed by Fox (2002). For example, in cross country productivity comparisons, it is possible for country A to have higher productivity in all sectors than country B and yet have lower aggregate productivity. This is due to the affect of sectoral share weights on the aggregation procedure. This aggregation problem manifests within countries as well. For individual firms or sectors productivity may increase yet at the aggregate level productivity can fall. This is what Fox describes as failure to satisfy the monotonicity property and is just the influence of share weights on the aggregation procedure. As we will see below share weights present further problems when calculating the free lunches that TFP growth ideally captures.

3.3. Distance function approach

This approach to measuring TFP seeks to separate TFP into two components. It uses an output distance function to measure the distance from the actual production of an economy or a sector to the production efficiency frontier.[15] Thus, in principle a change in TFP can be decomposed into that resulting from a move toward the efficiency frontier and a shift in the frontier. Caves, Christiensen and Deiwert (1982a,b) define a Malmquist index which is the ratio of two output distance functions with the numerator being the output distance function at time $t + 1$ using time t technology and the denominator being the output distance function at time t based on time t technology.[16] An alternative is to define the distance functions in terms of technology in time $t + 1$.[17] Fare, Grosskopf, Norris, and Zhang (1994) define a Malmquist index that is the geometric mean of these two indexes and this allows them to interpret two terms in there index, one as efficiency changes (movements toward the frontier) and the second as changes in technology (shifts in the frontier).[18]

In order to implement this technique, one must know everything about the state of technology at every point in time and at every level of aggregation that TFP is calculated. Unfortunately, this is not possible given the data available. However, this does not prevent attempts being made to implement the distance function approach. Fare, Grosskopf, Norris, and Zhang (1994) look at total factor productivity growth in seventeen OECD countries, constructing a production frontier nonparametrically using activity or Data Envelop analysis. The 'world' production frontier is constructed by looking at the total factor productivity input/output relations of the countries in the data set and letting those countries that produce the most output for given levels of inputs determine the frontier. All other countries in the set are then evaluated in terms of their distance from the frontier. Fare, Grosskopf, and Margaritis (1996) follow this approach but use sector level input and output data for New Zealand to produce the aggregate production frontier for the New Zealand market sector. Again this frontier is determined by the 'most efficient sectors' and all other sectors are evaluated in terms of their distance from that frontier.

Implicit in this technique is the assumption that all units being compared, countries or industries, have the same aggregate production function relating inputs to outputs. Evidence suggests that even firms within one industry do not have identical functions since productivity and profitability varies greatly among such firms. (See for example Jorgenson, Gollop and Fraumeni (1987).) If this is so within one industry, it is much more likely to be so across industries. Given what we know about technological complementarities and the need to adapt technologies for specific uses, identical production function across industries is not an acceptable assumption. For example, is it difficult to believe that the application of electricity to communications technologies can be considered to be the same production technology as the application of electricity to mining or machining? If all units, whether within or across industries or countries, do not have the same production function, then it becomes critical that the comparison of TFP across units is a comparison of averages not marginals. An efficient allocation of resources across units does not require that average productivities be equated but rather that productivity be equated at the margin. What matters is how much extra output can be produced by moving a marginal unit of resources from one unit to another. Only if the units have identical production functions does equality of marginal productivities imply equality of average productivities. If they have different production functions, then an efficient allocation resulting from an equality of marginal productivities of resources in each unit is quite consistent with different average productivities. For example, there is no reason to expect that the average productivity of resources in sheep farming should equal that of the computer software industry. An efficient allocation only requires that the total value of output cannot be increased by moving a marginal unit of resources from one to the other.

3.4. *Recognized Problems With TFP*

Many economists have identified problems associated with TFP both as a concept and with its measurement. Key references for measurement problems are Griliches (1987, 1994 and 1995), where he considers the many sources of error in TFP measurements. Griliches (1987, p.1010–13) outlines some conceptual and empirical problems concerning the measurement of TFP. These relate to the following issues: (1) a relevant concept of capital, (2) measurement of output, (3) measurement of inputs, (4) the place of R&D and public infrastructure, (5) missing or inappropriate data, (6) weights for indices, (7) theoretical specifications of relations between inputs, technology and aggregate production functions, (8) aggregation over heterogeneity. Concerning point (6), and as discussed in section 2.3, Diewert (1987, p.767–780) and Diewert and Laurence (1999) show that very restrictive assumptions have to be satisfied to generate these indices of output and input.

Griliches (1987) rewrites the TFP expression illustrating where these errors can occur.

$$TFP = \frac{\dot{A}}{A} = s\left(\frac{\dot{K}^*}{K} - \frac{\dot{K}}{K}\right) + (1-s)\left(\frac{\dot{L}^*}{L} - \frac{\dot{L}}{L}\right) + (s^*-s)\left(\frac{\dot{K}^*}{K} - \frac{\dot{L}^*}{L}\right)$$

$$+ h\left[s^*\frac{\dot{K}^*}{K} + (1-s^*)\frac{\dot{L}^*}{L} - f\right] + \alpha z + \mu + t$$

The symbols marked with asterisks denote 'correctly' measured inputs. The s is share weights of capital in total output. $((1-s)$ is the share weight for labour.) They are functions of elasticities of output with respect to specific inputs.

$$s^* = \frac{\alpha_k}{\alpha_k + \alpha_l} = \frac{\alpha_k}{1+h}$$

is the correctly measured share of capital. The α's are the true elasticities with respect to the inputs. $h = \alpha_k + \alpha_l - 1$ is a measure of the economies of scale with respect to the measured percentage rates of change of the conventional inputs (K and L). f is the rate of growth of establishments. z is the rate of growth of inputs which affect output, *but which are not included*. μ is errors in measurement. Finally, t is the 'true' rate of growth of the average level of disembodied technology, which includes externalities from technological change.

The first term:

$$s\left(\frac{\dot{K}^*}{K} - \frac{\dot{K}}{K}\right)$$

reflects the rate of growth in measurement error of capital.

The second term:

$$(1-s)\left(\frac{\dot{L}^*}{L}-\frac{\dot{L}}{L}\right)$$

reflects the rate of growth in measurement error of the labour input.

The third term:

$$(s^*-s)\left(\frac{\dot{K}^*}{K}-\frac{\dot{L}^*}{L}\right)$$

reflects the errors in assessing the relative contribution of each factor.

The fourth term:

$$h\left[s^*\frac{\dot{K}^*}{K}+(1-s^*)\frac{\dot{L}^*}{L}-f\right]$$

is the economies of scale term. It is zero if either $h=0$, constant returns to scale, or the rate of growth in the number of new establishments (f) just equals in the total weighted input, which implies that growth of output is by replication of identical establishments[19].

The fifth term, $\alpha_z z$, reflects the contribution of omitted inputs (private or public).

The sixth term, μ, is unspecified errors.

The seventh term, t, is the pure residual term. (i.e., the amount of growth not accounted for by the expanded list of possible sources.

Since we can be sure that there are errors in all these terms, some of which may be quite large, one must be extremely cautious in placing much reliance on any interpretation of changes in measured TFP. Griliches (1995) concludes that '[a]ll of the pioneers of this subject were quite clear about the tenuousness of such calculations and that it may be misleading to identify the results as 'pure' measures of technical progress.' (p. 6)

While we view these problems as cause for concern when people attempt to interpret TFP numbers we do not say more about them here. Instead, we focus our attention on a handful of specific issues that underlie the inconsistent interpretations of TFP made by the groups identified in the introduction.

4. TFP And Costly Technological Change[20]

In this section, we argue that TFP does not measure technological change but it may, ideally, measure the super-normal profits, externalities and some of the other 'free lunches' associated with such change.[21] Virtually all technological change is embodied in one form or another, in new or improved products, in new or improved capital goods or other forms of production technologies, and in new forms of organization in finance, management or on the shop floor. We speak in this section of capital goods although any embodied technology would do.

Although much theory proceeds as if these technological changes appear spontaneously, most are the result of resource-using activities. The costs of creating technological changes involve more than just conventional R&D costs. They include costs of installation, acquisition of tacit knowledge about the manufacture and operation of the new equipment, learning by doing in making the product, and learning by using it, plus a normal return on the investment of funds in development costs.[22] We refer to the sum of these as 'development costs.'

It was the important contribution of Jorgenson and Griliches (1967) to point out that TFP growth would only measure the gains in output that were over and above their development costs and, therefore, TFP growth would not measure the full contribution of new technology. While we accept their position that TFP growth only measures returns above development costs, we go on to argue, first, that these returns are not all 'free lunches,' second, that the measurable returns are not all of the free lunches that are associated with technological advance and, third, that what is measured by TFP growth may be quite large. This last point is in contrast to J&G who argued that these gains would, when properly measured, be close to zero. The unfortunate consequence was that the subsequent debate centred on whether or not the measure should approach zero, which obscured their really important contribution that TFP growth did not measure the full contribution of the new technology.

4.1. *A thought experiment*

Any time an investment is made to develop a new technology, the investors must at least be expecting to recover all of their development costs in the selling price of whatever embodies that technology. For concreteness, we assume it is a capital good. This implies that the price of the good, and thus the investment that the users must make in buying it, will capitalize all development costs. Consider an example in which an existing machine is improved so that it does more work on the same job than did its predecessor. Let the value of the fully perfected new machine's marginal product in the user industry be v. This is the maximum price that users will be willing to pay for each new machine. Let the development cost per unit of the new machine be w. There are three cases to consider for costly technological development:

1. $w > v$ implies perfectly foresighted firms would not invest in the technology. If they did TFP change would be negative.
2. $w = v$, implies TFP change is zero.
3. $w < v$, implies TFP change is positive.

In case 2 where full development cost are just covered, the returns to inventing in the new technology are just equal to the returns to investing in existing technologies since in competitive equilibrium characterised by risk (and no uncertainty), the returns to all lines of investment must be equal (and so only case 2 is possible in equilibrium). In case (3), there is a return over and above what is needed to recover the development costs that created the innovation. In a perfectly competitive, risk-only economy these extra returns must have been unexpected returns. They will be shared between the capital goods producers and the users in a proportion that will depend on the type of market in which the good is sold.

Importantly, there is technological change in all three cases while the change in TFP has only captured that portion of technological change that yields returns in excess of full development costs. Thus, zero change in TFP does not mean zero technical change. It only means that investing in R&D has had the same marginal effect on income as investing in existing technologies (investment with no technical change) and that there are no external effects that show up in increased output elsewhere without corresponding increases in inputs.

We might ask 'Where is the benefit in the new technologies when the marginal productivities of investing in new and existing technologies are the same?' Carlaw and Lipsey (2003a) show that the gain under these circumstances is not to be found at any current margin. Instead, it is to be found in the difference between the time path of GDP if technology had remained constant and the path of its actual behaviour as technology changes. If there were no technological change, diminishing returns to capital would result in a declining rate of growth of GDP for any given rate of capital accumulation. Assume, however, that there is technological change that just covers its development costs so that investment in new technologies yields the same rate of return as investment in existing technologies. Now capital accumulation does not encounter diminishing returns. The rates of return on investment in old and new technology hold constant and the growth rate of output does not fall for a given rate of capital accumulation. The gain for technological change is not, therefore, measured by any gap between investing in old and new technology but by the growing gap between the actual time path of old output and what the path would have been if technology had been static.[23]

4.2. *Free lunches and super normal benefits*

As noted above, in a perfectly competitive end-state equilibrium in which fore-sighted individuals invest in new technologies under conditions of risk, the expected return from all lines of expenditure are equated. Thus, the expected returns to investing in a new technology will just cover the opportunity cost of its full development and will be equal to the return to investing in new capital that embodies existing technologies. Under these conditions, additional returns would then only arise because of externalities (or unexpected events that are not consistent with full equilibrium). For this reason, Jorgenson and Griliches, and others who followed them, associated TFP change with the 'free lunches' of externalities.

In contrast, under the path dependent, process competition that characterises the real world of technological change in which new technologies are developed under conditions of Knightian uncertainty, investments in new technologies can, and often do, yield returns well above the going rate of return. Much of this extra return is a reward for facing the high degree of uncertainty associated with the development, the proving and the creation of applications for new technologies. *These are not free lunches*. Instead, they are the incentives required to persuade entrepreneurs to attempt technological advance in highly uncertain and often capricious environments. The concept of a free lunch can then be associated with externalities and other unpaid for benefits that accrue to others. In the case of GPTs these benefits typically spread over much of the whole economy and over long periods of time, because GPTs present a research agenda for applying them in myriad ways to new processes and new products. These are genuine free lunches. They bring benefits in term of new opportunities that agents typically do not have to pay for. (For example no one has to pay for the opportunity to incorporate electricity or a computer into the design of a new product or process.) To allow for this extra return, as well as genuine free lunch externalities, we define the 'super-normal benefits' associated with technological change as the sum of all associated output increases and cost reductions accruing to anyone in the economy *minus* the new technology's development costs.[24] These considerations do not alter the measured value of TFP changes, which remain increases in output in excess of measured increases in inputs, but they do suggest an alteration in how we view them. As long as one understands that TFP includes that part of the return on innovation that is a reward for undertaking uncertainty, there is no problem in calling it a measure of 'free lunches.' We prefer the term 'super normal benefits' since this term avoids the impression that they are strictly Manna from heaven that serve no purpose in the allocation of resources.

We make the distinction between free lunches and super normal benefits because it is so easy to misinterpret what TFP does measure once it is accepted that it is not a measure of technological change. For example, Hulten (p 9, n5) writes that the Hicksian shift parameter, A_t, '...captures only *costless* improvements in the way an economy's resources of labor and capital are transformed into real GDP (the proverbial 'Manna from Heaven'). Technical change that results from R&D spending will not be captured by A_t...'. In fact, that part of the gains from R&D that accrues to the innovators and that is in excess of the 'normal' rate of return on investing in existing technologies is potentially captured. For example, a new technology that is embodied in a new machine may equally increase the efficiently of labour and of capital and hence look empirically like Hick's neutral technological change. This does not imply either that it is disembodied or that it is costless.

5. When does TFP mismeasure super normal benefits?

In this section, we briefly summarise six situations reported in Lipsey and Carlaw (2002) in which TFP growth does not properly pick up the super normal benefits associated with technological change. In the first case, different timings of the arrival of the same free technological advance cause differences in measured TFP changes. In the second case, the accounting rules of certain statistical agencies imply that the free technological advances associated with R&D investment will not be included in TFP growth. In the third case, the omission of variables from the production function causes TFP growth to under estimate the technological gain. In the fourth case, the use of an aggregate production function to describe disaggregated activity causes TFP growth to under measure technological change. The fifth case describes the bias that can result in the TFP growth rate calculation of the technological gain when the economy takes time to adjust to the change in technology. The six cases cover all those delayed spill over effects that are not measured by a comparison of the current changes in inputs and outputs that characterises TFP growth measures. This is not an exhaustive list but it is surely sufficient to provide a note of caution to anyone who wishes to interpret TFP growth as anything other than an index of changes in output relative to changes in inputs.[25]

For analytical convenience, we assume that all technological changes considered in this section are costless. This implies that all of the effects on output should show up as changes in TFP. We find, however, that they often do not. (A similar but slightly more complex analysis produces the same results for costly changes.)

5.1. *Timing of Cost Reductions*

Lipsey and Carlaw (2002) provide a numerical illustration of a situation in which identical changes in technology give different changes in TFP and in free lunches depending only on the timing of the changes. A product costs $4,000 in year 0 and $540 in year 20 (an average cost fall of 10% per year). The resulting increase in output over the same period is an average of 10% per year. Consider two time paths for these changes.

In case 1, both the costs fall and the sales rise by 10% each year. The industry's TFP rises by 20% each year and its contribution to national TFP change will rise as its share of national income rises. Let total GDP be constant and the original weight be 0.02. Then the final weight will be 0.148.[26] Thus the contribution to the economy's TFP change will rise steadily from 0.4% in the first year to 2.96% in the final year.

In case 2, all of the cost reductions come in the first year while sales expand at 10% per year for 20 years. In the first year, the industry's TFP increases by nearly 100% (a .865 reduction in costs and an increase in sales of .1). With an initial weight of .02, this makes its contribution to the increase in national TFP 2% in that year and zero for the next 19 years.

All that differs between the two cases is the timing. Yet in case 1, the contribution to the increase in national TFP in the last year, when only 1/20th of the total change occurs, slightly exceeds the contribution in case two in the year when *all* of its cost reducing change occurs. Since in the first case TFP is rising for each of the 19 years prior to the final period, the total changes in TFP after 20 years is much larger than in the second case. The reverse is true for free lunches. In the second case, the costs are $540 in each of the 19 years following the technological advance, while in the second case they start at $4,000 and only reach $540 after 20 years, making the cumulative costs much higher in case 2 than in case 1, although the cumulative output is the same in both cases. So, given the identical final change in technology, costs, and output, TFP change is larger and the total of free lunches lower when the cost change is spread over many years than when it occurs all at once. The results suggest problems for people who wish to interpret TFP change as being a measure of free lunches since the nature of the nature of the free lunch (a fall in production costs) is the same for both cases but the effect on TFP growth is different.

As Lipsey and Carlaw (2002) note, '[this case] is more than a theoretical possibility. Something like this occurred in the automobile industry with the introduction of Henry Ford's Model T. The price of cars fell quickly while it took a decade for demand to respond fully.'[27] Indeed, some thing like it is common in cases where new durable commodities require a large slowly developed infrastructure before they can be widely used.

5.2. *The treatment of R&D*

Lipsey and Carlaw (2002) present another example of how TFP can be misleading with respect to capturing supernormal profits which involves the treatment of R&D investment in the national accounts of many countries. R&D is often recorded on the input side as a current cost and not given any direct output. Offsetting output appears only when the R&D results in reduced costs or increased output of final goods.

Treating R&D this way implies that if an established domestic industry shifts resources from making machines into R&D to design better machines there will be a measured fall in output with no change in input costs and hence, ceteris paribus, a reduction in its TFP. The resulting fall in TFP does not measure any technological regression.

This treatment also implies that a start-up firm that does only R&D in one year will have its input valued at cost and record an equal negative profit, since it has no sales. Thus it will have a negative contribution to TFP growth and show no contribution to current output. Yet, it may be contributing to technological change by producing new patentable technologies. If the patents produced are sold abroad, the transactions are recorded as capital transfers and no income is ever recorded. Hence there is no TFP gain at any point in the process. This is also the case if the start up firm is itself sold to a foreign multinational.[28] Selling the patent or the firm to another domestic firm is also treated as a capital transfer and there is no possible effect on TFP until after the new technology is put to use.

So in these respects, TFP measures nothing systematic concerning the value created by R&D until the new technologies are used to reduce costs or increase the production of final goods and services. Furthermore, there is a potential for getting temporarily misleading TFP measures as the economy switches resources from investment in producing hardware to investment in producing ideas. The figures may be permanently misleading if the intellectual property is sold to foreigners. (Lipsey and Carlaw, 2002)

5.3. *Omitted inputs: Natural Resources Made Explicit*

A third way TFP growth can mis-measure supernormal gains, pointed to by Lipsey and Carlaw (2002), concerns omitted variables. Failure to measure any input can bias TFP's measure of super normal benefits. The direction of this bias could be downwards when the omitted input is decreasing in size relative to the measured inputs as is the case with natural resources.[29] But the direction of the bias could be upwards as well for omitted inputs, such as informal R&D, that could be growing faster than the measured inputs. We illustrate the problem with Lipsey and Carlaw's example of omitting natural resources.

Since Solow (1957) growth theorists typically define physical capital to include natural resources, land, minerals, forests etc.[30] The treatment of physical and human capital that follows in growth models and accounting frameworks is appropriate for these two inputs but takes no account of the characteristics of natural resources. The stocks of plant and equipment can be increased more or less without limit but the stocks of arable land and mineral resources cannot. Appendix C has a version of the formal example provided in Lipsey and Carlaw (2002).

> The shortcomings of this treatment of resources can be seen in the contrast between two positions. The first is the prediction derived from the standard formulation in equation (I.2) above that measured capital and labour could have been increased at a common steady rate from say 1900 to 2000 with *constant technology* and no change in living standards. The second is the belief that the supply of some key natural resources and much of the environment's capacity to handle pollution could not have survived a six fold increase in industrial activity with 1900 technology. To reconcile these conflicting positions, we need to recognize that the capital that would need to grow would include such resource inputs as acres of agricultural land, quantities of mineral and timber resources, available 'waste disposal' ecosystems, supplies of fresh water, and a host of other things that are ignored by the standard theoretical treatments and most applied measurements of capital. (Since technology is assumed to be constant in the above exercise, this growth cannot be the result of increased efficiency in the use of natural resources due to new techniques.) (Lipsey and Carlaw 2002).

Lipsey and Carlaw then show that if the efficiency of use of any unmeasured resource is growing, this is likely to show up as an increase in the quantity of measured resource inputs. They illustrate by showing that in a case in which the quantities of measured capital and labour are increasing at some constant rate of x% per annum, while the efficiency with which unmeasured resources are being used is also growing at x% due to technological change in the resource industries, all of the increase in output will be ascribed to increases in the quantities of labour and capital inputs with no change in TFP growth.

5.4. *Aggregation of Inputs*

Lipsey and Carlaw (2002) provide a simple algebraic demonstration of the empirical findings of Jorgenson, Gollop and Fraumeni (1987) Chapter 8. Jorgenson *et al* find that failure to include quality effects results an upward bias in the contribution of inputs to output growth, when aggregation occurs. Lipsey and Carlaw tackle the point by assuming that the firm level production function has two types of labour and two types of capital.[31] They also assume that an aggregate production function (i.e., one with only one type of capital and one type of labour) is used to calculate TFP growth). The productivity parameter for the disaggregated production function is allowed to increase costlessly over time with the four inputs held constant. Because prices equal to marginal products must be used in the aggregation exercise, the TFP growth rate calculated using the aggregate production function shows zero change, whereas the free lunch associated with the actual underlying micro production function is the change in the productivity parameter. The result occurs because the act of aggregating causes the free lunch to be counted as an increase in the aggregate inputs.

Lipsey and Carlaw note that labour in different uses can be measured in physical units, such as labour hours, with different qualities being converted into labour hour equivalents. So the aggregation problem may not affect the labour input. However, capital in different uses is composed of physically different items that can only be aggregated in monetary units. The outcome is that increases in output due to a productivity increase will be divided between measured increases in the quantity of capital (in proportion to capital's share) and measured increases in TFP (in proportion to labour's share).

The important point is that because some amount of aggregation of inputs must *always* take place before any TFP growth index is calculated, some amount of technical change will *always* be recorded as changes in the quantity of inputs, especially capital.

Jorgenson and Stiroh (2000) argue for making disaggregated measures at the industry level. 'Productivity growth ... differs widely among industries.' (p. 161) so that disaggregation '... is especially critical in evaluating the validity of explanations of economic growth that rely on developments at the level of industries, such as technology-led growth.' (p. 166). However, even when calculations are made at the firm level, let alone the industry level, Lipsey and Carlaw show that substantial amounts of technological change will show up as increases in the measured inputs of either the firms or the industry.

5.5. *Aggregation When Calculating a TFP Index*

We now follow Lipsey and Carlaw and assume away the aggregation problem of the previous section so that the correct measure of the quantity of each type of input is available at whatever level of aggregation used to calculate TFP growth. The usual procedure of using expenditure share weights to aggregate over inputs and outputs can then be employed. An assumption that is critical for the validity of this procedure is that the marginal products of each factor of production are equated in all of their uses.

There are three possible reasons why this assumption may not hold. The first is the one we discuss below. The economy may be in a transition between competitive equilibria, causing marginal products not to be equated in all uses. The second is discussed by Hall (1988) and Basu and Fernald (1997). The presence of imperfect competition implies that marginal products will not be equated even when the economy is in equilibrium. Basu and Fernald (1995) show that under conditions of imperfect competition, aggregation of the sort done by Caballero and Lyons (1990 and 1992) will over estimate the free lunches that TFP is meant to capture. The third possibility is some combination of the first two.

Jorgenson, Gollop and Fraumeni (1987) empirically analyze the substitution of factors among sectors. Their findings may be a reflection of these problems. They find several problems, one of which is the hypothesis for Hicks neutrality (i.e., the rate of productivity growth is independent of quantities of intermediate, capital and labour inputs and the value shares are independent of time) is rejected in thirty-nine of the forty-five industries studied. None of the empirical tests conducted by Jorgenson, Gollop and Fraumeni ask the question dealt with by Lipsey and Carlaw (2002), the algebra for which is repeated in appendix E. They determine the nature of the bias in TFP's measure of super normal benefits in the presence of a free technological gain that causes a transition for one equilibrium set of marginal products to another.

Lipsey and Carlaw consider two concepts of equilibrium. Full equilibrium is the situation where all adjustments have been made and no agent wishes to alter his or her behaviour from period to period. Transitional equilibrium is the situation where each agent does not wish to alter behaviour in the current period but does whish to alter their behaviour across periods.

To study the first problem, that of an economy in transition from one equilibrium to another, Lipsey and Carlaw use a model with two sectors and two factors. A free technological gain is introduced into one sector making the marginal product of resources in that sector relatively higher than in the other sector. Two possible time paths by which the shock may work through the system are considered. In the first, all adjustments occur instantaneously and TFP growth exactly measures the free lunch associated with the technological change. In the second, the migration of resources into the sector with the higher relative marginal productivity takes time. During the transition the TFP measure of the free lunch is biased, the direction of bias depending on the returns to scale in the production functions in the two sectors. In the example used by Lipsey and Carlaw, the bias is downward for decreasing, constant and some range of increasing returns to scale. Beyond a critical value of increasing returns, however, the bias switches to being upward.

The algebraic example given by Lipsey and Carlaw allows them to encompass the results of Basu and Fermani (1995) by showing the conditions under which their upward bias in TFP growth in the presence of imperfect competition can occur (i.e., under conditions of sufficiently increasing returns to scale). In addition, the varying results of Jorgenson, Gollop and Fraumeni (1987) might be explained as differences in scale within the different industries they measured.

5.6. *Lagged spillovers*

A very different set of problems arise from the fact that the spillovers arising from radical new technologies are spread over long periods of time, decades even centuries. It is commonly pointed out that new GPTs present a research program for agents to improve its efficiency and develop its many possible applications to new products and new processes. Think, for example, of all the new products and processes that were, and are still being made possible by electricity, the computer and biotechnology. Decades after each of these GPTs was first introduced, entrepreneurs are still gaining free lunches by being able to freely incorporate some aspect of these GPTs into profitable ventures relating to new products and new processes. Because TFP (in levels or rates of change) measures only the difference between contemporary changes in costs and output, it misses all those spillovers that freely provide profitable opportunities that spread across the economy and over long periods of time.

5.7. *Summary*

Section 5 is based on a series of cases drawn mainly from Lipsey and Carlaw (2002) under which TFP growth is not an accurate measure of the supernormal benefits associated with technological change. There is no intention of providing an exhaustive list and we have noted examples provided by other authors of conditions under which TFP growth mismeasures the supernormal benefits associated with technological change. We conclude that although TFP is easily calculated it is difficult to interpret. Only under a very specific set of ideal conditions does it measure the super normal benefits associated with technological change. It is, therefore, at best only an indicator of how much measured output growth an economy achieves relative to measured input growth. It is not very helpful to policy makers who wish to test the efficacy of their industrial policies.

6. Relating Technological Change to Economic Growth

Economic growth is ultimately driven by technological change, in particular by a succession of GPTs.[32] There are spillovers and free lunches in the form of myriad opportunities for profitable investment in the development of new technologies that are complementary with the GPT (and often with each other as well).[33] There will be great economic gain because the opportunity for such profitable investments would not have existed without the GPT. It is the evolution of new technology in general and GPTs in particular that prevents declines in the marginal products of physical and human capital.

6.1. *GPT-driven growth*

Carlaw and Lipsey (2003b) provide a model of GPT driven sustained growth that is based on the historical evidence and stylised facts of how technologies affect the long run growth process. The assumptions of that model are as follows.
Assumptions

- Technology is not flat, it has a structure.
- Complementarities exist among different types of technological knowledge.

- We introduce randomness in outcomes of productive activity.
- There is uncertainty in that agents do not know enough to maximize over a complex process of knowledge accumulation and certainly cannot maximize over the life time of a GPT as in other models.
- There is no stationary equilibrium concept; a simulation model is used in which nothing is stationary. (This allows us to model a succession of GPTs in a path dependent historical process, rather than just being concerned with the evolution of one.)
- There are technological spillovers such that GPTs rejuvenate the growth process by making applied-R&D more productive and the productivity of fundamental research is increased over time by both applied-R&D and fundamental research.
- The knowledge that goes into developing new GPTs is developed endogenously rather then having GPT arrive costlessly.
- The arrival date of each new GPTs depends partly on the amount of pure knowledge produced and partly on random events.
- New GPTs increase the efficiency applied R&D and consumption production according to a logistic diffusion curve.[34]

Carlaw and Lipsey's model has three sectors, which are (1) a consumption good (2) R&D to develop applications of the GPTs to specific purposes, called 'applied-R&D' and (3) R&D that helps to develop GPTs, called 'pure research.' Each of the three sectors is represented by a single production function. Perfect competition is assumed to prevail dictating how agents allocate resources among these three sectors.

The GPT models in Helpman (1998) assume that agents are sufficiently foresighted to know the whole course of the evolution of a new GPT when it arrives. Thus they can maximize over the life time of the GPT, which produces a stationary equilibrium derived from their infinite horizon utility maximization. Even in Aghion and Howitt (1992) where new technologies arrive randomly, innovation is at a constant rate in equilibrium.[35] Carlaw and Lipsey's agents maximize their expected output in each period, but this is done subject to genuine uncertainty because they do not know the future payoff to resources allocated to pure research. They do not know the probability distributions that are generating the disturbances on the outcomes, nor can they infer them from past GPTs. So they assume that current marginal productivities will persist into the future.

This assumption of no foresight seems closer to what we observe. 'Nonetheless, faced with our assumption, one might wonder if, by learning over successive GPTs, agents might eventually be able to anticipate the course of each new one. But the facts suggest otherwise. Since GPTs are technologically distinct from each other, the history of past GPTs provides little quantitative evidence about how new ones will behave. For example, knowing how the steam engine affected the economy over the several hundred years of its evolution would tell agents virtually nothing about the evolutionary path to be expected for electricity at the time when the dynamo was invented in 1887.' (Carlaw and Lipsey (2003b))

Uncertainty in pure knowledge production is introduced in three ways. First, the flow of new pure knowledge generated by resources devoted to pure knowledge research in every period is uncertain. Second, the duration between arrivals of successive GPTs is uncertain (but typically long). Third, the productivity impact of a new GPT on the applied R&D sector is uncertain.

A logistic curve is used to represent the impact of the new GPT on the marginal productivity of resources in applied R&D through time. The interrelation between the production functions in each sector explicitly incorporates technological spillovers. GPTs rejuvenate the growth process by making applied-R&D more productive. The productivity of fundamental research is increased over time by both applied-R&D and fundamental research. These relations are intended to mirror the types of empirical observations discussed (Carlaw and Lipsey (2003b)).

Carlaw and Lipsey's model does not have a stationary equilibrium in either the levels or rates of change of the endogenous variables. This is because agents cannot foresee the consequence from their current decisions regarding resource allocations. Each period is characterized by a transitional competitive equilibrium where the marginal productivities of inputs in each sector are taken as given. But because of technological advance, the spillovers and uncertainty, the marginal products change from one period to the next unexpectedly. Thus the competitive equilibrium is different in each period and the economy never settles into a stationary equilibrium (neither a steady state nor a balanced growth path). A very productive new GPT can accelerate the average growth rate over its lifetime while a less productive new GPT can slow it.

To summarize GPTs arrive at randomly determined times with an impact on applied R&D productivity that is ultimately determined by the amount of pure knowledge that has been endogenously generated since the last GPT. The randomness in the model implies that short term outcomes are influenced by the realizations of the random variables, causing the average growth rate of output over the lifetime of each successive GPT to be variable. However, the long run average growth rate over a succession of several GPTs is determined by the accumulated amount of pure knowledge, knowledge that is determined partly by the endogenous allocation of resources to pure research and partly exogenously by random factors. While some GPT driven research programs are richer than others, there is no pattern to their growth rate and productivity effects. GPTs sustain growth as long as they continue to arrive.

6.2. *Calculating TFP from Simulated Data*

In this section we repeat a few of the TFP growth rate calculations made by Carlaw and Lipsey (2003b). We calculate TFP numbers from data simulated out of a version of Carlaw and Lipsey's model. Calculating TFP under these controlled conditions allows us to explicitly compare the rate of TFP change to the rate of change of technological knowledge and experiment with different measurement scenarios. Thus, we are able to make some progress towards developing a theory of TFP. We find, as Carlaw and Lipsey do, that only under certain, unrealistic conditions does TFP growth actually track technological change.[36]

The details of how to construct the TFP growth rate measure on the data simulated from the three sector model are provided in Carlaw and Lipsey (2003b) and are therefore not repeated here. We note that we use a Tornquist index to calculate TFP growth.

TFP growth can be calculated using various assumptions about how outputs from the pure knowledge sector are observed, about how knowledge is treated in the production function, and about scale effects.

Output of the pure research sector could be measured in one of three ways: (1) the actual flow of output from the pure research sector, (2) the input costs of creating that knowledge, and (3) as zero.[37] There are also two ways of treating the influence of knowledge: (1) as an input into the relevant production functions and (2) as a shift parameter in those functions. For any given rate of technological change in the model we get widely differing TFP results depending on which of these measurements conventions are adopted.

Carlaw and Lipsey (2003b) provide a full analysis of these possibilities. Here we provide some examples to demonstrate the potential for a wider research agenda to develop a theory of TFP. We plot the growth rate of the pure and applied knowledge stock, which are, aggregated using Tournquist index, against measured TFP growth. In all cases knowledge is treated as an input into production. Figures A and B show the accounting methodology where TFP growth is calculated using the perceived flow of output from the pure knowledge sector. 'Perceived' means that the uncertainty associated with the allocation of resources is not applied to the resources allocated to that sector. Figure A shows the case where there are constant returns to accumulated knowledge in all three sectors. Figure B shows the case where there are decreasing returns to knowledge in the consumption sector. Figures C and D show the case where output from the pure knowledge sector is measured at its resource costs. Figure C has constant returns to knowledge in all sectors. Figure D has decreasing returns to knowledge in the applied R&D sector. Figures E and F show the case where no measure of output from the pure knowledge sector is included. Figure E in the constant returns to knowledge case and F is the case where there are diminishing returns to knowledge in the consumption sector.

In all cases, TFP growth drops just at the time that there is an increase in knowledge growth, which in this model is technological change. TFP growth then stays low relative to knowledge growth. In some cases, after a prolonged period of time, TFP growth surpasses knowledge growth and overshoots it when knowledge growth actually declines. This is one possible explanation of the so called 'productivity slowdown' starting the mid-1970's, followed by the 'New Economy' boom, in productivity in the late 1990's, associated with information and communications technology.

In the few cases shown here TFP is persistently out of step with the actual knowledge creation process. In cases C, D and E TFP is persistently below knowledge growth. For the most part TFP has a low correlation with knowledge growth for example in case F the correlation between knowledge and TFP growth is 0.63.

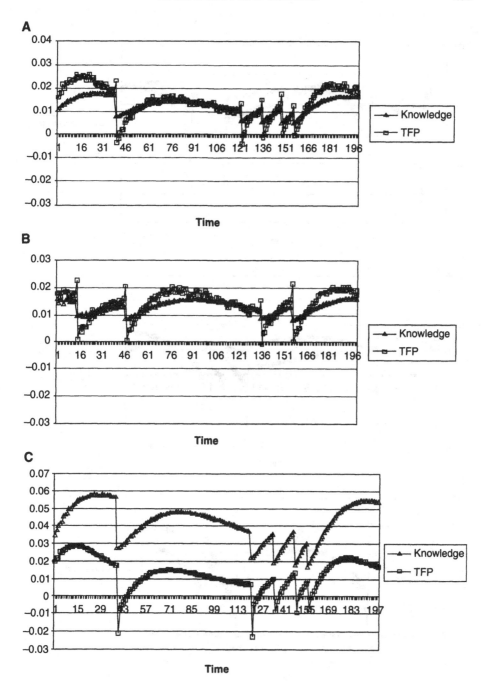

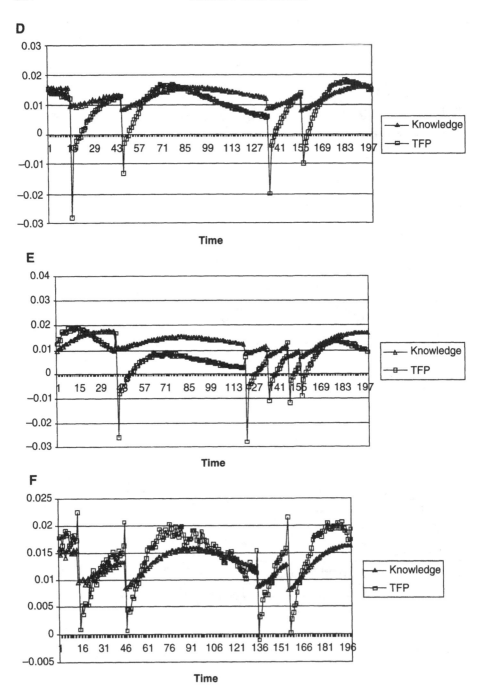

Figure 1. Growth Rates

As was reported in Carlaw and Lipsey (2003b) TFP growth seems to do the best job of tracking knowledge growth under the most unrealistic accounting assumptions (i.e., when the output flow from the pure knowledge sector is used to calculate total output). However these are the least plausible cases, because given the uncertainty that surrounds this sector, the measurer is unlikely to have data available to do such calculations. In the more realistic cases, TFP does not track knowledge growth well at all.

7. Conclusions

We set out in this paper to determine the relationship between economic growth, technological change and total factor productivity for a number of reasons. First because we wish to direct attention to alternatives to TFP as measures of technological change because we think technological change is the ultimate cause of long run economic growth. Second, because some people view TFP as a policy lever rather than an observation. Third, because many economists whose perspectives are based on an aggregate production function have argued that there is no 'new Economy' since the productivity numbers do not reflect big changes in technology.

We argue that TFP what ever else it may measure is not a measure of technological change. Much technological change involves the costly allocation of resources to lines of research and discovery and to the extent that those resources earn only normal returns when technologies are discovered and implemented the value of the technological change is capitalised in to input costs and TFP growth should be zero. TFP growth ideally can measure the super normal gains associated with technological change. However, we discuss several cases where TFP growth will not properly measure even the super normal gains. Finally we use the model of Carlaw and Lipsey (2003b) to simulate data and demonstrate under what conditions TFP growth will or will not track changes in technological knowledge. We confirm Carlaw and Lipsey's findings that TFP change does not measure costly technological change in the most plausible of measurement scenarios. We also discover that TFP growth seems to move in the opposite direction the rate of knowledge growth when GPTs arrive in the simulated economy. We pose the question as to whether this is the source of the so called productivity paradox.

Acknowledgements

The first author wishes to acknowledge Financial Support from the Royal Society of New Zealand, Masder Fund Grant UOC101.

Notes

1. The later being mainly the various papers of Bekar, Carlaw and Lipsey. See Lipsey, Bekar and Carlaw (1998b), Carlaw and Lipsey (2003a), and Carlaw and Lipsey (2003b)
2. In this paper we draw extensively on three interrelated papers, Lipsey and Carlaw (2003), Carlaw and Lipsey (2003a) and Carlaw and Lipsey (2003b).

3. See Lipsey and Beker (1995) Lipsey, Bekar and Carlaw (1998b) and Lipsey (2002).

4. The word 'associated' means different things in different contexts. In Solow's model there is causality running from productivity increases to economic growth. In any measuring context there is no such causality.

5. The three groupings and some of the quotations are borrowed from Lipsey and Carlaw (2003).

6. This notion is similar to that of Harberger (1998). His notion of 'real cost reduction' is a catch-all much like 'free lunch' and not narrowly interpreted as externalities.

7. We should make brief mention of the parametric approach to TFP. This approach estimates the parameters of an aggregate production function which is usually expressed in growth rate form. Schreyer and Pilat (2001) highlight the pros and cons of this approach. On the positive side it avoids imposing relationships between production elasticities and income shares, it allows for adjustment costs and adjustments in capacity utilization, it allows for the investigation of changes other than Hicks-neutral, and there is no a priori need for constant returns to scale in production functions. On the negative side there are a number of the usual econometric problems that are relevant. Small samples of data usually require the imposition of restrictions such as constant returns to scale in production functions. If productivity statistics are to be reported periodically, updating will require re-estimation of the entire system of equations. The complexity of the econometric methods used often hinders the explanation of method and interpretation of the productivity measures. For example, Szeto (2001) and Grimes (1983) produce results for New Zealand that are very different from each other with that difference being attributed to differences in method and time period.

8. For example, Alwyn Young (1995, p.8) uses five sub-categories of capital, residential buildings, non-residential buildings, other durable structures, transport equipment, and machinery and many categories of labour distinguished by sex, age and education, all of which are inputs into a single aggregate production function.

9. Often human capital is included as a third factor of production. But, for the purposes of simple illustration here we use the two factor (labour and capital) Cobb-Douglass production function.

10. Most work on TFP uses a Tornquist index, which is basically a discrete version of the continuous Divisa index. It is a percentage change index that averages base and given years weighted indexes, as does the Fisher Ideal index. For our purposes, in exposition of conceptual issues surrounding TFP growth we use the continuous Divisia index, which weights percentage changes in specific inputs by their share of total cost. Where we specifically wish to measure TFP growth using discrete real world or simulated data we use the Tornquist or Fisher indexes.

11. For a definition and full discussion of general purpose technologies see Bresnahan and Trajtenberg (1992) and the papers in contained in Helpman (1998)

12. In process competition '... firms jostle for advantage by price and non-price competition, undercutting and outbidding rivals in the market-place by advertising outlays and promotional expenses, launching new differentiated products, new technical processes, new methods of marketing and new organisational forms, and even new reward structures for their employees, all for the sake of head-start profits that they know will soon be eroded. ...[in short] competition is an active process.' Blaug (1997, p.255–6).

13. Note that in the growth accounting approach we were mainly defining TFP in terms of rates of change where as in the Index number approach TFP is discussed in either levels or growth rate terms and we will be explicit when we are defining TFP in terms of rates of change.

14. Diewert and Lawrence (1999) list the desired properties and discuss where the other three indexes have properties that fail to meet their criteria.
15. See appendix B for the definition of the distance function.
16. See appendix B for the formal definition of this index.
17. See appendix B for the formal definition of this index.
18. See appendix B for the formal definition of this index.
19. Griliches refers to 'f' as both establishments and firms at various parts of his argument. It seems to us that 'establishments', or 'plants', is the right concept. It is quite possible to replicate plants with no change in the number of firms so that his term would be zero when f is establishments and positive when f is firms,
20. This section is taken mainly from Lipsey and Carlaw (2002).
21. Others who have argued something close to this position include Nelson (1964), Rymes (1971) who discusses the need to measure technological change in a dynamic framework and Hulten (1979). Also, as we noted at the outset, this view is held by Jorgenson & Griliches (1967) and Hulten (2000). No one, however, seems to have argued that TFP measures what Frank Knight called the economic profits that were the return for facing uncertainty.
22. Radically new intermediate or final products rarely perform at full efficiency when first used. Instead, experience in producing and using them typically then reveals needed modifications in design and in production techniques.
23. Carlaw and Lipsey (2003a) and Carlaw and Lipsey (2003b) elaborate on this point.
24. Carlaw and Lipsey (2003a) provide a definition of technological complementarities which encompasses technological externalities and relate these to super normal profits in detail.
25. Hulten (2000) provides other examples where TFP does not properly measure free lunch. On page 34–5 he argues that where technological change induces some capital investment, part of the effects will be incorrectly assigned to an increase in capital. He considers a case of a balanced growth path with Harrod-neutral technological change. All of the growth in output is due to technological change in the sense that if there were no such change, output would be constant. But because capital is also growing in order to maintain a constant ratio of capital to efficiency units of labour, a proportion of the rise in output equal to capital's relative share will be attributed to more investment and only the proportion equal to labour's share will be attributed to technological change. We do not think this attribution to increased capital and to technological change is incorrect. If the capital stock were to be held constant by fiat while technological change continued, output would only be growing at the rate of increase in efficiency units of labour weighted by labour's share. The rest of the increase is due to more capital investment. Would this be a serious problem in practice if Hulten's argument for the under measurement is accepted? We think not because it is hard to locate any real technological change that enhances labour's productivity when combined with more and more units of capital that embody static technology. This problem is often overlooked because there is no tradition of relating such theoretical concepts as Harrod neutral technological change to the known facts about actual changes in technology as detailed in books such as Rosenberg's *Inside the Black Box* (1982).
26. If a series increases at 10% per year, it is 6.7 times as large in 20 years; hence the weight goes from .02 to .148.
27. The model T was introduced in 1909. In the first year when sales of the most popular model, the touring sedan, went over 100,000 (1913) its price was $600. Sales reached a peak of just under 900,000 cars at a price of $380 ten years later in 1923.

28. Particularly in small countries, many firms engage in start up behaviour and then sell out to foreign multinationals, realizing the return on their R&D expenditures from the sale price. Indeed, tax advantages given to small firms often encourage such activities. None of this value-creating activity will show up as income or as increases in TFP.
29. Hulten (2000: 51) makes a similar point in specific reference to the omitted negative effects of economic growth on the environment. He notes, however, that a solution to the omitted variables problem 'is an impossibly large order to fill.' This may be so but his observation serves to decrease confidence in the usefulness of the TFP measure.
30. Solow was aware of the omitted variables problem and warned that this could bias measurement of the residual (Solow, 1957).
31. The algebraic representation of this problem from Lipsey and Carlaw (2002) is repeated in appendix D.
32. We have made this point many times. For an early statement see Lipsey and Bekar (1995).
33. Technological complementarity is defined by Carlaw and Lipsey (2003a).
34. Carlaw and Lipsey (2003b) do not actually model the diffusion of GPTs logistically but the calculations of TFP growth presented later in this section are based on a model where logistic diffusion is used.
35. This is because their innovation arrival rate is derived from the expected value of the Poisson distribution with a parameter determined by the equilibrium flow of labor services into research.
36. In what follows, we use technological knowledge, pure and applied knowledge and technology interchangeably. In our model it is the technological knowledge generated in the pure and applied knowledge sectors that is technological change which drives growth.
37. The reason we consider various ways of measuring output from the pure research sector is because of the uncertainty there. Measurers cannot actually observe the flow of potentially useful knowledge that is accumulated but not released until the arrival of the GPT.

References

Abramovitz, M. (1956) Resource and Output Trends in the U.S. Since 1870, *American Economic Review*, 46, 5–23.
Barro, R. J. (1999) Notes on Growth Accounting, *Journal of Economic Growth*, 4, 119–137.
Basu and Fernald (1997) Returns to Scale in U.S. Productions: Estimates and Implications, *Journal of Political Economy*, 105(2), 249–83.
—— (1995) Are apparent productive spillovers a figment of specification error? *Journal of Monetary Economics*, 36, 165–88.
Bekar, Clifford, and Richard G. Lipsey (2001 Manuscript): Science, Institutions, and The Industrial Revolution, available at www.sfu.ca/~ rlipsey.
Blaug (1997) Competition as an End-State and Competition as a Process, in *Trade Technology and Economics: Essays in Honor of Richard G. Lipsey*, (eds) B. Curtis Eaton and Richard G. Harris, Cheltenham: Edward Elgar.
Caballero, R. and R. Lyons (1990) Internal and external economies in European industries, *European Economic Review*, 34, 805–30.
—— (1992) External effects in the U. S. procyclical productivity, *Journal of Monetary Economics*, 29, 209–26.
Carlaw, Kenneth and Steven Kosempel (2001 Manuscript): The Sources of Productivity Growth in Canada.

Carlaw, Kenneth and Richard G. Lipsey (2003a, forthcoming): Externalities, Technological Complementarities and Sustained Economic Growth, Forthcoming in *Research Policy*, Special Issue Honouring Nelson and Winter.

—— (2003b Manuscript): A Model of GPT-Driven, Sustained Growth available from www.sfu.ca/~ rlipsey.

Caves, D.W., L. R. Christensen and W.E. Diewert (1982a) Multilateral comparisons of output, input and productivity using superlative index numbers, *Economic Journal*, March 92(365), 73–86.

Caves, D.W., L. R. Christensen and W.E. Diewert (1982b) The economic theory of index numbers and the measurement of input, output and productivity, *Econometrica* 50, 1393–1414.

Chen, E. K. Y. (1997), The Total Factor Productivity Debate: Determinants of Economic Growth in East Asia, *Asian Pacific Literature*, 11, 18–38.

Crafts, N, and C. Harley (1992) Output Growth and the Industrial Revolution, *Economic History Review*, 45, 703–30

Diewert, E. (1987) Index Numbers, in Eatwell, *et al.*, 2, 767–780.

Diewert, E. and D. Lawrence (1999) Measuring New Zealand's productivity. Wellington, New Zealand Trasury. http://www.treasury.govt.nz/workingpapers/1999/99–5.asp

Eatwell, J., M. Milgate, and P. Newman, eds. (1987) *The New Palgrave, a Dictionary of Economics*, London: Macmillan.

Fare, Grosskopf, Norris, and Zhang (1994) Productivity Growth, technical progress, and efficiency change in industrialized countries, *American Economic Review*, March 84(1): 66–83.

Fare, Grosskopf, and Margaritis (1996) Productivity growth, in B. Silverstone, A. Bollard and R. Lattimore (eds) *A study of economic reform: The case of New Zealand. Contributions to economic analysis*, Vol. 236, Amsterdam: Elsevier, 73–100.

Fox, K. (2002) Problems with (dis)aggregating productivity, and another productivity paradox, unpublished manuscript.

Freeman, Chris and F. Louca (2002) *As Time Goes By: From the Industrial Revolution to the Information Revolution*, Oxford: Oxford University Press.

Gordon, R.J., (2000) Does the 'New Economy' Measure up to the Great Inventions of the Past? *NBER Working Paper #7833*, National Bureau of Economic Research: Washington.

Greenwood, J., Z. Hercowitz and P. Krusell (1997) Long Run Implications of Investment-Specific Technological Change, *American Economic Review*, 87, 342–62.

—— (2000) The Role of Investment-Specific Technological Change in the Business Cycle, *European Economic Review* 44, 91–115.

Griliches, Z. (1987) Productivity: Measurement Problems, in Eatwell, *et al.*, (1987) 3, 1010–1013.

—— (1994) Productivity, R & D, and the Data Constraint, *American Economic Review*, 84, 1–24.

—— (1995) The Discovery of the Residual, *NBER Working Paper #5348*, National Bureau of Economic Research: Washington.

Grubler, Arnulf (1998) *Technology and Global Change*, Cambridge: Cambridge University Press.

Hall, Robert E. (1988) The Relation Between Price and Marginal Cost in U.S. Industry, *Journal of Political Economy*, 96, 921–947.

Harberger, A. (1998) A Vision of the Growth Process, *American Economic Review*, 88(1), 1–32.

Helpman, Elhanan (ed) (1998) *General Purpose Technologies and Economic Growth*, Cambridge: MIT Press.

Hulten, Charles R. (1979) On the Importance of Productivity Change, *American Economic Review*, 65, 126–136.

—— (2000) Total Factor Productivity: A Short Biography, *NBER Working Paper*, 7471, National Bureau of Economic Research: Washington.

IMF Staff (2000) *Country Report No. 00/34.*

Jorgenson, Dale (1995) *Productivity, Volume 1: Postwar U.S. Economic Growth* Cambridge: MIT Press.

—— (2001) Information Technology and the U. S. Economy, *American Economic Review*, 91(1), 1–32.

Jorgensen, Dale and Z. Griliches (1967) The Explanation of Productivity Change, *Review of Economic Studies*, 34, 249–83.

Jorgensen, Dale and B.M. Fraumeni (1995) The Accumulation of Human and Nonhuman Capital 1948–1984, Jorgensen (1995), 273–331.

Jorgensen, Dale and K.J. Stiroh (2000) U.S. Economic Growth at the Industry Level, *American Economic Review*, Papers and Proceedings, 90, 161–167.

Jorgensen, Dale, Frank Gollop and B.M. Fraumeni, (1987) *Productivity and U.S. Economic Growth*, Cambridge MA, Harvard University Press.

Krugman, Paul (1996) The Myth of Asia's Miracle, in *Pop Internationalism*, Cambridge: MIT Press.

Law, M. T. (2000) Productivity and Economic Performance: An Overview of the Issues, *Public Policy Sources Number 37*, Vancouver BC: The Fraser Institute.

Lipsey, Richard G. (1992) Global Change and Economic Policy, in *The Culture and Power of Knowledge: Inquiries into Contemporary Societies*, ed. by Nico Stehr and Richard V. Ericson, Berlin: Walter de Gruyter.

—— (1993) Globalisation, Technological Change and Economic Growth, in *Annual Sir Charles Carter Lecture*, Ireland: Northern Ireland Economic Council, Report #103.

—— (1994) Markets, Technological Change and Economic Growth, *The Pakistan Development Review*, 33, 327–352.

—— (2002) The Productivity Paradox: A Case of the Emperor's New Clothes, forthcoming in *ISUMA: Canadian Journal of Policy Research*, Special Issue on Policies for the New Economy, 3(1), 120–6.

Lipsey, Richard G., and Clifford Bekar (1995) A Structuralist View of Technical Change and Economic Growth, in *Bell Canada Papers on Economic and Public Policy* Vol. 3, Proceedings of the Bell Canada Conference at Queen's University, (Kingston: John Deutsch Institute), 9–75.

Lipsey, R. G., and K. I. Carlaw (2002 manuscript) The measurement of technological change, available from www.sfu.ca/~rlipsey.

Lipsey, Richard G., Clifford Bekar and Kenneth Carlaw (1998a) What Requires Explanation, Chapter 2 in Helpman (1998).

—— (1988b) The Consequences of Changes in GPTs, Chapter 7 in Helpman (1998).

Metcalf, S. (1987) Technical Change, in Eatwell, *et al.* (1987), 4, 617–20.

Nelson, Richard R. (1964) Aggregate Production Function and Medium-Range Growth Projections, *American Economic Review*, 54, 575–606.

Pack, H., and L.E. Westphal (1986): Industrial Strategy and Technological Change: Theory or Reality, *Journal of Development Economics*, 22, 87–128.

Pomeranz, Kenneth (2000): *The Great Divergence: China, Europe and the Making of the Modern World Economy*, Princeton: Princeton University Press.

Prescott, E.C., (1998) Needed a theory of Total Factor Productivity, *International Economic Review*, 39, 525–51.

Rosenberg, Nathan (1982) *Inside the Black Box: Technology and Economics*, Cambridge: Cambridge University Press.

Rymes, Thomas K., (1971) *On Concepts of Capital and Technical Change*, Cambridge: Cambridge University Press.

Schreyer, P. and D. Pilat (2001) Measuring productivity, *OECD Economic Studies*, 33, 127–170.

Solow, R. (1956) A Contribution to the Theory of Economic Growth, *Quarterly Journal of Economics*, 70, 65–94.

—— (1957), Technical Change and the Aggregate Production Function, *Review of Economics and Statistics*, 39, 312–20.

Statistics Canada (1998), 13–568.

Szeto, K.L. (2001) An econometric analysis of a production function for New Zealand, *Wellington, New Zealand Treasury, Working Paper 01/31*.

Wade, Robert (1990) *Governing the Market: Economic Theory and the Role of Government in East Asian Industrialization*, Princeton: Princeton University Press.

Westphal, L. (1990) Industrial Policy in an Export-propelled Economy: lessons from South Korea's experience, *Journal of Economic Perspectives*, 4, 41–60.

Womack, J.P., D.J. Jones and D. Roos (1990) *The Machine that Changed the World*, New York: Rawson Associates.

Young, Alwyn (1992) A Tale of Two Cities: Factor Accumulation and Technical Change in Hong Kong and Singapore, in *NBER Macroeconomic Annual*, Cambridge: MIT press.

—— (1995) The Tyranny of Numbers, *Quarterly Journal of Economics*, 110, 641–80.

Appendix A

Laspeyre's index:

$$Y_L(p^0, p^1, y^0, y^1) = \frac{\sum_{i=1}^{m} p_i^0 y_i^1}{\sum_{i=1}^{m} p_i^0 y_i^0} = \sum_{i=1}^{m} s_i^0 \frac{y_i^1}{y_i^0}$$

where

$$s_i^t = \frac{p_i^t y_i^t}{\sum_{i=1}^{m} p_i^t y_i^t}$$

The Layspeyre's index is the value of period 1 output measured using period 0 prices divided by the value of period 0 output measured using period zero prices.

Paasche index:

$$Y_P(p^0, p^1, y^0, y^1) = \frac{\sum_{i=1}^{m} p_i^1 y_i^1}{\sum_{i=1}^{m} p_i^1 y_i^0} = \left[\sum_{i=1}^{m} s_i^1 \left(\frac{y_i^1}{y_i^0} \right)^{-1} \right]^{-1}$$

The Paasche index uses period 1 prices to weight the output from period 1 and period 0.

Fisher index:

$$Y_F(p^0, p^1, y^0, y^1) = \left[Y_L(p^0, p^1, y^0, y^1) Y_P(p^0, p^1, y^0, y^1) \right]^{\frac{1}{2}}$$

The Fisher index is the geometric average of the Laspeyre's and Paasche indexes.

Tornqvist index:

$$Y_T(p^0, p^1, y^0, y^1) = \prod_{i=1}^{m} \left(\frac{y_i^1}{y_i^0}\right)^{0.5\left(s_i^0 + s_i^1\right)}$$

The Tornqvist index geometrically weights the output of the two periods using an average of the two period share weights.

Appendix B

$$D_0^t(x^t, y^t) = \inf\{\theta : x^t, y^t/\theta) \in S^t\} = (\sup\{\theta : (x^t, y^t/\theta) \in S^t\})^{-1}$$

where x^t is a vector of input quantities at time t and y^t is a vector of output quantities at time t. S^t is the production feasibility set given the available technology at time t. The term $D_0^t(x^t, y^t)$ is the output distance function. The superscript t is the index of time that also denotes the state of technology being used to calculate the distance function. To calculate $D_0^t(x^t, y^t)$ one must find the largest factor that all the outputs in the output vector could be increased by and still have all of the output and input combinations in the feasibility set. $D_0^t(x^t, y^t)$ is the reciprocal of that number. The closer the economy is to the production possibilities frontier the smaller will be $D_0^t(x^t, y^t)$.

The Caves, Christensen and Deiwert (1982a, b) Malmquist index is defined as follows:

$$M^t = \frac{D_0^t(x^{t+1}, y^{t+1})}{D_o^{t+1}(x^t, y^t)}$$

An alternative way of expressing this Malmquist index is in terms of period $t + 1$ technology.

$$M^t = \frac{D_o^{t+1}(x^{t+1}, y^{t+1})}{D_o^{t+1}(x^t, y^t)}$$

The Fare, Grosskopf, Norris, and Zhang (1994) Malmquist index is the geometric mena of the previous two.

$$M_o^t = \frac{D_o^t(x^{t+1}, y^{t+1})}{D_o^t(x^t, y^t)} \left[\frac{D_o^t(x^{t+1}, y^{t+1})}{D_o^{t+1}(x^{t+1}, y^{t+1})} \frac{D_o^t(x^t, y^t)}{D_o^{t+1}(x^t, y^t)}\right]^{\frac{1}{2}}$$

It is interpreted as follows:

Efficiency change $= D_o^t(x^{t+1}, y^{t+1})/D_o^t(x^t, y^t)$

Technical change $= \left[\frac{D_o^t(x^{t+1}, y^{t+1})}{D_o^{t+1}(x^{t+1}, y^{t+1})} \frac{D_o^t(x^t, y^t)}{D_o^{t+1}(x^t, y^t)}\right]^{\frac{1}{2}}$

Appendix C

Let the underlying production function be:

$$Y = BK^{\alpha}(nR)^{(1-\alpha)}, \tag{C.1}$$

where K is accumulating factors, R is natural resources and n is an efficiency coefficient standing for the technology of resource use. Differentiating with respect to time yields:

$$\dot{Y}/Y = \dot{B}/B + \alpha\dot{K}/K + (1-\alpha)(\dot{R}/R + \dot{n}/n). \tag{C.2}$$

The assumed production function for the purposes of measuring TFP is:

$$Y' = AK, \tag{C.3}$$

so that

$$\dot{Y'}/Y' = \dot{A}/A + \dot{K}/K$$

Calculate TFP_m from equation (II.3):

$$\frac{\dot{\text{TFP}}_m}{\text{TFP}_m} = \frac{\dot{A}}{A} = \frac{\dot{Y'}}{Y} - \frac{\dot{K}}{K} = \frac{\dot{B}}{B} + \alpha\frac{\dot{K}}{K} + (1-\alpha)\left(\frac{\dot{R}}{R} + \frac{\dot{n}}{n}\right) - \frac{\dot{K}}{K}.$$

Letting $\dot{B}/B = 0$, yields

$$\frac{\dot{A}}{A} = (1-\alpha)\left[\left(\frac{\dot{R}}{R} + \frac{\dot{n}}{n}\right) - \frac{\dot{K}}{K}\right]$$

So

$$\dot{A}/A = 0 \text{ if } \dot{R}/R + \dot{n}/n = \dot{K}/K$$
$$\dot{A}/A > 0 \text{ if } \dot{R}/R + \dot{n}/n > \dot{K}/K$$
$$\dot{A}/A < 0 \text{ if } \dot{R}/R + \dot{n}/n < \dot{K}/K$$

The measured TFP changes depend only on the above relation not on any cost associated with changing n. To illustrate, let $\dot{R}/R = 0$ and $\dot{n}/n = \dot{K}/K$ so that measured TFP remains constant, indicating, on the standard interpretation of TFP growth measures, that there is no technological change. First, assume that the technological change represented by $\dot{n}$ is free, coming with no resource cost. Then all of the benefit is a free lunch, yet TFP growth remains zero. Second, assume that there is a positive resource cost equal to xK% ($0 < x < 1$). Now the level of Y will be lower by xKα but the rates of growth of Y and A will be unchanged so that (II.3) will still fit the data giving no change in TFP. In this case, changes in TFP do not measure free lunches. Instead, they measure the extent to which the rate of increase in the use of resources measured in efficiency units exceeds the rate of increase in the accumulating factors.

Appendix D

Let the firm's real microeconomic production function be

$$Y = BM^\gamma N^\delta P^\varepsilon R^\eta \quad 0 < (\gamma, \delta, \varepsilon, \eta) < 1 \text{ and } \gamma + \delta + \varepsilon + \eta = 1$$

where M and N are two types of capital and P and R are two types of labour used within the firm and B is a productivity parameter.

Now we assume that an aggregate production function is used to calculate the firm's TFP:

$$Y' = AK^\alpha L^\beta \quad \alpha + \beta = 1.$$

Note that Y and Y' measure the same output but we wish to keep track of the production function (aggregated or disaggregated) on which we are taking derivatives. Let the firm's aggregate capital be calculated as $K = p_m M + p_n N$ where prices are equal to marginal products: $K = (\gamma BM^{\gamma-1}N^\delta P^\varepsilon R^\eta)M + (\delta BM^\gamma N^{\delta-1}P^\varepsilon R^\eta)N = (\gamma + \delta)Y$. Similarly, let the firm's aggregate labour be $L = p_p P + p_r R$, or $L = (\varepsilon + \eta)Y$.

Now let B in (I.4.1) change continuously through time with unchanged inputs of M, N, P, and R. Then $\dot{Y} = (dY/dB)(\dot{B}) = (M^\gamma N^\delta P^\varepsilon R^\eta)(\dot{B})$. Any change in B now shows up as changes in the two aggregate inputs, K and L:

$$\dot{K} = (dK/dY)(dY/dB)(\dot{B}) = (\gamma + \delta)(dY/dB)(\dot{B}), \text{ and}$$
$$dL/dt = (dL/dY)(dY/dB)(dB/dt) = (\varepsilon + \eta)(dY/dB)(dB/dt).$$

So, using the fact that Y' is homogeneous of degree one in K and L:

$$\dot{Y}' = (dY'/dB)(\dot{B}) = (dY'/dK)(\dot{K}) + (dY'/dL)(\dot{L}).$$

Thus a Divisia index based on the two aggregated inputs in the firm's aggregate production function gives:

$$\text{TFP} = \frac{\dot{Y}'}{Y'} - \alpha\frac{\dot{K}}{K} - \beta\frac{\dot{L}}{L} = 0.$$

If instead, we had calculated a Divisia index from the firm's disaggregated production function, we would have obtained the correct answer:

$$\text{TFP} = \frac{\dot{Y}}{Y} - \alpha\frac{\dot{M}}{M} - \beta\frac{\dot{N}}{N} - \gamma\frac{\dot{P}}{P} - \delta\frac{\dot{R}}{P} = \frac{\dot{A}}{A} = \frac{\dot{B}}{B}$$

since all four percentage changes in the disaggregated inputs are zero.

Appendix E

Consider the following stylization of a two sector economy. Let the primary production sector be

$$X = A(L_x)^\alpha (K_x)^\beta$$

Let the manufacturing production sector be

$$Y = B(L_y)^\gamma (K_y)^\sigma$$

Let the resource constraints in the economy be

$$L = L_x + L_y \text{ and } K = K_x + K_y$$

The aggregate accounting identity for this economy is

$$P_x X + P_y Y \equiv w_x L_x + w_y L_y + r_x K_x + r_y K_y$$

The P_i are output prices and the w_i are input prices for each sector where $i = (x, y)$. If we take P_y as the numerare price for the system, then

$$\frac{P_x}{P_y} X + Y \equiv \frac{w_x}{P_y} L_x + \frac{w_y}{P_y} L_y + \frac{r_x}{P_y} K_x + \frac{r_y}{P_y} K_y$$

is the accounting identity.

Assuming full perfectly competitive equilibrium, we can relate prices to marginal products in the following well known way:

$$\frac{P_x}{P_y} = \frac{MP_{L_y}}{MP_{L_x}} = \frac{MP_{K_y}}{MP_{K_L}}$$

$$\frac{w_y}{P_y} = \frac{w_x}{P_x} = MP_{L_x}$$

and

$$\frac{r_y}{P_y} = \frac{r_x}{P_y} = MP_{k_y}$$

Simplify further by normalizing P_y to be 1.

Now consider what happens when the productivity parameter for the manufacturing sector costlessly increases. There will be an immediate increase in the marginal product of labour in manufacturing causing labour to migrate from primary to manufacturing production. If we maintain the assumptions of the full equilibrium, implicitly assuming that the adjustment takes place instantaneously, we can calculate the change in TFP in the following way:

$$\frac{\dot{\text{TFP}}}{\text{TFP}} = \left(\frac{P_x X}{P_x X + Y}\right)\frac{\dot{X}}{X} + \left(\frac{Y}{P_x X + Y}\right)\frac{\dot{Y}}{Y} - \left(\frac{w_x L_x}{w_x L_x + w_y L_y}\right)\frac{\dot{L}_x}{L_x}$$

$$- \left(\frac{w_y L_y}{w_x L_x + w_y L_y}\right)\frac{\dot{L}_y}{L_y} - \left(\frac{r_x K_x}{r_x K_x + r_y K_y}\right)\frac{\dot{K}_x}{K_x} - \left(\frac{r_y K_y}{r_x K_x + r_y K_y}\right)\frac{\dot{K}_y}{K_y}$$

which is simply the Divisia index for TFP.

The assumption of full perfectly competitive equilibrium along with some straight forward algebraic manipulation implies

$$\frac{\dot{\text{TFP}}}{\text{TFP}} = \frac{1}{P_x X + Y}[P_x \dot{X} + \dot{Y}] - \frac{w_x}{w_x L_x + w_y L_y}[\dot{L}_x + \dot{L}_y] - \frac{r_x}{r_x K_x + r_y K_y}[\dot{K}_x + \dot{K}_y]$$

From the resource constraints we know that

$$\dot{L}_y = -\dot{L}_x, \text{ and } \dot{K}_v = -\dot{K}_x$$

so the second and third terms are zero. Substituting the time derivatives of the production function and the definition of P_x implies:

$$\frac{\dot{\text{TFP}}}{\text{TFP}} = \frac{1}{P_x X + Y}\left[\frac{\dot{B}}{B}Y\right].$$

In this case, TFP growth exactly measures the gains associated with the free productivity increase in sector Y.

Now consider the second type of equilibrium. What happens if the transition is not instantaneous? When the productivity change occurs, marginal products are driven out of equilibrium. But now prices do not instantaneously adjust because labour and capital are not instantaneously mobile. We can determine the direction of bias in the prices:

$$\frac{P_x}{P_y} < \frac{MP_{L_v}}{MP_{L_x}}, \text{ and } \frac{P_x}{P_y} < \frac{MP_{K_v}}{MP_{K_x}}$$

Again $w_y/P_y = MP_{L_v}$, and $r_y/P_y = MP_{K_v}$.

However now, $w_x/P_x = P_x/P_y MP_{L_x} < MP_{L_y}/MP_{L_x} MP_{L_x}$, and $r_x/P_y = P_x/P_y$ $MP_{K_x} < MP_{K_v}/MP_{K_x} MP_{K_x}$

Let $G \in (0,1)$ be the gap between the marginal products of labour and full equilibrium prices and $\hat{G} \in (0,1)$ be the gap between the marginal products of capital and full equilibrium prices so that:

$$\frac{P_x}{P_y} = \frac{G(MP_{L_y})}{MP_{L_x}}, \frac{P_x}{P_y} = \frac{\hat{G}(MP_{K_y})}{MP_{K_x}}$$

and

$$\frac{w_x}{P_y} = \frac{P_x}{P_y} MPL_x = \frac{G(MP_{L_y})}{MPL_x} MPL_x = G(MP_{L_y}), \frac{r_x}{P_y}$$

$$= \frac{P_x}{P_y} MPK_x = \frac{\hat{G}(MP_{K_y})}{MPK_x} MPK_x = \hat{G}(MP_{K_y})$$

Once again normalize P_y to be one. The change in TFP is expressed as:

$$\frac{\text{T}\dot{\text{F}}\text{P}'}{\text{TFP}} = \frac{P_x X}{P_x X + Y} \frac{\dot{X}}{X} + \frac{Y}{P_x X + Y} \frac{\dot{Y}}{Y}$$

$$- \frac{w_x L_x}{w_x L_x + w_y L_y} \frac{\dot{L}_x}{L_x} - \frac{w_y L_y}{w_x L_x + w_y L_y} \frac{\dot{L}_y}{L_y}$$

$$- \frac{r_x K_x}{r_x K_x + r_y K_y} \frac{\dot{K}_x}{K_x} - \frac{r_y K_y}{r_x K_x + r_y K_y} \frac{\dot{K}_y}{K_y}$$

Now substituting in the new definitions of the prices and the time derivatives of the production functions yields:

$$\frac{\text{T}\dot{\text{F}}\text{P}}{\text{TFP}} = \frac{1}{P_x X + Y} \left[G(MP_{L_y})\dot{L}x + \hat{G}(MP_{K_y})\dot{K}_x + MP_{L_y}\dot{L}_y + (MP_{K_y})\dot{K}_y + \frac{\dot{B}}{B}Y \right]$$

$$- \frac{1}{w_x L_x + w_y L_y} \left[G(MP_{L_y})\dot{L}_x + MP_{L_y}\dot{L}_y \right]$$

$$- \frac{1}{r_x K_x + r_y K_y} \left[\hat{G}(MP_{K_y})\dot{K}_x + MP_{K_y}\dot{K}_y \right]$$

We can now subtract the original TFP growth calculation from the second to determine if there is any bias between the full equilibrium and the transitional equilibrium. If

$$\frac{\text{T}\dot{\text{F}}\text{P}}{\text{TFP}'} - \frac{\text{T}\dot{\text{F}}\text{P}}{\text{TFP}} < 0$$

then the transitional calculation under estimates the gains. If the inequality is reversed, then TFP growth overestimates the gains.

First we note that $\text{T}\dot{\text{F}}\text{P}/\text{TFP}$ is a positive term in $\text{T}\dot{\text{F}}\text{P}/\text{TFP}'$ so that we can eliminate $1/P_x X + Y[\dot{B}/BY]$ from both TFP growth calculations leaving just the remaining terms in $\text{T}\dot{\text{F}}\text{P}/\text{TFP}'$. Making use of the fact that $\dot{L}_x = -\dot{L}_y$ and $\dot{K}_x = -\dot{K}_y$ we get the following:

$$\frac{\dot{\text{TFP}}}{\text{TFP}'} - \frac{\dot{\text{TFP}}}{\text{TFP}} = \left[\frac{G(MP_{L_v}) - MP_{L_v}}{P_xX + Y} - \frac{G(MP_{L_y}) - MP_{L_v}}{w_xL_x + w_yL_y} \right] \dot{L}_x$$

or

$$+ \left[\frac{\hat{G}(MP_{K_v}) - MP_{K_v}}{P_xX + Y} - \frac{\hat{G}(MP_{K_v}) - MP_{K_v}}{r_xK_x + r_yK_y} \right] \dot{K}_x$$

$$= \left[\frac{1}{P_xX + Y} - \frac{1}{w_xL_x + w_yL_y} \right] [G(MP_{L_y}) - MP_{L_y}] \dot{L}_x$$

$$+ \left[\frac{1}{P_xX + Y} - \frac{1}{r_xK_x + r_yK_y} \right] [\hat{G}(MP_{K_y}) - MP_{K_y}] \dot{K}_x$$

We are interested in signing this expression to determine if there is any bias in the Divisia index when the marginal products are not fully adjusted to long run perfectly competitive equilibrium. To do this note the following

$$[G(MP_{L_y}) - MP_{L_y}] \dot{L}_x > 0, \text{ and } [\hat{G}(MP_{K_v}) - MP_{K_v}] \dot{K}_x > 0 \text{ since}$$
$$[G(MP_{L_y}) - MP_{L_y}] < 0, \dot{L}_x < 0, [\hat{G}(MP_{K_y}) - MP_{K_v}] < 0, \text{ and } \dot{K}_x < 0$$

Thus the two expressions left to evaluate are:

$$\left[\frac{1}{P_xX + Y} - \frac{1}{w_xL_x + w_yL_y} \right], \text{ and}$$

$$\left[\frac{1}{P_xX + Y} - \frac{1}{r_xK_x + r_yK_y} \right]$$

By evaluating the expressions around zero we get:

$$\left[\frac{1}{P_xX + Y} - \frac{1}{w_xL_x + w_yL_y} \right] = G(MP_{L_x}) \left(1 - \frac{1}{\alpha} \right) + (MP_{L_y}) \left(1 - \frac{1}{\gamma} \right) < 0$$

$$\text{if } \alpha < 1 \text{ and } \gamma < 1 \text{ and}$$

$$\left[\frac{1}{P_xX + Y} - \frac{1}{r_xK_x + r_yK_y} \right] = \hat{G}(MP_{K_x}) \left(1 - \frac{1}{\beta} \right) + (MP_{K_y}) \left(1 - \frac{1}{\sigma} \right) < 0$$

$$\text{if } \beta < 1 \text{ and } \sigma < 1.$$

This says that $\dot{\text{TFP}}/\text{TFP}' - \dot{\text{TFP}}/\text{TFP} < 0$ for $\alpha < 1, \gamma < 1, \beta < 1$ and $\sigma < 1$. We can also see that there is no bias if all of these parameters are just equal to one, which implies that the production functions have increasing returns to scale. This implies that there is a negative bias in TFP growth calculations where marginal products are in transitional equilibrium. This negative bias exists for decreasing returns to scale, constant returns to scale and even for some parameterizations leading to increasing returns to scale. Furthermore, for sufficiently large increasing returns to scale there will be an upward bias of measured TFP growth.

9

THE LONG-RUN IMPLICATIONS OF GROWTH THEORIES

Jonathan Temple

University of Bristol

1. Introduction

This paper draws attention to some misunderstandings that can arise in the discussion and analysis of theoretical growth models. The paper gives especial attention to the place of long-run outcomes in growth theory, and argues that the traditional emphasis on these outcomes can be misguided. This emphasis has led some commentators to assign too much importance to the presence of knife-edge assumptions. It could also lead us to dismiss useful models, to develop new models of the growth process that have little practical relevance, and to ignore effects that are of critical importance for welfare.

The underlying viewpoint of the paper is that growth models are best seen as tools for thought experiments. Examining long-run solutions provides a means of conducting these experiments that is analytically tractable. In this light, knife-edge assumptions are helpful because it can be simpler to think about a long-run solution with growth effects than to investigate the magnitude of level effects.

From this perspective, the use of knife-edge assumptions and long-run solutions is a convenient way of organising our thoughts. The resulting models are inevitably slightly artificial, but what makes them useful is the ability to hold some things constant, such as the quality of ideas and the productivity of researchers, as in a laboratory experiment. It is this high level of abstraction which permits insights into such issues as the impact of a given parameter change on welfare.

Problems arise when researchers take the models too literally, and interpret the long-run predictions of growth models in a different light. At least tacitly, too many researchers seem to believe that the ability of a model to generate perpetual balanced growth is a useful criterion on which to judge different growth models. Yet it should not surprise anyone that perpetual balanced growth is only possible in these models under restrictive, knife-edge assumptions. Similarly, as will be discussed later, it would be a serious mistake to criticise certain models simply because their predictions about long-run growth effects also depend on restrictive assumptions.

Neither should one be surprised if the long-run outcomes indicated by growth models turn out to have limited predictive power. It is not altogether sensible to ask whether real-world growth can be sustained indefinitely by using models which hold such things as the quality of ideas and the productivity of researchers constant over time, and that often abstract from natural resources. It should be clear that such a model can tell us very little about the growth rate we should expect in future centuries. Accordingly, the answers given by standard models to such questions, and their relation to knife-edge assumptions, may be of little practical relevance.

This uncertainty in looking forwards also applies in reviewing historical evidence. The strength of the models, their high level of abstraction, now becomes a weakness. It is difficult, perhaps impossible, to find empirical counterparts for the long-run growth rate and the other variables at the heart of the models. As a result, one should probably be rather sceptical about exercises in which researchers try to compare the long-run predictions of different models with empirical evidence. Agnosticism may be the best we can hope for.

This is less worrying than it might sound. Although some have argued that the distinction between different growth models is a crucial question for policy, these discussions often give far too much weight to what happens in the long run. It is possible that the popular distinction between growth effects and level effects has begun to distort our thinking on these issues. Instead of worrying about the effects of policy on the growth rate in a hypothetical long-run equilibrium, perhaps far distant in time, we should analyse the impact on welfare. It is entirely possible that models which yield very different long-run outcomes are in much closer agreement on welfare implications.

The rest of the paper will discuss these arguments in more detail. Section 2 provides the necessary background concerning knife-edge assumptions. Section 3 contains some sceptical observations on the place of long run outcomes in theoretical analysis. Section 4 discusses the connections between growth theory and reality, while section 5 draw on this perspective in looking at the recent debate surrounding scale effects. Finally, section 6 proposes five 'Obvious Rules' to apply when thinking about the long-run implications of growth theories.

2. Knife-edge assumptions

Growth models are often set up to yield a balanced growth path, in which growth can be sustained indefinitely, and this seems like a valuable property for such models to have. A typical long-run outcome is that capital and output grow at the same constant rate into the indefinite future, and the real interest rate is constant. It should be clear, however, that such an outcome is a special case, and so will usually require highly restrictive assumptions.

This is true even in the Solow model. Although it is usually seen as a general and flexible model, the existence of the conventional balanced growth path requires knife-edge assumptions. Either the production function must be Cobb-Douglas, or technical progress must be restricted to the labour-augmenting type.

Cobb-Douglas technologies are widely used because they are so easy to analyse, but we lack persuasive evidence that the elasticity of substitution between capital and labour is always and everywhere equal to unity, and such a result would be a remarkable coincidence. The alternative assumption, that all technical change is labour-augmenting, is also restrictive. In an interesting precursor of recent arguments, Akerlof and Nordhaus (1967, p. 343) use this kind of point to argue that 'balanced growth in the presence of steady technological change may be, in a well-defined sense, a razor's edge case'.

A more familiar knife-edge assumption is that found in the more recent AK models of endogenous growth. The problem here is that the exponent on capital (K) must be exactly one for constant steady-state growth. Otherwise, growth usually either declines to zero (given an exponent less than one) or keeps on rising (given an exponent greater than one). Since it is highly unlikely that the relevant parameter will be exactly one, McCallum (1996) writes that this requirement 'must be regarded as implying that the endogenous growth approach does not actually generate steady, everlasting growth in the absence of exogenous technical progress' (p. 60).

One interpretation of McCallum's remark – quite possibly a misinterpretation – is that the presence or absence of steady, everlasting growth is somehow a relevant criterion on which to judge a model of growth. It seems a natural requirement; surely if we want to think about growth, we need a model in which growth takes place in the long run? As I will discuss later in this paper, the long run is a theoretical abstraction that should not be taken too literally. As a result, it is not sensible to discriminate among models according to whether or not they yield perpetual growth. Moreover, it is quite possible that a model in which growth eventually ceases would be the best approximation to the real world.

Since steady growth in AK models rests on a knife-edge assumption, the approach initially seemed more restrictive than the research-driven endogenous growth models introduced by Romer (1990) and Aghion and Howitt (1992). Then Jones (1995a, b) made the simple but important point that there is a fragile assumption at the heart of these research-driven models, too. Typically such models include an equation for the accumulation of ideas, essentially equivalent to

$$\dot{A} = \delta L_A^\lambda A^\phi$$

where A is the stock of ideas and L_A is the number of workers generating new ideas. If ϕ is greater than one, growth is explosive. If it is less than one, per capita growth depends on population growth, rather than the policy parameters that endogenous growth theory has traditionally emphasised. Hence endogenous growth that is sensitive to policy, without being explosive, rests on the knife-edge assumption that $\phi = 1$.

One question is whether knife-edge assumptions, and particularly the need for exact linearity, only arise because we usually examine steady-state growth that is

both sustained and constant, rather than just sustained. Jones and Manuelli
(1990, 1997) have pointed out that exact linearity is not essential for sustained
growth in AK models. What is crucial is that the marginal product of capital does
not become too low. For example, CES technologies are capable of generating
sustained endogenous growth for certain parameter values. What these different
technologies have in common is that they are asymptotically linear, and hence can
deliver sustained growth, even though the growth rate will typically fall over time.

Dalgaard and Kreiner (2003) make much the same point in relation to the
process for generating new ideas in research-driven growth models. As long as the
accumulation of new ideas is asymptotically linear in the existing stock, sustained
growth is possible. Early on in the endogenous growth literature, Grossman and
Helpman (1991, p. 75–78) also analysed the assumptions about knowledge needed
to generate sustained growth, in a model with an increasing variety of goods.
They concluded that growth can be sustained in the face of decreasing returns to
research, provided that the ratio of knowledge to cumulative research remains
sufficiently high as the marginal product of research declines.

Overall, though, it is clear that perpetual growth is not a particularly general
implication of growth models, and a balanced growth path even less so. This
should not be surprising. These outcomes are special cases, and are likely to
demand restrictive assumptions. If we see growth theories as primarily a tool
for thought experiments, we can easily defend knife-edge assumptions as a way of
making the analysis relatively tractable.

One way of seeing this is to consider the arguments surrounding constancy of
the long-run growth rate. The Solow model is sometimes rather naively criticised
for its association with constant growth in the long run, contrary to the historical
evidence. Yet every theorist knows that this aspect of the model is not intended as
a prediction about the actual growth process, but just as a convenient way of
setting up the analysis. In practice, it is more plausible that technology evolves
stochastically, but the model can accommodate this feature, as in the real business
cycle literature.

The key point is that apparently restrictive assumptions are useful precisely
because they allow us to abstract from matters not directly relevant to the
problem at hand, and to carry out experiments holding certain variables constant.
In this respect, the models are the laboratory we otherwise don't have. As I will
argue later in the paper, using models for this purpose casts a rather different light
on the role of knife-edge assumptions. Furthermore, these assumptions are not
unique to research-driven models, and their presence or absence may not be
a useful criterion in discriminating between rival explanations of the growth
process.

3. The long run: a sceptical perspective

In this section of the paper, I will argue that theoretical ideas concerning long-run
outcomes are less fundamental than is usually thought. The long run is a theoretical abstraction, and its use should be approached with care. The long-run

equilibrium of a (deterministic) growth model is an outcome that can be sustained indefinitely. This does not mean that we are likely ever to observe it, or that it should be central to the analysis of policy.

At present, the long-run implications of stylized models are taken very seriously. Theoretical implications about what can be sustained indefinitely are given a great deal of attention, and are taken to transfer in a meaningful way to interpretations of the past and predictions of the future. My argument is that this kind of speculation takes the theoretical concept of the long run too literally, just as the more naive interpretations of the Solow model take the idea of constant growth too literally.

For policy purposes, what happens indefinitely (in the long run) may often be of comparatively little interest. It should be remembered that the rate of convergence to the long run equilibrium can be extremely slow. This is the case for the Solow model for certain parameter values, which can imply that the convergence process stretches over many decades. In more complicated models, with endogenous human capital accumulation, or in which research intensity must converge to some long-run level, the rate of convergence will often be even slower.

This observation has an important consequence. An excessive focus on the long-run properties of a stylized model may well distract us from the welfare effects of a given parameter change. Imagine the following scenario: a policy-maker asks an economic theorist to suggest a means of increasing the growth rate. Ah, replies the theorist, you are looking for what we call a growth effect: that is, a policy intervention which will raise the growth rate of the economy indefinitely. The theorist suggests a number of policies, but adds that these will only increase the growth rate indefinitely if a number of knife-edge parameter conditions are satisfied, ones which are unlikely to hold in practice and that relate to parameters or variables that are essentially unobservable. The policy-maker leaves, shaking her head and muttering remarks about the ivory tower abstractions of academic theorists.

This is, admittedly, a caricature, but it is a surprisingly accurate one. This can be seen in the importance that some recent papers assign to the distinction between endogenous and semi-endogenous growth models. In an endogenous growth model, the rate of innovation depends on the allocation of resources, and policy can affect the long-run growth rate. In a semi-endogenous growth model, innovation is again a process that requires the use of resources, but the long-run growth rate is independent of policy. As a result, one can find references to 'policy invariance' results, and claims that the distinction between endogenous and semi-endogenous models is of profound theoretical and practical importance. The debate is at its least sensible when participants argue that we should look at the data and see whether the knife-edge conditions required for endogenous growth are actually met in practice.

This debate shows how too much emphasis on long-run outcomes can distort our thinking. As a result, too much emphasis is given to growth effects over level effects. The terminology alone leads us astray: since we are often asked to think about 'growth', a growth effect has an intrinsic glamour that level effects lack. Thus growth models are typically set up in slightly artificial ways so that growth can be sustained into the indefinite future, and so that the long-run growth rate responds to parameter changes.

Yet it should be remembered that genuine growth effects would be extremely powerful, and we have no good prior reason to believe in their existence. Consider what a growth effect implies: a favourable parameter change today means that, holding all else constant, today's forecast of output per capita in a thousand years from now, or ten thousand years from now, will be many, many times higher than it would otherwise have been. It should not surprise us if the parameter changes which can actually give rise to such powerful effects are few and far between.

If this seems like a strange point, it is worth remembering that, before the recent endogenous growth literature, genuine growth effects were effectively absent. In the Solow model, sustained growth can be seen as the outcome of a series of level effects. That is, growth relies upon a steady stream of innovations, each of which feed through into a higher level of productivity. More generally, we have no reason to dismiss the idea that past history and future experience can all be explained in terms of level effects. In research-driven growth models, the rate of convergence to the long-run outcome can be very slow, and even centuries of sustained growth may be consistent with a long-run equilibrium in which growth comes to a halt. As I will discuss further below, it will be very hard to distinguish empirically whether or not this is happening, and we may never be able to decide which models come closest to the truth in their long-run predictions.

This casts a different light on the presence of knife-edge assumptions in recent endogenous growth models. If we see these assumptions as unrealistic, this just returns us to an earlier position, namely that long-run growth does not respond to policy. This does not matter, because the central question of interest is the relationship between parameter changes and the level of welfare, not the long-run behaviour of the growth rate. This may seem so obvious as to hardly bear repeating. Yet the debates about knife-edge assumptions, and the frequent tendency to neglect level effects, implicitly assign special importance to long-run outcomes, often at the expense of studying the more fundamental consequences for welfare.

4. Growth theory and reality

The prominence given by theorists to long-run outcomes has an unfortunate consequence. As we have seen, sustaining growth indefinitely requires fairly special assumptions. Long-run growth at a constant rate inevitably sits on a knife-edge. A naive response is that, because of these knife-edge assumptions, growth models are not a useful way of thinking about the world around us, and a more general approach should be sought. It is hard to imagine what form such an approach would take, however.

A more sophisticated response is that models which make restrictive assumptions about parameters may be good approximations to a world in which the parameters take other values.[1] On this interpretation, ultimately any theory of endogenous growth might really be capturing something that is 'only' a level effect in practice. The use of restrictive parameter assumptions is then just one way of simplifying the analysis.

It is sometimes argued that, for policy evaluation, we need to go further than this, and establish which available model is the best approximation to the truth. For example, is growth endogenous or semi-endogenous? Unfortunately it is difficult to see how we could ever conclude in favour of one type of model or the other. We do not observe the long-run growth rate, and there is a considerable distance between other key theoretical concepts and observable variables.

The usual suggestion is that we look at average growth rates over long periods, and then examine how these long-term growth rates have varied over time. Even leaving aside the difficulty of slow convergence to a steady state, it will be very hard to use this approach to gauge the effect of a specific parameter change on the long-run growth rate. This analysis will typically have to assume that variables such as the average quality of ideas, or the productivity of researchers, or even the whole process by which ideas are generated, are constant over time. This is not an attractive set of assumptions, and it is therefore hard to see how predictions about long-run outcomes can be tested in a genuinely rigorous way.

As a result, it will be virtually impossible to test the long-run predictions of growth models against the data. Instead, we will have to retain a kind of agnosticism about the long-run properties of actual growth processes, and this agnosticism is almost certainly the best we can hope for. Given this difficulty, one approach would be to calibrate a variety of models, under a range of assumptions. In the unlikely event that knife-edge restrictions are met in the real world, and hence long-run growth is endogenous, a suitably parameterized semi-endogenous model could still provide a reasonably good approximation to actual welfare effects. This should be true provided that the welfare calculations discount the future at a sufficiently high rate, or if convergence to the long-run equilibrium is slow.

Another useful perspective would be to consider the apparently competing models as ultimately complementary. Different models provide different insights, and the usefulness of a specific model will depend on the context and the question being asked. In this light, even if agnosticism is the best we can hope for, that is less of a problem than it may seem at first glance.

In practice, even though long-run predictions are impossible to test, some theorists seem to be inexorably drawn to thinking about outcomes that can be sustained indefinitely. The desire to develop a theory in which even long-run growth is responsive to policy might well lead to some unappealing models. For example, in order to generate endogenous growth under fairly general parameter assumptions, one route is to make population growth endogenous. Such a model can yield interesting and counter-intuitive responses to policy interventions, but it is hard to believe that such responses will take place sufficiently quickly to be of practical relevance.

There are other justifications sometimes given for assigning a special place to long run outcomes. One argument is that we have observed growth for over two hundred years, so that a good model should be potentially consistent with perpetual growth. Another argument is that we should be keenly interested in what our models predict about future growth rates. If it seems likely that growth might cease, or be dependent on continued population growth, or even explode, that is something we need to know.

The problem here is that theoretical models necessarily hold many things constant, in a way that inevitably undermines any attempt to make sensible practical forecasts. Growth models are constructed in unusually abstract terms, and it would therefore be a mistake to take them too literally, either in analysing the past or making predictions about the future.

In that case, what use is growth theory? Returning to a key theme of this paper, the true usefulness of growth models is that they stand in for the laboratory we otherwise don't have. They allow us to examine and quantify the effects of parameter changes and policy interventions while holding other things equal. Those things held equal typically include such crucial variables as the quality of ideas and the productivity of researchers. Although these are very helpful simplifications for thought experiments, the approach is necessarily too stylized for us to learn very much by comparing the long-run predictions of the models with the available evidence.

For example, consider the familiar point that we have observed sustained growth for more than two centuries. This does not mean that the best approximation to the data is necessarily a model that yields perpetual growth. It is quite possible that we are in the course of a lengthy transition to a long-run equilibrium in which growth eventually ceases, and I see no good prior reason to rule this out. Equally, it is possible that growth might have already ceased, were it not for changes in the quality of ideas, the productivity of researchers, and so on.

The usual explanation of the historical record appeals to technical progress, occurring at a remarkably steady rate. As an explanation of the data, this at least has the advantage of economy, but the data remain compatible with a large class of models, with very different long-run predictions. Admittedly, it might be possible to discriminate among these models by looking at other implications that can be tested against the data. It is far less clear, however, that we will ever have enough data to discriminate between models based solely on their long-run predictions.

With this in mind, there is perhaps not much hope of deciding which model yields the most accurate predictions regarding long-run outcomes. This may seem unfortunate, since in principle, a finding that growth will eventually cease or explode could be of great importance in a wide range of areas. Yet consider our actual forecasts of growth over the next hundred years. Perhaps researchers will find it harder and harder to make useful progress, and the generation of useful new ideas will fall relative to the existing stock. Alternatively, as Dinopoulos and Thompson (1999) point out, perhaps the generation of knowledge will itself undergo technical change, for instance through the introduction of computer technology. We simply don't know.

These brief examples are intended to expose the inevitable uncertainty about the building-blocks of these models: ideas, knowledge, the productivity of researchers, the whole process by which today's inputs are turned into tomorrow's new technologies. Analyses of the models and their long-run predictions will necessarily hold constant some of these components, in a way which is too stylized and unrealistic when one uses the models to approach the empirical evidence or to make predictions about the future.

It is essential to remember that this difficulty in mapping between the models and the real world does not necessarily render invalid any insights into policy that the models can yield. If the quality of ideas and the productivity of individual researchers are pretty much independent of policy interventions, we can go on using the models to think about policy in thought experiments which hold these things equal. It is only when we come to the retrospective analysis of policy effectiveness, or the testing of different models against each other, or predictions about future growth rates, that the high degree of abstraction will become a central and probably insurmountable difficulty.

To reiterate, the implication of all this is that we should remain agnostic about the 'right' growth model, and not waste our energies trying to discriminate between them based on their long-run predictions. Instead, we could examine the welfare effects of policy in a range of models, whether endogenous or semi-endogenous, with or without scale effects, and be wary of recommendations that are too closely tied to a single framework. Although different models will generate very different answers about long-run outcomes, we have no reason to give special priority to these answers in discriminating between the models, or in assessing the overall impact of a parameter change. Crucially, it is entirely possible that models which yield very different long-run outcomes are in close agreement on the welfare implications of specific parameter changes.

5. The debate on scale effects

The debate surrounding knife-edge assumptions in growth models is closely connected to the rapidly growing literature on scale effects. That is, does the scale of the economy, as captured by a variable like population size, affect the long-run growth rate? There are an increasing number of papers in this vein. Dinopoulos and Thompson (1999) and Jones (1999) provide very useful introductions to the issues.

The papers on scale effects often take as their inspiration the observation of Jones (1995a) that the number of people employed in research in the US has increased substantially, with apparently rather little change in the growth rate, at least as yet. This contradicts a prediction of the simplest endogenous growth models, namely that productivity growth should be proportional to employment in the research sector.

Furthermore, researchers like Young (1998) have indicated that, in models without any kind of scale effect, policy may not affect the long-run growth rate. Howitt (1999), among others, has shown that this conclusion is not necessarily a particularly general one, and that it is possible to construct a growth model with no scale effects, but which still retains a role for government policy in determining the long-run growth rate. In turn, Li (2000) argues that such conclusions again rest on knife-edge assumptions.

Empirically, the question of whether or not long-run growth depends on scale is probably unanswerable. A widely-read paper by Kremer (1993) provides some of the best available evidence, using data far back in time, but we have no reason to believe that the same processes continue to govern the production of ideas in the modern era. The problems in settling this debate should now be familiar. We do not observe the long-run growth rate; even if we could, we cannot test long-run predictions against the data, unless we make some truly heroic assumptions about relevant unobservable variables; and the long run equilibrium may be so distant in the future that we have neither the ability to resolve the debate, nor any practical need to do so.[2]

The debate about scale effects could again lead to some odd-looking models, if too much emphasis is given to long-run outcomes. In thinking about certain growth models, such as that of Jones (1995b), one might argue that population growth is the key constraint on long-run growth rates. After all, the role of population growth initially appears central, if the number of researchers is to be increased indefinitely.

Yet the number of researchers may be expanded in other ways, even over a very long time span. Between 1950 and 1993, the measured fraction of the US labour force engaged in research trebled. Since the figure went from 1/4 of one percent to 3/4 of a percent, there is clearly room for continuing expansion, perhaps taking place over hundreds of years (Jones 2002). Furthermore, the world's research population could be swelled by drawing on the OECD member countries, and ultimately on the populations of India and China. It is therefore hard to see the population constraint on the number of researchers as central to thinking about future growth, except perhaps over millennia. This is another example of how a focus on long-run outcomes could lead to models that are not wholly sensible, and that emphasize the wrong set of constraints.

There is a different and perhaps more useful way of looking at the evidence of Jones (1995a). He draws attention to the long-term rise in research intensity in the USA, as the number of researchers has steadily risen relative to the total population. In more recent work, he has analysed this rise as part of a lengthy transition to a new steady-state (Jones 2002). More generally, in the light of his evidence, one could stipulate that a good model of endogenous growth should be compatible with changing research intensity over time. Some models of this type might imply that growth can only continue if research intensity increases. This is clearly an outcome that cannot be sustained indefinitely, and therefore rules out a balanced growth path.

This brings the arguments of this paper full circle, by making clear once again that a balanced growth path is a special case, which is likely to demand restrictive assumptions. It is not clear that we should expect models with this property to be the best approximation to the data, and so it would be a mistake to assume that a good model of growth necessarily gives rise to a balanced growth path. Instead, the widespread use of such a path in theoretical work, together with the knife-edge assumptions that make it possible, are best seen as useful devices that allow for simpler analysis, if not for greater realism.

6. Conclusions

Readers of earlier drafts of this paper gave a wide range of responses, and often differed in their interpretation of the key points. With this in mind, it may be useful to provide a summary of the main arguments in the paper. The summary appears below, in the form of 'Five Obvious Rules for Thinking About Long-Run Growth'.[3] All have a common point of departure that I see as self-evident, namely that our primary research interest should be in the welfare consequences of parameter changes, and not simply in long-run outcomes. Another running theme is that growth models are often best seen as laboratories for thought experiments, and apparently competing frameworks can form a useful complement to one another.

Obvious Rule 1. Remember that the long run is a theoretical abstraction that is sometimes of limited practical relevance.

For some parameter values, convergence to the long-run equilibrium is slow in the Solow model. In models with endogenous human capital accumulation, or that require research intensity to converge to a long-run equilibrium level, convergence is likely to be even slower. The implication is that the long run equilibrium may be a distant prospect. Much of the variation in growth rates, as observed over time and across countries, will be due to transitional dynamics. In thinking about welfare effects, the transitional path taken by the economy will often be more important than the final resting point of the growth rate.

Obvious Rule 2. Don't assume that a good model of growth has to yield a balanced growth path, or that long-run growth has to be endogenous.

The main piece of evidence we have for the existence of a balanced growth path is that the real interest rate does not display any clear trend. That does not mean, however, that only models with this property are of interest. We may be slowly converging to a growth path along which the real interest rate eventually shows different behaviour. Moreover, when we consider growth models in which research intensity can vary over time, the case for emphasizing the balanced growth path looks weaker, simply because convergence to such a path might take many centuries.

That is less worrying than it sounds, because the interest in balanced growth paths is often driven by theoretical convenience. Outcomes that can be sustained indefinitely, such as balanced growth paths, have been studied so widely partly because they are inherently convenient to analyse. The predictions of such models about actual, long-term outcomes may well be inaccurate, because we don't have strong reasons to believe that perpetual balanced growth is the only possible real-world outcome. This does not preclude such models from telling us valuable things about the growth process. What a specific growth model predicts about the long run is just one of its properties, and in some instances, one of the least interesting.

Furthermore, the perceived need for a useful growth theory to yield sustained endogenous growth is a potentially dangerous misconception. Again, we have no prior reason to believe that the long-run growth rate (in the sense of a growth rate that can be sustained indefinitely) should be sensitive to parameter changes. Placing such demands on growth theories may lead to models that are of little practical relevance, while some genuinely useful models are wrongly dismissed.

Obvious Rule 3. Don't dismiss a model of growth because the long-run outcomes depend on knife-edge assumptions.

Among the set of possible outcomes, perpetual balanced growth seems like a very special case. It should not surprise anyone that such an outcome rests on highly restrictive assumptions. Importantly, this does not imply the models are useless, because the necessary assumptions are just one way of setting up a laboratory for thought experiments. We can use them when it simplifies the analysis, recalling that the answers to key questions will often be similar in more general circumstances.

Few people criticise the Solow model for the restrictive assumptions needed to generate steady growth, and the knife-edge assumptions in endogenous growth models should be seen in a similarly forgiving light. These models can still have very useful things to say about the evolution of welfare, even when they require special assumptions to generate conventional 'growth effects' that can be sustained indefinitely. This point was made quite explicitly by Jones (1995b) but has too rarely been acknowledged in more recent work.

Obvious Rule 4. Remember that long-run predictions may be impossible to test. It will be extremely difficult to discriminate between models based on their predictions about long-run outcomes.

Within a theoretical model, the long-run growth rate is one to which the economy will eventually converge, holding various things equal. We never observe an empirical counterpart to this quantity. The usual suggestion is that we look at average growth rates over long periods, and how they respond to parameter changes. Even leaving aside the difficulty of slow convergence, the problem here is that we have no reason to believe that the various determinants of the long-run growth rate are constant over long spans of time. For example, the average quality of ideas, or the productivity of researchers, or even the whole process by which ideas are generated, are all likely to be subject to important changes over time. The prospects for finding empirical counterparts to these variables are not strong.

As a result, it will be very difficult, perhaps impossible, to test the predictions about the long run made by different growth models. We will probably have to show a degree of agnosticism in thinking about long-run outcomes, and hence in choosing which model to use. This may not matter, because it is quite possible that models with very different long-run outcomes will be in much closer agreement on the welfare impact of a given parameter change.

This reminds us that we should think mainly about overall welfare effects, and much less about long-run implications. It also reminds us that we should see long-run solutions to growth models primarily as results of thought experiments, and we should not ask too much of the models in this regard. The long-run solutions are just one set of implications among many, and involve an unusually high degree of abstraction. We should be cautious before expecting them to explain past historical experience, or to be useful in predicting the future.

From the alternative 'models-as-laboratory' perspective, many of the problems apparently associated with knife-edge assumptions, or with the widespread use of abstract concepts such as the 'stock of knowledge', or with the analytical device of a balanced growth path, immediately disappear. Moreover, this viewpoint clarifies that 'exogenous' and 'endogenous' growth models are not necessarily rival explanations for the data. The models are tools for thinking about the world, and the most useful framework will depend on the context. Attempts to distinguish which model is 'correct' will tend to run aground on the inherent difficulty of testing long-run predictions. Even if a model's predictions about long-run outcomes could be comprehensively rejected, it might still retain some usefulness – not least because alternative models might be worse approximations to the data in other respects.

Obvious Rule 5. Don't undervalue level effects.

If our prime concern is the level of welfare, as it should be, then we have little reason to investigate only changes in the long-run growth rate. Yet researchers (and textbooks) too often imply that a particular effect must be relatively unimportant because it is 'only' a level effect.

This is fundamentally misguided. Genuine growth effects would be extremely powerful forces, and we have no prior reason to believe in their existence. As several articles have demonstrated, endogenous growth models often require knife-edge assumptions to generate such effects. As a result, it is quite plausible that past and future developments rest entirely on level effects, some large, some small. In the Solow model, growth can only be maintained by a sequence of level effects, as a constant stream of technical innovations feeds through into higher output. It should not worry us that long-run growth in research-driven models is similarly hard to sustain, or unresponsive to policy. These models will continue to yield level effects that should be central to policy analysis.

Looking at these five rules together, it should be clear that the concept of the long run can often exert a dangerous hold on our thinking. Giving too much emphasis to long-run outcomes could lead us to dismiss useful models, to develop new models of the growth process that have little practical relevance, or to ignore effects that are of critical importance for welfare. Ultimately, all that a long-run equilibrium of a model denotes is its final resting point, perhaps very distant in the future. We know very little about this destination, and should be paying more attention to the journey.

Acknowledgements

An earlier, rather different draft of this paper first circulated under the title 'Growth theory on a knife edge?'. I am grateful to Chad Jones, Chol-Won Li, Pietro Peretto, Stephen

Redding and Peter Thompson for helpful comments on that earlier draft. The paper's perspective on the long run owes much to my undergraduate tutor, Geoff Harcourt. Any errors or misunderstandings are my responsibility.

Notes

1. See for example McCallum (1996).
2. There is rather more hope of settling a related and perhaps more sensible question, namely whether the *level* of productivity is independent of scale. This is one example of how some popular hypotheses about long-run growth should perhaps be reformulated and tested in terms of level effects.
3. The device of listing 'Obvious Rules' is borrowed from Ayckbourn (2002).

References

Aghion, P. and Howitt, P. (1992) A model of growth through creative destruction. *Econometrica*, 60, 323–351.

Akerlof, G. and Nordhaus, W. D. (1967) Balanced growth – a razor's edge? *International Economic Review*, 8(3), 343–348.

Ayckbourn, A. (2002). *The crafty art of playwriting*. Faber and Faber, London.

Dalgaard, C.-J. and Kreiner, C. T. (2003) Endogenous growth: a knife-edge or the razor's edge? *Scandinavian Journal of Economics*, forthcoming.

Grossman, G. M. and Helpman, E. (1991) *Innovation and growth in the global economy*. MIT Press, Cambridge, MA.

Howitt, P. (1999) Steady endogenous growth with population and R&D inputs growing. *Journal of Political Economy*, 107, 715–730.

Jones, C. I. (1995a) Time series tests of endogenous growth models. *Quarterly Journal of Economics*, 110, 495–525.

Jones, C. I. (1995b) R&D-based models of economic growth. *Journal of Political Economy*, 103, 759–784.

Jones, C. I. (1999) Growth: with or without scale effects? *American Economic Review*, 89, 139–144.

Jones, C. I. (2002) Sources of U. S. economic growth in a world of ideas. *American Economic Review*, 92(1), 220–239.

Jones, L. E. and Manuelli, R. E. (1990) A convex model of equilibrium growth: theory and policy implications. *Journal of Political Economy*, 98, 1008–1038.

Jones, L. E. and Manuelli, R. E. (1997) The sources of growth. *Journal of Economic Dynamics and Control*, 21, 75–114.

Kremer, M. (1993) Population growth and technological change: one million B.C. to 1990. *Quarterly Journal of Economics*, 108, August, 681–716.

Li, Chol-Won (2000) Endogenous vs. semi-endogenous growth in a two-R&D-sector model. *Economic Journal*, 110, C109–C122.

McCallum, B. T. (1996) Neoclassical vs. endogenous growth analysis: an overview. *Federal Reserve Bank of Richmond Economic Quarterly*, 82/4, Fall.

Romer, P. M. (1990) Endogenous technological change. *Journal of Political Economy*, 98(5), S71–S102.

Young, A. (1998) Growth without scale effects. *Journal of Political Economy*, 106, 41–63.

INDEX